Cambridge Studies in Oral and Literate Culture   7

XHOSA ORAL POETRY

Cambridge Studies in Oral and Literate Culture

Edited by PETER BURKE and RUTH FINNEGAN

This series is designed to address the question of the significance of literacy in human societies; it will assess its importance for political, economic, social, and cultural development and will examine how what we take to be the common functions of writing are carried out in oral cultures.

The series will be interdisciplinary, but with particular emphasis on social anthropology and social history, and will encourage cross-fertilization between these disciplines; it will also be of interest to readers in allied fields, such as sociology, folklore, and literature. Although it will include some monographs, the focus of the series will be on theoretical and comparative aspects rather than detailed description, and the books will be presented in a form accessible to nonspecialist readers interested in the general subject of literacy and orality.

XHOSA ORAL POETRY

Aspects of a
black South African tradition

JEFF OPLAND

*Professor and Director of the Institute
of Social and Economic Research,
Rhodes University*

CAMBRIDGE UNIVERSITY PRESS

CAMBRIDGE

LONDON NEW YORK NEW ROCHELLE

MELBOURNE SYDNEY

Published by the Press Syndicate of the University of Cambridge
The Pitt Building, Trumpington Street, Cambridge CB2 1RP
32 East 57th Street, New York, NY 10022, USA
296 Beaconsfield Parade, Middle Park, Melbourne 3206, Australia

First published 1983

Printed in the United States of America

Library of Congress Cataloging in Publication Data
Opland, Jeff, 1943–
Xhosa oral poetry.
(Cambridge studies in oral and literate culture; 7)
Includes index.
1. Folk poetry, Xhosa – History and criticism.
I. Title. II. Series.
PL8795.5.064 1983   398.2'049636   82–22058
ISBN 0 521 24113 8

The following scholars, publishers, and institutions have generously given permission to use extended quotations from copyrighted works: From "The Traditional Praise Poetry of Xhosa: Iziduko and Izibongo" by Wandile F. Kuse (Univ. of Wisconsin, diss., 1973), by permission of the author. From *A Companion to Homer* by Alan J. B. Wace and Frank H. Stubbings (Macmillan, 1962), by permission of the publisher. From "The Praises of Xhosa Mineworkers" by Alexander Theodore Wainwright (Univ. of South Africa, diss., 1979), by permission of the author. From *Reminiscences of Kafir Life and History* by Charles Brownlee (1916); *Poems of an African* by James J. R. Jolobe (1946); *The wrath of the ancestors*, trans. by A. C. Jordan (1980); *Umhlekazi UHintsa* by S. E. K. Mqhayi (1937); and *Lovedale South Africa 1824–1955* by R. H. W. Shepherd, by permission of the publisher, Lovedale Press. From *The Singer of Tales* by Albert B. Lord (Harvard Univ. Press, 1960), by permission of the publisher. From *Rituals of Rebellion in South-East Africa* by Max Gluckman (Manchester Univ. Press, 1954), by permission of the publisher. From "The Power of Words in African Verbal Arts" by Philip M. Peek (*Journal of American Folklore,* 1981), by permission of the American Folklore Society. From *Towards an African Literature: The Emergence of Literary Form in Xhosa* by A. C. Jordan (Univ. of California Press, 1973), by permission of the publisher. From "The Religious System of the Ndlambe of East London District" by E. H. Bigalke (Rhodes Univ., diss., 1969), by permission of the author. From *Reaction to Conquest* by Monica Hunter (1936), by permission of the author. From "The role of the bard in contemporary African community" by Archie Mafeje (*Journal of African Languages,* 1967) by permission of the publisher. From "African education and society in the 19th century eastern Cape" by Michael Ashley (in *Beyond the Cape frontier: Studies in the history of the Transkei and Ciskei,* ed. C. Saunders and R. Derricourt, Longman, 1974), by permission of the publisher.

FOR DANIEL

CONTENTS

PREFACE

Since Xhosa oral poems generally locate their subjects in a genealogical context, it seems appropriate to start with a genealogy. Xhosa was the great-grandfather of Tshawe, who was the great-grandfather of Togu, who was the father of Ngconde, who was the father of Tshiwo, who in turn fathered Phalo. Phalo's senior son was Gcaleka, and Rharhabe was one of his junior sons. Gcaleka was the father of Khawuta, the father of Hintsa, the father of Sarhili; Rharhabe fathered Mlawu, the father of Ngqika, who was the father of Sandile. These men were all royal chiefs, who came to settle with their followers in the southeast of what is today the Republic of South Africa, displacing Khoi and San inhabitants (formerly known as Hottentots and Bushmen). According to custom, the members of a chiefdom were known by the names of their founding chiefs, so that all followers of these chiefs could be called *amaXhosa,* the Xhosa people; after the major split in the royal line, the followers of Gcaleka, Khawuta, Hintsa, and Sarhili were known as *amaGcaleka,* the Gcaleka people, and the followers of Rharhabe, Mlawu, Ngqika, and Sandile were known as *amaRharhabe,* or, consequent upon the split between Ngqika and his uncle Ndlambe, *amaNgqika.* The language they spoke was transcribed and printed for the first time by Christian missionaries who settled in Ngqika's chiefdom, and was identified in name with the Xhosa people. The Xhosa people, however, were not the only ones who spoke the language called Xhosa. Dialects of Xhosa were spoken by various peoples living to the northeast all the way through present-day Transkei to the Umzimvubu River. All these Xhosa-speaking peoples, known as the Cape Nguni to distinguish them from the Natal Nguni, who speak the Zulu language, are ethnographically related though distinct, constituting separate clusters under independent chiefs, although both the Cape and the Natal Nguni peoples as well as their languages were originally called Kaffir by their European neighbors. The major members of the Cape Nguni or Xhosa-speaking peoples are the Xhosa (Gcaleka and Rharhabe), Thembu, Xesibe, Bomvana, Mpondomise, and Mpondo. It is the traditions of oral poetry current among these Xhosa-speaking peoples – and not just among the Xhosa people – that form the subject of this book: The "Xhosa" of the book's title thus refers to a language and not to a nation.

ix

Xhosa is a member of the Bantu family of languages spoken in Africa roughly south of the Congo; the family includes such languages as Kikuyu, Luba, Luganda, Mongo-Nkundu, Nyanja, Shona, Swahili, Thonga, and Umbundu. The southeastern Bantu languages include the Sotho family (Tswana, Southern Sotho, Pedi, for example) and the Nguni family (such as Zulu, Swazi, Xhosa, Ndebele, Ngoni). The Xhosa language, spoken by the Cape Nguni, and the Zulu language, spoken by the Natal Nguni, are sufficiently close to be mutually intelligible, though a Zulu- or Xhosa-speaker would not be able to understand a speaker of Tswana or Southern Sotho. Perhaps the most famous of Zulu rulers was Shaka, the Harald Fairhair of southern Africa, who early in the nineteenth century embarked on the conquest and subjugation of his neighbors, driving large numbers of Zulu-speaking refugees in all directions in a disruptive movement known as the Mfecane. Those who moved southwest settled down somewhat uncomfortably in Cape Nguni territory, and although they intermarried and came to speak Xhosa, they generally supported the white colonists in their frontier wars against the Cape Nguni; these people, known collectively as the Mfengu (Bhaca, Bhele, Hlubi, Ngwane, Zizi, etc.), are here treated as Cape Nguni, and their poetry is treated as Xhosa poetry.

My own interest in Xhosa oral poetry derives from the comparative study of Anglo-Saxon poetry and other oral poetic traditions. I commenced my fieldwork among the Cape Nguni in 1969 in order to draw comparisons between Xhosa and Anglo-Saxon poetry; the living Xhosa tradition was used to illuminate the dead Anglo-Saxon tradition. That line of inquiry culminated in a book on Anglo-Saxon oral poetry (Opland 1980a), the completion of which has now freed me to concentrate on the Xhosa tradition in its own right. The impulse to write the present book came in the form of a suggestion from Ruth Finnegan, to which I responded favorably largely because it gave me the opportunity to formulate a general statement on the tradition of Xhosa oral poetry. This book is not an edition of Xhosa texts in my collection; I have taken the opportunity here of offering a preliminary analysis of the Xhosa tradition as I see it. I call this a "preliminary analysis" since much of my fieldwork was conducted in the framework of my comparative research, and in writing this book I have become aware of painfully large areas demanding further research that I have not yet myself undertaken. Hence I have relatively little to say here about the meter of Xhosa poetry, for example, or about the poetry of women, or the relation of the poetic tradition to Xhosa song. I have tried to express here my own fascination with Xhosa oral poetry through an exhibition of some of its aspects, each of which may be apprehended with profit from a number of disciplinary vantage points. A study of the tradition of Xhosa oral poetry should hold interest for the likes of anthropologists, folklorists, historians, political scientists, psychologists, sociologists, and persons interested in the history of religion and education, poetry, and comparative literature, but I believe that a rounded view of the tradition cannot be gained exclusively from within any one of these disciplines. My approach to Xhosa oral poetry is essentially interdisciplinary.

I have quoted the original Xhosa texts only where necessary; original material in both German and Xhosa is here generally presented only in translation. For assistance with the German translations I am indebted to Dietrich Hofmann and Dieter Welz; for assistance with Xhosa translations I am deeply indebted to Sydney Zotwana, Buntu Mfenyana, Wele Manona, and Vuyani Mqingwana. As far as possible, translations of Xhosa texts have been checked with the poets themselves. My early fieldwork was facilitated by the award of a Lestrade Scholarship from the Department of African Languages at the University of Cape Town in 1970 and 1971; I am grateful to Ernst Westphal for his support. It is my pleasure here to acknowledge my gratitude to friends and colleagues who accompanied me on my field trips: Norman Mearns, Richard Moyer, Morton and Caroline Bloomfield, John Leyerle, Fred Robinson, Roberta Frank, and my sons Russell and Daniel. Assistance and encouragement were willingly offered to me by many people, some of whose names I now forget; among those who come to mind are Michael Berning, Martin and Gill Browne, Trevor Cope, Derek Fivaz, Sandra Fold, Jackson Magopeni, Richard Mfamana, Douglas Mzolo, P. M. Ntloko, Herbert Pahl, Rudolph Schwarz, and Silas Tindleni. I am grateful to Oakley West for drawing Map 1. Of course, this book could not have been written without the cooperation of chiefs, poets, and others in Transkei, Ciskei, KwaZulu, and Cape Town, to all of whom I am grateful for their support and to some of whom I am in addition indebted for their friendship.

I started thinking about this book during a year spent on sabbatical from August 1980 to June 1981 at Yale University, where I inflicted some of my thinking on participants in the Southern African Research Program; I am grateful to Leonard Thompson, director of the program, for according me fellowship status. I started writing the book in Kiel during the latter six months of 1981 as a Fellow of the Alexander von Humboldt Foundation; I am deeply indebted to the foundation for affording me the freedom from commitments that enabled me to complete the bulk of my work, and to the Board of Management of the Institute of Social and Economic Research at Rhodes University for recommending my leave. While I was free to write, Derek Fivaz and Renee Vroom carried the administrative burden back home. I am grateful to them both, but especially to Renee Vroom, who not only kept things going in my absence but also typed the manuscript on my return: To exploit a Xhosa turn of phrase, *ungunobhala woonobhala,* she is a secretary among secretaries. I am also indebted to Michael Whisson and Simon Bekker, who read and commented on the manuscript; to Janis Bolster, who copyedited it; and to Susan Allen-Mills of Cambridge University Press, for her courteous and efficient handling of both the manuscript and its author. But my deepest debt of gratitude is and will always be to my wife, Cynthia, who continues to tolerate so much more than it is fair of me to expect, and who provides me with a reason and a purpose for it all. This book is dedicated to my son Daniel, who wasn't with us while it was being written.

Grahamstown   Jeff Opland
March 1983

1

DOCUMENTARY PERSPECTIVES

The first Europeans to see the coast of land occupied by Xhosa-speaking people were Portuguese explorers who sailed round the Cape of Good Hope in the fifteenth century. (Bartholomew Diaz raised a stone cross on the coast of southern Africa during his voyage in 1488; not far from the spot where the ruins of that same cross were discovered in 1936 – see Axelson 1938 – lies the grave of Nongqawuse, who, some four centuries after Diaz's voyage, was the principal figure in the most disastrous event in Cape Nguni history, the cattle-killing episode of 1857.) In the middle of the seventeenth century the Dutch East India Company established a permanent settlement at Cape Town some five hundred miles to the southwest of land occupied by the Xhosa. Thirty years later the first expedition of white settlers from the Cape traveled eastward until they were attacked by a party of Xhosa who were amazed at their first sight of white men and of horses, and at the capacity of bullets to pierce their oxhide shields; they fled "with hellish cries," they were pursued, and many were killed (Kropf 1889a:2). From the latter part of the seventeenth century date a number of descriptions of Xhosa-speaking people written by survivors of coastal shipwrecks. By the end of the eighteenth century there were Dutch settlers living not many miles to the west of Xhosa territory. Early in the nineteenth century the Cape passed into British control, and in 1820 a large contingent of British settlers was located to the west of the Fish River. The Dutch and the British engaged in a series of wars fought against their black neighbors across the eastern frontier, the last of which ended in 1878 (see Elphick and Giliomee 1979 and Lamar and Thompson 1981).

Descriptions of or references to poetic activity among the Xhosa-speaking peoples date from the early nineteenth century (for a survey of nineteenth-century references to Zulu poets, see Gunner 1976). We have observations of Cape Nguni practices by European travelers who pass through their territory on hunting expeditions in search of game, scientific specimens, or souls; we also have accounts of Cape Nguni practices by Europeans – colonial administrators or missionaries – who lived for extended periods in close contact with their charges; and we have references to their own traditional customs written by native Xhosa-speakers themselves.

1

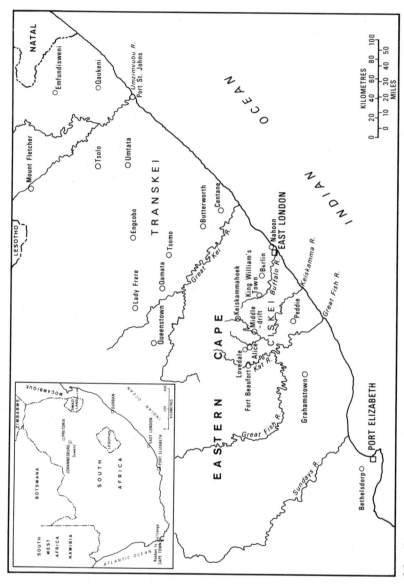

Map 1.

The accounts of passing travelers are the least reliable, tending to be superficial and based on chance observation. Even what passes for personal observation is often of questionable authenticity, since most travelers write for a foreign market – their works are published in England or Germany – and incorporate into their narratives, often without acknowledgement, sections from the published accounts of their peripatetic predecessors. Many are at pains to spice their writing with exotic descriptions of primitive behavior or pagan savagery, and most describe Cape Nguni culture* from a dogmatically ethnocentric perspective: As Katherine George put it, "The observer of alien cultures has tended to be prejudiced, in the simple sense that he has preferred his own to all other existent cultures and has viewed the strange as a malformed deviant from the familiar" (1958/1968:23). Cowper Rose offered his brother in England the following anecdote in a letter written from the Cape in the early nineteenth century: "When a Kaffer returned to his own country from Cape Town, to which he had been taken by an English officer, and, full of the strange things he had seen, told his tale to the dark group around him, describing the wonders of a ship, which he called 'a waggon that moved upon the waters, and that never *uitspan'd*,' (unyoked,) and many other marvels; he was greeted at the close of each story, when he expected applause, by a unanimous comment, '*That's a lie!*' – a very common fate with travellers" (1829:156–7). Certainly many early travelers among the Xhosa-speaking peoples richly merit that common fate, but not all. I shall start my selection of perspectives on Xhosa poetry with extracts from the narratives of transient travelers.

Ludwig Alberti described the return of a Xhosa hunting party in 1807:

> When the hunting party has returned to the neighbourhood of its village, the one who inflicted the first wound on the Lion that was killed, is hidden from view by shields held in front of him. At the same time one of the hunters leaves the troop and praises the courage of the slayer with a screaming voice, accompanied by a variety of leaps, and then returns again, when another one repeats the performance, during which the others incessantly shout hi! hi! hi! and beat their shields with knobkirries at the same time. This is continued until one has really reached the village. [1968:77]

The screaming voices might have been producing "heightened prose," but I am confident that we are dealing here with a description of poetic utterances in praise of the courage of the hunter. The performances are histrionic in that they are excited and accompanied by vigorous gestures. A number of individuals separately extol the virtues of the same man, and their performances are accompanied by nonverbal shouts and noise from their companions. Since none of the performers is especially singled out, we may assume that these poets (if poets they are) are amateur rather than professional performers; whether or not they each repeat the same words or produce separate poems of their own, whether the poems are improvised for the occasion or memorized, we cannot say, though in view of the excitement of the performers and their reference to "the courage of the slayer," it is likely that the poems refer to the recent hunt and to the slayer's prowess in it.

Henry Lichtenstein visited the Cape from 1803 until 1806, but the account of his travels was published after that of Alberti, from whom he quotes at times. Lichtenstein notes that "the Koossas, when they want to affirm anything very solemnly, or to utter any malediction, make use of the name of their king, or of some of his ancestors, as *Non Geika! Non Chachábe! Non Khambuhsje*" (1812/1928:310). This practice participates in a ritual system that also provides a context for Xhosa poetry, as we shall see. Lichtenstein's comment about the invocation of a chief or his ancestors is closer to the mark than his later statement about salutations: "Though the Koossas have no mode of saluting each other when they meet, yet there is a courtesy practised towards the king wherever he is seen, by pronouncing his name with the syllable *Ann* before it, thus, Ann-Geika. His title is Inkoossi, which signifies *ruler*" (p. 353). Established modes of salutation are universal among the Cape Nguni, although it is true that the chief (Xhosa *inkosi*) is greeted in the manner described, a form of salutation that generally is incorporated into poems in praise of the chief; Ngqika, however, would not have been greeted by a commoner with his given name, but with his praise name, *A! Lwaganda!* The practice of honoring people with praise names is alluded to elsewhere by Lichtenstein: "When the Koossas wish to do honour to anybody, they give him a new name, the meaning of which nobody knows but the person who gives it. This is particularly done by any white people, who come among them, and remain with them for any time. Vander Kemp had in this way three names given him, *Jinkhanna, Gobuhsso,* and *Tabeka-Kelehre.* It is incomprehensible how soon a stranger is known throughout the country by his new appellation" (p. 318). As we shall see, names of one kind or another are a significant ingredient of Xhosa poetry. Generally, praise names are commemorative of a significant deed or striking characteristic (*Nyengana* refers to the shining bald head of J. T. van der Kemp, the first missionary to visit the Xhosa in 1799, and *Ngobuso* refers to his countenance), and their meaning would accordingly be evident to the bearer of the name and to his contemporaries who use it, though the reference might well become obscure in transmission over distance and time.

Recollections of a visit to British Kaffraria is a fascinating, anonymous, undated account of a tour of mission stations undertaken – it is evident from the content – by a lady in 1857, the year of the disastrous cattle killing, to which she frequently alludes. The author clearly has her prejudices, but her concerns, fortunately for our purposes, are not exclusively evangelical. She is an interested observer of and inquirer after Xhosa culture, as the following description of the singing of unconverted Xhosa reveals ("red Kafirs" retained their garments traditionally dyed with ochre, which converts to Christianity abjured): "I could not hear of any traditional songs. The wild chant in which the red Kafirs uplift their united voices when they assemble for a feast, is most monotonous. A sort of see-saw chant, from highest pitch to lowest bass, continued without variation, except as it is now and then broken by a shrill whistle or a long-drawn howl. One cannot imagine it expressing any kind of sentiment, yet the Kafirs soon learn to sing hymns pleasingly, when taught by the missionaries" (p. 90). African musical rhythm is cyclical rather than linear, and might well strike a passing Western observer as monotonously repetitive. Elsewhere, the author muses on the presence of poetry among the Xhosa after receiving a striking welcome at St. Luke's mission station near present Nahoon on 15 July 1857:

> I was then introduced to the women, who looked at me with as much curiosity as the girls had done. One of them made a speech which, being interpreted, signified that I was a chief's daughter, pleasant as a river of water or a flower in the bush. Now, I think that a more poetical effusion than that with which the governor was greeted – they told him he was the great cow. Nevertheless that was the highest eulogy that could be pronounced, as the cow is held in the highest estimation. I think the Kafirs are a poetical people, though Mr Greenstock will not allow that; he says they have practical, reasoning minds, which suggest questions it is sometimes very difficult to answer; but they express themselves figuratively, as do all the uncivilised, and that is associated with poetry in our minds. [p. 115]

On her return to Grahamstown, the author attends a missionary meeting on 29 July and records the exhortations of Bishop Cotterill: "The Bishop said the conversion of the heathen must be a work of time. No great progress can be made till missionaries are acquainted with the natives, and understand their language thoroughly. He recommends them to collect and preserve proverbs, legends, and tales illustrative of their history and national character" (p. 140). The bishop's progressive exhortation might well have been taken to heart by some individuals, but, as we shall see later, in the seventh chapter, a good fifty years were to elapse after the arrival of the missionaries before mission presses published Xhosa folklore.

Gustav Fritsch toured South Africa from 1864 until 1866 in order to gather enthnographic and physiological material for his description of the inhabitants. His book contains a long section on the Cape Nguni, as well as sections on the Natal Nguni, Tswana, Herero, and Khoisan and a linguistic and a historical section. Given the range of his endeavors, the generally high quality of his information is all the more commendable. He is the first of our foreign travelers to refer explicitly to Xhosa poetry: "The ideal of the Kaffer, the object of his daydreams and the favorite subject of his songs (*Liedern*), is his oxen, which are his most valuable possession. With the praise songs (*Lobgesängen*) of the cattle those of the chief mix themselves, and in these in turn the chief's cattle figure prominently. In these praises (*Preisen*) of his ruler he does not so much express loyalty as – deriving from the awareness of his dependence – a fear of the despot, who can ruin him" (1872:50). Cattle form the basis of the traditional economy of the Nguni, and are always used for the most significant sacrifices to ancestors; women from other clans, and therefore the wives as well, are denied access to the cattle and to the cattle enclosure (kraal) of the homestead. (The vocabulary of Xhosa includes scores of adjectives to describe the colors of cattle, but does not distinguish between blue and green.) Each animal in a herd is known individually, and a dancer often imitates the movements of his favorite ox. Just as men or women compose poems in praise of each other, so too men compose poems about their cattle. Such poems might well share stock descriptions of cattle with other poems in the tradition, including those that refer to chiefs; this seems to be what Fritsch is referring to when he writes that poems about chiefs "mix themselves with" the poems about cattle.

Fritsch also offers us an intimate description of a typical evening's entertainment in a hut:

> At night or in cold, unfriendly weather the hearth fire in the huts forms a point of attraction around which the company gathers, and for hours on end they pursue their harmless entertainment in an atmosphere which – because of the secretions of the compact mass of people, the smoke of the fire and of tobacco – is hardly likely to afford the European much opportunity of drawing a breath. If the gathering is at its

ease, communal singing (*Gesänge*) might well commence –
provided that one dares to use that word for the ear-shatter-
ing noise that has little more in common with music than the
beat; humming, hand-clapping or foot-stamping enrich the
musical pattern and only thereby afford the proper emphasis
which stirs the performers at the very least to unbelievable
enthusiasm. The words of the songs are pretty indifferent and
highly repetitive, as a rule turning to the chief's power and
strength, his wealth in cattle or to their fanatical passion for
their own cattle. Translators of such songs have laboured
hard to avoid triviality; success comes only partially . . . If
women are admitted [to dances in general], they form the
outermost circle around the dancers or a compact group, and
establish the time with hand-clapping and ululating songs in
which they more or less express their admiration of the men's
performance. [Pp. 90–1]

Fritsch depicts here the typical context for the production of many
forms of folklore, the central hearth in the circular, single-roomed,
wattle-and-daub hut with a conical, thatched roof. It is not clear
whether Fritsch's *Gesänge* are songs (*amaculo*) or poems (*izibongo*); to
the comment on translation is appended a footnote referring the
reader to a published translation of a poem in praise of the Zulu chief
Mpande, so perhaps it is izibongo that are alluded to. The practice
described is known as *ukutshayelela*, the encouragement – usually poetic or nonverbal – of men shouted out by women. Fixed poems in
praise of individuals might be uttered on such occasions, and their
utterance would account for Fritsch's comment about the recurrence of
words, although he might equally well be referring to the stock phrases
common to poems in the tradition. The women in this passage are
doing what the hunters did in the Alberti passage, expressing poetically their admiration for the performance of another. The anonymous
lady traveler observed that to call someone a great cow was a sincere
form of flattery; Fritsch emphasizes the prominence of cattle in the
Cape Nguni world view and in their poetry. Lichtenstein noted that the
Cape Nguni invoke their chief or his ancestors; Fritsch emphasizes the
prominence of the chief in Xhosa poetry. As we shall see in the fifth
chapter, the chief and cattle play a significant role in the ritual belief
and practices of the Cape Nguni; poetry participates in this system.

Ralph Deakin's perspective is of particular interest, since he is the
first of the travelers whose testimony I have selected who mentions a
specialist poet, someone distinct from the common man or woman.
Deakin was a British journalist who accompanied the Prince of Wales

on his tour of the empire in 1925. He offers this description of part of
the ceremonies attendant on the prince's visit to Port Elizabeth:

> Elsewhere there was a huge gathering of natives – Zulus, Xo-
> sas, Basutos, and Fingos; and their deep-toned thunder of
> salutation to the "Great Son of our Sovereign Lord and Pro-
> tector, the Great White King over the Seas" preluded the first
> native welcome the Prince had received in an important native
> area of South Africa. The *mbongo,* the poet who walks before
> any great chief, summoned the tribesmen to bow down and
> tremble. He chanted the *Izibongo,* or song of greeting, and at
> the end of each of his stanzas, the whole assembly burst in,
> chanting in unison. [1925:83]

And when the prince passed on to King William's Town:

> Opposite the rose-smothered stand sat the ubiquitous *mbongo,*
> official tribal chanter of praises, who wore a vermilion cape
> and sat with a look of dread uneasiness on his wizened counte-
> nance. Behind him were lined chiefs of the Imidushani, Aman-
> tinde, Imiqayi and other Cis-Keian tribes . . . Then the
> *mbongo* drew himself up to his full height and opened his
> capacious mouth; with teeth shining in his black visage he
> half-recited, half-chanted the Prince's praises and gave him
> greeting into the land. "*Imvula Mayine!*" (Let the heaven drop
> blessings!) shouted the natives of Dortrecht and the chiefs
> clapped hands and the ten thousand voices cheered merrily.
> [Pp. 91–2]

In place of the man or woman praising or encouraging the efforts of
others or of his cattle, we have here an official personage, the tribal
poet, *imbongi,* who greets in poetry the visiting dignitary on behalf of
the assembled gathering, awarding him poetic titles. Deakin's account
depicts the warm and harmonious welcome offered to the prince by
his loyal black subjects. There is considerable irony in this portrait, as
well as some significance: The imbongi in King William's Town was
S. E. K. Mqhayi, the greatest figure in Xhosa literature, and we have
a text of the poem Mqhayi produced about the Prince of Wales
(Mqhayi 1943/1957:59–61). A. C. Jordan translated as follows the
climax of this poem, a poem that does not quite express the servile
loyalty Deakin readily assumed:

> Ah, Britain! Great Britain!
> Great Britain of the endless sunshine!
> She hath conquered the oceans and laid them low;
> She hath drained the little rivers and lapped them dry;

She hath swept the little nations and wiped them away;
And now she is making for the open skies.
She sent us the preacher, she sent us the bottle;
She sent us the Bible, and barrels of brandy;
She sent us the breechloader, she sent us cannon;
O, Roaring Britain! Which must we embrace?
You sent us the truth, denied us the truth;
You sent us the life, deprived us of life;
You sent us the light, we sit in the dark,
Shivering, benighted in the bright noonday sun.

[Jordan 1957–60/1973:27]

Missionaries or colonial administrators share many of the prejudices of the travelers who observed the Cape Nguni at home, but
their testimony promises to be more informed as a result of their
greater intimacy with the people and especially with the language.
Dr. J. T. van der Kemp of the London Missionary Society spent
fourteen months preaching among the Xhosa from 1799 until 1800
before withdrawing to establish a mission at Bethelsdorp near present-day Port Elizabeth, where he ministered largely to the Khoi
population; Joseph Williams established a mission station near present-day Fort Beaufort, but on his death two years later in 1818 his
Kat River Mission closed (see Holt 1954). In 1820 John Brownlee
established a station in the Tyhume Valley near present-day Alice
that after a change of site became Lovedale, the first permanent – and
the most important – mission station among the Xhosa-speaking
people (see Holt 1976). It was the dialect of these descendants of
Xhosa that the Lovedale missionaries transcribed and used in their
early publications; it is this dialect that has given its name to the
language and that has become the standard literary dialect of all the
Xhosa-speaking peoples. Brownlee John Ross describes the work of
his grandfather John Ross and of John Bennie, who soon joined John
Brownlee at the Tyhume Mission Station:

> Mr Ross had brought out with him a small printing press, the
> first ever set up among the Eastern tribes. His energy is shown
> by the fact that it was unpacked and set up the day after he
> arrived, and fifty copies of the alphabet were thrown off two
> days later.
>
> Owing to good work already done by Mr Bennie, a lay
> agent, but a man of remarkable talent and genuine poetic
> gifts . . . a small spelling-book, a portion of Brown's cate-
> chism, a few hymns, and the Lord's Prayer were printed in
> Xhosa within fourteen days of Mr Ross's arrival.

Very soon there followed a grammar and a vocabulary; and by 1825 translations of the Scriptures had made considerable progress. A solid foundation for Native literature was thus early laid. Mr Bennie may well be regarded as the pioneer; Mr Ross made the work scholarly, sound, and final. [Shepherd 1948:8]

Ross testifies to the intimacy with which his uncle Richard, John Ross's son, learned to know the Xhosa, to the extent that he could address them in the appropriate manner:

He also acquired the ability, considered by them the peculiar mark of a man of high rank, to ask an African a few questions and then say: "I know you: you are of the house A, clan B, tribe C, your chiefs were D, E, F, and G; of them your bards sang thus, and thus . . ." To this kind of talk no man on earth, with the exception of the old-time Scottish Highlander, is more susceptible and responsive than the African of good blood who knows his people's past. It is fine to see how a disreputable-looking, broken-down old Native pulls himself together, stands erect, and realises once more his manhood when a White man meets him thus. [P. 16]

The ethnocentrism aside, this passage is interesting for the testimony it affords of the effect of reference to clan and group relationships and a recital of the traditional, memorized poems about chiefs.

Clearly Charles Brownlee, a Xhosa intimate who was the son of the pioneer missionary John Brownlee and who served as commissioner to the Xhosa under Ngqika, intended to achieve much the same effect when he wrote a letter in Xhosa to the newspaper *Imvo zabantsundu*, jointly thanking all those who had sent him messages of condolence on the death of his son in 1889:

I thank you, Makaula, chief of the Bacas,
    The deliverer who has rescued
    Flame in the hearth of Madikana,
    Being quenched by the borders of Ngqungqushe.
    The deliverer who rescues till succour is accomplished.
    Who delivers repeatedly:
    Who delivers and wearies not.
    There is the dragon gloating over the children!
To you, Albert White Makaula, I give thanks.
    Grandson of Ncapayi,
    Who takes the path that leads up the mountain slope.
    Upon whom gaze many eyes.
    Disappoint them not!

To you, Qebeyi, I give thanks:
  Son of a mighty one,
  Whose horns they would blunt,
  Yet whose horns they have sharpened:
  Who runnest foremost in the race of man,
  Who lettest fall words that strengthen men of honour.
  Who upholdest the truth with thy substance.
  Who upholdest and waverest not,
  Stand thou in the foot-print of thy father:
  Of Mekeni of the Embo country.
To you, N. C. Umhala; and to you, H. E. Tshatshu; and to
you son of Nozwane:
  Sons of the great ones
  Of the city of Palo,
  I give thanks.
To you, Rev. W. Philip; and you, offspring of Nkovu. – To
you also, son of Jabavu, and to you of Xiniwe. – To you also,
son and grandsons of him of Jotela. – To you also, Nana, son
of Ganya, and to the great wealth of names that stand with
you – I give thanks.
  Ye awakeners and leaders of the nation,
  Seed that fell upon good ground,
  Grain that has produced a tree great as the world,
  Leaven that has stirred up the ignorance of the dusky races,
  To you all I give thanks.
I thank you for your letters in which you give me your sympathies in the bereavements which have befallen me, and
have let fall your tears upon the graves of my children, and
have come to visit my sorrow and my sufferings. They have
brought me words of consolation and sympathy.

                        [1896/1977:75–6]

Clearly, individuals are thanked here by the production of poems in
their honor; some may be current throughout the tradition, but the last
is evidently Brownlee's own composition for the nonce.

    William Shaw was a young Methodist minister who came out to
South Africa with the party of British settlers in 1820. He soon conceived the idea of a chain of mission stations reaching to the northeast
throughout the territory occupied by the Cape Nguni, and in April
1825 he paid a visit to Hintsa, the paramount chief of the Gcaleka,
near present-day Butterworth, in order to secure the chief's permission
to establish a station among his people. In his memoirs Shaw described
his first evening at Hintsa's great place, in so doing affording us our
earliest description of an imbongi at work:

About sun-set, "the fool" or "jester," kept at this great place and the residences of all Chiefs of great power and authority in Southern Africa, as a similar functionary was formerly kept in the courts of more civilized countries, repeatedly cried aloud his usual public announcement of the events of the day. Mixed up with many highly complimentary praises of his master, he said, "Our Chief is a great Chief, &c. When the white men came to see him, he received them. He looked at them. He shook hands, and gave them an ox to eat." This was followed by another long rigmarole, consisting of a recital of the pedigree, titles, virtues, and glorious deeds of the Chief. I have often been amused on other occasions, and at the kraals of other Kaffir Chiefs, with this strange burlesque on the cries, proclamations, and formal announcements still made during great state ceremonies by the heralds and pursuivants of much more highly civilized courts. [1860:480]

Just as the imbongi in King William's Town in 1925 greeted the Prince of Wales with titles, so a century earlier Hintsa's imbongi recites a "rigmarole" consisting of his titles, his actions, his qualities, and his genealogy. Interspersed with this performance in honor of his chief are references to current events. Shaw explicitly compares the imbongi's function to that of the herald in European courts; a century after the publication of Shaw's memoirs, scholars compared the Xhosa imbongi to the Celtic bard (see Mafeje 1967) and the Anglo-Saxon poet (see Opland 1971 and 1980a).

Lichtenstein noted that chiefs and prominent commoners merit honorific names. In his reminiscences, Henry Dugmore, another of the British emigrants who were settled on the eastern frontier in 1820, writes of the chief Mqhayi, son of Ndlambe, that his "name of honour, when saluted by his subjects, was Umjengalanga–'he who resembles the sun.' " This tells us little more than we learn from Lichtenstein, but a few sentences later we read that in December 1834 Mqhayi was in the Cape, and "He had left the tribe in charge of his brother Zetu, a man of different stamp from himself, whose salutation name was 'Heart of Rock,' and whom the people were accustomed to speak of as 'the man who goes into battle smiling' " (1958:67). Not only do chiefs have praise names (Xhosa *izikhahlelo*, singular *isikhahlelo*), which are used as salutations, but here we learn that a chief is also referred to by a phrase commemorative of one of his characteristics, and that this phrase serves as an alternative name. Trevor Cope calls the commemorative sentences that a Zulu is given by others in the course of his career or that he composes about himself "praises," and he maintains that a Zulu oral poem (izibongo), whether of a commoner or a chief, is a collection of such praises (1968:26); following Cope, I shall use the noun "praise" in this book in the sense of a commemorative phrase that, as we see from Dugmore, can be used as an alternative form of reference.

Perhaps the most intimate description of the practice of poetry and its significance among the Xhosa-speaking peoples by an outsider comes from Albert Kropf, who spent over forty years in the eastern Cape as superintendent of the Berlin Missionary Society, who was involved in an early effort to translate the Bible into Xhosa, and who compiled what remains today the standard Xhosa dictionary. Kropf's description of the Xhosa peoples, *Das Volk der Xosa-Kaffern im östlichen Süd-Afrika nach seiner Geschichte, Eigenart, Verfassung und Religion* (1889a), quotes without specific acknowledgement from previous writers (such as Fritsch, for example, on p. 121), but his descriptions are generally marked by their detail and originality as independent of his predecessors. Like Lichtenstein, Kropf notes that the Xhosa swear by the chief's name (p. 33); like Lichtenstein and Dugmore, Kropf observes that prominent men merit praise names – the hero Gxulume son of Gcagana is called "Weapon and axe of the place of Nomtshwaka" (p. 32) – and chiefs assume praise names with which they are saluted – Sandile is greeted as Mgolombane, and Qeya on his accession assumed the honorific title Ngangelizwe, "Big as the world" (p. 43). Fritsch, Deakin, Ross, and Shaw all refer to poems about chiefs or visiting dignitaries; Kropf quotes a poem about a chief at the end of his narrative of the career of Rharhabe:

> So died Rarabe, who is sung about as follows:
>   A small moon, brittle (waning), –
>   The council place mourns. –
>   He lives at home and does not see what is outside;
>   The raven, who takes care of the fodder,
>   The hawk, who longs for prey,
>   The grass which, from the cliff
>   Consumed by hare and badger,
>   Fathers Ntsusa and Kote.   [P. 41]

Like Alberti, Kropf refers to poetry in the context of the hunt:

> Nqeno was a prince who was also much loved by the Gcaleka for his eloquence and fairness. In his old age, when he might have been away hunting, he lay back in ambush, and if the game did not come straight to him, he had it driven into the hunting area where the hunters wanted it, and as soon as it

was there, he claimed the biggest as his, perhaps a bushbuck, he stood up and let fly his spear and called out, when it had struck home: "Tsi, ha, ha, ha, weapon of Langa, of Tshiwo, of Nomagwayi from the east!" Then his followers carried it home and praised him, until they ran out of breath. [P. 17]

It is noteworthy not only that the chief is praised effusively for his performance by his followers, but also that Nqeno himself praises his spear by reference to his own ancestors. Later, Kropf refers again to the invocation of ancestors during the hunt: "Before they enter the forest one of them imitates in mime the quarry calmly grazing and others imitate catching it; then they enter the forest with many invocations to the spirits of the ancestors" (p. 112).

Kropf's description of the Cape Nguni contains a remarkable account of their attitude to cattle. Favorite cattle are given praise names and are honored in poetry, the name of the tribal ox serves as an alternative name for the tribe, men are honored by comparison with cattle, and intimate relationships link a man to his favorite head of cattle. In many respects, then, cattle are treated like people:

Cattle-breeding, although still carelessly practiced, is the Kaffirs' greatest passion and religious observance and a great obstacle to improved agriculture. They feast their eyes on the cattle with so great a lust that their imagination is occupied with it day and night. They sing about it and praise its qualities and compare it to the loftiest ideas of rational people and of still loftier powers. They believe that a special sympathy exists between them and it not only on earth but even after death. The bellow or cry of the cattle, its lust for battle and strength, its victories or defeats in battle are for them omens of good and evil. Ox, bull and cow have become titles of honor for strong, generous people. The bull was formerly the property of the chief alone, and symbolized his power and strength; the cow represents wealth, luck and generosity. Each tribe has a tribal ox, after which it is called in order to honor the tribe, just as each distinguished man has such an ox to which he accords all kinds of titles of honor, which is protected in battle and must not be killed, but has to be brought back home again. The illness and death of a beloved ox often occasions moaning and crying quite as loud as over a sick or dead person, and one might then hear from the mouth of the afflicted Kaffir: "Death has broken into our place with much greater might than when he wants merely to carry off a person. Our great ox is sick, and when he who is stronger than all others dies, what will become of us? We shall all perish!" And just as they do at the death of a person, the Kaffirs often abandon the place where the beloved great ox died. [Pp. 108–9]

Kropf offers descriptions of Xhosa amusements such as dancing and cattle racing that are significant for our purposes because they afford examples of the content of the poetry that tends to be produced on such occasions. Women *tshayelela* their dancing husbands, comparing their attributes to those of animals, and men incite their cattle by reference to their ancestry, and to their qualities and achievements:

> In daytime dances in the open at the cattle kraal or near the dwelling, the women on one side in Eve's costume beat the time with sticks on a dried ox hide to the accompaniment of humming and growling, and on the other side the young men and girls, each with a spear in hand, leap into the air, contort their limbs and utter cries of joy. At some remove a cluster of elderly and ancient women sits together. A little old lady praises with the greatest satisfaction the movements of her naked dancing daughter or granddaughter. On the right hand side the men sit silent and serious, as if giving attention to an oracle, at most an earnest scolding escapes their mouth when the gesticulations of a son displease a father. When the young have had their fill of this amusement, which has bathed them in sweat, the men raise themselves to demonstrate their skills and to strive with each other. Now the wives open their mouths; one shouts out the praises of her husband: "Behold my man, how he strides about, is that not the gait of an elephant, etc.?" Another: "Behold, my man struts about like a lion." A third: "That one of mine surpasses all, he flies around like an eagle" . . .
>
> Racing with cattle is high entertainment for the Kaffirs and usually takes place at the conclusion of weddings. Even as calves they are egged on to race by youngsters with whistles and shouts. In the races of oxen the men whistling and shouting all the time run on foot or ride ahead on horses, behind and here next to the oxen. The galloping animals are all inflamed by praise, while the individual is inspired by reference to its lineage: "You ox, you who were born of N., your father was black and white in appearance, he earned praise at such and such races; you are not yet shown to be inferior to him, demonstrate today your power, speed and endurance; today you will yet prove superior to all others!" and so on. The ox who gains the victory is praised now in the most comic and

exaggerated manner, in the course of which his movements are imitated. It is an exciting scene, and the sweat flies down in torrents. [Pp. 110–11]

Kropf offers us intimate depictions of poetry as it operates generally in Cape Nguni society. Only once in *Das Volk der Xosa-Kaffern,* in passing, does he refer to poets – *Barden,* "bards" (p. 5) – who stand apart from the everyday poet, such as Shaw observed among the Gcaleka and Deakin observed in Port Elizabeth and King William's Town a century later. In his dictionary, Kropf's entry for the verb *ukubonga* reads: "To praise, extol loudly and impromptu by songs or orations; to praise, magnify, laud, celebrate the deeds of a chief, or the feats of race oxen, or the valour of an army. Old men of the chief's clan, though distant, creep out of their huts at daybreak and loudly celebrate his praises. Phr. *lento umntu iyemka noko ibongwayo,* man goes away, though he is celebrated, i.e. the most renowned must die" (1899/1915:42). The noun *imbongi* is defined as "the poet who praises; an improvisator," and the joint entry for *isibongo* and *umbongo* is "praise, poetry; the song or hum of a nurse to lull a child to sleep. *Plur. izibongo,* poems descriptive of the feats and character of chiefs or heroes. Among the Abambo, *isibongo* is the clan name, e.g. *Mabengu, Dlamini, Radebe;* in greeting or in thanking a person the clan name is used" (p. 42). (The Abambo or Mfengu were originally Zulu who fled from Shaka and settled in the south among Xhosa-speaking people; in my experience the singular form *isibongo* is not current in Xhosa either for a surname, as it is in Zulu, or for a poem.)

"Bards," poets whose specific task is to deliver poems about chiefs, are also referred to in passing by George McCall Theal, a noted historian who taught at Lovedale from 1871 to 1877. Theal's collection of Xhosa folktales is a rich compendium of customs, beliefs, pastimes, and verbal lore in general. In his introduction to the volume he refers to battle tactics, and notes of the warrior that "the height of ambition is to be mentioned in one of the rude chants which the bards, whose principal employment is to sing the praises of the chief, compose on the occasions of festivals, and to hear one's name received with applause" (1882:14).

William Charles Scully was a colorful literary figure (see Marquard 1978) who once served as a colonial administrator among the Bhaca, another group who fled from Shaka early in the nineteenth century. Despite his condescending ethnocentrism and his patent effort to play to the galleries of his English readers, Scully's extended account of his encounters with a Bhaca imbongi are of value because they refer to the animal imagery, genealogical data, and allusions to personal qualities and deeds that constitute staple ingredients of the Xhosa eulogy:

> In those days the "imbonga," or "praiser," was still a recognized institution. Each chief had his praiser, and as I ranked as a chief I did not escape the embarrassing attentions of this functionary. It was rather a tax on both one's modesty and one's patience to be constrained to listen, from early morning till dewy eve, to a man of strong lungs declaiming about one in terms of the most exaggerated hyperbole – comparing one to the lion for bravery, to the serpent for subtlety, to the greatest of the great men of the past for wisdom, and to the thunderstorm for power. I was, like nearly all human beings, amenable to flattery, but one soon got tired of it when laid on so thickly. After I had heard a circumstantial account of my own supposed mighty deeds and a catalogue of quite mythical illustrious ancestors, recited over and over again with ever-increasing poetic licence for several days in succession, I felt I had had more than enough, so I presented my "imbonga" with an old blanket, and he departed, apparently content. As he went up the hillside he paused every few yards, turned round, and shouted newly coined epithets of praise at me. Fainter and fainter grew his voice until it could no longer be heard.
>
> A few months afterwards, however, the "imbonga" returned. Again he extolled me to the skies; again he called upon the heavens above and the earth beneath to do homage to my majesty and worth. Again he compared my beauty to that of a lofty tree and my somewhat meagre figure to that of the fattest black ox in the Baca pastures. But my self-esteem was unmoved: the novelty had worn off; I had heard it all before, and too often. I ordered him to depart, but he praised me all the more. I determined not to give in and buy him off, so he praised me steadily for a fortnight. I afterwards found out that my servants fed him, secretly, from my kitchen. I had him removed by the police, but as soon as he was released from custody he returned. In the end I surrendered, but not unconditionally. I agreed to give him a half a crown and an old shirt, he making a solemn promise never to praise me again. After the sum agreed upon and the garment had been delivered, my praiser once more ascended the hillside, rending the heavens with the clamour of his poetic eulogy. But he kept his promise, for I neither saw nor heard of him more. [1913:270–2]

Descriptions of or references to poetic activity by native speakers of Xhosa are generally scant. One of the earliest occurs in a series of accounts of Ntsikana based on oral tradition but written by John Knox Bokwe and originally published between 1878 and 1879. Bokwe confirms what we learn from Lichtenstein and Dugmore about Cape Nguni practices, for Ntsikana had a nickname, Nokonongo, which could be coupled with a praise to encourage him:

> In the afternoon Ntsikana at last appears, stalking slowly from the company of lookers on towards the dancing party. For some reason or other, he appears today not to be quite in the humour for this dancing. One of his admirers notices this, and by way of trying to put him right, shouts out a flattering address, well known to, and greatly appreciated by Ntsikana: – *"Wesuka u-Nokonongo, imaz' egush' ibele"* (There goes Nokonongo (nickname), cow that conceals her udder, i.e. keeps back her milk, hinting at great reserve of power). [1900/1914:11]

Elsewhere, Bokwe mentions that the whole Soga family, from among whom the earliest converts to Christianity came, could be referred to as *Lo mzi kaKonwana siwubizile*, "We have summoned this village of Konwana" (p. 16).

One member of the Soga family, Tiyo Burnside Soga, wrote a book about Xhosa traditions entitled *Intlalo kaXhosa*. In the Lovedale archives, now housed in the Cory Library for Historical Research at Rhodes University, there is a translation by C. S. Papu of the second edition (1917) that includes this passage on the imbongi:

> *Ukubonga* (To praise)
> To praise is a natural thing with the Bantus. The one versed in praising was seen and noticeable whilst still a little boy because he would begin at that age praising other boys; he would continue as he grew up and when he was now a man, he praised them properly and he would be styled "Imbongi" (Praiser). He praised when there was no war in preparation for a time when war broke out. He used to be employed by the Great Place to praise the circumcised young men (abakweta) and on their coming out from their hut, he would then be paid. The National praiser used to praise at the Great Place and he would get a beast and even in war he would praise the Warriors of his Chief. If he wanted to get anything from the Chief, he would start praising him without being asked to do so and he would get whatever he wanted at the Great Place. The

Chief used to be very fond of this Praiser. In this way the Praiser is a prominent server of the Chief also a great soldier in War. He learnt his profession by going about and listening to other Praisers when praising in a certain Festival. The next thing you would hear him using exactly the same expression in his praises tomorrow. The Xhosas had very good retentive memories. Today you don't find any more Praisers, they have sunk down with the Kingdom and humanity of Xhosa. [Cory MS 16369]

Soga, of course, has a perspective of his own, one quite different from those of the Europeans we have cited, but from this passage we learn of the connection, sometimes mercenary, between the imbongi and the chief, of his training and his performances in peace and war, and of his free use of phrases common to the poetry of other poets in the tradition. The contemporary imbongi does not involve himself as a poet in the rite of initiation, and this, together with Soga's intriguing concluding remark on change, hinted at also in the first sentence of the extract quoted from Scully, may suggest a radical break toward the end of the nineteenth century in the tradition of the imbongi, which he shall have to consider in the final chapter.

In 1936 Margery Perham published ten African oral autobiographies, including one collected by Monica Hunter Wilson from a Xhosa woman, Nosente. In the course of her narrative, Nosente describes her seclusion during first menstruation and refers, as does Kropf, to men praising their oxen during races: "Before sunset cattle were driven from all the neighboring kraals. The young men took them to a distance, then raced them back past our home. They swept down on us. As they passed the men shouted praises of their oxen, and women made trilling shouts. After that day I came out of the hut" (Perham 1936/1963:123). Later Nosente refers, again as does Kropf, to praises uttered during the dancing that follows the brewing of new beer, but whereas Kropf depicts women praising the dancing men, Nosente has the men praising themselves in terms of their heroic achievements: "When they had drunk men began to sing and dance. They danced in a line, and were led by a young man with a concertina, which he had brought back from the mines. When I first saw a concertina. The dust rose from the floor of the hut as they danced and the sweat poured down their bodies. Men danced alone praising themselves for their exploits in battle, and each woman danced her own dance" (p. 132).

There are a few other significant accounts of poetic activity, notably by the imbongi S. E. K. Mqhayi in his novel *Ityala lamawele* and in his autobiography, and by the anthropologist Archie Mafeje, but these sources will be cited elsewhere in this book. I want to pass on finally to consider depictions of practices incorporated into the greatest Xhosa novel, *Ingqumbo yeminyanya,* "The wrath of the ancestors," written by the greatest Xhosa scholar-critic, A. C. Jordan. *Ingqumbo yeminyanya* concerns tensions in the Tsolo district, tensions between the native Mpondomise and the immigrant Mfengu, between Western and traditional ways, between those with formal education and those without; it narrates the accession of the young Zwelinzima to the paramount chieftainship of the Mpondomise, the consequences of his progressive policies and ultimately of the disastrous destruction by his educated wife of a snake held by the Mpondomise to be the chief's ancestral spirits.

Jordan's *Ingqumbo yeminyanya* is a rich source of evidence on the way people – albeit fictional characters – address each other. Friends may have nicknames for each other, but they may also be addressed by patronymics or by their clan names; elders are addressed respectfully by ancestral names (on the Zulu naming system see Koopman 1976: chap. 1). Thus, in the opening scene of the novel, Mzamo welcomes a party of horsemen to his home: "By this time all the men were laughing. So Mzamo went round shaking hands, greeting the seniors respectfully by their ancestral names, and teasing the younger men calling them by their nicknames. He knew them all intimately, for he had been brought up at Mbokothwana where, along with Maqhubela and a few others in this group, he had taken part in all the pranks of boyhood. In fact, Maqhubela was his bosom friend, and the two used to call each other 'Thole lenkunzi' " (Jordan 1980:5). Maqhubela belongs to the Nozulu clan, and Mzamo is a Dlamini; a Lovedale student in the party from Mbokothwana, Mphuthumi, is a Mashiya. In the following exchange, Mzamo addresses Mphuthumi and Maqhubela by their clan names, knowing Maqhubela well but having only just learned the name of Mphuthumi's father, and Mzamo is in turn addressed by his clan name:

> When the turn of the college student came, the host said: "Come and have a drink, young man. What is your name, by the way?"
> "I am Mphuthumi, father."
> "You look very much like Dumakude. Are you his son?"
> "Yes, I am, father."
> "Come and have a drink, then Mashiya!"
> "No, thank you, father. I don't drink."
> "What! Are you a schoolmaster, then?"

"What do you mean, 'schoolmaster,' Thole lenkunzi?" exclaimed Maqhubela. "Is it not these very teachers who tell us where beer is to be found these days?"

"No, Nozulu," replies Mzamo. "What I mean is that teachers drink on the sly."

"Nonsense! Not these of the days of gaslights. Teachers drink with us nowadays."

"Then why not let Dumakude's child drink? Come, have a drink, my boy. This stuff doesn't tell tales. And all of us here are your fathers."

At this point Dabula intervened.

"No, Dlamini," he said. "This child doesn't drink, and I don't want him to. He has so far escaped the habit."

[Pp. 5–6]

Mphuthumi is also called Mashiya and the son of Dumakude by Zwelinzima (on pp. 33 and 34, for example). Zwelinzima, son of the late paramount chief Zanemvula, is the central character of the novel; he grows up concealed from his ill-intentioned uncle Dingindawo, who has usurped the chieftainship on Zanemvula's death. As students at Lovedale, Mphuthumi and Zwelinzima are close friends; they are in love with Nomvuyo and Thembeka, respectively. The four students call each other by their given names and also by the nickname Sibali; Zwelinzima is also known to them as Major. Thus, when Zwelinzima is acknowledged as the rightful heir of Zanemvula and installed as chief, Jordan comments, "Poor Thembeka! She little knew that Zwelinzima could no longer be the 'Major' of Lovedale" (p. 132), and Thembeka starts a letter to Zwelinzima, "I don't know how I should address you in this letter: whether to call you 'Major' or 'Most Excellent One' " (pp. 134–5). In his last speech to Zwelinzima before he makes public his claim to chieftainship, Zwelinzima's foster-father says, "Zwelinzima, Jola, this is the last time I address you by your personal name. Hereafter I shall be obliged to address you according to your rank. You and I must part today, for the time has come when you must go and take up the position for which your father asked me to prepare you" (p. 113).

In addition to these modes of address, chiefs and men of royal blood are called by their praise names (izikhahlelo), which they receive on accession. Dabula, for example, a minor chief of Mfengu descent among the Mpondomise, is called Dlangamandla, "Mighty Feaster," when he is addressed directly and when he is referred to in the third person, as in this exchange between Mzamo and his old neighbor Ngxabane:

> "Is this ochre man showing you those tiny huts of his, Dlanga-
> mandla?" remarked Mzamo. "Are those things fit to show
> anybody, Ngxabane?"
> "No my son," rejoined the old man. "Dlangamandla knows
> my old home in the kingdom of Zanemvula. He knows very
> well that I was not always like this." [P. 8]

Immediately after his accession, Zwelinzima introduces impressive innovations: "Even the resident magistrate at Tsolo remarked that, since
the coming of the Chief, the discussions at the District Council had
been of a very high standard. Indeed, the name, *Langaliyakhanya*
(Shining Sun), by which the people had greeted Zwelinzima at the
installation, seemed to suit him very well!" (p. 161). And later, after
Zwelinzima's first appearance in the parliament at Umtata, Jordan
remarks, "When the Bhunga adjourned, his name was on the lips of all
members from far and wide. Previously they had known him only by
reputation, and now all agreed that he did indeed deserve to be known
as the Shining Sun!" (pp. 162–3).

The chief's wife also receives a new name. At the wedding of Zwelinzima and Thembeka, not entirely approved of by the traditional Mpondomise, "The witty Nomvuyo was bubbling over with fun and Mphuthumi simply refused to address Zwelinzima as 'Chief' but called him
'Major' and 'Sibali' " (p. 157), and "after the wedding the Mpondomise
leaders began all over again to instruct Zwelinzima in his duties as
Chief, as if they had not done so at the time of his installation. His wife
also came in for much advice. She was not Thembeka any more, but, as
the custom was, she received the new name of Nobantu, Mother of the
People" (p. 158). In the flush of early enthusiasm for the energetic new
chief, even his car is accorded a praise name:

> Meanwhile, unknown to Zwelinzima, members of various or-
> ganizations – among which he was known as *Ndawo-zonke*
> (Mr Everywhere) – protested that he could not carry out his
> many duties unless they found him "a pair of feet," as they put
> it. So they came together and discussed the matter, with the
> result that Zwelinzima was one day most pleasantly surprised
> to find himself presented with a beautiful car, the joint gift of
> the various organizations that had been formed since his mar-
> riage, and now it was the car that came to be known as
> *Ndawo-zonke*. [P. 161]

In addition to their praise names, the Mpondomise chiefs are addressed or referred to by the name Jola, "Raider," or Jol' inkomo,
"Raider of cattle," a name applied also to men of royal blood who are

not chiefs. Zwelinzima and his uncle Dingindawo, for example, who are chiefs, are addressed in this way, as is Gcinizibele, who is related to the royal house (p. 20) but is not a chief. Dabula, a Mfengu ultimately of Zulu origin, and now a chief in an area of Mpondomise settlement, is called by his praise name, Dlangamandla, but is also addressed as Zulu. Both Jola and Zulu are royal ancestral names, the Mpondomise royal line descending from Majola and the Zulu from Zulu himself. These names are to the chiefs and their relatives what the names of clan ancestors are to commoners. Chiefs may be addressed as descendants of their ancestors: Zwelinzima, for example, is called Son of Ngwanya (his grandfather) by a Thembu chief (p. 181). (Given the ritual relationship between the chief and his people, the Mpondomise may themselves be addressed formally as descendants of the royal line, as when Gcinizibele greets his guests with "Honourable countrymen, sons of Ngwanya Majola, today I find myself unable to speak . . ." on p. 112.) Finally, all chiefs may in addition be addressed by formulaic titles such as Child of Kings, Most Excellent One, Most Excellent of the Excellent, or simply My Chief.

The dialogue of *Ingqumbo yeminyanya*, then, displays the system of alternative names and forms of address current among the Mpondomise (and other Xhosa-speaking peoples). There are also a number of passages describing poetry in action. In the first, Jordan narrates the first meeting between Mphuthumi and Zwelinzima at Lovedale after Mphuthumi has learned that Zwelinzima is heir to the Mpondomise paramountcy:

> Mphuthumi recalled his first meeting with Zwelinzima and the various incidents that had strengthened the ties of friendship between them. And, thinking of what he had recently learned of his friend's true origin and position, he could not help exclaiming to himself: "This world we live in! Up till a short time ago – just two months – Zwelinzima and I separated for the holidays with every hope of meeting again on the same happy footing as of old, but today when we meet there will be a gulf between us – he a chief, and I – "
>
> "Say so, Sibali!"
>
> The greeting came from a voice he knew better than any other voice in the world – the voice of Zwelinzima. There was Zwelinzima standing in front of him, smiling. Mphuthumi leapt to his feet, saluted Zwelinzima in a manner befitting a chief, and began a praise-song in his honour:
>
> "Bayethe, Offspring of the house of Majola!
> Mighty monster of the blood of Vukuz' umbethe!

Tough-snouted, even as the wild boar.
It plunged into the Mthatha water
And tunnelled its way through the earth
To emerge beyond the Xesi of Rharhabe:
You whose arm is nauseating from the spittle of Dingin-
    dawo's dogs!
Beware, Gcinizibele, lest mongrels snarl at his excellency!
Hail, worthy prince! Hail, Child of Kings!"

Having thus spoken, Mphuthumi took Zwelinzima's outstretched hand in both of his and kissed it fervently. Zwelinzima was overwhelmed. He did not know what to do, and his
friend, still treating him with the deference he would give to a
chief, supported him gently, helped him to a seat on a rug he
had spread for him on the ground, and covered him with
another rug. Then he continued his praise-song:

"See Zanemvula's flocks and herds ravaged by hyenas and
    wild dogs!
Why do you tarry here,
Why do you linger,
Fondly trusting they're guarded by the drongo bird?"

At these words Zwelinzima flung himself on the ground
and covered his face. "Oh, Mphuthumi!" he cried, "Please
stop, Mashiya!"

Mphuthumi was not unfamiliar with national gatherings. He
had attended several of them and had listened to the great
national bards speaking in honour of their chiefs. But he himself had never tried to sing any praises. On this occasion, the
praise-poem he recited seemed to come spontaneously and he
was unable to say where it came from. When he saw his friend
moved almost to tears, he also felt deeply moved himself. But
he "hardened his liver" and, assuming a firm tone, he un-
covered Zwelinzima, and said: "There's no need for me to tell
you why I called you here. You know. Sit up and let's talk.
Wipe away those tears! The house of your father is in a state
of desolation and confusion. It's no place for a cry-baby of a
girl. It needs a man! "

These words stabbed Zwelinzima and he roused himself immediately and sat up, for it had come home to him very forci-
bly that the "majorship" had come to an end this day. From
now on he was the son of Zanemvula, Chief Supreme of the
Mpondomise. The very events to which Mphuthumi had al-

luded in his praise-poem convinced him that it would be futile
to conceal his identity any longer.

For a long time Zwelinzima sat silent, gazing at his friend
who sat in front of him. When at last he spoke, he said: "Son
of Dumakude, you are a man! You've hit me right on the
head! Tell me, what is this all about? How did you get to
know all these things you have been saying? What has happened at home? Oh, speak, please!" And he turned his face
away. [Pp. 32–4]

Of the two poems Mphuthumi utters, the first refers to Zwelinzima's
ancestor Majola in six lines, then refers specifically to the enmity of
Zwelinzima's uncle Dingindawo, and cautions his foster-father Gcinizibele. The second poem is addressed directly to Zwelinzima, inciting
him to action in response to the dilemma confronting the land of his
father. Later, as he reflects on his situation, Zwelinzima recalls the
direct appeal embodied in the second poem:

> The more he thought over the whole matter, the more fantas-
> tic it became. Mphuthumi's voice was still ringing in his ears. It
> was like the voice of one calling to him from a great distance,
> out of sight; it was no longer the familiar voice of the Mphu-
> thumi he knew so well. It was the voice of one who had gone
> out in quest of a vagabond who had disappeared many years
> ago, leaving his father's cattle and sheep at the mercy of ravag-
> ing beasts of prey.
> "See Zanemvula's flocks and herds ravaged by hyenas and
>   wild dogs!
> Why do you tarry here,
> Why do you linger,
> Fondly trusting they're guarded by the drongo bird?"
>   While the other students slept soundly, Zwelinzima was
> haunted all night long by that cry. [P. 36]

Later again, when Zwelinzima's foster-mother rebukes him for hesitat-
ing to appear before his supporters in his claim for the chieftainship,
Zwelinzima recalls Mphuthumi's poem:

> Her words had the desired effect. Zwelinzima pulled himself
> together, recalling the incident at the Black Hill when Mphu-
> thumi reminded him that the House of his father was no place
> for a cry-baby of a girl. He remembered the words that Mphu-
> thumi had used in his praise-song:

> *"See the flocks and herds of Zanemvula ravaged by hyenas*
> *and wild dogs!*
> *Why do you tarry here,*
> *Why do you linger,*
> *Fondly trusting they're guarded by the drongo bird?"*

> Zwelinzima sprang to his feet, put on his coat and walked
> straight to the guest-hut. [P. 110]

Mphuthumi appears again as a poet in a passage describing his
horse, which has a name, a praise name, and a poem that Mphuthumi
has composed and memorized about him:

> You might have said that Mphuthumi's horse, Goloza, (the
> Lingerer), was actually conscious of the admiring eyes which
> followed his cavortings. He even had a trick of affecting lame-
> ness, the rogue, and it was such a convincing performance that
> more than once his rider had been held up by the police for
> riding a lame horse. Mphuthumi derived so much satisfaction
> from thus making fun of the police that he had named the
> horse "Destroyer of the Peace." He would tell the tale of this
> clever trick when he sang his praise-song. [P. 87]

Jordan follows this with an example of a humorous narrative spun by
Mphuthumi about Goloza, in the course of which he recites the poem
he has composed in his honor:

> You who linger at the trysting-place in vain,
> You shameless serpent who destroyed the peace of Paradise,
> Hear the chickens screeching, terror-stricken
> As the hen-mother skids away, out of your path!
> Scamper away, baby-fowl, scamper after your mother!
> Howl away, dog's head, and tonight I'll feed you on mphothulo.
> [P. 87]

As an Mpondomise, albeit educated, Mphuthumi is not especially
marked for his poetic gifts. He praises his horse with a poem he has
composed and memorized, and on one emotional occasion he bursts
into unpremeditated poetry on greeting his friend for the first time as a
chief. It is the duty of the imbongi, on the other hand, to produce
poetry on occasions of significance, such as at the ceremony installing
Zwelinzima as a chief:

> As early as daybreak, the national bard could be heard singing
> praises to the Mpondomise people. He alluded to great na-
> tional events that were known only to the oldest men. His
> narrative moved these veterans deeply. For was he not re-

calling the days of their early manhood, those days of battle in the Hope War, or the days of the annihilation of the invading Nonzaba and his warriors at Mbutho?

The bard alluded to the darkness that had temporarily enveloped Mpondomise people during those years when the king's child, Zwelinzima, had vanished. He compared the return of the young chief to the coming of the dawn, and the rays of the sun to the farflung benefits flowing from the benevolence of a true chief. Then he broke forth into ecstatic song:

"Make way, for the Ngwanya offspring of Majola bestirs himself!
Arise and behold, most glorious of glorious suns!
Arise and gaze in admiration,
Glittering eye of the Prince of Heaven!"

He paused. Then from the throats of all the men of the visiting clans there thundered forth the royal salute, while the womenfolk chanted ceaselessly. Novices in the art of praise-song also tried to emulate the national bard, declaiming their praises while he took his rest. But these were but poor imitations of those of the master. Then once again the voice of the bard arose, swelling into praise so majestic and strong that the fiery youth felt their blood tingling, and their spirits burning with new courage.

The weather was clear and calm, and as the day moved towards noon the sweat could be seen pouring down the bard's face, for he did not spare himself, but gesticulated vigorously in the ecstasy of his praise-song. [Pp. 133–4]

The distinction that Jordan draws in this passage between the imbongi and unofficial, amateur poets in the community is noteworthy.

After the installation and the wedding, Zwelinzima's popularity steadily declines. When he stands opposed to the power of the diviners, and favors a move to exterminate goats, the traditionally minded Mpondomise voice their protest at a meeting:

And when the meeting broke up, feeling was still running very high. Even the praise-song delivered by the national bard on this occasion was indirectly critical of Zwelinzima. The praise-song concluded . . .

"Say!
What manner of rain is this we have this day –
This rain that moistens only portions of land
Alas! We die of drought, we simple fools
Who thought today we lived in a rainy land!" [P. 176]

Here the imbongi, whose function includes the expression of blame as well as praise, plays on the suggestions in the names of Zwelinzima (*Langaliyakhanya,* "Shining Sun") and of his father (*Zanemvula,* "Bringer of Rain") in voicing his criticism on behalf of the people. (Jordan glossed the allusion more fully in his translation of this passage, which was altered after his death for publication. His translation in the typescript runs:

> Even the praise-song delivered by the national bard on this occasion was waddling, in step with the general discontent. Subtly suggesting with his imagery of *rain* that the chief was unworthy of his late father, Zanemvula (Bringer-of-Rain), the bard concluded his praise-song as follows:
>
> > *Say!*
> > *What manner of rain is this we have this day –*
> > *This rain that moistens only rainless lands?*
> > *Alas! We die of drought, we simple fools*
> > *Who thought today we lived in a rainy land!")*

Thembeka (now Nobantu) unwittingly contributes to the decline of her husband's popularity. She fondles the royal ox, which

> was greatly beloved of the Mpondomise because it was the last of the ancient stock of the House of Majola . . . It was little wonder then that this ox, derived of such famous stock, and the last of its kind, should be held in such reverence by all the Mpondomise, both in the Qumbu and the Tsolo regions, while the People of Majola swore by it . . . The young men had always resented Nobantu's playfulness towards the ox, for to them it was unseemly that the ox should be treated like a toy. Nobantu, on the other hand, was puzzled by their reaction, for she felt sure they did not love the animal more dearly than she did. But the reason for their objection was that it was a violation of a sacred custom for a woman ever to approach the ox. Moreover, her love differed from theirs. She loved it merely as a tame creature, a pet, with which she might now and again amuse herself, while they on the other hand revered it. [Pp. 171–2]

Apart from the disrespect she innocently displays toward the royal ox, Thembeka's disdain for traditional beliefs has disastrous consequences one day as she sits outside with her baby son:

> While they were sitting, there came two men with a lawsuit. On being prompted in the customary manner, the complainant was stating his case when he suddenly stopped, looked at the

sleeping child and fell on his knees in an attitude of worship
and began to recite traditional praises of the House of Majola.
Turning their eyes and looking at the child, the other men also
fell on their knees and joined in the praises, while the women
who had let down their shawls on account of the heat covered
their bodies, readjusted their head-cloths becomingly and
moved away quietly. Nobantu had been concentrating on her
knitting, but, becoming aware of these movements, she looked
up. Why, everyone was gazing at her child! She turned quickly
to see what it was. As the child lay sleeping, a yellowish-brown
snake had crept on to the pillow and coiled itself at the head of
the baby close to the fontanel. Horror-stricken at this sight,
the mother uttered a piercing scream.

"God of the Heavens! My baby!" she cried.

And seizing the snake, she flung it far away, picked up the
child and ran hysterically this way and that, still cryng, "My
baby! My baby!"

By this time the child was naturally crying too, having been
rudely awakened by the mother's quick harsh touch. Mean-
time the men were running after Nobantu and shouting "Nobantu! Nobantu! What are you doing? Why all this agitation?
This is not a snake. This is Majola!' . . .

Then rushing into the house and seizing a stick, she made
for the snake amid the cries and protests of the horrified
people. Seeing her determination to attack it, all the men
sprang forward and tried to hold her back. Even Dingindawo
had no time to remember the customary taboos forbidding him
to touch the body of his daughter-in-law. Everybody protested
and appealed to her, crying "Nobantu! Don't you realize that
you are doing? This is your father! This is the Chief–Majola
himself!' . . .

But Thembeka writhed and struggled in their grasp.

"Leave me alone!" she shouted. "None of your snake-
ancestors for me and my child!"

Horror-stricken at this blasphemy, the men momentarily
shrank back, and in that split second Thembeka broke away
and flew at the snake. All the people hid their faces as she
crushed the snake's head to a pulp. [Pp. 183–4]

Later, the old royal counselor Ngxabane addresses the stunned
crowd that gathers:

"People of Zanemvula, of Ngwanya, of Majola, if I am
silent, it is not because I don't want to speak. It is because I

cannot find words to express all that I feel in this matter . . .
This is no calamity, for calamities we know. This is worse than
calamity. Say, rather, it is the curse of death. For it is the
doom, aye, the very annihilation of a people. Who can speak
when an entire people has been destroyed? To whom is he to
address himself? And how has he survived the general destruction, that he is able to speak? . . ." [P. 188]

The snake is Majola, father of Ngwanya, father of Zanemvula, father
of Zwelinzima, and as such is saluted with the praises of the royal
house, for the praises, as we shall see, ritually are the chiefs, and the
chiefs ritually are the people. With Majola dead, the people are destroyed, for they have no ancestors to protect them.

In the agonized debate that follows Thembeka's action, old ethnic
cleavages between the Mpondomise and the immigrant Mfengu arise:

"Who are the true Mpondomise of the ashes?" pressed
Ngubengwe.
"Oh, *now* we're getting somewhere," said Jongilanga. "The
true Mpondomise of the ashes are all those men who have
Mpondomise clan-names and praise-names. And the matter
we've come to discuss concerns those people and those people
only. Ask the men on those seats there what their clan-names
and praise-names are, and see how many of them, besides the
royal chiefs with them, are true Mpondomise."
"Oh! Is that where you stand, Jola!" said Dabula, laughing
scornfully.
"Yes, that's where I stand, Tolo. *That's* where I stand,
Zulu. *That's* where I stand, Dlangamandla. *That's* where I
stand, Ngwenya-nkomo."
"Yes, *I* can see that *that's* where you stand. In fact, Jola, by
praising me so profusely with my clan-names, you want me to
understand that I am also an outsider?"
"That's for you to decide."
"*This* is the day, I swear by Zulu!"
This was the day indeed! for until this day no one in the
land of the Mpondomise had ever referred to Dabula's Mfengu
origin. It was no wonder then that all the men felt that a crisis
was approaching. [Pp. 206–7]

A sequence of tragedies follows the split that ensues. In an effort to
placate the traditionalists, Zwelinzima agrees to take a Bhaca wife.
"That day a herd of cattle was going to Bhacaland as *lobola* for the
Chief, and just as the morning sun was leaving the eastern mountains

behind, the shrill voices of the women pierced the silence in praise songs. They sang all the praise names of the Royal House of Majola, while from out of the gates of the Royal Place the herd of cattle – the bride tribute of the people – moved along slowly, with the counsellors of the Mpondomise following behind" (p. 259). But even this effort comes to nothing, and *Ingqumbo yeminyanya* ends on a note of unrelieved tragedy as the Mpondomise ancestors wreak vengeance in their wrath.

2
A COMPLEX TRADITION

We have assembled before us in the previous chapter a number of documentary perspectives on the practice of poetry among the Xhosa-speaking peoples classified fairly arbitrarily but for convenience into three groups (travelers, intimates, and native Xhosa-speakers), each arranged internally and roughly into chronological order. In surveying this evidence, I have been able to signal the major concerns of this book, and to introduce topics that will be taken up for detailed discussion subsequently, but I have probably succeeded at the same time in confusing the reader with the variety of impressions I have selected for presentation. The purpose of the present chapter, therefore, is to rearrange some of the material, adding new material where necessary, in order to achieve a more coherent overview of the Xhosa tradition of oral poetry.

The simple thesis of this chapter has already been demonstrated by the evidence adduced in Chapter 1: There are many kinds of poets and many kinds of poetry. Interest in the poetry of the southeastern Bantu peoples has tended (perhaps for good reason) to concentrate on the poetry about chiefs and prominent men: Such poetry was usually of historical significance from the European perspective in that it often concerned individuals who forced their way into the arena of colonial history. Recent collections and studies by Isaac Schapera on Tswana poetry (1965), by Cope on Zulu (1968), by D. P. Kunene (1971a) and by M. Damane and P. B. Sanders (1974) on Southern Sotho all concentrate exclusively on the poetry of chiefs and prominent people. Refreshingly different scholarly perspectives have recently been advanced by Douglas Mzolo (1978) on Zulu clan praises and by Elizabeth Gunner (1979) on the poetry produced by Zulu women, and by Aaron C. Hodza and George Fortune (1979), whose collection of Shona poetry from Zimbabwe places clan praises in the forefront but also includes examples of poems composed by the poet about other people and poems composed by the poet about himself ("boasts"). In many ways the poetry of the Xhosa imbongi is more polished and impressive than the poetry composed or transmitted by others in his community; but in this chapter we shall consider the imbongi as only one of many kinds of poets in Xhosa society (see Opland 1975): The Xhosa tradition of oral poetry is complex, not monolithic.

Three brief clarificatory remarks are warranted before we start. First, I must of necessity offer generalized remarks at this stage and write of an ideal time, perhaps in the middle of the nineteenth century, in rural territory. The actual situation today is complicated by social processes and forces such as urbanization, assimilation, and formal education; changes in the tradition over time will be treated in the final chapter of this book. Second, I shall write about an unspecified Xhosa-speaking group, suppressing the insistent fact that the individual history of some groups might alter the generalized and therefore somewhat simplified picture presented here. Again, the true situation is complicated by consistent social upheaval, especially by the incursion of refugees (some more militant than others) from the Zulu chief Shaka (died 1828) who settled throughout Transkei and Ciskei and became collectively known as the Mengu or Mbo (see Ayliff and Whiteside 1912, Kawa 1929, Moyer 1976, and Ncwana 1953). As a consequence of these disruptive migrations, there are Xhosa-speaking emigrant Bhaca and Hlubi in Transkei today, as well as Zulu-speaking Bhaca and Hlubi who remained northeast of the Umzimvubu River. A detailed exposition of the distinctions between Xhosa and Zulu poetry (both known as izibongo) and of Zulu influences on the Xhosa tradition is beyond the scope of this book, though I shall find occasion to compare aspects of the two traditions, and I shall, with only minor reservations, stress the similarities between the two traditions and their likely common origin by introducing some Zulu evidence in this chapter. Third, I am describing here a phenomenon that I call oral poetry, begging entirely the question whether it is "prose" or "poetry": The verb defining the action of uttering poetry in both Xhosa and Zulu is *ukubonga*, and I am describing that activity. In the previous chapter the English verb most frequently employed for this purpose was "praise," but the currency of that verb in that sense is doomed in this book from here on, if only because the poetry, as we shall see, deals in criticism as well as praise. The withdrawal of the verb "praise" from the lists leaves a yawning gap in our technical vocabulary, since no suitable substitute immediately suggests itself: "Recite" smacks of memorization, "utter" is too general, "declaim" too formal, "chant" too musical, and so on. At the risk of falling victim to pedantry I shall simply use the Xhosa verb "bonga" to mean "to utter a poem (about)" and accept shamelessly derivatives like "bongas," "bonga'd," and "bongaing."

The observations on Xhosa poetry cited in the previous chapter serve to convey the impression that izibongo treat three main topics. We encounter poetry concerning chiefs and dignitaries in Charles Brownlee, Deakin, Fritsch, Jordan, Kropf, Ross, Scully, and Shaw; poetry concerning ordinary individuals in Alberti, Bokwe, Fritsch, and Kropf; and poetry concerning cattle in Fritsch, Jordan, and Kropf and in the testimony of Nosente. Let us seek further testimony on the subjects of izibongo in order to amplify this range. In his autobiography, S. E. K. Mqhayi (1875–1945) writes of the time when as a boy he and his friends produced poetry to relieve the tedium of herding cattle. "I had always liked the poems in honour of persons or objects or events. It was pleasant when someone chanted a poem in praise of me, and I used to chant poems about some of the cattle I herded, about dogs and about my companions" (Scott 1976b:27). A. C. Jordan notes that "the subject of a praise-poem may be a nation, a tribe, a clan, a person, an animal, or a lifeless object" (1957–60/1973:21). In the course of a research project conducted on two gold mines near Johannesburg, A. Wainright, P. McAllister, and P. Wallace (1978) collected over 250 izibongo from poets who "were invited to *bonga* (praise) on any topic they chose . . . The subject of the poetry included the praises of chiefs, dogs, horses, cattle, *iinduna* (tribal representatives), as well as personal and clan praises" (Wainwright 1980:372). Xhosa poems, on this evidence, are produced about chiefs and dignitaries; about families, clans, and other social groupings; about individuals, animals they encounter, and objects in their daily lives worthy of commemoration. This is a broad list, but it is immediately apparent that fit subjects of Xhosa oral poetry are people, animals, and objects; in general izibongo does not concern itself with landscape and emotion in the manner of romantic or lyric poetry. Izibongo is a poetry rooted, in subject and imagery, in the concrete: In his obituary of the greatest of Xhosa oral poets, S. E. K. Mqhayi, Jordan observed that Mqhayi, "essentially a poet of the traditional type," was "almost wholly confined to concrete subjects, usually human beings" (1945/1973:111) in his written poetry, and that " 'Nature for Nature's sake' hardly has a place in *izibongo* of the old type, and Mqhayi's nature poems are on the whole disappointing" (p. 115). In this chapter we shall consider traditional Xhosa oral poetry "of the old type" as it operates in three interlocking spheres of social activity: the poetry of the individual in home and everyday life; the poetry of the clan, which cuts across village and domestic boundaries; and the transcendent poetry associated with the chief and his court.

First, we consider man in his domestic setting, the unexceptional tribesman as he grows up in a traditional rural environment. In the course of her fieldwork among the Mpondo, Monica Wilson elicited the following testimony from Geza:

> Geza told for whom, and in honour of what sort of deeds, praises are made.

People and animals are praised for gallant deeds. Never
have I heard a man, who is a coward, with praises. The man
who runs from a fight is looked upon as a woman, and
women have no praises. Those who are praised are men and
boys, bulls, oxen, cows, horses, dogs, cocks, and certain
birds.

Once I asked an old man who had fought with my grandfather Geza, about him. He answered, "You call him Geza
now, but I used to call him 'Breakerdown of the Cattle Kraal
of Mkinwana, he who stabs first, he who cuts with the spear
until the intestines come out.' "

Isaiah is good with his gun, and is fond of hunting. After the
sound of his shot had died away you will hear him say, "The
stone that has been stained red by the ochre it usually grinds,
the ragged-winged crow, and the swallows that make their
nests with mud."

A boy also has praises when he is good at aiming. Once I
went bird hunting with many other boys, including my
mother's brother's son Isaac. We made a long line so that
those who were at the end could not see each other. Isaac
was at one of the ends. A dove flew past us, and we all
missed it, except Isaac. I heard him shout, "Well aimed. I
(resemble?) dishes and plates, sugar basin, Europeans' uten-
sils, the old men's bald heads, which are burnt by the sun,
near Mswakeli's *umzi"* (the Regent). Some of us also joined
in praising him.

A man who owned a bull which was always victorious over
other bulls praised him thus: "Ngqolosa the cunning, an old
Mtshawu (a clan) man! The hut of the lazy person at Nomcok-
awana's burns. I saw Maqaqa taking his overcoat, and going to
buy me a hoe."

The ox gets its praises when it is good in yoke. A man had
a brown Afrikander with long horns named Ndulubantshi
(Waistcoat). In times of hardship he would pull hard, and
groan, so that the man became proud of him and praised
him, saying, "What! Bolokodlela, a river near Senxela's
umzi! The old white woman who is stingy to me with the
salt."

I have a cow at home which I praise for lowing nicely when
she has a calf. The first time she lows I say, "A new Noah." She
lows again: I say, "A new Noah. From the first generation to
the third generation, from A, B, C to 1, 2, 3" . . .

Every morning at dawn people are wakened by the crowing

of cocks. The cocks are praised during the day when people
are happy, and have got rid of sleep. When the cock crows at
noon you may hear grown-ups or children say, "Crow cock,
Maqobolokazana, Maqobolokazana (the name of a girl), your
sweetheart gave an axe in place of a beast for *umnyobo*. The
chest of a fowl!"

Among the birds which have praises is the *nqilo* (Cape long
claw). If the bird sings in front of one walking he expects luck
where he is going. He then says, "Say, sprig of a Sparrow, I
have not tasted the meat. The boys have been stingy to me."
[Hunter 1936/1961:371–2]

Omitted from this testimony for lack of space are "praises of good
horses, and dogs keen at hunting" (p. 372), but for our purposes Geza
covers well the range of poetry a man might encounter in a domestic
milieu. Let us start with the autobiographical izibongo.

In the course of his career from boy to veteran, a man may assemble
a poem about himself. His autobiographical poem will consist of a
series of allusive (and often cryptically elliptical) phrases, as in the
poems Isaiah and Isaac utter about themselves in Geza's testimony;
Nosente referred to men dancing "alone praising themselves for their
exploits in battle" (Perham 1936/1963:132). Although there is no differentiation in the Xhosa vocabulary, I shall refer to these poems as
"boasts," thereby following the precedent established by Hodza and
Fortune for Shona poetry and the precedent well established by commentators on classical and medieval literature. Let us assemble a few
more examples of such boasts. In 1909 James Stuart recorded the
testimony of Lunguza kaMpukane, a member of the Thembu group
living among the Zulu, which included an account of a battle during
which Nombona the son of Marama stabs his captors with their own
spear, "shouting 'I have eaten, I, the finch of the ridge, the waterfowl
of Marama, I, whose forearms do not break!' as one of Mzilikazi's men
fell dead" (Webb and Wright 1976:319). C. L. S. Nyembezi quotes a
boast from a novel by B. W. Vilakazi:

It always became a warrior to praise himself. Dr. Vilakazi
gives a good picture of this in his *Nje-Nempela* where Chakijana ka Gezindaka praises himself. As this is a novel the incident need not be historically accurate, but a very realistic picture is portrayed. After narrating his exploits, Chakijana sums
up by saying:
That is myself; he who wants me, here I am; I am here, I:
"Backward mover like a wizard,
The slippery one on whom the soldiers slipped at Bobo,

The greatly talked of, who has tired the judges,
The one who moves together with constables."   [1948:111]

In his article on Xhosa-speaking miners, Wainwright cites extracts
from two boasts. In the course of the first, the poet comments on his
motive for seeking work on the mines:

The bull that left carrying baggage
But was brought back by his eyes.
The crab that skirts the water's edge.

The poet explains that he came to the mines empty-handed, but returned home with the fruits of his labor; the poverty that he saw at
home sent him back to the mines to seek temporary work like a crab
just dipping into the water (unlike a fish, which needs the water to
live). In the second extract, the poet expresses satisfaction at having
earned sufficient to purchase a car (cf. Wainwright, McAllister, and
Wallace 1978:21–2)

No child of Mzimkhulu!
Speaking as he praised himself here at work.
Car of mine that I bought for forty (pounds)
Have you ever seen the likes of it, my child?
[Wainwright 1980:380]

To the boast a man composes about himself he may add praises
commemorative of his deeds, qualities, or physical characteristics
coined for him by others. Boys and men honor their companions by
composing and reciting such phrases. Geza says that an old man used
to call his grandfather "Breakerdown of the Cattle Kraal of Mkinwana, he who stabs first, he who cuts with the spear until the intestines
come out" (Hunter 1936:371); Bokwe noted that one of Ntsikana's
contemporaries tried to humor him by reciting a phrase well known to
Ntsikana, "There goes Nokonongo, cow that conceals her udder"
(1900/1914:11). Moses Ngubane, a Zulu from Empangeni, recited for
Alison Oettlé a poem about his brother, which she set out with commentary as follows:

The breaker or conquerer (this was his praise name, given to
him while very young by his grandfather)
By breaking or overcoming men (this man usually overcame
any opponent)
The drinker of zulu beer
When the beer is still hot (a person who could drink this
"hot" beer would be an extraordinary person in courage.
The Zulu custom was to leave the beer for a day before it
was drunk.)

The snake that has stood on the Igqulo mountain (Indlondlo
   was a vicious black mamba that used to chase people)
Warriors are afraid of this snake.
Mbanda shouted (he was a famous man who lived at Gqulo
   mountain)
He said, Dont impede that snake
Because it is a magic snake.
   The heifer of Ngcazi (his grandfather)
That has looked over the Illovo river,
And the beautiful girls followed it. (this refers to his popularity)
Crooked legs
   Because they have made the enemies crooked. (ie, the ability
   of the man to conquer enemies was likened to his crooked
   legs.   [1973:6–7]

During my first field trip in August 1969, I asked Ndzima, a Mfengu
living in the Qeto location near Peddie, to bonga; he responded:

I am going to start with my equal:
   Bushman son of Makhabane
   An elephant with an overgrown foot
   A puff adder with a beard
   The offspring of the daughter of Mzanywa
   Up the Fish River this side of the Ngqumteshe.
Let me come back to Salonti son of Singqoto:
   He who constantly turns over while sleeping, like a dog
   He who dies and rises again like the moon
   A last waist-garment that is desired by all the women of
      Qeto
   The child of the daughters of the Jwarha at Farmers, near
      the sea, River.

One man's boast, which he recites about himself from time to time,
usually as an expression of pride in an action or an achievement, would
be heard often and known by his associates and could accordingly be
identical to the biographical poem they utter to encourage or honor
him. His boast might consist of phrases he has composed about himself, as well as phrases his associates have composed and habitually
utter about him. These biographical and autobiographical poems are
related to the practice of honoring men with praise names referred to
by Lichtenstein, and to the system of alternative names evidenced in
the dialogue of Jordan's *Ingqumbo yeminyanya,* for the poems consist
in large part of a sequence of praises related to each other in that they
refer to the same man; sometimes the praise is preceded by or other-

wise associated with a praise name or patronymic. Cope notes that a Zulu izibongo consists of a sequence of praises that a man composes about himself or that have been composed about him by others; Oettlé comments on the poem given her by Moses Ngubane that "in this poem, each section starts with a praise-name and is followed by facts relating to the praise-name, or details about it" (1973:7). The fullest collection of such biographical and autobiographical poems in Xhosa can be found in W. B. Rubusana (1906/1911:379–468).

Generally, then, the poem about a person will refer to him, his achievements, and his qualities in a sequence of praise names and commemorative praises. Sometimes, however, a poem about a person uttered by another will incorporate, or indeed consist entirely of, phrases from poems about others and thus strictly be irrelevant to the subject. For example, in the same area near Peddie in which I collected the poems from Ndzima, I recorded a poem from Nophumzile Magopeni. This poem consisted of a sequence of names of various people, followed by their praises:

> Oh Vondovayile
> He punishes the Mpondo
> Folodayisi
> He beckons with his eyebrow
> He exposes himself and thrusts himself forward
> The one who buys a blanket for a shilling
> You women of Qeto
> Harvest and gather the better ones and leave the rags
> Here is Mahonono Mahono's mother
> Oh the women's snake is a belt for a skirt
> Zapoqopoqo
> One without education who makes the cat's hair fall out
> Pilapila of Godogo.

Nophumzile said that she uses the poem to bonga her son Mbambeli. She had not herself composed the poem; in fact, she remembered it from recitations by her grandmother: "I heard it. My grandmother used to praise someone else. Then I kept it so that in case I get married and I have a son then as well I'll praise my own son." Not only is the poem irrelevant to Nophumzile's son, it was even more irrelevant to the boys who were dancing one night and whom she encouraged by reciting the poem, for her son was not among those present. In her excited recitations of the poem that night, Nophumzile sometimes varied the order of the praises. It seems that in such a situation the *sound* of the izibongo is what encourages the dancers, rather than the words themselves. As Monica Wilson remarked,

"Praises are gabbled so that many, even of a Pondo audience, do not catch half of what is said, and the allusions are not understood by many. Geza insisted that 'the words do not always refer to the deeds the person is praised for, but are only a collection of phrases referring to remote or recent events' " (Hunter 1936/1961:372). The recitation of biographical or autobiographical poems frequently forms part of some other noisy activity, such as dancing or fighting; they are uttered in an excitable manner, in a rush, and the words are often lost in the surrounding noise.

An individual's boast may consist of phrases he has composed about himself, phrases he has heard others use when they bonga him, and/or phrases he has adopted from poems about third parties. Any individual will know his own boast, as well as those of his contemporaries, which he hears them reciting about themselves and to which he might himself contribute. Thus the old Mpondo knew the izibongo of Geza's grandfather, Moses Ngubane knew that of his brother, and Ndzima those of two of his friends. As he grows up, a boy will also hear his father reciting his boast from time to time, and will come to know this poem too, just as his father knows the izibongo of his father. The male head of a household usually knows at least the izibongo of his father and of his grandfather, and if they are dead (as they will be if he is the head of the household) these izibongo will then be the poems of his ancestors. These poems have special ritual significance and are recited in the kraal when a head of cattle is slaughtered to conjure the presence of the ancestors so that they may be addressed and supplicated. During such recitations there is no competing noise, and the words are repeated reverently in a normal voice. A man's boast, which he recites about himself during his lifetime, will be used in this way by his eldest son when he is dead.

P. A. W. Cook commented on the evolution of boasts and personal poems into ritual izibongo of the ancestors among the Bomvana: "A sacrifice, *idini*, is without efficacy unless the officiant calls out the *insinqulo* [*sic*] or praise names of the ancestor to whom the sacrifice is being made" (1931b:109). The imbongi gives a series of names to boys emerging from the rite of initiation: "These names are the names of the man who owns this *sibongo* and not of ancestors" (p. 110).

> When a man dies his *isibongo* becomes an *isinqulo*. *Ukunqula* is to call on the ancestors by name and to use their praise names, their *izinqulo*, which are the same as the *izibongo* were before they died. The *isinqulo* is thus a means of making an intimate contact with the ancestral spirit. Their praise names are parts of their very selves.

If a man makes a sacrifice he *nqulas* his ancestors, beginning as far back as he can. If his father is still alive he cannot, of course *nqula* him.

A man uses the *isibongo* or *isinqulo* of an ancestor whenever he sneezes, when a dog is chasing a buck or when his oxen are racing. If a man or woman stumbles or lets anything drop they cry out the name of an ancestor. This is a prayer for help. Simply the name is used, e.g., "Ah Mbelu!"

Women have no *sibongo* and thus no *isinqulo*. [P.111]

An individual will thus know poems about himself, about his associates, and, especially if he is an eldest son, about his ancestors. He also learns or composes poems about animals he encounters in his day-to-day activities, especially, as we learn from Fritsch and Kropf, about his cattle; Kropf noted that oxen galloping in a race are particularly inspired by reference to their ancestry, and Geza recited three izibongo about cattle to Wilson. Nyembezi quotes two Zulu izibongo recorded by Stuart, one about a bull:

> Headring of a man
> As it is sewn it crumbles,
> Spots that are hollows
> Nomalevu of Nomalekete
> Clothes which both show well
> The one below and the one above
> Snakes that climbed trees without limbs

and one about a dog:

> A woman that has frowns like a man
> Man, you would give freely
> You fear the frowns of the woman
> A woman that frowns upon her husband
> Hand that touched in an evil place
> For it touched the groin.   [Nyembezi 1948:111]

The fullest collection of Xhosa izibongo recited by individuals about their cattle and horses can be found in Rubusana (1906/1911:365–78).

As we learn from Mqhayi's autobiography, boys are especially fond of composing and/or reciting poems while herding, poems about themselves and each other, about their livestock and their dogs, and about the birds of the veld. Geza gave Wilson the izibongo of a cock, and of the Cape long claw: "Say, sprig of a Sparrow, I have not tasted the meat. The boys have been stingy to me" (Hunter 1936/1961:372). These poems about birds may be original compositions, or they may be transmitted within the tradition; if, as Geza testifies, both adults and children recite the same poem about a cock, then it would seem that that poem at least is traditional in that location. But there are indications that traditional izibongo of certain birds have a wider currency. Robert Godfrey cites a number of variants of the izibongo of the Cape long claw, one of which, collected from a schoolboy (probably a Mpondo) in Emfundisweni, contains a line that the Mpondo Geza used in his izibongo of the same bird:

> This is the bird whose flesh I have never tasted
> With the councillors who were eating it;
> Bird with the blood-spot on your throat,
> Better luck-bringer than other birds.   [1941:104]

Godfrey cites extracts from the izibongo of a number of birds, including one on the fiscal shrike collected from a Thembu in 1910, "picturing the sway held by this species over the majority of birds":

> Tshoko ji! I'm a hangman!
> Fear not, little chap!
> I'm the courageous bird,
> Well-versed in warfare!
> Even the pied crow is under my sway,
> For I get under his wings
> And stab him with my bill, –
> And off he gets!
> Most of the feathered tribe is under my sway,
> For I am the bravest of birds;
> With my bill I stick my prey by its head on the thorns,
> Hanging it on a tree.   [Pp. 110–11]

Like the poems about people, the izibongo of birds are sometimes in the first person, sometimes in the third person. All the poems about animals, like the poems about people, refer to characteristic qualities and traits, to deeds or actions.

All these poems associated with an individual in the course of his day-to-day domestic life, whether about people or about animals, may be original compositions recited by the composer, original compositions recited by an associate who has learned the poem from the composer's recitations, traditional poems transmitted by word of mouth and composed by persons unknown to the reciter, or mixtures of some or all of these. Every boy, Jordan remarks, "was expected at the very least to be able to recite his own praises, those of the family bull, those of the favourite family cow, even if composed by someone else, and was also expected to know the traditional praises of certain species of animals and birds. Any boy who lacked these accomplishments was held in contempt by the men as well as by other boys" (1957–60/1973:21–2). These poems tend to be memorized and repeated verbatim from performance to performance, though the order of the phrases they consist of might vary, since such poems in general are singularly lacking in logical coherence.

Every individual in traditional Xhosa society lives with his extended family in a homestead (*umzi*), a group of huts and a cattle kraal sometimes within a larger enclosure. These homesteads tend to be discrete, though all are subject to the jurisdiction of the headman of the location. In his day-to-day intercourse, a man comes in contact with people in his location, and it is in this social sphere closest to his homestead that the boasts, personal poems, and poems about animals tend to operate. By virtue of descent, however, every man and woman is in addition associated with members of his or her clan, and such ties of affiliation operate within a location as well as throughout the chiefdoms, for clans consist of various families often geographically scattered though claiming descent from common ancestors. Each clan has a traditional poem associated with it, and it is to these clan praises that we now turn.

Kropf defines the Xhosa word *isiduko* (plural *iziduko*) as "family name or honour, such as *i-Tshawe* or *i-Gqwashu;* a name of the ancestor or stock from which a clan or tribe is descended, used as an exclamation by members of that clan or tribe" (1899/1915:86). We saw how these names of ancestors were used in Jordan's *Ingqumbo yeminyanya* as alternative names, so that Maqhubela of the Nozulu clan could be addressed as Nozulu, Mzamo of the Dlamini clan as Dlamini, Mphuthumi of the Mashiya clan as Mashiya, and Dabula as Tolo, Zulu, and Ngwenya-nkomo (1980, pp. 5–6, 207). Use of such a name or a recital of a sequence of such names, as Ross noted, honors the clan member to whom they are addressed. The use of patronymics or a recital of the izibongo of his ancestors in a sequence by the head of a homestead relates an individual to the immediate genealogical context of a specific nuclear family; recital of the sequence of iziduko relates an individual to the more distant genealogical context of his clan, an affiliation that he shares with individual members from many other nuclear families living in his location and elsewhere.

To the name of a clan ancestor can be added a few of the praises he earned during his career, in order to produce for each clan ancestor named an izibongo, just as Ndzima produced izibongo about his two friends or the old Mpondo about Geza's grandfather. If they are recited in a genealogical sequence, we have a poem about the ancestors of the clan precisely analogous to the poem a household head would recite about his ancestors. These are the clan praises.

The fullest collection of Xhosa iziduko is that of Henry Masila Ndawo (1939); the most detailed study of Xhosa iziduko is by Wandile F. Kuse (1973) and that of Zulu clan praises by Mzolo (1977; cf. Mzolo 1978 and 1980). "It is customary," Ndawo writes in his introduction, "for everyone to be known by the isiduko which applies to him. It is rare to encounter someone without an isiduko, without an *isinqulo.*" Kropf does not gloss *isinqulo,* but he defines the verb from which it is derived, *ukunqula,* as "to call on the departed ancestors (*iminyanya*); to utter incantations for help, as is done by doctors for their patients; hence, to worship, pray; to call upon God for blessings" (1899/ 1915:286). Ndawo equates the isiduko with an isinqulo, implying that the use of an isiduko is a form of invocation, just as Cook equates isibongo and isinqulo; this and other ritual aspects of names and poetry will be discussed in the fifth chapter. Ndawo goes on to note that "these iziduko are names of people and of places" (1939:1). The clan name, isiduko, used as a surname, is the name of one eponymous ancestor. The list of ancestral names sometimes linked with places (usually of burial), iziduko, can be amplified by the addition of the praises of the ancestors named: "A person usually embellishes his isiduko by reciting its izibongo" (Ndawo 1939:intro.). The isiduko is thus the clan name, the name of the founding ancestor; the plural, iziduko, refers to a list of names of clan ancestors; and the addition of izibongo of these ancestors produces the clan poem, or the clan praises. Clan affiliations imply common descent, and transcend geographical locations: Ndawo notes that a man leaving his relatives to serve in another chiefdom would retain his clan affiliation but become a member of the chiefdom he served; thus many clans are distributed throughout the provinces (p. 2). Ndawo then proceeds to present and discuss the praises of fifty-five Hlubi clans, which he calls *izibongo zeziduko,* "poems of the clans."

Kuse, citing Ndawo, affirms that iziduko are a set of names of ancestors. "They are of special importance to members of the clan since they are the names by which clansmen reaffirm their identity and distinguish themselves from other clans" (1973:5). One may inquire after another's clan affiliation, as in the following hypothetical exchange: "For example, in response to the question, 'Ungumni?' (Of what clan are you?) a Dlomo would say, 'NdingumDlomo' (I am of the Dlomo clan). The inquirer might then in turn respond, 'Aha! Madiba!' The answer 'Dlomo' would have triggered a recognition of a set of names within the inquirer, enabling him to select any one of them as he responds, 'Aha! Madiba!' citing one of the Dlomo *isidukos*" (p. 2).

Kuse testifies to the serious contexts in which iziduko are produced, reinforcing Ndawo's suggestion of ritual significance:

> The recitation of *iziduko* [clan praises] then, is not a frivolous exercise, even if they are sometimes invoked only for entertainment. Often times they are brought to bear in transactional encounters between people as indications of earnestness when one is making a solemn statement or oath. The *isiduko* (or the *iziduko* implied by an *isiduko*) functions as an endorsement of a verbal commitment to a transaction or mutually agreed-to plan or course of action contemplated seriously. When one uses one's *isiduko* as in "MaRudulu!" or "Ndifunga amaRudulu" (I swear by the Rudulu clan), one is giving or pledging his (her) honour and the reputation of his/her clan. He swears by all that is holy and sacred. One's word is not to be taken lightly. [P. 8]

Kuse presents and translates with brief discussion some ten clan praises, four of which are common to Ndawo's collection, and proceeds to analyze them structurally after the system advanced by Daniel Kunene (1971a). Here, for example, are the praises of the Dlomo clan based on Kuse's translation:

> Dlomo
> Dlange
> Ngqolomsila
> Sopitsho
> Myem-myem
> Madiba
> The one begrudged by enemies
> Appearer and they expose their loins to him; they expose
>   themselves to him no longer; they fear white men.
>   [P. 13]

Kuse notes that "the praise name *uVela-zimbentsele* [Appearer and they expose their loins to him] is, in this case, elaborated upon with the praise phrase *azisambentseli zoyik' abelungu* [they expose themselves to him no longer: they fear white men]" (p. 5).

Although the clan praises may in origin be the names of ancestors to which their praises might be added, in transmission lines concerning clan characteristics or history might be coined, or striking and perhaps apposite lines from other clan praises might be incorporated. Thus Jordan remarks that the clan praises "make reference to heroic incidents in the history of the particular clan" and cites an example:

In order to join the Hlubi, the Masingila clan had to fight their way across one of the big rivers that flow into the Indian Ocean. They slew so many of the enemy that the water turned red. They are therefore praised as follows:

Beautiful as the blades of grass in summer
They came, from the seas, the blood-red sea,
That might river unfordable to men,
Crossed only by swallows, because they have wings.

[1957–60/1973:23]

And Ndawo notes that

sometimes the people who share the same clan praises are not related. This results from the fact that iimbongi [plural of "imbongi"] do not easily forget. When they hear the imbongi of another area uttering new and attractive praises, they adopt them.

That is why many people have the same clan praises and clan names, although they are not related . . .

In many izibongo phrases like "The woman with long breasts who suckled beyond the stream," "They no longer close the door at . . . 's place since men's heads provide the barricades," "Of Ziyane," "Of Mpofana and Thukela," "Of the woman who ate the zebra when no man could" appear often. [1939:3–4]

There is generally little room for innovation in the transmission of clan praises: Because of their ritual significance, the praises are usually passed on passively as received, with variations occurring in the course of memorial transmission. Such variations are revealed, for example, in a comparison of Ndawo's and Kuse's versions of the Zengele praises (the latter collected from Phyllis Jordan, A. C. Jordan's widow). In Ndawo:

The Zengele previously had their own chieftainship. They all swear by Zulu. Dlomo once fled to them when he was expelled by Zulu the son of Radebe. They gave him a hearty welcome. From that day they became Hlubi. Today they are known as the Hlubi proper.

"They are Zulu.
They are of Jili's place – the son of Mama – we wondered!
They are of Thiyani's place, of the place of The one that welcomes,
Because they welcome the chief who appears.

They are of Nomphumela's place, of The mat of the old
   women:
They avoid it until they forget it.
They are of the place of The one who cries blood, of Dun-
   jane's place.
They are of the place of Poison of the snake." [1939:33]

And in Kuse:

A Zengele person
Thiyane
The one that welcomes because he welcomed the chief who
   appears
The one who cries blood
Of Dunjane's place
Poison of the stick, while other nations shed only tears he
   sheds tears of blood. [Based on Kuse 1973:14]

In the course of his career, as we have seen, a man may collect
commemorative phrases or praises that are coined by others for him or
that he himself composes, and others may bonga him by reciting his
praise name(s) and these praises; this izibongo identifies him as an
individual. Others may also bonga him as a member of a clan by
reciting the clan izibongo, which consists of the names, praise names,
and praises of ancestors of the clan, as well as praises commemorating
events in clan history or physical or moral attributes of clan members
in general. This izibongo identifies him as a member of a clan, an
affiliation he shares with many others. Since praises commemorate
qualities or characteristics, where apposite these praises may be transferred from one poem to another, whether from clan praise to personal
izibongo or between clan praises: some phrases, in other words, are
current throughout the tradition and constitute a common stock. These
phrases may also occur in the izibongo of chiefs, to which we now turn.
   In the last chapter we encountered passing references to bards in the
writings of Kropf and Ross; a description of the activities of such
personages, known as iimbongi, in Shaw and Soga; descriptions of
iimbongi bongaing Europeans in Deakin and Scully; and fictional rep-
resentations of the imbongi operating in a traditional setting in Jordan's *Ingqumbo yeminyanya*. It is the imbongi's special task to bonga
the chief and dignitaries. Cope sees a difference only in degree of
refinement between the izibongo of a Zulu commoner and the izibongo of his chief. A collection of the praises that a man composes
about himself or that he earns in the course of his career constitutes his
izibongo; the izibongo of chiefs or prominent men tend to be longer

and more polished because they are subject to refinement by an imbongi whose duty it is to refine them:

> When a man of distinction is rewarded for his services by the chief with grants of cattle and land and with political position, he then establishes a great kraal and appoints a personal praiser, who will collect, polish, and perfect his praises, so that they constitute what we call a "praise-poem." The development from praises to praise-poems is not paralleled by the development of any new word to designate the product so that the praises of the meanest man, which could comprise something in the nature of "long-legged one who ran to Zungu's without stopping," and the praises of the kings, which occur as stanzas of several verses in strings extending up to twenty minutes' time in recital, are likewise known as *izibongo*. Certainly there is no difference in kind, but there is a considerable difference in development. The praises of chiefs and important men benefit from the services of professional praisers, whereas the praises of the common man are simply the spontaneous tributes of his fellows. [1968:26–7]

The task of the Zulu imbongi is to collect the praises of the chief: "Anyone can tell tales, anyone can sing songs, anyone can shout out praises to encourage a man engaged in a fight or performing an exhibition dance . . . Anyone can also compose tales, songs, and praises. But the praise-poem of a chief requires a specialist for its composition and proper performance. The specialisation is more in the performance than in the composition, for the composition of a praise-poem is a matter of collection and perfection rather than of creation" (p. 27). By collecting the praises of the chief, which are of the same order as those of ordinary tribesmen except that there are more of them because of the social prominence of the chief, the Zulu imbongi produces an izibongo. On ceremonial occasions he must recite the izibongo of the chief and of the chief's ancestors fluently, so that his principal talent is a good memory: "The art of the professional praiser requires natural ability and special application. An excellent memory is an essential qualification, for he has to memorize not only the praises of the chief but the praises of all his ancestors as well, and he has to memorize them so perfectly that on occasions of tribal importance they pour forth in a continuous stream or torrent" (p. 27). Thus one imbongi may better another by knowing more of the praises of a chief. Hoye kaSoxalase, the imbongi of the Zulu king Solomon son of Dinuzulu, told Stuart on 16 September 1921 that "Solomon once set me to compete with Sehla, but I subdued him completely, for he only knew

Dinuzulu and Cetshwayo. I know as much as he knew of Dinuzulu and Cetshwayo" (Webb and Wright 1976:171).

No one to my knowledge has established precisely in what proportion the composition of the izibongo of a chief is "a matter of collection and perfection rather than of creation." Certainly the Zulu imbongi memorizes the izibongo of chiefs long dead and recites them on occasions of national importance in a fixed, often genealogical sequence (see the testimony of Hoye in Webb and Wright 1976:168–70). A comparison of versions of the izibongo of Zulu chiefs readily reveals that they are primarily memorized, although the order of praises may vary. The fullest collection of Xhosa izibongo of chiefs is in Rubusana's anthology (1906/1911:229–348). Ndawo assembled the izibongo of thirty-six Hlubi and seven Bhaca chiefs (1928), three of which are common to Rubusana's collection. A comparison of the versions common to Rubusana and Ndawo reveals precisely the same pattern of variations ascribable to memorial transmission that is revealed through a comparison of variants of the izibongo of Zulu chiefs (see Opland 1974).

This would suggest that the Xhosa izibongo of chiefs, like those of Zulu chiefs, are merely polished and memorized by the imbongi, but there is in fact considerable latitude for creativity in both the Zulu and the Xhosa traditions. In 1974 Trevor Cope, Douglas Mzolo, and I interviewed two Zulu izimbongi (the Zulu plural) at the home of Chief Gatsha Buthelezi, chief minister of KwaZulu, the "homeland" designated for the Zulu people by the South African government. Each imbongi in turn produced at our request the izibongo of the Zulu kings; the poems about each king were to a large extent identical except for the order of the praises. When I broke the general sequence and asked one imbongi to bonga his present chief, Gatsha Buthelezi, he hesitated and then said that he would do so, but that his poem would not be the same as that which his fellow imbongi would produce. Through his apology, the imbongi demonstrated that he believed that izibongo of chiefs *ought* to be verbally identical; he also demonstrated that one imbongi's izibongo of a living chief may vary considerably from those of other izimbongi. On testing, we found a high degree of congruence in the izibongo they produced about Chief Buthelezi's grandfather, relatively less in the poems they produced about his late father, and little in the poems they produced about Chief Buthelezi. This finding bears out Cope's observation that the Zulu imbongi's task is one of collection and memorization of the praises of a dead chief (all the poems in Cope's collection, originally assembled by Stuart, are about dead chiefs or dignitaries), but indicates that there is greater latitude for creative composition of praises of living chiefs.

Xhosa izibongo of chiefs, like those of Zulu chiefs, and like those of any person in the community, are often clearly recognizable as a set of praise names and praises, as in the izibongo of Rharhabe quoted by Kropf, and the izibongo of his grandson Ngqika incorporated by the late J. J. R. Jolobe into his poem *UThuthula:*

> Lwaganda, hail to thee.
> The *Tshulubembe* great,
> Who laughs until the last.
> The wooden pole for gate
> At Phalo's cattle fold,
> The ringtailed monkey of the Nkwebus.
> The black serpent,
> Which crosses pools.
> The vulture with the dark brown wings.   [1946:15]

Rubusana prints a nineteen-line izibongo of Ngqika (pp. 245–6); the first line of Jolobe's version is the form of salutation using Ngqika's isikhahlelo, the second and third lines are the first line of Rubusana's version, the fourth and fifth lines are Rubusana's thirteenth line, and the remainder are Rubusana's lines 3 to 5 (cf. Yali-Manisi 1952:126). This indicates once again that an izibongo, even of a chief, is basically a set of praise names and praises, the praises succeeding each other in no fixed order. In this respect, as Cope notes, the izibongo of chiefs are no different in kind from the izibongo of any individual in the community. The individual memorizes and does not deliberately alter the izibongo of his ancestors, but during his own career he composes praises for himself or assembles the praises composed in his honor by his colleagues, and to these he might add relevant or attractive praises from other poems he chances to hear. These boasts (or personal poems about others) will alter on the occurrence of new events worthy of commemoration in praises. It is the imbongi's task to bonga his chief. He will know the fixed poems transmitted to him through the tradition about his chief's ancestors, but he must himself compose or collect praises about his living chief; these will alter as the chief involves himself in new actions or events worthy of poetic commemoration, or perhaps when one imbongi adopts appealing or apt phrases he has heard in the izibongo of another.

Any one living chief may have more than one imbongi, and their izibongo of the chief are likely to differ substantially. In fact, the imbongi might be expected to compose the poem he performs about his living chief, for part of his function is to report and comment on current affairs and their significance as he sees them, as Hintsa's im-bongi did on the first day of Shaw's visit: His poetry is in honor not so much of the chief as of the chiefdom, just as the clan izibongo about the ancestors of the clan honors the present members of the clan. The imbongi is a tribal poet, and his poetry concerns the chief as representative of the members of the chiefdom. As Jordan put it,

> It must be repeated that the African traditional praise-poem is not, as most white people think, just a song of praise in which the bard showers flattering epithets on his chief. The "praises of the chiefs" deal primarily with the happenings in and around the tribe during the reign of a given chief, praising what is worthy and decrying what is unworthy, and even forecasting what is going to happen: rivalries for the chieftainship within the tribe; the ordinary social life; alliances and conflicts with neighbouring tribes; military and political triumphs and reverses, etc. Thus the African bard is a chronicler as well as being a poet. The chief is only the center of the praise-poem because he is the symbol of the tribe as a whole. [1957– 60/1973:59–60]

Again, in his obituary of Mqhayi, Jordan wrote that "one of the essential qualities of *ubumbongi* [being an imbongi] was true patriotism, not blind loyalty to the person of the chief, but loyalty to the principles that the chieftainship does or ought to stand for" (1945/1973:112). The imbongi comments in his poetry on current affairs, expressing his attitude as one member of the chiefdom to the events and circumstances that affect the chiefdom, criticizing, when he sees fit, behavior that he considers excessive or beyond the norm. In order to act in this way as a spokesman, as a political commentator, he must be the composer of his poems. In this capacity the nineteenth-century iimbongi recorded in their poems about chiefs their reactions to white missionaries and colonial administrators and the innovations they introduced. When Ndimba, for example, transferred his chiefdom to the magistracy of Charles Brownlee, the imbongi commented caustically:

> He helplessly lives in the House of Tshalisi [Charles]
> Whom he loves for paying a wage;
> This child may be found in Kelly's canteen,
> Bearing patiently the kicks of the German.
> [Jordan 1957–60/1973:62]

These poems offer us a salutary corrective to the perspectives of Europeans, often offering us what W. D. Hammond-Tooke (1969) called "the other side of frontier history."

In this chapter the tradition of Xhosa oral poetry has been presented as complex, rather than monolithic: Many people participate as active or passive bearers of the tradition, men, women, children, amateurs, and specialists. This chapter has also presented Xhosa poetry in three intersecting domains of social activity: In the day-to-day life of the homestead and village, a man composes poetry about himself or about others and about his livestock and transmits poems he learns about others, about his ancestors, or about wild creatures such as birds; as a member of a clan at home, in his village or throughout the territory of the Xhosa-speaking peoples, his wife, friends, or strangers can honor him by reciting the poem about his clan; as a member of a chiefdom that may include a number of locations, he serves a sacral chief who embodies the well-being of all members of the chiefdom and in whose honor the imbongi performs izibongo on behalf of the chiefdom. All poetry basically consists of a collection of commemorative praises alluding to qualities and characteristics both physical and moral, and to significant events. The boast a man assembles about himself in the course of his career is similar in kind to the poem commemorating his associates; to the poem commemorating his ancestors; to the poem in honor of his clan, his chief, or his chief's ancestors; even to the poem he composes about his cattle. Any tribesman might actively compose poems about himself, about his associates, about his cattle, or, especially if he is an imbongi, about his chief; he might passively bear and transmit poems composed by others about himself, about his associates, about his ancestors, about the chief's ancestors if he is an imbongi, or about wild animals. Poems about his own or about the chief's ancestors, about his clan, or about birds are *traditional* in that he and his associates will know them and transmit them much as they receive them; poems about himself, about his associates (including the living chief), or about his livestock might be called *original* as distinct from traditional in that they are composed and freely altered by an individual or by his contemporaries. Original poems might incorporate traditional phrases, and original poems (for example, about individuals) can become traditional (when individuals die and become ancestors). The imbongi might bonga the chief but as an individual be honored in turn through the recitation of his clan praises. Whether they are active or passive bearers of the tradition, whether the tradition in them is active or inactive (see Goldstein 1971/1972, extending the concepts of Von Sydow), the lives of the Cape Nguni are permeated by poetry at home, in their location and their chiefdom, and throughout the territory inhabited by the Xhosa-speaking peoples.

If I have presented the Xhosa tradition of izibongo as complex, and in a three-part classification according to interlocking domains of social activity, I have also presented the tradition as rather static. That impression must now be corrected and an element of dynamism introduced. I have not made much effort to dispel the impression that Xhosa poetry is either traditional and transmitted in fixed form as received, or original and composed by individuals who compose it with deliberation and then transmit it in largely fixed form – that Xhosa poetry, in other words, is like the productions of medieval Celtic bards who composed poetry in isolation with blankets over their heads prior to public recitation (see J. E. Caerwyn Williams 1971); or like the poetry of the late-seventh-century Englishman Cadmon, who retired to convert to poetry a dictated biblical narrative by "memorising it and ruminating over it, like some clean animal chewing the cud" (see Opland 1978); or like the Icelandic skald Egil's *Head Ransom*, which he composed in captivity one night to flatter his captor and secure the remission of his sentence of death (*Egilssaga*, chap. 60); or even like the poetry of the blind Milton, composed and dictated to an amanuensis. Basically, such a description is accurate if we withdraw poetry from the realm of social interaction; such a description has become traditional in its own way, for with very few exceptions scholars have simply assumed that Nguni poetry is memorized and transmitted in a fixed form. In fact, we already have evidence before us that in a live social situation, in performance, Xhosa poetry often embodies a high level of spontaneity, so that we must now modify to a certain extent the impression of a largely static tradition.

A man has in mind his boast. Ask him to repeat it for you, and if he is Nombona the son of Marama he might offer you something like

> The finch of the ridge
> The waterfowl of Marama
> He whose forearms do not break;

but as he stabs an opponent in battle he might well shout out in exultation,

> I have eaten
> I, the finch of the ridge
> The waterfowl of Marama
> I, whose forearms do not break. [Webb and Wright 1976:319]

The example is hypothetical, but it is intended to show how a memorized set of praises can be employed with reference to the unique context in which they are uttered. Cattle might have fixed praises; in the heat of a race an owner might encourage his ox with those praises:

> You ox, you who were born of N.,
> Your father was black and white in appearance,
> He earned praise at such and such races;

but he might go on to exhort the ox in that specific race

> You are not yet shown to be inferior to him,
> Demonstrate today your power, speed and endurance:
> Today you will yet prove superior to all others.
> [Kropf 1889a:111]

Again, Kropf's words are hypothetical, since he carried no tape recorder with him to nineteenth-century cattle races, but I have used them to show how a memorized set of praises could form the basis of an improvised poem relevant to its specific context. These memorized poems could be about cattle or people or clans. They might have formed the basis of the spontaneous productions of men in praise of a victorious hunter referred to by Alberti, or of women in praise of their dancing men referred to by Kropf. Mphuthumi might thus exploit fixed praises when, on seeing Zwelinzima, he bursts into a poem the first six lines of which seem to be traditional Mpondomise royal praises and the balance of which refers to the predicament confronting the House of Majola and urges Zwelinzima to action. Mphuthumi, Jordan remarks, had heard iimbongi at national gatherings but had never himself "tried to sing any praises. On this occasion, the praise-poem he recited seemed to come spontaneously and he was unable to say where it came from" (1980:33). Such mixtures probably constituted the spontaneous productions of the amateur poets at Zwelinzima's installation, those "novices in the art of praise-song" who "also tried to emulate the national bard, declaiming their praises while he took his rest. But these were but poor imitations of those of the master" (p. 134). Kropf, as we have seen, defined "ukubonga" as "to praise, extol loudly *and impromptu* by songs or orations" (1899/1915:42).

The imbongi is a poet marked as such in the vocabulary and by virtue of his function and the characteristic garb he wears on festive occasions; he is expected to appear and perform at such ceremonies in the presence of the chief. But it is not unusual to hear men and women, boys and girls, burst into poetry with little apparent forethought, like Mphuthumi, in order to express verbally their high emotion. They might make use of memorized poems such as clan or personal praises, or the performance might be entirely spontaneous. Chief S. M. Burns-Ncamashe, himself an imbongi, confirmed the existence of this element of spontaneity in a conversation we held on 9 July 1971:

> OPLAND: You said that just about any Xhosa person has the ability to compose a poem if he's inspired.
> NCAMASHE: Yes.

OPLAND: This means that the imbongi is just sharing in a sort of common heritage?

NCAMASHE: I should say that, you know, because you take for example on a festive occasion among the Xhosa people, when everybody is full of joy and in a very happy mood, you should listen to the Xhosa women – and this is more particularly so among the abaMbo; you know, they are more poetic than the pure Xhosa ones – when they do what is called ukutshayelela.

OPLAND: I was going to mention that.

NCAMASHE: You know, they say excellent, sometimes original poetry. There are fixed izibongo of certain tribes, you know, which everybody knows: A Radebe is *Ndlebe-ntle zombini, Iimpundwan' ezingathiwa manqa-manqa,* etc., etc. [Two beautiful ears, Small buttocks that can be cupped in the hands]. But the women in that joyous mood would even go further and say something that is original, which is poetic, which is wonderful.

Such performances, of course, have rarely been recorded, though I have been fortunate enough to have a tape recorder ready at six gatherings at which persons other than iimbongi stood up to bonga. Later, each denied being an imbongi, and declined to repeat the poem because the particular moment that had inspired him had passed.

The modern Xhosa imbongi is primarily an improviser of poetry. In performances about his own chief certain lines will tend to recur. I have recorded one poem by the Thembu imbongi D. L. P. Yali-Manisi about his paramount chief, Kaiser Matanzima, almost every line of which can be matched in other poems about Matanzima that I have recorded from Manisi (see Chapter 6). But if you ask him or virtually any other Xhosa imbongi to produce a poem on a subject about which they do not habitually bonga, they have the ability to do so and their poetry will then be almost entirely original in diction. This ability to improvise freely in poetry is essential to the modern imbongi if he is to operate to maximum effect in social situations, if he is to express the opinion of the people or comment on an event in the course of that event, as we see the imbongi doing in *Ingqumbo yeminyanya,* when at a meeting he criticizes the progressive policies Zwelinzima insists at the meeting on following (Jordan 1980:176). The imbongi may know the praises of the chief's ancestors, he may coin and repeat from performance to performance certain praises commemorative of his chief, but in general he has the ability to produce polished poetry on the spur of the moment, he is, in Kropf's definition, "the poet who praises; an improvisator" (1899/1915:42).

This ability, however universal, might well be relatively recently acquired. I have met, interviewed, and recorded the poetry of over one hundred iimbongi, only two of whom, the late Edmund Goduka Sihele of Tsomo and Waraya Ranuka of Grahamstown, could produce from oral tradition praises of Thembu and Xhosa chiefs such as Rubusana collected. Sihele claimed to have learned the poems from his father, who was also an imbongi; Ranuka, over eighty years old and blind, decried the modern iimbongi who do not know the old praises of the chiefs. The imbongi will receive more detailed treatment in the next chapter, and changes in his tradition will be considered in the final chapter of this book.

3
THE IMBONGI

Among the perspectives gathered in Chapter 1 there were some that referred to the bard, the imbongi. Ross informs us that bards sing about chiefs, and Scully says that among the Bhaca each chief has his praiser. Deakin calls the imbongi "the poet who walks before any great chief" and "the official chanter of praises," and notes that the imbongi who performed at the reception for the Prince of Wales in 1925 wore a "vermilion cape" (1925:83, 91–2). Shaw compares Hintsa's imbongi to the herald in European courts, and notes that his poem consists of his chief's titles, attributes, genealogy, and deeds, and also refers to the events of the day. Theal makes it clear that it is not only chiefs who are the subject of the imbongi's poetry: For any warrior "the height of ambition is to be mentioned in one of the rude chants which the bards, whose principal employment is to sing the praises of the chief, compose on the occasions of festivals" (1882:14). Jordan's references to the imbongi in *Ingqumbo yeminyanya* confirm that iimbongi perform at "national gatherings" where they "speak in honour of their chiefs," as the imbongi does at Zwelinzima's installation: On that occasion the imbongi refers in his poetry to the battle history of the Mpondomise and to the current circumstances affecting the chieftainship in words "so majestic and strong that the fiery youth felt their blood tingling, and their spirits burning with new courage" (1980:134). Soga also refers to the role of the imbongi in raising military morale: "He praised when there was no war in preparation for a time when war broke out" (Cory MS 16369).

This set of impressions suggests that the imbongi was a poet markedly distinct from others in the community; he was associated with a chief, his poetry dealt with history as well as current events, he wore a distinguishing costume, and he had the power to inspire strong emotions in his audience. This picture was amplified somewhat in Chapter 2 by the suggestion that the imbongi served not so much the chief as the chiefdom, since in his poetry he criticized as well as praised. In Chapter 2 the imbongi's poetry was set within the context of all poetry current throughout the tradition; here the imbongi moves center stage as I cast the spotlight on his education as a poet, his relation to the chief, and his functions in the community. The previous chapter presented the Xhosa tradition of oral poetry in general; in this chapter I concentrate on the specialist poetry of the imbongi in particular. Having then treated the izibongo of the imbongi in general, I will proceed in Chapter 4 to a consideration of the poetry and careers of four iimbongi in particular.

We have seen that Kropf defined "imbongi" as "the poet who praises; an improvisator" (1899/1915:42), and I have asserted that in general the modern imbongi has the ability to compose his poetry in performance, as the imbongi seems to do in *Ingqumbo yeminyanya* when in the course of a meeting he criticizes the policies espoused by Zwelinzima at the meeting. Let us place before ourselves an account of a modern Xhosa imbongi in action, not in the vague rural setting of the previous chapter, but in the harsh world of black urban townships. Langa is such a black township, a segregated dormitory for workers in Cape Town and its surrounding areas (see M. Wilson and Mafeje 1963). In the urban townships there are no tribal chiefs, and in the largely detribalized milieu there is generally scant regard for the agents and for the politics of the black homelands the South African government is establishing on ethnic lines. In 1963 Transkei was granted self-governing status, a hotly debated step that culminated in its achievement of "independence" in 1976 under Kaiser Matanzima, a member of the Thembu royal family. In 1961 Mtikrakra Matanzima, a cousin of Kaiser, visited Langa to raise funds; his entourage included Melikaya Mbutuma, a Thembu imbongi. The reception of the chief in Langa is the subject of an article by Mafeje (1963) that in passing provides the only extant scholarly account of an imbongi's participation in a meeting, a factual counterpart of Jordan's fictional scene in the chiefdom of Zwelinzima.

Mafeje defines an imbongi as "a praise poet who frequented the chief's great place and travelled with him in the traditional Nguni society. His distinctive feature is that he can recite poems without having prepared them beforehand" (p. 91). (As we shall see shortly, in a subsequent article Mafeje abandoned as misleading the English term "praise poet.") Mafeje notes that the visit of Chief Mtikrakra Matanzima was resented by the Langa residents. At a meeting in the Langa Hall organized by the Chief's Reception Committee, the atmosphere became increasingly tense as two church ministers and then two members of the committee spoke. The atmosphere "exploded"

> when a young man from Thembuland, despite protests from the chair, stood up and said, "I am X's son, a member of the Ndungwane clan from Engcobo, and therefore a true Thembu." He went on, "I am not going to address myself to those men at the table, for I see that they think this is a church

service. Get this straight, this is not a church service, this is a forum (*inkundla*)." He politely, but determinedly addressed himself to the chief and said, "Honoured scion of the royal house (*mntwan' omhle*) give us some light! What is your mission here? We, as your people, would like to know." As he spoke, the chairman was ordering him to sit down, but some members from the audience, with equal persistence, demanded that he be allowed to speak for they said, "he is a man like any other man." Immediately he had finished speaking, the *imbongi* dramatically jumped forward onto the stage, and recited a praise poem, addressing himself to the chairman:

"Mlambo [a clan name], you know how to handle royal affairs,
Refrain from giving ministers all the chance to speak,
For they are going to preach, as they are wont to.
Be advised and give way before the Thembu burn one
    another."

He went on praising the chief and introducing him to the audience. After the *imbongi* had sat down, one of the Mgudlwa chiefs . . . said a few words of welcome to the chief . . . The next speaker was a Joyi chief. He also welcomed Mtikrakra . . .

This speech touched everybody, and most of all the *imbongi,* who stood up, and burst into a praise poem with great emotion:

"I have been wondering what is happening to everybody else,
That up to now nobody has made any reference to Joyi,
The dark bull that is visible by its shiny horns,
Horns that to-day are besmeared with streaks of blood.
It is for that reason that to-day he is not amongst us,
As I am talking to you now, he is far away in a
Lonely desert. But, to me, it seems that even that
Loneliness will not stop his bellowing."

The Joyi the *imbongi* was referring to is one of the Thembu chiefs who have been uncompromisingly opposed to such schemes as rehabilitation and stock limitation. He has been banished. [Pp. 91–2]

After the meeting, Mafeje asked two women teachers why they had attended the chief's reception, and they "said that they came out of curiosity, and that they wanted to see what happens in such gatherings. Their only comment was that the one thing they liked was the *imbongi:* they were impressed by his oratory" (p. 92).

Later, a farewell meeting was held for the chief outside the police station: "The chairman invited people to come to the table with their donations, but only a trickle of men did so. The *imbongi* was also encouraging them to go to the table. People were delighted with his praise songs, and he seemed to be getting more money from them than the chief" (pp. 92–3). The Joyi chief delivered a long and frank speech expressing the people's unhappiness in general and their disillusion with chiefs. Mtikrakra addressed the people for the first time, saying that he did not yet know whether he would choose the path to "salvation" or to "doom," so he could not promise them anything except that he would remember their advice.

> The moment the chief had said his last word, the *imbongi*, who could hardly contain himself, burst forth and said:
>
> "Yhe-e-ha-a! Nongcekulana ["tiny man"] has spoken,
> The dark bull of Mtikrakra has spoken,
> The daring and fearless son of Ngubengcuka
> has spoken. The one with a wrinkly forehead
> Like a lion has spoken. He has spoken, the
> One that they marked as soon as he appeared.
> He would have said a lot more, but only that
> European dishes [i.e., conditions under the white administra-
>   tion] have made my chief's son's
> Tongue sore. I am experiencing terrifying
> Things in this land of Phalo. It appears
> As if civilization knows no chieftainship.
> There is no need for panic, male issue of my nation, do not
>   be
> Unnecessarily perturbed multitudes of Rarabe, for I have not
> Foreseen anything, but all I am saying to you is that you
>   should
> Stay in readiness, because you do not know what might
> Happen tomorrow. I vanish like a submarine in the sea."
>
> The *imbongi* was making his last impression at the last gather-
> ing during their visit to Cape Town. [P. 94]

Here we see the imbongi Mbutuma commenting in poetry in the course of a meeting, pacifying an inflammable situation, focusing attention on a victimized absentee, introducing his chief to a strange and hostile audience and later supporting his appeal for money, and commenting in farewell unfavorably on the harshness of life for blacks under the white regime and on the absence of traditional values in the urban areas ("It appears as if civilization knows no chieftainship"). The functions served by the imbongi are complex, but we shall start with perhaps his most remarkable attribute, his ability to compose poetry spontaneously, for it is evident that Mbutuma could not possibly have prepared his poetry in advance but responded poetically to the situation confronting him. How general is this ability, and how does the imbongi learn to do it? How does a man become an imbongi?

Although they might mull over the general content, very few of the iimbongi I have met prepare the words and memorize their poetry in advance of a performance; often they bonga at occasions they attend without having intended to do so beforehand. Like other tribesmen, they know the fixed izibongo of clans and of their ancestors and other poems they have learned at school or elsewhere; but in general when they perform in their official capacity they produce spontaneous poetry relevant to the context. Whether or not the individual imbongi is conscious of this, the difference can readily be established through a comparison of separate performances by the same poet of poems about the same subject. I commenced my fieldwork in 1969, and I have never recorded two poems from the same imbongi concerning the same subject that are identical. Certain passages and phrases will recur from performance to performance, but they are not consciously memorized as the Zulu imbongi believes the izibongo of his kings should be. These variations occur not only over time, as the chief involves himself in new events about which the imbongi coins praises for incorporation into poems about him, but even between performances about the same chief recorded from the same imbongi within minutes of each other. On 9 July 1971 I spoke to S. M. Burns-Ncamashe, a Rharhabe imbongi who was at that time assisting the Xhosa Dictionary Project at the University of Fort Hare in Alice, and discussed among other things the difference between improvisation and memorization:

> OPLAND: Do you think [these poets] had composed and memorized certain praises which they would always repeat word for word?
>
> NCAMASHE: Well, in some cases they would repeat more or less the same phrases, but with new phrases each time, because usually izibongo do include a description of the appearance of a person or thing, and naturally, since the appearance doesn't change, you'd always refer to a man with that long nose or thin legs and so forth – he'd still have them, you know, a big tummy and so forth. So, in addition to the appearance, then there would be the events that may have taken place which would be included naturally in the subject of the izibongo.

Ncamashe offered as an example a twelve-line izibongo about the late
Archie Sandile, paramount chief of the Rharhabe, whose salutation
(isikhahlelo) was Velile. I pursued my theme:

> OPLAND: In that little *Velile* that you sang, if you had to sing
> *now* another *Velile,* you would use sometimes some of the
> same words, but it would be verbally not an identical poem,
> would it, although it would be praising the same man? In
> other words, when you praise you don't memorize, every
> time you praise you make up what you're saying while
> you're saying it?
>
> NCAMASHE: You take for example what I have said here. Now
> what I have said has stuck onto me, because when Velile
> was alive that's what I'd often said to him, and it sticks. But
> I say other things as well. But there are those others which,
> because of repetition – you see, I was always in contact with
> Velile as *imbongi yamaRharhabe* [imbongi of the Rharhabe
> people]. I was always with him, whenever I could [be]. So
> there is this question of, this matter of words fixing them-
> selves in a natural manner, imperceptibly, you see. You find
> yourself repeating yourself without actually sitting down to
> memorize this.

The latent imbongi as he grows up might produce poetry on the
spur of the moment, as do many of his associates. Like his associates,
too, he memorizes poetry, and sometimes conscious variations and
then improvisations develop from those fixed phrases. Edgar Dontsa,
a young Hlubi imbongi, himself the son of an imbongi, said in an
interview at his home near Mount Fletcher on 28 December 1970 that
he improvises on the fixed clan praises:

> OPLAND: When you learn to praise your clan, do you always
> praise it using exactly the same words? In other words, is it
> memorized like a recitation?
>
> DONTSA: No, I don't use the same words. If I am praising
> perhaps you, I will use different words, just because now
> you happen to be somebody and then if I happen to stick to
> someone then I have to use different words.
>
> OPLAND: But if you praise your clan, let's say, iziduko.
>
> DONTSA: Yes, I know. There I'll have to use different – in fact,
> the same words there.
>
> OPLAND: *Exactly* the same words?
>
> DONTSA: Yes.
>
> OPLAND: Do you think if you have to praise your clan now, I

came back in a week's time and asked you to praise your clan again, would you use exactly the same words?

DONTSA: Yes.

OPLAND: You would?

DONTSA: Yes.

OPLAND: So that it's memorized?

DONTSA: No, there *are* words, the words which were memorized and which are still there. There are those words. Then now I recite those words. Having done it I add new words, yes, to that, in order to make it be more, more impressing.

Lungisila Gibson Vuma is an Mfengu who was a sixteen-year-old schoolboy with a strong desire to be an imbongi when I met him on 10 December 1970. He produced two izibongo for me, both of which were based on poems he had learned in school: "I learnt this from school, and then I added some thoughts to the poems I learnt at school." With us during the interview were Gibson's chief and Lungisa Wilberforce Msila, a Gcaleka imbongi working in the area as an agricultural consultant, who served as imbongi for a number of the local Mfengu chiefs. Msila acknowledged that like Gibson he had learned to bonga spontaneously by first adding phrases of his own composition to poems he had learned from books:

MSILA: He's starting doing what I started doing when I first became imbongi, because I was fond of quoting from these poems written by these authors.

OPLAND: Now if he keeps on like this and he goes the way you're going, in a few years' time he will be singing his own poems?

MSILA: I was older than him, because I was taking books from the library. He says now he just passed Standard 5 [the seventh year of schooling] this year. I was doing my J.C. [the tenth year] at that time when I adopted this system.

The latent imbongi is thus but one of many in his community who enjoys the by no means unusual talent to compose poetry on the spur of the moment, whether he achieves this ability through subconscious absorption of the phrases and rhythms of the traditional memorized or written poetry or through conscious imitation and experimentation. There comes a time, however, when the boy or man develops an ambition to exploit his natural talent and to become an imbongi. For some, the impulse for this decision comes suddenly in the form of a dream. Benjamin Hoza, for example, was fifty-three years old and illiterate when I interviewed him in his home in the Qongqotha loca-

tion outside King William's Town on 10 December 1970. He had
started to act as an imbongi only ten years earlier, as he told me
through an interpreter:

> There was a ceremony that day I started to become imbongi,
> at Zwelitsha. I was present there also. Then I came back home
> from there. I slept. I dreamt, as if I was preaching. In the
> morning I didn't know anything about that. Now when an ox
> was being slaughtered for that particular occasion at Zwelit-
> sha, it suddenly came into my mind, all clear. I started praising
> at the same time, and I praised, and I praised, till the ox was
> wholly slaughtered. It appeared as if I was reading all the
> words of praising. And after that there was another ceremony
> at the chief's great place. They came to fetch me. Sangotsha
> came to fetch me. When I came there I praised the chief, and I
> had more words. Since then I've been, it's my duty till today,
> going up and down, up and down, Cape Town, Johannesburg,
> everywhere. Even now I'm on duty: this is the chief's counse-
> lor, of the imiDushane, he's come to fetch me to go on duty
> praising. That's how I began to become imbongi.

Ncamashe and A. M. S. Sityana are other iimbongi who have told me
that their original impulse to become specialist poets came to them in
dreams, as it did for Max Khamile, who likens his experiences to those
of a diviner in the process of being visited in dreams and being summoned by the ancestral spirits, a process known as *ukuthwasa*. For
most, however, this decision comes slowly. A person bongas his associates and his livestock. He appears at ceremonies and festivals and
perhaps bongas his chief and visiting dignitaries. If he does this often
enough he may become a regular feature of such occasions and become accepted by the chief and the people, and he may find himself
gravitating toward the chief's residence (his "great place," *komkhulu*)
and performing there frequently, and perhaps the chief may invite him
to form part of his entourage when he travels; he may then have
become an imbongi.

There are a number of critical features in this paradigm: There is no
formal apprenticeship or training for an imbongi; he needs the tacit
acceptance of the people to become an imbongi; rarely is he officially
appointed imbongi by the chief, merely acknowledged or recognized if
he chooses to present himself; and though he may associate himself
intimately with the chief and the affairs of the great place, as imbongi
he is never paid a salary by the chief. Aspirant iimbongi may listen to
and learn from others, but they do not attach themselves to a practic-
ing imbongi in order to learn their craft. The process is strictly infor-

mal: There are no guilds of poets; iimbongi do not form a separate class or caste; their status is not hereditary. Alfred Sityana says that no amount of training can make an imbongi of a boy lacking a special talent:

> OPLAND: If a boy came to you and said to you "I want to be an imbongi," what advice would you give him?
>
> SITYANA: Well, I'm going to advise him to, not to try, I mean not try to get in touch with anybody, because this thing comes itself.
>
> OPLAND: So it's a gift: He either has the gift or he hasn't?
>
> SITYANA: Yes. It shows that he has no gift.

On 20 December 1970, in response to much the same question, D. L. P. Yali-Manisi stressed the necessity of listening to the izibongo of elders and went on to support the point made by Sityana that an imbongi must simply have a special talent:

> OPLAND: If a young man came to you and said that he wanted to become an imbongi, what advice would you give him? What would you tell him, how would you instruct him?
>
> MANISI: Well, as far as I'm concerned, there are no proper instructions, but I would dare say there are instructions, only that I would advise him to listen to the elders, to the elders when they praise the chief or when they are praising one another and then from that they may get experience.
>
> OPLAND: Just listen?
>
> MANISI: Yes.
>
> OPLAND: And to practice?
>
> MANISI: Yes.
>
> OPLAND: How do they practice? Did you practice when you were a young boy with your father's sheep and cattle? You know, did you try to fit words together and try to –
>
> MANISI: No. I praised. From the moment I had something that I can now praise then I praised.
>
> OPLAND: So this is a special gift?
>
> MANISI: I take it as a special gift, yes.
>
> OPLAND: And not everyone has it?
>
> MANISI: No.

Manisi himself underwent no formal training:

> OPLAND: Where did you learn to sing?
>
> MANISI: Actually, I didn't learn it. I grew up as a young boy in this location looking after my father's cattle and sheep. Then

I used to hear old men singing praises when you bring in cows for milking. From that I got such little experience. Then from it I see myself now being called a poet.

The aspirant imbongi exercises his talent in public and may come to be accepted by the people: He attaches himself to the great place, as the Bhaca imbongi attached himself to William Scully (to Scully's unsympathetic embarrassment), and his appearance on ceremonial occasions might come to be a regular feature of such events. Mafeje described this process thus: "He was self-appointed, and his success was determined by the response of the people to what he had to say. If the people felt that what he said was representative or reflective of their interests and aspirations, then he was generally accepted as the 'national poet,' *imbongi yakomkhulu* (the poet of the main residence), or, more recently, *imbongi yesizwe* (the poet of the nation)" (1967:195). A popular chief might well attract more than one imbongi to his great place; many chiefs have none. The process is left to chance, although Khamile told me that after a performance a visiting chief once issued an invitation to him to settle in his chiefdom. At some stage in the process, the poet who has won popular acceptance by chief and chiefdom (rarely explicitly acknowledged) assumes for his public appearances a distinctive traditional costume of animal-skin cloak and hat, and brandishing two spears or fighting sticks he performs thus garbed before his chief. His transition from everyday poet to imbongi is complete.

It is generally accepted that the imbongi enjoys the license in his poetry to use ribald language otherwise unacceptable in public. Hence Rubusana wrote in the preface to his collection of Xhosa folklore:

> The book consists chiefly of poetry, as that is the main form of literature filled with Xhosa eloquence, and it is that part of the language that includes all figurative speech in Xhosa.
>
> To some, perhaps, it will be difficult to comprehend because of the obscure terminology and because they lack poetic acumen. The bulk of the praises by the red-ochre people will be found to consist of terminology that is offensive to the educated people who have a euphemistic taste, and who do not like calling a spade a spade. We have attempted to excise some of these words, or to conceal them beneath a cloak of euphemism. We could not do so everywhere, because it became evident that by so doing we would be assassinating the very spirit and emotion of the poet.
>
> To those whose feelings might be hurt, we can only say, like the English poet Tennyson,

Vex not thou the poet's mind
　With thy shallow wit:
Vex not thou the poet's mind;
　For thou canst not fathom it.

To those who might be obsessed with evil thoughts on en-
countering such words we say, "Evil begets evil." [1906/
1911:vi–vii]

Not only can the imbongi use ribald language, he also enjoys the
license to criticize with impunity persons in positions of power. Both
licenses seem to be acknowledgements that the imbongi in performance is not to be held responsible – perhaps *is* not responsible – for
what he says. His public performance is always dramatic, accompanied
by sometimes vigorous movement and gesture and uttered in a strained
growling voice designed to carry in a crowd; in performance the imbongi often works himself into an ecstatic transport of inspiration.
Many iimbongi I have recorded in public are unaware of what they
have said in performance, and subsequently listen attentively to the
tape recording as if they were hearing the poem for the first time. The
Thembu imbongi Nelson Title Mabunu produced a poem for me on 20
December 1970. When I returned on 16 February 1971 to check my
transcription and translation with him, I first played him a recording of
a poem by Manisi and invited his reaction. Mabunu liked Manisi's
poem, but felt that the criticism Manisi had voiced about the duplicity
of the nineteenth-century missionaries, although fair, ought not to
have been expressed, as whites would not understand and blacks
would be aroused; yet when a few minutes later we checked the transcription of the poem Mabunu himself had produced two months earlier, we found that he had expressed precisely similar sentiments (see
Opland 1975:202).

The imbongi distinguishes himself from other poets in the community in that he exercises his talent and follows his calling, assuming a
distinctive costume, attaching himself to the great place, and performing before his chief and visiting dignitaries on festive occasions. But if
he is distinct from the throng of "amateur" poets from which he
emerges, he is not a "professional." The modern imbongi is by occupation a full-time teacher, clerk, policeman, laborer, or entrepreneur,
and an official poet only in his spare time. In his capacity as imbongi
he is not a retainer of the chief and is not paid for his services. His
poetry chronicles the deeds and qualities of his chief and inspires his
audience to loyalty for the chief, but it is essential that the imbongi
distance himself from the chief, for he must praise what he sees as
laudable in him but also decry what is worthy of condemnation. He

must be free to speak the truth as he sees it: His poetic assessment of
the chief is not blindly adulatory. He has the ability to inspire strong
emotions and also to sway opinion. If he criticizes excesses in the
behavior of his chief, he also exhorts his audiences to mend their
errant ways. He is loyal especially to the chiefdom; he is the bard,
the tribal poet, and he sees the welfare of the chiefdom as his concern. He incites warriors to courage in battle, or pacifies inflamed
emotions. He establishes the moral norm, urging tribesmen to respect
their chief, his ancestors, and their own forefathers but decrying whatever threatens the ideal polity. From this central role in society flow
others. Since his poetry is concerned with his contemporaries as well
as their antecedents, the izibongo of the imbongi incorporates the
history of the chiefdom. His poetry can identify the chief he serves,
and he functions therefore as a herald; he is a cheerleader, custodian
of lore, mediator, prophet, literary virtuoso. His essential role, however, is political, concerned with the well-being of the polity.

   In fulfilling this political function the imbongi bears a striking resemblance to tribal poets of other cultures, in Africa, ancient Israel,
ancient Greece, or medieval Europe (see, for example, Hollander
1945/1968, A. R. Johnson 1944/1962, Nagy 1979, Opland 1980a, and
J. E. C. Williams 1971). Mafeje draws parallels between the functions
of the imbongi and of the medieval Celtic bard in an article entitled
"The role of the bard in a contemporary African community" (1967).
In this milestone in scholarly commentaries on the Xhosa imbongi,
Mafeje discards the term "praise poet," which he used in his 1963
article, in favor of the term "bard":

> While it is true that the traditional bard, amongst other things,
> praises the chief and gets rewards, this does not appear to have
> been his major function or role. Therefore, my main objective
> in this paper will be to demonstrate that his role went further
> than just praise of the chief. The English term "bard" has
> been used here to translate the Xhosa word *"mbongi,"* a name
> that was given to a poet who frequented the chief's main resi-
> dence (*komkhulu*) and travelled with him in traditional Nguni
> society. The reason for this is the similarity between this insti-
> tution and the institution of bards and their role in certain
> ancient and medieval European societies. [P. 194]

Mafeje sees the functions of the imbongi as complex, but asserts that
the main function was political:

> If the people felt that what he said was representative or re-
> flective of their interests and aspirations, then he was generally
> accepted as the "national poet," *imbongi yakomkhulu* (the

poet of the main residence), or, more recently, *imbongi yesizwe* (the poet of the nation). It is, therefore, apparent that the main function of the South African bard is to interpret public opinion and to organize it (once he has been firmly established), failing that, he does not achieve the status of "national poet" . . .

The method of the South African bard, in carrying out his duties, is not unlike that of the European bards. Like them, he celebrates the victories of the nation, he sings songs of praise, chants the laws and customs of the nation, he recites the genealogies of the royal families; and, in addition, he criticizes the chiefs for perverting the laws and the customs of the nation and laments their abuse of power and neglect of their responsibilities and obligations to the people. The only important difference between the European and the South African bard is that the position of the latter, unlike that of his European counterpart, is *not* hereditary and whatever privileges he enjoys, in view of his services at the main residence, are not heritable. Secondly, there is no evidence that the South African bards ever organized themselves into special societies; the vocation has always been one followed by lone individuals.

In summary it may be stated that (i) both the European and the South African bards came from the commoner rank; (ii) their positions depended on their general acceptance by the people; (iii) the roles of both types are characterized by some measure of freedom to criticize, whether subtly or openly, those in authority, i.e. Kings and Chiefs. In contemporary western societies this role seems to have been taken over by the newspaper cartoonist. The significance of all these public "critics" (the European bard, the medieval court jester, the South African bard, and the newspaper cartoonist) is considerable, since they serve as a check against abuse of power by those in authority; they represent the opinions of the ruled. [Pp. 195–6]

Mafeje then proceeds to analyze the izibongo produced by Melikaya Mbutuma on six occasions between September 1959 and March 1963, as Transkei moved along its controversial path to self-governing status. These were the first published Xhosa izibongo to be captured in performance by means of a tape recorder and presented in a scientific framework that explicitly denied the assumption that all Xhosa oral poetry was memorized and that demonstrated the relevance of the izibongo to the context in which it is performed.

In serving "as a check against abuse of power by those in authority," in representing "the opinions of the ruled," the Xhosa imbongi enacts through his public performances what Max Gluckman calls a "ritual of rebellion." Gluckman considers ceremonies

> among the South-Eastern Bantu of Zululand, Swaziland, and Mozambique. Here there are (in some cases, were) performed, as elsewhere in Africa, national and local ceremonies at the break of the rains, sowing, first fruits, and harvest. In one ceremony the idea of a goddess who is propitiated by the rites is clearly expressed; usually the ceremonies are directed to the ancestral spirits of the tribal chiefs or the kinship groups concerned. But whatever the ostensible purpose of the ceremonies, a most striking feature of their organization is the way in which they openly express social tensions: women have to assert licence and dominance as against their formal subordination to men, princes have to behave to the King as if they covet the throne, and subjects openly state their resentment of authority. Hence I call them rituals of rebellion. I shall argue that these ritual rebellions proceed within an established and sacred traditional system, in which there is dispute about particular distributions of power, and not about the structure of the system itself. This allows for instituted protest, and in complex ways renews the unity of the system. [1954:3, but see Norbeck 1963]

Drawing on descriptions by Hilda Kuper, for example, Gluckman analyzes the Swazi first-fruits festival, *incwala:*

> The political structure, as the source of prosperity and strength which safeguards the nation internally and externally, is made sacred in the person of the king. He is associated with his ancestors, for the political structure endures through the generations, though kings and people are born and die. [P. 19]

> The ceremony states that in virtue of their social position princes and people hate the king, but nevertheless they support him. Indeed, they support him in virtue of, and despite, the conflicts between them. The critically important point is that even if Swazi princes do not actually hate the king, their social position may rally malcontents to them. Indeed, in a comparatively small-scale society princes by their very existence have power which threatens the king. Hence in their prescribed, compelled, ritual behaviour they exhibit opposition as well as support for the king, but mainly support for the kingship. This is the social setting for rituals of rebellion. [Pp. 21–2]

Central to these ceremonies are public expressions of protest on behalf of the ruled directed against a sacral king and designed ritually in fact to assert the validity of the kingship. Later, Gluckman returns to Nguni belief in the sacral chief and in the continuing influence of his ancestors over the well-being of the chiefdom:

> The first fruits ceremony is a political ritual organized by the state which is an enduring group: hence it exhibits different beliefs and processes. The Bantu believe that the ancestral spirits of the king are in the end primarily responsible for the weather, and for good crops. These spirits have been in life part of the society, and they are always about certain sacred spots inside men's habitations. They may be wayward in their actions, but they are inside society. The earthly king is their representative who supplicates them in a small-scale ceremony at sowing; and again the first fruits ceremony to celebrate a successful season involves the king and his ancestors. [Pp. 27–8]

Although Gluckman does not refer specifically to the Xhosa-speaking peoples, they are members of the Nguni group and support aspects of the systems of belief of other Nguni groups such as the Zulu and Swazi. In exercising his license to voice publicly on behalf of the people criticism of their ruler, the Xhosa imbongi enacts a ritual of rebellion, operating within a system similar to that described by I. M. Lewis, who sees marginal female mediums possessed by spirits voicing opposition to–and tolerated by–a male-dominated society: "Whatever the possessed person does is done with impunity since he is considered to act as the unconscious and involuntary vehicle of the gods" (1971:105).

The clear counterparts of such spirit-possessed mediums in Xhosa society are the (male and female) diviners, *amagqirha* (singular *igqirha*), who like the imbongi wear animal skins in the course of their duties and who commune with the ancestors through tutelary spirits. There are indications that the imbongi, although he is distinct from the igqirha, is also held to be possessed in performance. His license to criticize and to use ribald language might be an acknowledgement of this. Some iimbongi claim initial inspiration from dreams, and dreams feature in the poetry of many iimbongi; the imbongi is also expected to deal in prophecy. N. J. van Warmelo (1938:7) once asserted that the Zulu imbongi always smoked marijuana before performing, and this claim is confirmed by the testimony of the Zulu imbongi Hoye kaSoxalase, who told Stuart on 15 September 1921 that "izibongo are learned over the smoking horn, where people are sitting smoking. Today they are still learned like that" (Webb and Wright 1976:169). These hints, as well as my personal observations of iimbongi in performance and their reactions on subsequently hearing recordings of their performances, suggest that the imbongi frequently produces his poetry in an ecstatic, trancelike state of inspiration. Add to this the predominance in the imbongi's izibongo of animal imagery and the fact that he wears animal skins and brandishes spears or fighting sticks, and one is left with the suspicion that the modern imbongi is a vestigial shaman (see Eliade 1957/1964).

Ritual aspects of the imbongi's connection with the chief and with the chiefdom will be taken up for further discussion in the fifth chapter; here it is necessary merely to allude to certain aspects of the role of the imbongi in society. Information in the preceding paragraphs derives from the aggregate of numerous conversations I have held with iimbongi and informed persons. Later I present four individual iimbongi, but this chapter concludes with illustrative extracts from some of these conversations. On 11 December 1970 my assistant Jackson Magopeni and I met Max Khamile in his home in Middledrift. Khamile is an Mfengu teacher, a member of the Dlamini clan, who was at the time sixty-two years old.

> OPLAND: Have you been bongaing for a long time?
>
> KHAMILE: Oh for quite a long time: I started when I was about thirty years of age. Anyway, even still further than that I studied it during my school days.
>
> OPLAND: You studied praise singing? Mqhayi?
>
> KHAMILE: He was still alive.
>
> OPLAND: Did you know Mqhayi?
>
> KHAMILE: I knew him and he knew me too.
>
> OPLAND: He was born here, wasn't he?
>
> KHAMILE: He was born in the Alice district, Tyhume Valley, at a place called Melana . . .
>
> OPLAND: First of all, how does a man become an imbongi?
>
> KHAMILE: Well sir, I can't definitely say, because as for myself I take it for something that comes from the ukuthwasa way of inspiration. Because, with me, I am a man who can read and write. I can write you a passage now. But now you tell me to recite the passage, I might not touch a word of it. Or else, when I'm about to finish, I might take a word or two from the passage I gave you on the same topic, I will not change it.
>
> OPLAND: So when you bonga, you haven't, you're not memorizing?
>
> KHAMILE: No, I'm not memorizing.
>
> OPLAND: You make up what you sing while you're singing?

KHAMILE: It comes just of its own. As a matter of fact, with me it's the occasion that inspires itself into me. Then the words automatically come. At a time then when I'm warmed by it, you know, I continue. It takes a long time sometimes. It will take about half an hour or so at times.

OPLAND: This must take quite a lot of training, or practice?

KHAMILE: No, it's not practice and training.

OPLAND: It just comes naturally?

KHAMILE: It just comes naturally. As for myself then I was never trained by anybody. But what I noticed with me, you see, from my childhood, I, in me, there was the inclination, you see, of being ukuthwasa. I took it from my father and mother.

MAGOPENI: Supposed to be a witchdoctor.

KHAMILE: Yes, of course, and the witchdoctors liked me very much.

OPLAND: So how did you start praising? I mean when you were a young boy, a small boy.

KHAMILE: When I was a small boy.

OPLAND: You couldn't sing like you sing now?

KHAMILE: Well, of course the voice then differed, you see.

OPLAND: No, but you said that when you sing now you never, you make up what you say while you're singing.

KHAMILE: It comes of its own.

OPLAND: Of its own?

KHAMILE: Yes.

OPLAND: Could you do that when you were a boy?

KHAMILE: Yes, I could do, of course. Yes.

OPLAND: Because I've spoken to many boys and they say that they start off by memorizing.

KHAMILE: Well, people who memorize, I just hear from their own self, just when they begin, "Oh, that's a memorizer. He won't go much."

OPLAND: He won't go far?

KHAMILE: No, he won't go far.

OPLAND: You don't think it's a start, if he starts by memorizing?

KHAMILE: If he starts by memorizing, when the end of his memory comes he goes no further . . .

OPLAND: So you don't read, well, you read poetry but you don't memorize?

KHAMILE: No, I don't memorize.

OPLAND: So would you say that there are two different kinds

of iimbongis, the one who memorizes and the one who makes up?

KHAMILE: Well sir, with me, I don't recognize the memorizer as an imbongi, you see.

OPLAND: What would you call the memorizer?

KHAMILE: I don't know.

OPLAND: He just bongas?

KHAMILE: He's a wisher, you see, you can tell he's a wisher because, you see, that's a schoolboy: As his teacher I give him a passage to memorize and then that's where his visions end.

OPLAND: Mr. Khamile, who is the imbongi, then? Can you tell me in your own words what the imbongi is, what he means in the tribe, what his function is?

KHAMILE: Oh yes. The imbongi is a great man in the tribe. He has indirectly the tribe in his powers. He has the power to urge them to get warmed up with something. Or when it comes in occasions of let's say fighting, the imbongi can make a tribe to rise up against the chief or even when the chief is inclined to be haughty, he stands up, he has the power upon him to subside him, you see.

OPLAND So he can criticize the chief?

KHAMILE: Not exactly criticize, but he can control him to some extent, you see, not to divide.

OPLAND: So does the imbongi have special powers?

KHAMILE: He has those powers. They just go into the man's spirit, you know: He feels changed.

OPLAND: Yes, I've seen this: People get quite worked up when you bonga. There's something else, if I can just change the subject slightly: When men were dancing, then the women bonga them, to incite them. Now this is memorized praising, isn't it?

KHAMILE: No, it's not, by the women. They know nothing of memorizing.

OPLAND: So do they just sing what comes?

KHAMILE: Just sing. It come out automatical with them.

OPLAND: Would you say in Xhosa that they are bongaing?

KHAMILE: In Xhosa I would say they are tshayelela, *bayat-shayelela.*

OPLAND: Shouting.

KHAMILE: Just to give certain courage, in other words.

OPLAND: So you wouldn't use the word "bonga"?

KHAMILE: No. I wouldn't use the word "bonga" because

with them, as I am an old Dlamini here and I have an
occasion here, they will only refer to my clan only,
"AmaDlamini, amaNdlovu, amaGuma," you see, and they
won't go further.

OPLAND: Yes.

KHAMILE: Ukutshayelela.

OPLAND: Yes . . . So that they're not praising, really?

KHAMILE: No, they're not praising, really.

OPLAND: You see, in the books that I have read they call that
praising and I think they're not understanding what is
really –

KHAMILE: They don't understand the difference. Here's the
difference between tshayelela –

MAGOPENI: *Imphililisa* ["The imbongi really invigorates"].

KHAMILE: Yes, imphililisa. Well, the imbongai can have that
power, can make people change their views to some extent.
But even then it's not easy. If there's nothing that attracts
them into the action from you, well, they're just as cool as
anything, say, "Ach, what does he do now? I can't do that."

OPLAND: So you must be dramatic and inspirational?

KHAMILE: Oh yes, oh yes. That is the idea, sir.

OPLAND: Can you tell me something then about how a man
becomes an imbongi?

KHAMILE: I did tell you, sir. You see, as for myself, I don't
know with other men, but –

OPLAND: Let's say officially.

KHAMILE: Officially. Well, to be officially recognized by imbongi is, the chiefs will recognize you first, and then they
will refer you to the ruling body, that is the Bantu Administration officials, like the great man at Umtata, Mr. Abra-
hams. He knows me too; I've been with him many times.

OPLAND: And in ancient days before there were the white
administration, how do you think, how was the imbongi
recognized?

KHAMILE: He was recognized by the chief.

OPLAND: By the chief?

KHAMILE: Yes, and the counselors.

OPLAND: And then he appoints a man an imbongi?

KHAMILE: No, he is never appointed. You see, he just, he
rises up in power, you know, in power, rising up, rising up,
and then a time will come when he will picture as the best of
them all because there are generally more than one in a
tribe. Yes, but the tribe will automatically be interested with

that particular being, and now all the others will just subside of themselves.

OPLAND: When there're two people who're trying to be an imbongi, what makes one better than the other?

KHAMILE: Well, this is what they, it's how they dramatize.

OPLAND: How they dramatize?

KHAMILE: Yes, and it's how, the language, it's the dramatization, the topic, and the inspiration.

OPLAND: And the words that they use?

KHAMILE: The words that are used too.

OPLAND: Are these important?

KHAMILE: Oh yes, the words are very important, sir, because nowadays people do say that the imbongi has freedom of speech. I do agree with them to some extent, but not fully, because with me I study first of all the, it's the *occasion* that reveals itself and now all my talks then are based on the, it's the occasion, it's the occasion that –

MAGOPENI: Is taking place.

KHAMILE: Yes, that's taking place. Now then with the words, you see, we hear a man praising you sometimes, you see, they say

Wau! Andingeyizek' intomb' 'omLungu	[I may not marry a white woman
Kub' umLung' unyel' endlini	Because a white shits in a house]

because you people are the first people who showed us the toilets, you know, and now then that imbongi says, "Would you marry your daughters, because you ran into your houses when you wanted to relieve yourselves?" Well, such things then, sir, are general, such words don't appear in any topic.

OPLAND: So he uses unusual words?

KHAMILE: Those words, they are nasty to use. They are meaningless, but an insult to somebody, you know.

OPLAND: But when he bongas, it's not an insult?

KHAMILE: Well, when he bongas it's not an insult, people say, but as for myself I say it is to use words that are meaningless, words that are far from the occasion . . .

OPLAND: Do you think that the tradition of praise singing will continue or die out?

KHAMILE: It will continue, sir, as far as my judgment, it will continue, because today since the government has brought the chiefs to the front, many youngsters now are springing up as praisers.

OPLAND: But thirty years ago was this the case?

KHAMILE: Well, thirty years ago it was sort of dying out, it was dwindling. Yes. Because the tribe, you see, had no pride in them . . .

OPLAND: So that the imbongi from what you say is very intimately connected with the chief and with the power of the chief?

KHAMILE: The chief, and the tribe, and also the current events.

OPLAND: So if you take away, if you break the power of the chiefs, let's say, take away the chiefs, the imbongis will die out?

KHAMILE: Well, they might not, they might not, because the fact that they should be under chiefs won't die out in their spirits . . .

OPLAND: Now the imbongi carries nowadays two sticks always, you carry two sticks when you sing.

KHAMILE: I carry one. Well, it all depends with what one feels. As for myself, I am of the opinion that it's not my clothing that bongas, my attire, it's myself. I sometimes bonga in a suit, just as Mr. Magopeni here. Yes.

OPLAND: Now what do these sticks that the imbongi traditionally carries, what do they signify?

KHAMILE: Oh, the sticks, they signify his position. And also they signify that the one behind him is of royal blood, is a royalist, the chief. Being imbongi, you can even be charged and a beast taken from you, you know, charged a beast to pay, if you go in front of a chief with bare hands. Oh yes.

OPLAND: Is this tribal law?

KHAMILE: Yes, that's tribal tradition.

OPLAND: But you're not as it were a bodyguard?

KHAMILE: Of course, being not a bodyguard, but as a matter of fact we are the head of the bodyguard because you should have enough powers to sense the danger that's below there. You should have enough power to sense the man that you might meet today, and now the bodyguard then gets wiser from your visions.

OPLAND: So the imbongi, you've spoken to me now about the imbongi's role as far as the chief and the tribe are concerned. You do other things: Do you ever prophesy when you sing?

KHAMILE: Well, that's always, yes, that's always.

OPLAND: You do that too?

KHAMILE: It does, yes, it does come to me too at times.

OPLAND: Do you think that the imbongi is also an entertainer? Or is he always serious? Does he make people laugh or are you always serious?

KHAMILE: Well, sometimes, but with me I generally never make them laugh. People laugh when you hear words, funny words as I have referred to in the past. These things make people laugh. But let's say there's a cripple, he happens to pass. One imbongi will say, he has the power to make that man forget himself that he is a cripple, when he bongas him, yes, though he refers to his disability in walking. But there are times he can make that man very fearsome by making the audience laugh at him. Now he'll begin to know, "Well, I'm only an intruder here, because I'm a cripple." Well, then it's when I say that a man who has no control, who has no powers to control him, how to handle his singing, that man is very unfortunate . . .

Later that day we traveled with Khamile to interview Justice Mabandla, an Mfengu chief who was at that time chief minister of the Ciskei Territorial Authority, at his great place near Alice.

MABANDLA: . . . My experience of an imbongi is that firstly he is a praise singer of a chief. Well, about the difference of the present imbongi and the imbongi of the olden days, I would only say it is in dress only. The imbongi was used in the olden days to encourage amongst other things the warriors when they had to go to war, in the same fashion that our women do; they do something similar to it but they are not praise singers or imbongis, but they have some, I wouldn't know what to call it, we call it ukutshayelela in Xhosa. But it gives the same thing to men when a woman does it as much as the imbongi when he does it gives to the men. Well, men usually are much, well, like anybody, they fear death. But once an imbongi sings his praises even the worst coward will definitely go into it. Again the imbongi as I know him is one who introduces his chief to whatever community the chief is unknown. From what he says the people, without him speaking normally they are, I mean our people, they understand what he says and they then, I mean they usually know who the chief is through the imbongi. Say now when the great place, that is, the place of residence for the chief, is built again, when there's some misunderstanding say between or amongst the tribesmen about that particular thing that is being undertaken or introduced, if the imbongi understands or learns that there is some ill-feeling or something he starts singing his praises and the people understand him and again bridge their differences and they do what is good for their tribe or for the chief. So the imbongi is used in many different categories, even sometimes as I have said if, as I have done before, I go along with him, he, Mr. Khamile now, is one of our accepted imbongis, if we go say to a city, the people, that is, the Xhosas, need not necessarily be told who that chief is. Through his praise singing they will know. And if the aim is say to collect funds to build a church or to build the great place as I have said, the people just automatically do it because he, *he* has spoken. Well, the actual introduction of the whole thing, if it is done at all, the people will have understood it before even say the master of ceremonies introduces the affair, through the praise singer.

OPLAND: So he acts as a spokesman of the tribe?

MABANDLA: He is.

OPLAND: A spokesman of the chief?

MABANDLA: That's right, in a different way of course of speaking, but the people understand him.

OPLAND: You said that Mr. Khamile is one of your accepted imbongis: What qualities do you look for in an imbongi to make him acceptable?

MABANDLA: Well, I would not be accurate in my answer, but people usually feel. You know, they have a license, the praise singers or the imbongis, they have a license of theirs which they give themselves. He can say anything, and the people sometimes took exception to what the imbongis say. Now they take exception because from what he says they can hear what he means. Do you understand my point?

OPLAND: Yes.

MABANDLA: And yet another imbongi can say the same thing in a different tone. Now those who insult people are never accepted.

OPLAND: Yes, Mr. Khamile made a big point of this when we discussed this.

MABANDLA: Yes, these people, and they too, they do it.

OPLAND: Yes, so the imbongi can criticize in a particular way?

MABANDLA: Exactly.

OPLAND: But he has the license to criticize?

MABANDLA: Well, he has. You can do nothing about it.

OPLAND: You can't do anything to Mr. Khamile if he says you're a bad chief or something?

MABANDLA: No, especially during that time when he is singng his praises I can't. But the people, even if he refers that straight to me, the people will understand him and they will just not, they will comment after he has been quiet and show that they resent what he has said and that type of an imbongi is never accepted by the people. So this one I can assure you is accepted throughout by all the sections, Xhosas, the Fingoes, and the Thembus, because he hasn't got that tinge, that insulting tinge in his praises.

OPLAND: Now there would be something else surely: There are other qualities which make a good imbongi, his ability with words, or his fluency?

MABANDLA: And his nonrepetition and his history about the other tribes, his knowledge about the, say this one, he happens to know my family tree: That is why he is accepted by the people here. Now he knows again the family tree of the Hlubi chief, and he is there accepted. He happens to know also the family tree of the Rharhabe line and even there he has been used two occasions, they have invited him to sing his praises at the occasions . . .

OPLAND: Can I just ask you one other question: Let's say there was a competition of two imbongis. What would make one imbongi better than another?

MABANDLA: It is his fluency, his nonrepetition, his wider knowledge of not only his chieftainship but with, I mean who has got a good knowledge of even the family trees of other chieftainships.

On 20 December 1970 Jackson Magopeni and I travelled to Queenstown to interview the Thembu imbongi Nelson Title Mabunu in his home. Mabunu, who was then fifty years old, is a member of the same clan, the Hala, as the Thembu royal family that includes Chief Kaiser Matanzima and former Paramount Chief Sabata Dalindyebo. Mabunu, who served as the urban representative of eight chiefs of Emigrant Thembuland, was nominally a butcher but actually a sergeant in the security police. Chief George Matanzima, Kaiser's brother, then minister of justice and now prime minister of Transkei, who had suggested I meet Mabunu, was spending the first day of his vacation with Mabunu in Queenstown, and sat in on the interview.

MABUNU: I started as imbongi, that is, praise singer, for Chief Kaiser Matanzima since 1958.

OPLAND: Before that, did you do any singing?

MABUNU: Before that, you know when I grew up as a boy, herding cattle and sheep, that is how I think the thing started. I used to praise other boys, praise my father's cattle, and so on. But I did not attach any importance to that. But when I contacted the chief and was connected to him I started singing praises . . .

OPLAND: Can I just start on one aspect now: I'm interested in the education of an imbongi, not the school education, but how a young boy becomes an imbongi. When you were praising your cattle, your father's cattle, were these, did you make up your own words yourself?

MABUNU: It comes in this way: Some people think perhaps an imbongi sits down and studies. That is not the thing: It's an inspiration. When you see something, you know, it's like a preacher in church when he preaches the gospel, you feel touched, then you feel like saying some words yourself, you know, that's an inspiration. It's nothing else and it can be nothing else. You can judge a recitation done by schoolchildren, I mean by a schoolchild, something that he has learnt and that he'll recite. But singing praises for a chief or anything, it's an inspiration. You talk about things, but you must have knowledge of the whole setup, say if you have been herding cattle, you know the colors of the cattle, you know perhaps this is an ox which is, in Afrikaans you say it's a *vooros of 'n agteros* ["a front ox or a back ox"], you know those things, you know how it pulls, you know what it must do, pulls, you know, small things count a lot afterwards because you must have a background nearly of all the things you are going to praise. You have perhaps the same. A marriage, you must know what a marriage is, if it's now at a funeral of course you must be used to that and you must know how the people, the mourners and others feel about it. And you must know in fact what this, of the deceased, what deeds, what his deeds were.

OPLAND: . . . In what ways do you think the earlier imbongi was different from what you are today?

MABUNU: In the first place an imbongi, I would say compare him with an orator, in a way, he must have been an eloquent man, an eloquent speaker. As I have said he must have quite a good knowledge of the things, I would say of the past history.

OPLAND: Now you can look up that history in a book, you can

go to Soga or you can go to Hammond-Tooke or something and you can read that.

MABUNU: You can read that and then when you sing praises you can quote directly or indirectly. But the people, that is now, your audience, will understand what you really mean in their own language.

OPLAND: But the imbongi two hundred years ago couldn't read all this knowledge.

MABUNU: He couldn't read and most of the people of course couldn't read, but they had knowledge of their history, where their nation came from, generation after generation, because they imparted that knowledge, you know, the fathers to the sons, and so it carried on.

OPLAND: Verbally?

MABUNU: Verbally.

OPLAND: Now in what way do you think the singing of an illiterate imbongi differs from the singing of a literate imbongi?

MABUNU: It differs in fact today. You know an imbongi has that freedom, even if today, of using at times somewhat vulgar language. But actually it's not vulgar, it's vulgar to-day because it's a civilized society. You cannot call those things or those articles by their names, in fact their actual names, you have to modernize now and people will know "Oh he means this, he means that." That was the differ-ence, but those days he would say anything, he had that liberty.

OPLAND: So there was a freer approach to the use of lan-guage?

MABUNU: A freer approach to the language.

OPLAND: I recorded a song, I don't know if you know this word, Mr. Ntloko didn't know, in which the imbongi ended up, excuse me if I'm being rude, with the word *mhlumba, mhlumba kwaTshiwo.* Now this was as you said a, well, he wasn't a very literate man, but he stays in Langa. Is this the kind of word that you're talking of?

MABUNU: That's the kind of word that you wouldn't, in this, today's society, you wouldn't mention those words because they really mean private parts.

OPLAND: Yes, but the imbongi in traditional life could, he had the liberty to do that?

MABUNU: He had the liberty to do so.

OPLAND: Did he have any other rights or privileges which the ordinary tribesman didn't have?

MABUNU: Yes. You know, an imbongi in a way could swear at a chief.

OPLAND: At a chief?

MABUNU: Yes, swear at anybody. But like, I would say as it is today in Parliament, you can be excused when you say some things in Parliament, things which you cannot say outside the parliament house. I think it was the same thing.

OPLAND: He didn't actually *swear* at them?

MABUNU: He didn't actually use, not actually *swearing* at them, but in a way which could be interpreted that way. You know, if he wants to tell perhaps a chief or somebody his faults, he is the only man who could in public tell his chief his faults and praise him for what he has actually done and deserved praising.

OPLAND: What is the function of this kind of criticism in tribal life? This obviously has an important role in tribal life.

MABUNU: The criticisms?

OPLAND: Yes.

MABUNU: Criticisms, as it is even today, I think there is not much change, because today if you criticize a man he might take an exception, but some other men like criticisms because they improve on criticisms.

OPLAND: You're talking of the imbongi now?

MABUNU: Of the imbongi now. Now the imbongi's aims in criticizing the chief were that, he even criticized the counselors, you know, that is why he was recognized as an important figure because he is the man who's regarded as intelligent, he's regarded as intelligent by his people. He can criticize the counselors, he can criticize the chief, and he can tell them, "This is the way it should have been done," and based on knowledge received from ancestors, even if in those days they were not reading. He's the man who used to sit by the cattle kraal with the older people and listen to them: That was education in those days, that's how he was regarded as a better man.

OPLAND: A sort of tribal history book.

MABUNU: Tribal history, tribal history.

OPLAND: Now what you say indicates that the imbongi is a very special man who's got special rights and privileges. This means that not anyone can be a chief's imbongi. How does a man become an imbongi?

MABUNU: Well, it goes according to ability, if he's able to do it, but not everybody, you know, like ordinary people, they're not alike in eloquence.

OPLAND: Yes, I've seen quite a number of tribesmen who *can* praise, but they're not imbongis.

MABUNU: They're not imbongis.

OPLAND: Now what do you think a chief would look for in making a man an imbongi? What qualities would an imbongi have? Eloquence you've mentioned.

MABUNU: Well, actually it is not the chief who chooses that "I want this man to be my imbongi" because he might choose a man who cannot do the job. It is the imbongi who comes forward to bonga a chief and the chief appreciates and the tribe appreciates; then they regard him as the chief imbongi.

OPLAND: He just sort of comes from the people?

MABUNU: Ya, it comes from the people, in fact it comes from him.

OPLAND: Now the imbongis that I see wear skins and sort of ritual dress.

MABUNU: Skins and tribal dress.

OPLAND: At what stage of their development do they start wearing that? Can they just put on the skins any time they think they're ready?

MABUNU: They can put on their skins at certain, I would say if there is a certain event, a gathering or a chief's meeting or any other important event that is taking place.

OPLAND: I was getting at more, as a chap is growing up.

MABUNU: I know exactly what you want.

OPLAND: You know, at what stage does –

MABUNU: You want to know if perhaps, like I would say in education.

OPLAND: That's right, if there's any sort of qualifications.

MABUNU: If there's any sort of a qualification. You see, there is no qualification of imbongi. The qualification is their acceptance, his acceptance *by* the people *as* imbongi. Correct, Chief?

OPLAND: For various reasons.

MABUNU: For various reasons.

OPLAND: Now only after he's been accepted can he put the skins on, or can he wear them of his own accord beforehand?

MABUNU: Well, actually in those days nobody could simply put on and pretend to be an imbongi whereas he is not, he is not.

OPLAND: So there are no real rules or regulations, this is a sort of question of custom, everybody just does, sort of conforms to the custom?

MABUNU: That is the thing. If he is gifted, if he has got that inspiration, then he praises, he sings praises, and he is recognized as a – There are many who just praise or sing praises for a certain thing and it ends there. He cannot sing praises for this and that, this and that, this and that, as an accepted imbongi [can].

OPLAND: Now that raises a very interesting point, because I met a man who could sing a whole lot of praises, he could sing praises of his son, he could sing praises of himself and praises of his age-set, you know, the boys who used to stick fight when he was a young boy, but every time he sang he sang the same words. You know, he had memorized that particular song. Now it happened one night that there was dancing in an office and the imbongi – this man wasn't an imbongi – praised the chief "A! Zwelinzima!" And this man was terribly jealous, so he got up and he wanted to praise the chief too because he was full of emotion, but he couldn't, he could only memorize, and he just found that he couldn't praise the chief, but he started babbling off a whole lot of words from the praises of his son. Now this means that there are two different kinds of people: There's a man let's say who will make up a song and keep it in his mind –

MABUNU: I would put it this way: Perhaps it will be clear. We as a nation have clans and each and every one is an imbongi of his clan. He can bonga himself as a Cirha, then he calls the izibongo of his ancestors. Or he is a Dlamini, then he will sing praises *as* a Dlamini. Then one would think, "Oh this is an imbongi," yet he is not an imbongi. What I am coming at, I think you have touched on an important point, that is, singing memorized praises and praises an imbongi will, say if you say, "Praise this, sing praises," he will do it.

OPLAND: If it inspires him.

MABUNU: It is a, what I'm coming to now is that, I'm just losing the point which is very important: praise singing of memorized, that is, now you study and sing praises, but there is that, what I called emotional, but I call it inspiration.

OPLAND: Impromptu, or spur of the moment.

MABUNU: Ya, impromptu. Ya, that is the thing. Now memorized praises or, this is the point I'm coming to: In praise singing like in any other thing you must not be out of subject, that is the point you were driving at. It is a dance, you are praising at a dance, function, then you start praising at

that man, you see. That is the difference: you must not be
out of subject . . .

OPLAND: When you act as an imbongi, that is, at a special
function or affair, do you always improvise?

MABUNU: No.

OPLAND: You do sometimes sing –

MABUNU: You just sing praises.

OPLAND: Yes, but these are not memorized praises?

MABUNU: These are not memorized praises in so much that
after praising if a man comes to you and says could you
repeat what you said, it's not easy, it's not easy.

OPLAND: Yes. Do you *ever* memorize? Will you ever, say,
recite something?

MABUNU: Well, you don't memor – I don't know with the
others, but you don't memorize. What you do is to know
what you're going to talk about.

OPLAND: But not the words?

MABUNU: Not the words. You know what you're going to talk
about.

OPLAND: This I understand: If you want to praise Mzimvubu
[Chief George Matanzima] you will know something that he
did.

MABUNU: Yes.

OPLAND: So you will know *what* you're going to say but the
actual words are –

MABUNU: The actual words just come.

OPLAND: Just come out. Now when Mr. Schwarz played me
that record, you know, he's got a whole record of you, I
could just by listening to it, I could tell when someone was
reading a praise song that had been written down or when
he was improvising. He's got songs, tapes of you improvising. So already I can *hear* a difference in delivery. Do you
think there would always be a difference?

MABUNU: Yes, there will always be such a difference.

OPLAND: Could you develop that? What kind of difference
would you expect?

MABUNU: Well, in fact, when an imbongi is reading from
something that is written down there will be hesitation,
there will be, you know when you read and read and read
and read and read you sometimes have something in mind.
You think, "I should have said this here, I should have said
this here," then you hesitate at times. But when you bonga

you just carry on. Yes. I don't know whether I'm answering your question fully.

OPLAND: Yes, but let me try and, this is part of an answer; there's another aspect too. For the imbongi to bonga there are characteristics of his way of singing.

MABUNU: Of singing, yes.

OPLAND: Could you perhaps talk about that, about the tone that he uses or his method of delivery.

MABUNU: You see, an imbongi could be useful in delivering a message. Say you are perhaps a candidate, you want to be elected for a seat in Parliament. Then you have your imbongi. That imbongi before you speak he can sort of, I don't want to use this English word, to "hypnotise" people, he could –

OPLAND: Inspire them.

MABUNU: *inspire* the people so that when you stand up and deliver your address they are already having confidence in what you are going to say. An imbongi could be dangerous: He could incite people. He can incite people, because in the olden days when there's going to be a war or I would say a battle between two sides, you would always find an imbongi. That is where and when the imbongi was regarded as a very important man, because he would sing praises that even those who have got water in their hearts could go out fully and fight. Yes.

OPLAND: Yes. I met an old man who said that praising was a bad thing because if an imbongi praised him then he would hit a man even though he didn't want to hit him.

MABUNU: Isn't that the same thing? That's the same thing. This imbongi, if there's a meeting here, take for instance the Transkei National Independence Party and the Democratic Party, now perhaps the man who is for or pro-government is going to address a meeting where there are people who are in opposition, then the imbongi gets up. He inspires, in so much that if anyone of those dare stands up he could be assaulted. I think in that manner it is the same way with the Europeans, say now there is a brass band, people, there is a war and people do not want to come out to join the soldiers, but if that band is playing right through the town you would find many coming up to sign on.

OPLAND: Play military music.

MABUNU: Play military music.

MATANZIMA: One thing, I was thinking, once happened in Cape Town: A man was drunk during the war and a brass band was playing. He went to join.

MABUNU: He went to join. That is the work of the imbongi arranging things.

OPLAND: Now how does the imbongi do this? Is it just by his eloquence?

MABUNU: His eloquence, his eloquence . . .

OPLAND: Perhaps we could go back over this idea of composing spontaneously, how a young man learns to compose. Does he ever go through any sort of formal period of training? If there's a great imbongi in his district, would he ever, do you think, go and listen to that man and study him?

MABUNU: That's very important, that's very important, that's very important. Not even the young man, also the well-known imbongis, also the well-known iimbongi. If you do not attend big occasions, then you feel, you sort of cannot be very competent when you meet imbongis because there are imbongis from Pondoland, imbongis from the Ciskei, that is, the Gcalekas, there are imbongis from the Rharhabes, the Thembus and the Fingoes, etc., etc. Now if you don't meet them at certain occasions, perhaps three or four occasions a year, then you feel that you are not, you're losing the what's 'is name. But if you meet at times, it keeps you in touch, you improve, you hear that one praising and you hear this one praising. Say now you are about five or six praising at the same function. Now if he sings his praises, you want to do it better, and then the third man wants to do it better, then there is that competition and it is at those occasions when the chief says you cannot stop them, you cannot stop them . . .

OPLAND: Chief, I think there's only one other thing I want to ask and perhaps you can answer it. It develops from what I was saying here now: The imbongi today is frequently, or his praising is sort of a part-time activity, as it were, it's not his occupation. I assume in the early days the imbongi was a professional and it was his full-time occupation. Is this true?

MATANZIMA: Although he was not paid at all. He wasn't paid.

OPLAND: No, but this was his job, as it were.

MATANZIMA: That was his job, yes, and occasionally the chief looked after his imbongi, occasionally gave him a beast, he gave him something in appreciation of his services . . .

MABUNU: To add to what you have said in fact in the way of a question: Is there now any change, is there now any development? This reminds me now of last Sunday's occasion when at Mount Arthur at the service, there was a conference there of the Ciskeian Izenzele Women's Association, and it was in church, and the minister after delivering a sermon, the people and myself were so moved that I found myself singing praises, I just found myself singing praises in church . . . It's not usually done in church. You find the whole congregation clapping hands and so on, because they were so touched and inspired. Even myself, I found myself, it comes that way, it comes that way, it comes that way.

OPLAND: Your question to me then was?

MABUNU: Was that you asked me if there is any change in the izibongo and the imbongis of today as compared with those of those days. Some other imbongis, as the chief said, still think that you cannot bonga at a funeral, but even myself I go to a funeral not intending to sing praises –

OPLAND: Yes, but you find yourself moved.

MABUNU: but you find yourself moved to such an extent that you sing praises there, and you will find that you receive letters afterwards. It's a pity I'm not in the office where I would show you letters written to me afterward, people thanking me for what I have done, in fact which I did not intend doing. Now at a funeral, when you sing those praises, you know, you show them the greatness of God, you –

And at this point Mabunu broke off the conversation by launching into a spontaneous izibongo that lasted nine minutes (Opland 1975:196–9), even though on two occasions in the course of our conversation he had declined my request to bonga.

In this chapter we have looked at the imbongi in general; in the next chapter we shall concentrate by way of example on four iimbongi in particular.

4

FOUR IIMBONGI

The imbongi might have much in common with other participants in the tradition, but each imbongi is at the same time both a type and an individual. This chapter presents four individual iimbongi. However, since to consider the poetry of even one poet is to generalize, the movement from the general to the specific developed in the preceding two chapters and in this chapter will then conclude with the izibongo produced by one imbongi on one particular occasion. We have almost no information about specific nineteenth-century Xhosa iimbongi such as Gunner assembled about Zulu izimbongi (1976). The earliest imbongi about whom we know rather more than his name is S. E. K. Mqhayi, and it is with Mqhayi that we start.

Samuel Edward Krune Mqhayi dominates Xhosa literature. His novels and poetry are read by every schoolchild, and many people still remember his oral performances with a respect bordering on awe. We have met him already in Deakin's florid prose as the imbongi who greeted the Prince of Wales in King William's Town in 1925, and we have noted his reference to the izibongo he learned as a boy herding cattle. The subject of two dissertations (Kuse 1978 and Qangule 1979), an obituary by A. C. Jordan (1945/1973) that is the finest piece of writing in the meager body of Xhosa literary criticism, a bibliography (Scott 1976a), and a number of articles or sections of studies many of which present English translations of his work (Bennie 1936, Gérard 1971, Shepherd 1955), as well as poetic tributes in Xhosa (Jolobe 1936/1957:121–3, Mbebe 1951, Tayedzerhwa 1951, Yali-Manisi 1952:106–9 and 121–3 and 1980:76–81), Mqhayi is the most studied and most respected figure in Xhosa literature. In Jordan's assessment, "His contribution to Southern Bantu Literature is easily the largest and most valuable that has hitherto been made by any single writer" (1945/1973:105). We know much about Mqhayi from these studies and also from his autobiography (1939), extracts from which W. G. Bennie translated into English (Scott 1976b); this translation formed the basis of a translation into German (Westermann 1938). Understandably perhaps, since he left so substantial an output, Mqhayi is coming more and more to be viewed as a figure significant in the history of Xhosa written literature, and that is only just. Considerably less is known about Mqhayi as an imbongi. Reminiscences from people who heard

90

A BANTU POET.—This is the native who delivered an oration to the Prince of Wales at King William's Town.

Figure 1. Samuel Edward Krune Mqhayi. Photo: *Cape Times*, 29 May 1925.

him perform could still be collected, but no one has done this systematically. Recordings of only two of Mqhayi's oral poems are extant (Opland 1977b), made in a studio in about 1934. Some hitherto unpublished material in manuscript might yet supplement the canon of Mqhayi's writings, and poetry originally printed in Xhosa newspapers merits collection and republication, but at this stage we are unlikely to add appreciably to our limited knowledge of Mqhayi as an oral poet.

Mqhayi tells us about his ancestry and his early life in his autobiography, in an article in *Imvo zabantsundu* on the death of his father, and in his biography of Chief Nathaniel Cyril Mhala, *USoGqumahashe* (1921). He traces his descent back five generations to Ntshezi, a Thembu of royal blood of the house of Bhomoyi of the Zima clan. Ntshezi's son Sheshegu first crossed the Kei to settle in the land of Phalo near Alice, giving his name to the district; in migrating, Sheshegu became a member of the Dange chiefdom. Sheshegu's son Mqhayi was a seven-foot giant who distinguished himself in singing wedding songs, outshining acknowledged singers, including the chief Ngqika. The Dange accordingly honored Mqhayi with the izibongo

> He that taunts the wild animal
> The mouthpiece and the horn
> The thong and the milkpail
> The brindled buck from Jadu,

for Ngqika (the "wild animal"), after being bested, invited Mqhayi to settle in his chiefdom, where he became one of Ngqika's intimate counselors (the two as inseparable and mutually dependent as a mouthpiece to a horn, as a thong to a milkpail); Ngqika paid the Dange a large herd of cattle in compensation. Mqhayi died in battle at Jadu in 1834. His son Rune was converted to Christianity by Henry Calderwood, a missionary in the territory of Maqoma the son of Ngqika, and Rune became an elder of the Macfarlane congregation in the Tyhume Valley. He died in 1895 at the age of ninety-six. Rune's son Ziwani, born in 1830, was a teacher who eventually settled in Grahamstown, where he became an elder in the Methodist Church. Like his grandfather Mqhayi, Ziwani displayed musical talent, though unlike his son he lacked eloquence: As his son put it, "He was no orator, for he was too quiet a man" (Mqhayi 1921:10). Ziwani son of Rune, son of Mqhayi, son of Sheshugu, son of Ntshezi,

> The dark Boer,
> He that has a heavy load,
> The feverish flea,   [Mqhayi 1921:8]

died at his home in Grahamstown on 11 February 1920 at the age of ninety, transmitting to his son Samuel an ancestral legacy of service to chiefs and two generations of Christian education.

Samuel Edward Krune (Rune) Mqhayi was born in the Tyhume River Valley near Lovedale on 1 December 1875. At the age of seven he started attending school near his home, but three years later he traveled across the Kei to Centane, where he lived for the next six years. Here in Gcaleka territory, an area still notable for its high incidence of red-blanketed inhabitants (those who refuse conversion to Christianity and acceptance of Western ways), Mqhayi avidly absorbed the traditional folkways. He returned to the Tyhume Valley at the age of fifteen to enter Lovedale, where he studied to become a teacher. He taught, then became subeditor of the newspaper *Izwi labantu,* returned to teaching, became editor of the newspaper *Imvo zabantsundu,* and returned yet again to teaching, this time at Lovedale. Mqhayi came to object so strongly to the way Xhosa history was presented in the school that he resigned from Lovedale and withdrew to settle on an isolated hill just outside Berlin, a few miles from King William's Town in Ndlambe territory. The hill was known by the Ndlambe as *Isixhoba sikaTilana,* "Tilana's rocky outcrop"; Mqhayi renamed it *Intab' ozuko,* "The mountain of glory." From this "Mount Helicon," Jordan wrote in his obituary in 1945, Mqhayi "descended in his impressive kaross on great tribal or state occasions to sing the praises of important personalities. The last of such occasions was the meeting held by the Minister of Native Affairs at King William's Town last July" (1945/1973:106).

Mqhayi died on Ntab' ozuko on 29 July 1945, and he was buried there two days later. On 26 March 1951 a tombstone was unveiled over his grave, an occasion attended by many dignitaries as well as a young imbongi, D. L. P. Yali-Manisi. In his poetic re-creation of the scene, the late St. John Page Yako criticizes literary figures who absented themselves and accordingly missed Manisi's performance:

> Even Jordan of *The Wrath of the Ancestors* has seen nothing
> Since he has not seen the edge of Yali-Manisi's hair,
> As he gestured and acted up as if to stab the heaven of heavens.
> Even Mdledle hid himself at Lovedale
> Fearing for his egg-head
> Lest Manisi's dust should fall on and soil it.
> [Trans. Kuse 1978:261–2]

Thirty years later the dust has settled, and Ntab' ozuko is occupied by a lonely homestead near the unidentifiable site of Mqhayi's mud house; the impressive tombstone barely breaks through the heavy undergrowth of scrub and thorn trees that sprawls wild across his untended grave.

Mqhayi's career as an oral poet started when as a boy herding cattle he used to compose and recite poems about his companions and the animals of the veld. His career as a literate poet began when he started contributing to *Izwi labantu,* a newspaper that commenced publication in 1897 in opposition to *Imvo zabantsundu,* established in 1884. Walter Benson Rubusana had been associated with *Imvo,* but after he had fallen out with its editor he contributed to the establishment of *Izwi.* In his early contributions to *Izwi,* Mqhayi styled himself *Imbongi yakwa-*

Gompo, "The imbongi of the East London area," a name apparently given him by Rubusana. An editor of a Johannesburg newspaper, Selope Thema, seems to have felt that the geographical appellation was too restrictive for a poet whose concerns were more universal, and dubbed him *Imbongi yesizwe jikelele,* "The imbongi of the whole nation," a phrase that Mqhayi readily adopted in reference to himself.

The chronology of Mqhayi's canon is complicated, but his earliest – certainly his most influential – published novel seems to have been *Ityala lamawele* (1914), "The case of the twins," an account of a legal dispute between twins over rights of succession set in the court of Hintsa, the Gcaleka paramount chief, not far from Centane. Bennie offered Mqhayi his criticism of this short work, and a second edition appeared extending the historical novel by the addition of biographical and historical notes as well as relevant poetry Mqhayi had published in newspapers. The result is a curious blend of historical fact and fiction that adds up to a history of the Xhosa intellectual from intricate legal disputation in a sheltered traditional milieu through the arrival of the foreign Mfengu, first contact with the white man, escalating involvement in his affairs and ultimately in World War I in spite of a radical and historically deep-seated doubt about the honor of his intentions with regard to South African blacks. Mqhayi subsequently published translations of *Aggrey of Africa* (1935) and *Adonis of the Jungle* (1949); biographies of N. C. Mhala, the first editor of *Izwi* (1921), and of John Knox Bokwe (1925); two political allegories, *Samson* (1907) and *Don Jadu* (1929); incidental essays and fragments on Ntsikana (1926) and on sacrifices (1928); his autobiography, *UMqhayi wase-Ntab' ozuko* (1939); and four volumes of poetry, in 1923, 1927, 1937, and 1943. Other poems by Mqhayi were included in the anthologies of Rubusana (1906/1911) and Bennie (1935). This output in Xhosa is matched only by the various publications of the late J. J. R. Jolobe (Scott 1973).

Mqhayi was the first Xhosa oral poet to exploit fully the new technology of printing introduced by Scottish missionaries in the Tyhume Valley in 1823. Most early published poetry in Xhosa is in form and sentiment influenced by Western models; Mqhayi committed to writing original poetry in style and purpose hardly distinguishable from the oral poetry of the traditional imbongi. Mqhayi did write poetry in Western mode, but he is always most successful with his traditional poetry (see Jordan 1945/1973:111–12). His earlier publications in *Izwi* as Imbongi yakwaGompo elicited a revealing broadside fired by Jonas Ntsiko, who wrote for an earlier newspaper, *Isigidimi samaXhosa,* "The messenger of the Xhosa people," and for *Imvo* under the name *Uhadi waseluhlangeni,* "The harp of the nation." On 26 November

1900 *Imvo* carried eighty-six rhymed four-line stanzas by Ntsiko preceded by the following statement:

> The Bard of the Gompo area in the recent past has, in entertaining himself, done grievous harm in that
> (1) he painted in ugly colours two people, needlessly;
> (2) he caused to be printed in a newspaper of a section of the brown people horrendous expletives;
> (3) he has plagiarized the praises of the scion of Tshoni declaiming King Sarili, while he still lived.
> Therefore, because I am incensed and scandalized, and because I am offended by the plagiarism, this fellow eminently deserves
>
> A SOUND THRASHING.
>
> [Kuse 1978:19–20]

Ntsiko's poem (much of it translated in Kuse) readily reveals the influence of Western poetic structure. He takes Mqhayi to task for criticizing two contemporaries, for using strong and offensive language, and for quoting without acknowledgment from the izibongo the son of Tshoni had composed about Sarhili, the Gcaleka paramount chief and son of Hintsa. Ntsiko writes in Xhosa but from within a milieu that has accepted Western literary sensibilities: What appears in print should not be offensive (cf. Rubusana's grounds for bowdlerizing some of the izibongo he prints), and should be one's own original composition. Xhosa oral poets, as we have seen, have no conception of literary copyright and borrow freely apposite words or phrases they might have heard elsewhere; and the imbongi traditionally deals in criticism of public figures, sometimes using abusive language. Ntsiko opposes Mqhayi then for exercising his traditional prerogatives as imbongi, in print. Mqhayi succeeded in reconciling within himself the traditional ways he absorbed in Centane and the Western Christian education he received at Lovedale. He was the first Xhosa imbongi to write his traditional poetry for publication in Western media. Mqhayi thereby erected a bridge that succeeding poets tread; and posterity reveres him while Ntsiko's poems lie unread in yellowing nineteenth-century newspapers.

Sipho Mangindi Burns-Ncamashe knew Mqhayi and often heard him perform: He recollects that Mqhayi was "a man endowed with a stentorian voice" who in performance tended to stand still, supplementing his oral poetry with dignified gestures. Ncamashe himself is an imbongi of considerable interest if only because he has attained higher educational qualifications than any other imbongi, he has been installed as a chief, and he has become involved in Ciskeian politics. He was born on 1 December 1920 at the Pirie Mission near King William's

Town, the eldest son of Mountain Ntaba Nzimana and Elsie Nobanzi Burns-Ncamashe. He is a direct descendant of Gwali, the eldest son of Tshiwo the son of Ngconde in the Xhosa royal line. As a result of a dynastic dispute, Phalo, Tshiwo's youthful son and heir, and his uncle Mdange opposed Gwali, Ngconde's son Ntinde, and Khwane (the newly created chief of the Gqunukhwebe), and drove all three with their followers westward across the Kei, initiating thereby the first Xhosa settlement in the Ciskei.

Sipho Burns-Ncamashe grew up as a member of a royal family, greeted with the Xhosa royal clan name Tshawe, but without a chief-dom: The Gwali chieftainship was disbanded as a consequence of the ninth and last frontier war in 1878. He pursued a distinguished school career, earning first-class passes and winning scholarships. At St. Matthews Teachers' Training College he was awarded the Native Primary Lower Teachers' Certificate in 1938 and the Native Primary Higher Teachers' Certificate in 1940. He taught at St. Matthews and studied further at Lovedale. In 1948 he graduated from the University of Fort Hare with a B.A. degree, majoring in Xhosa and native administra-tion. This was followed by a University Education Diploma from the University of South Africa and in 1954 a B.Ed. degree from the Uni-versity of Cape Town. He served as principal of three schools before becoming a lecturer in the Department of African Languages at the University of Fort Hare and later senior editor on the Xhosa Diction-ary Project. He entered Ciskeian politics in 1968 and became minister of education in the Ciskei Territorial Authority when Lennox Sebe defeated Justice Mabandla in the 1974 election. The Gwali chieftain-ship was restored in that year, and on 1 November Ncamashe was installed as chief by the late Paramount Chief Apthorpe Mxolisi San-dile; in the absence of an imbongi, Ncamashe himself bonga'd his guests. When he lost his position on the cabinet, Chief Ncamashe entered opposition politics, but in 1981 he settled his differences with the ruling party and accepted appointment as studio manager of Radio Ciskei in King William's Town.

In his youth, Ncamashe often heard performances by iimbongi, in-cluding Mqhayi, but he himself started to bonga only in 1944. His first poetic impulse was to write poetry, which he started to do as a result of a dream he had in about 1938. On 15 April 1982 he described his early poetic career in these words:

> As for education as an imbongi, I don't know what to say because, as far as I can remember about myself, this came as inspiration. In fact, I didn't show much interest in izibongo or poetry of any kind except in recitations prescribed for school

purposes by teachers, until I was between 18 and 20. To be specific, I think it was in 1938 when this started in a dream I had while I was a student at St. Matthews College near Keis-kammahoek. I estimate that that was during the year 1938. In the dream, I was sitting or standing in the shade of an oak tree at my Pirie Mission home, where I was born, in the district of King William's Town, now Zwelitsha. I looked in the direction of Ntaba kaNdoda near Debe Nek and saw, coming at a dis-tance, about a mile away, two men, distinctly. They were walking towards my home and wore blankets and carried what looked like sticks, as a Xhosa man will do. A voice told me they were Sarhili and one counselor, and were coming to my home. "Stand up and bonga the great son of Hintsa. Why are you quiet?" The voice said something like that. From that moment an incessant stream of poetic phrases flowed profusely from my mouth until the strangers arrived and suddenly disap-peared. Something disturbed me in my sleep and on being awakened I felt very much strained, as if I had been physically engaged in actual praise singing. More strange still, my voice was subsequently literally hoarse for the whole of the following day. This is true: This is no made up story.

Ncamashe's initial response to this dream was to write poetry. He established and edited a student magazine, the *Scholar's own*, which published his first poems. Later poems were published in the news-papers *Umteteli wabantu* and *Imvo zabantsundu*. In 1944 for the first time he began to bonga people

as the spirit moved me. I say this because some people are not aware that it is not always that all iimbongi are inspired to sing praises. There are moments when they don't want to say any-thing. The inspiration comes, but words don't come. Strange to say, but with me in any case that is so. This singing of praises of people, like the dream, also started at St. Matthews College where, even during mealtime in the dining hall, when I felt the compulsion then I sang the praises of anybody, of the students or somebody who was not there that I thought of at the time, or some incident of the past.

In 1946 Ncamashe became the general secretary of the Rharhabe Council, a position that brought him into contact with chiefs and their iimbongi from Ciskei and Transkei. These contacts inspired him to bonga in public, and in 1947 he bought leopard and jackal skins and, carrying spears, appeared without notice to bonga a Hlubi chief at the installation of a headman. (The chief was on that occasion accompanied by an imbongi of his own, Max Khamile.) Ncamashe's travels as secretary of the council with Paramount Chief Archie Sandile afforded him opportunities to bonga, and shortly after Mqhayi's death in 1945, Ncamashe says, "I came to be regarded as his successor and was referred to as *imbongi yamaRharhabe* ["imbongi of the Rharhabe people"] from that time." Ncamashe performed as imbongi during the baptism in Grahamstown of the son of Paramount Chief Apthorpe Mxolisi, Archie Sandile's son and heir; the ceremony is referred to by Victor Tonjeni in a book that includes poems by Ncamashe and a photograph of him in his imbongi's outfit (1959:57).

Apart from poetry published in newspapers and in Tonjeni's book, Ncamashe's poems can be found in his collection of essays and poems *Masibaliselane* (1961), "Let us tell each other stories"; in two volumes of *Dimbaza*, which appeared in 1969 and 1970 and then ceased publication; and in *Izibongo zakwaSesile (Rhodes University)* (1979), a collection of poems written in the course of a year spent undertaking research into Rharhabe history as university fellow at Rhodes University in 1977. Ncamashe does not feel that his high level of education affects his ability to perfórm as an imbongi: "When I do bonga – and not writing – the words come spontaneously. It makes some difference when I sit down to write, because then I read over it and have time to think and revise." Ncamashe's poetry, both oral and written, is characterized by an intellectual wit expressed in a rich vocabulary. A few of his written poems exhibit Western stanzaic structure and meter, but the overwhelming bulk of his published poetry is in the form and style of izibongo such as the imbongi produces. He prefers traditional style because it comes naturally to him:

> NCAMASHE: You see, in writing Western style, you think, you calculate, you measure, as it were, but in one's own traditional method that doesn't come into the picture at all.
>
> OPLAND: When you write traditional poetry, do you write it as if you were bongaing?
>
> NCAMASHE: Yes, that is true. In fact I don't think it is possible to write it outside that spirit, if I might so say, because I see myself saying this, but instead of saying it I write it. That is actually how I choose to put it.

Thus much of Ncamashe's written poetry can be used as the text of izibongo performed in traditional style. In fact, in 1977 Ncamashe wrote a poem about the chancellor-elect of Rhodes University, a portion of which he subsequently performed during the installation ceremony in a style indistinguishable from the spontaneous lines that followed smoothly from the read text. Again, in preparing a radio talk on izibongo on 15 April 1982, Ncamashe read two extracts from a poem about iimbongi he had written in traditional style (1979:38–50). He followed the text closely, but toward the end became involved in the rhythm of his reading and interpolated two spontaneous lines of his own. He was amused by this experience, remarking that it reminded him of Mqhayi reading from his published poetry to Ncamashe's St. Matthews students and casting aside the book as he launched into a spontaneous izibongo.

Ncamashe's elevation to a chieftainship and his political status have meant that he rarely performs in public now as an imbongi. In August 1976, when a U.S. professor visited his great place, he was encouraged by the performances of Max Khamile to assume Khamile's cloak and spear and produce an izibongo honoring his guest; in 1977 he performed two oral poems about the new chancellor of Rhodes University. Since then he had not bonga'd until he read his poetry for broadcast in 1982. He acknowledges that an imbongi who lacks practice, as he does, is less effective, but in spite of the rarity of his performances, he has not lost the ability to produce spontaneous, highly crafted poetry. His talent, though it rusts unburnished rather than shining in use, has not left him. Theoretically, he could still perform in public: "Nothing stops me from doing so. An imbongi has no limits to his performance. When he feels like doing so, he does so. And if conditions permit – I'm thinking of a state of health such as I'm in now: I'm in no mood to do that – then he can just carry on." Inspired by the day's discussion on 15 April 1982, Ncamashe has in fact on three subsequent occasions donned his skins to bonga in public, resuming his career as an imbongi.

We have already met Melikaya Mbutuma as the imbongi whom Mafeje observed in Langa and whose oral poetry he used as the basis for his subsequent article on the role of the imbongi. Mbutuma was born on 25 June 1928, he attended the Matanzima Secondary School in Cala and then Blythswood, and after ten years of schooling he spent two further years undergoing a teacher training course. He now lives in the Egoso location in Transkei, where he owns a store, and he operates a taxi service from the nearby town of Engcobo. Mbutuma claims that "an inborn instinct" led him to start his poetic career, and in 1955 he was recognized as an imbongi of the Thembu chiefs. He has traveled widely as an imbongi, "studying from old men," and owes a particular loyalty to ex-Paramount Chief Sabata Dalindyebo. Mbutuma considers it his duty as an imbongi to criticize a chief when he is in the wrong, and to sway people; certainly he is one of the most fearless and outspoken iimbongi I have met: Mafeje notes that, "like

Figure 2. Chief Sipho Mangindi Burns-Ncamashe performing at his great place KwaGwali on 15 August 1976. Photo: J. Opland.

so many of those who are critical of the South African Government policies and articulate the aspirations of the mass of the people in South Africa," Mbutuma "has received several warnings from the police and the officials in the Transkei, asking him to stop 'sowing seeds of dissension between the people and the chiefs, or between the people and the Government' " (1967:220). Mbutuma has consistently voiced in his poetry firm opposition to Kaiser Matanzima and support for his senior relative and political opponent, Sabata Dalindyebo. For example, in March 1963, as Transkei was moving toward self-government under Matanzima, Mbutuma produced a poem that presented Chief Sabata as a focal point of the resistance to Chief Kaiser's collaboration with the white Republican government:

> I dreamt that the royal scion [Sabata] was standing at the top of the Qetume Mountains,
> With his arms outstretched and his eyes looking upwards to the heavens.
> He was praying because of the terrible wailing and the bitter tears of his people;
> Because of their torture and persecution;
> 15 And because of the misery of the black masses . . .
> I came across the ancestors at the top of Xhalabile's Mountains,
> They said we were subverting the country by our great desire for power.
> Things are so critical because of Kaizer Matanzima's ambitiousness.
> 25 How could he strive to get a higher position than the paramount chief of all the Thembu?
> He has shocked me by unleashing such destructive forces.
> He has destroyed the reputation of the Thembu nation.
> He imagines himself as all powerful and important.
> He reveals his true colours by accepting a position that does not legitimately belong to him.
> 30 For his coercive ways, he will never be forgiven or forgotten.
> No democratic government ever forces people to do things against their will.   [Mafeje 1967:216]

Later in the same poem he pursues his criticism of Matanzima (who in 1966 was made "Paramount Chief of Emigrant Thembuland," a position without precedent created by the South African government to place Matanzima on equal footing with Sabata) and urges Matanzima to change his course as the agent of Pretoria's policies:

Worthwhile decisions come from the people themselves;
They never come from the chief alone.
80 Nowadays the chiefs make unilateral decisions,
And the result is their having to be protected.
Please tell me, Chief Kaizer Matanzima,
If you express the people's views, why have you been pro-
vided with a bodyguard?
As a spokesman of the nation, I deny your claim.
85 You have deviated from the views of the people.
Turn back and you will see that you are alone, you have no
following.
Your chieftainship is founded on a precarious base.
The white Government is your source of strength,
90 Time and again we find you, son of Mhlobo, in lofty posi-
tions,
You fly over us like an eagle.
Honourable chief, take stock and reconsider your position.
Crudeness and barbarity never make a man.
Kaizer Matanzima, you are one of us but you have been mis-
led by our enemies.
95 You have been misled by foreigners.
You are now too proud and stubborn.
You thought you were being educated, and yet you were be-
ing brain-washed.
Chieftainship is one course that is not studied in the class-
room.   [P. 218]

Mbutuma speaks on behalf of the Thembu people as *imbongi
yesizwe* (line 84), "the imbongi of the nation." Pained by the division
within the ranks of the Thembu, he seeks to reunite Matanzima and
Sabata under Sabata's legitimate paramountcy, in accordance with custom. Certainly he does not criticize Matanzima out of blind loyalty to
Sabata, simply because Matanzima stands politically opposed to Sabata: Sabata too comes in for sharp censure. In the same poem Mbutuma reflects on his own paramount chief's response to the plight of
the Thembu:

When their voice reached Jonguhlanga, he responded in a sur-
prising way.
He does not drink European liquor, he swims in it.
He says the difficulties facing him are alarming, and at times
he dreads the thought of them.
I found him using brandy as a quencher of his worries.
110 He has found it a suitable substitute for the traditional *amasi*.
I found this depressing and distressing.

What can one do? These people [chiefs] are born in their
   positions!   [P. 218]

Mbutuma is intimately involved in the current affairs of his people.
He is an astonishingly fluent improviser who can produce a poem on
any subject that takes his fancy with no premeditation whatsoever.
This makes him a particularly valuable imbongi, for he has the ability
to comment poetically on events in the course of those events, as
Mafeje saw him doing in Langa; his participation is designed to influence the outcome of the issues he comments on. In subject matter, his
poetry is almost exclusively contemporary; he may cite historical
precedents or refer to historical characters or events, but only when he
sees such references as relevant to the present situation. As he puts it,
"I don't praise with a thing that is not happening," or again, "Praising
is through eyes: It's what you see."

Mbutuma's oral poetry, then, is immediate and fearlessly outspoken. Time and again in his izibongo Mbutuma refers to dreams and
to animals, especially birds. He claims that much of his poetry is inspired by dreams. When he has been summoned to Chief Sabata's
great place to perform, on arrival he goes into seclusion in a hut and
sleeps: Chief Sabata has issued orders that no one is to disturb Mbutuma while he is sleeping. On waking, he emerges to join the gathering
and to interject poetic comments on the proceedings from time to
time. His dreams are often prophetic, and on occasion he is so disturbed by them that he feels compelled to travel to Engcobo, to stand
in the street and to bonga. On 10 July 1977 Mbutuma incorporated
reference to a dream into a poem he produced as part of a public
lecture I delivered in Grahamstown:

30   Listen, men, let me tell you a dream:
       I saw a mystery!
       I see things that are not seen by men;
       I know things that are not known by women.
       It is my chief's son: I came upon men in a house,
35   I came upon Vorster and Koornhof
       And Graaff and other dignitaries and men sitting.
       Then there was a knock at the door.
       Knock! Knock! Knock!
       Koornhof went and opened
40   And when he opened he came upon the son of Mhlobo
         hammering at the doorway, hammering on the door.
       Koornhof turned and told Vorster:
       He said "The son of Matanzima is standing at the door
       Wanting to come in."
       Yeha!

Figure 3. Melikaya Mbutuma in the 1820 Settlers Monument, Grahamstown, on 10 July 1977. Photo: Hepburn and Jeanes, Grahamstown.

45   A strange thing happened before my eyes:
      The son of Mhlobo just burst in,
      He came inside,
      And Vorster rose to his feet,
      And he gave him his own seat.

50   The son of Mhlobo sat down at the table.
     Yeha!
     What shall I say?
     He said,
     Graaff said, "I told you so."
55   And the world continued to exist,
     And the world continued in cooperation,
     And the world continued happily.

Immediately after this performance, Chief S. M. Burns-Ncamashe offered the audience a commentary on the Xhosa poem that included a summary of the scene between B. J. Vorster, then prime minister of South Africa, Dr. P. Koornhof, his minister of plural relations and development, Sir De Villiers Graaff, leader of the opposition, and Chief K. D. Matanzima, prime minister of the newly independent Transkei. Ncamashe interpreted the parable of Mbutuma's dream as follows: "In other words, he is prophesying political changes in the country where the whites will eventually yield to black rule. Vorster there is a representative of white authority, white political dominance, and Kaiser Matanzima represents the threat that the blacks are, the political threat that the blacks are to all whites in this country."

Spontaneity is the essence of Mbutuma's oral poetry, but he has also found time to write. However, very little of his work has been published, so that Mbutuma is little known as a poet outside Thembu circles; his reputation rests almost exclusively with those who have heard him bonga. Some of his poetry has been published in the now-defunct newspaper *Umthunywa,* and transcriptions of his oral poetry have appeared in articles by Mafeje and me (Opland 1974). In 1967 Mbutuma sent a collection of his poems to a university, but they were returned to him; rebuffed by that rejection, he declined to send his work to any other potential publisher. In 1974 the manuscripts of two novels that he had written, one collection of short stories, two collections of poetry, a history of the Thembu, and a set of newspaper clippings were deposited for safekeeping in the Cory Library for Historical Research at Rhodes University. One of the collections of poetry, largely Western in form, was published in 1977 as *Isife somzi,* "The garden of the nation." Only 300 copies were printed; by the end of 1981, 194 had been sold.

David Livingstone Phakamile Yali-Manisi is, like Mbutuma, a Thembu, and like Mabunu a member of the royal Hala clan. He lives in the Khundulu Valley between Queenstown and Lady Frere and works as a clerk in the magistrate's office in Lady Frere. He was educated at the Matanzima Secondary School and at Lovedale. While he was at Lovedale he wrote his first book of poetry, *Izibongo zeen-kosi zamaXhosa,* "Izibongo of Xhosa chiefs," which was published by the Lovedale Press in 1952 and is now out of print. Manisi gathered material for the poems in this collection by visiting the Thembu, Gcaleka, and Rharhabe chiefdoms and interviewing "the old people." The book contains poems that Manisi wrote in traditional style about three dozen chiefs living and dead; about nineteen dignitaries like John Knox Bokwe, Rubusana, and Mqhayi; and on the deaths of seven dignitaries such as Rubusana, Mqhayi, and B.W. Vilakazi. There are also six narrative poems in traditional style on historical subjects like Ntsikana and the Mfengu migration, and eighteen poems in Western style on miscellaneous subjects like peaće, Satan, and humanity. Two years later, in 1954, the Khundulu Methodist School at Bolotwa published Manisi's second volume of poetry, *Inguqu,* "A return to the attack," also now out of print. This is a collection of twenty-three poems on various subjects, some narrative, some religious, some about Chief Kaiser Matanzima, one on Mqhayi's home, two on the Ntsikana Day celebrations of 1948 and 1954, and one on Nelson Mandela. Manisi's third collection of poetry was sent to Chief Matanzima, who handed it to his secretary, who handed it to the minister of education, who has since retired; the manuscript is lost. In October 1976 Manisi performed in Umtata at the celebration of Transkei's "independence" and subsequently wrote a long poem on the subject in traditional style that was published in 1977 as *Inkululeko: Uzimele-geqe eTranskayi,* "Freedom: independence in Transkei." His latest volume of poetry, *Yaphum' ingqina* (1980), "Out goes the hunting party," contains four lyrical poems and one other in Western style, and the bulk consists of izibongo in traditional style about chiefs and dignitaries living and dead.

A comparison of Manisi's traditional written poetry and his oral poetry, as we shall see later, reveals a network of phrases, lines, and passages in common. It is not easy to declare whether these repetitions are conscious premeditations for written compositions that find their way thence into his oral poetry, or whether they derive from the exigencies of his oral performances, which he recognizes as such and works into his writing in imitation of his oral style; the existence of these common elements does serve to make his written poetry generally indistinguishable in style and diction from his oral poetry. Manisi does not write easily: "When I write I write with head aching and pains before I put a word down." As an oral poet, on the other hand, he is as fluent in improvisation as Mbutuma, often prepared to produce with no hesitation izibongo on nominated subjects (see Opland 1975:200–2, for example). His reputation, probably the highest of any of the iimbongi I have worked with, depends on his oral performances as an imbongi rather than on his written poetry, much of which falls victim to the politics of publishing in Xhosa. As we have seen, St. John Page Yako praised poetically the performance of the young Manisi at the unveiling of Mqhayi's tombstone in 1951, and Mbutuma remembers Manisi's izibongo at the Matanzima Secondary School. Chief Nca-mashe recollects that Manisi's performances as a schoolboy at Love-dale occasioned his punishment by an unsympathetic housemaster. The imbongi Max Khamile remembered Manisi's performances as a youth-ful supporter of the African National Congress: In the course of the conversation from which I quoted at the end of the previous chapter, Khamile and I were discussing other iimbongi, and he responded to my mention of Benjamin Hoza: "Yes, I've known Hoza. There was one chap up in Thembuland. I don't know whether that man still lives. You know, I heard him just before the fiery days of the Congress move-ment. Ah, that boy I took him for good. He was up in Thembuland. I don't know, now after that I hear nothing of him now. I don't know whether he belongs to the group that is in detention . . . That was Yali-Manisi, Manisi I think." And in his introduction to Manisi's sec-ond volume of poetry, *Inguqu,* Dorrington Nobaza wrote: "This gentleman, D. L. P. Yali-Manisi, revealed himself as a gifted imbongi at an early age when he was a boy of 16 years. He was recognized at Lovedale, at Stewart's place, where he praised at a large gathering at the St. Ntsikana Memorial Service, under the influence of Mr. J. T. Arosi, B.A., in 1946. Since then he has become known as the new imbongi of the nation. He has been in demand at all national festivi-ties, where he has praised both chiefs and the nation" (p. [i]).

Mbutuma is concerned in his poetry with current events; Manisi too is a poet with his feet firmly planted in the contemporary world, but his sense of history and its relevance to the affairs of the present is more marked than Mbutuma's. He expressed his attitude to his calling in a question-and-answer session conducted in Xhosa after a lecture I delivered with Manisi to a class of black urban schoolchildren, most of whom had never before met an imbongi or heard one perform, in Grahamstown on 11 June 1979; after avowing his belief in the necessity for an imbongi to be thoroughly familiar with the history of his people, Manisi went on to talk about his own personal evolution, more tradi-tional than and quite distinct from that of iimbongi like Msila, who started off learning izibongo from books:

> MANISI: You cannot be an imbongi if you do not know your nation. To be an imbongi of the nation you have to know the nation's history, its origins and the main events. You should know how its leaders, like chiefs, are related to one another. You must be familiar with the battles that your

great-grandfathers and their chiefs waged, fighting for their land and the nation of which you are a member. If you do not have that history, what would be the basis of your izibongo?

Of course, you can be an imbongi even if you do not know the history of your people, but then you won't bonga your nation: You will bonga the toktokkie, you will bonga the gait of the rock lizard, and talk about the crab's dancing in the river. But if you are going to bonga a nation, you must know its origins, the course of its history, where and when it experienced setbacks and difficulties until there was you, its member of today.

QUESTION: Is it possible to be an educated imbongi or an imbongi who has learned his art at school, or is bongaing something you have to suck during early childhood?

MANISI: Yes, I understand your question. Bongaing is of different kinds. First, you don't suck it. It is not something people can hand on to each other through the breast. As you grow old, by birth you have excitement in your blood and passion about domestic affairs. Long before you participate as a member of the nation, it will be clear from your habits that you are likely to be a certain thing. You will grow up then. When you are involved in national affairs, and if you have a keen mind, you will absorb the practices of your nation, and you'll like them. You will hate what is bad among your people; you will like what is an incentive to progress among your people. You will find yourself gradually appreciating what is good until you become what you were destined to be by the Almighty.

Well, if you have a love of your people, you could start by learning. You can derive inspiration from the poems that have been written for us. For example, if you can read Mqhayi's *Ityala lamawele*, *Inzuzo*, and *Imihobe nemibongo*, and come across two or three words, or four or five lines, these could inspire you. And then you use these as a springboard in order to be an imbongi. But it is not something that is acquired through education. No, you don't go to school for it. If it's not inborn, it's just not there, son of the nation. You must have it in your veins. If you carry it in your veins and if I suddenly appear when you had been thinking of me, and if you know me you will exclaim, saying, "I recognize you," and then go on bongaing. If you have learned it, then it's not inborn. And if you prepare it when you are attending rites and ceremonies, you'll get there having made your preparations and find that the rite has taken a different course, and you will bonga on the way to Ndenxa while the nation is going to Hala.

Manisi was forty-four years old when I first met him in December 1970; I have seen him fairly regularly since then, recording and then discussing his poetry with him. Manisi traces his ancestry back six generations (see Yali-Manisi 1952:103). His father, Yali-Manisi, was the son of Nobathana the son of Nobaza, all counselors to the Hala chiefs. The elder Yali-Manisi was wont to give instructions to his relatives, who would say to him, *Siyale,* "Give us instruction," from which it was said, *Unguyali Manisi,* "He is Instructor-Manisi," whence Yali-Manisi. The imbongi's maternal grandfather, Jim Mcinziba, had been a counselor to the Gcaleka chief Mcotama, and left Centane after the last frontier war in 1878. The young poet learned Gcaleka traditions from his grandfather, and he learned about the Thembu Hala from his uncle Mdubane Manisi. The first chief that Manisi came to know well was Ndabemfene Maqoma of Ntselamanzi near Alice, with whom Manisi spent weekends while he was at school at Lovedale from 1945 until 1948; from his association with Chief Ndabamfene, Manisi learned about the Rharhabe. All this oral information was grist to the mill of the young man who had started to bonga in 1943 when he saw the initiates of his Khundulu location returning from seclusion and he "praised them and their fathers": "I felt it was a very good time for me to praise these fellows because they were looking nice and their fathers were happy because they were coming from the mountain all well." He described these early days in replying to a question from a schoolboy in Grahamstown in 1979:

> QUESTION: Did your inspiration start at Lovedale, or did it start elsewhere?
> MANISI: I was inspired as a small boy, younger than you are. I was herding cattle above those fields below the small ridges of the location where I live. We used to hunt grass-warblers. Do you know a grass-warbler? We were hunting those birds, and chasing the widow-birds, riding and racing with donkeys. We would compete, and the donkeys would throw us down and we would graze our backsides. I started at that time. By the time I came to Alice, I had already started to *thwasa.*

"Ukuthwasa" was a term Khamile used for his calling, strictly, the process of inspiration and summoning by the ancestors experienced by the neophyte diviner; Manisi later glossed his use of the term here as "any learning through personal meditation."

The performance of an oral poem by Manisi is an impressive event. He is a compact man who exudes an aura of barely contained energy. Just before a public performance he is tense and taciturn, seeming to be searching deep within himself. Release comes when he explodes into poetry, forcing his words out in a rich and fluent torrent, in a measured and urgent style that demands attention. His knowledge of the Xhosa language and of the history of his people is deep, and his poetry is filled with arcane and allusive descriptions characteristic of the old izibongo of the chiefs, filled with intricate and inventive rhetorical patterning, infused with imagery that is always natural and earthy. In spite of his powerful talent, Manisi performs in public now all too infrequently, occupied as he is with his full-time work in Lady Frere. In 1979 Manisi spent five weeks at the Institute of Social and Economic Research at Rhodes University in Grahamstown as Mobil Traditional Artist in Residence. Before he arrived at the institute in May, he had performed on two occasions in the course of the year. He produced eight oral izibongo in Grahamstown before he returned to Lady Frere. When I visited him early in November to check transcriptions and translations of his poems, Manisi told me that since leaving Grahamstown he had performed twice at local weddings. When I returned again in the middle of December, Manisi had not performed in public since my last visit. At that time I recorded a snatch of poetry and a long poem in the course of conversation with Manisi, and two poems in the evening at a ceremony to which I took him in honor of the late Benjamin Tyamzashe, an eminent composer. I again saw Manisi on 30 May 1980; he had not performed in public as an imbongi since my December visit.

We moved from a consideration in Chapter 2 of all poets in the tradition to a consideration in Chapter 3 of the imbongi in general; in this chapter we passed on to consider four iimbongi in particular. With Manisi we ended by narrowing the focus to the output of one imbongi in the course of one year. Now in conclusion I should like to narrow the focus still further by presenting the poetry produced by one imbongi at one particular function. Over the weekend of 20 and 21 April 1974, I learned that Manisi would be accompanying Chief Kaiser Matanzima to bonga on the occasion of the award of an honorary doctorate to Matanzima by the University of Fort Hare the following Saturday. So on 27 April I took my place expectantly in the hall. The academic ceremony was long, but proceeded without any interruption by iimbongi; I was worried that Manisi might not have accompanied Matanzima. As I slipped out of the hall ahead of the procession,

Figure 4. David Livingstone Phakamile Yali-Manisi performing in Grahamstown at the opening of the International Library of African Music, Rhodes University, on 17 May 1979. Photo: Fotonik Studio.

however, Manisi began to bonga, pacing up and down before the
crowd of onlookers:

>   Hail Daliwonga!
>   Hail Daliwonga!
>   This then is the paramount chief of the Thembu of Rhoda,
>   This then is the dignitary of the mountains of Mngqanga.
> 5   He is All blankets look alike,
>   But you can tell them apart by the width of the stripes;
>   Sheep look alike because of the dust,
>   Those who know them distinguish them by their markings.
>   This then is the lofty one of Tato's place.
> 10   He is The stars who do not agree with the sun,
>   Because they are used to traveling with the moon;
>   They fear the sun because of the heat.
>   I understand that he is The powerful land;
>   Though it is powerful it has been defeated by the heavens,
> 15   Because they brought drought and the rivers dried up.
>   However, things can lie, oh poets:
>   The stones dry out leaving pools.
>   So then, crowds of Ntu,
>   So then, crowds of our countrymen,
> 20   I have nothing to say because I have seen the boy.
>   Away went the boy of Mhlobo,
>   He cleaved rivers,
>   But he skirted the forests of Hoho.
>   And so on went the great one,
> 25   And he entered beneath Qelekequshe,
>   The hill in the land of Sandile and Dondashe.
>   So then, fair-skinned son of Mhlobo's wife,
>   You who keep black sticks in safety,
>   Which will be reclaimed
> 30   On the day we reclaim our people's rights below Table
>   Mountain;
>   But we are given that stick,
>   That stick which is small,
>   To rule over the eastern rivulets,
>   And yet the land of Xhosa extends to below the sentinel
>   mountain,
> 35   By the sentinel mountain I mean Table Mountain,
>   Because that is where our nation's heroes lie,
>   Because that is where Mfanta the Xhiba of Mtikrakra lies,

There lies Makana son of Gwala.
Those then need to be reclaimed.
40   We'll not reclaim them with arms,
We'll reclaim them by watching the shooting of the stars.
Lead them then, fair-skinned son of Mhlobo,
Teach them of the shooting of the stars,
Because this land needs blood no longer,
45   But we will go direct,
Because we are directed.
When I say so, go home with them for they are your country-
men.
I stop and I sit, then I disappear!
I disappear!

Manisi starts his poem with the isikhahlelo given to Matanzima on accession to the chieftainship, *Daliwonga*, "Creator of grandeur," and locates Matanzima as paramount chief of the Emigrant Thembu (Rhoda), whose great place is at Qamata in the lee of Mngqanga. Lines 5 to 8 constitute two complex metaphors with the same import. Superficially, all blankets and all sheep look alike, but discriminating inspection or familiarity reveals differences; Matanzima is generally criticized for his policies, but a less superficial, more discriminating examination might reveal his better qualities. Line 9 characterizes Matanzima as tall and a descendant of Tato, one of the ancestors of the royal Hala clan of the Thembu. Lines 10 to 12 metaphorically depict Matanzima as the sun: Others (the stars) felt they had legitimate claims to the chieftainship on account of their popularity, but when Matanzima became chief instead, they feared him because they were accustomed to dealing with chiefs lacking in education (the moon). In lines 13 to 15 Matanzima is likened to the land whose fruitfulness is subject to the control and authority of the South African government. However, when poets liken Matanzima to the sun (as in lines 10 to 13) they err, for, continuing the metaphor of the land and the drought (lines 13 to 15), even in times of drought when the rivers run shallow, the sun dries the rocks but still leaves pools in the river beds: The pools in lines 16 and 17 are what is left over after the sun (Matanzima) has acted, the laws that tie Transkei to Pretoria even after "independence" might have been achieved.

Manisi then addresses his black audience (lines 18 to 19), descendants of the eponymous Ntu known as *abantu*, "people." Kaiser the son of Mhlobo, he says, journeyed from his home to the University of Fort Hare in Alice, which lies below the hill Qelekequshe (Sandile's

Kop) in the land once ruled by Sandile and Dondashe the sons of Ngqika (lines 21 to 26). It is to Kaiser Matanzima now that the essence of the nation is entrusted, the symbolic black fighting stick that is hidden in times of trouble to be retrieved when all is well once again. All is not well at the moment because Transkei is small, confined to the eastern portion of the Cape Province (lines 31 to 33), and because the heroes of the nation lie buried below Table Mountain on Robben Island, where they died as prisoners of the whites (lines 36 to 38); all will be well again, the time to reclaim the hidden stick of pride will have arrived, when all the country down to Cape Town is in black hands (line 34), and when reparation is made for the national heroes who died in exile and were not accorded traditional burials on ancestral land (lines 30 and 39). This settlement will come not through armed struggle (lines 40 and 44) but through inspired leadership that will bring the Xhosa to the destiny prophesied by Ntsikana, who spoke mystically of the shooting star as portent (Hodgson 1980:37). Manisi affirms his belief in this inevitable destiny (lines 45 and 46) before he ends his poem with a traditional formula of closure.

At the conclusion, Manisi strutted off into the crowd, the academic procession with Matanzima in its midst having moved off to disrobe. Manisi remained keyed up after his performance, aloof and withdrawn as he acknowledged the numerous expressions of congratulation. A white boy handed him a pen and an opened autograph book; Manisi grandly made a cross in the book, handed it back disdainfully and said to me in explanation, "What for must I sign my name in his book?" a supreme gesture of contempt for all those whites whose prejudice leads them to expect blacks to be so inferior to them that they must make a cross where their signature is required. One woman in the milling crowd asked Manisi to bonga again. The academic ceremony had been protracted, it was growing late, and Manisi had a long road to travel with Matanzima back to Transkei; in response to the request Manisi immediately expressed his impatience in a second izibongo produced within minutes of the first:

> Hey! Hey, my fellows!
> Pay attention, crowds of my country!
> Where is this chief of mine,
> Who lives below the mountains of Mngqanga?
> 5 Where is this lofty one of Matanzima,
> The son of the bearded puff adder of Tato,
> Which was seen by Mbanga's women on the way to work?
> Oh what a pity I lack wings,
> So that I could hover like a kestrel!

10   Oh what a pity I lack wings,
      So that I could float like a kite!
      So then, fair-skinned son of Mhlobo's wife:
      Lend me a polecat, men,
      Since my baboon has collapsed at Ndakana;
15   Lend me a polecat to ride on,
      So that I can go home to Qamata,
      For we left our families in trouble.
      So then, son of Mhlobo, let's go home,
      For the mountains are casting long shadows.
20   Here then is this chief of Tato's place,
      Even from afar he's beautiful as the Pleiades,
      The chief who's adorned with clay
      While others are adorned with leopard skins.
      He's the one who wears clothes smeared with clay
25   When he goes to his home at Bumbana;
      But when he returns from there
      He'll be riding the clumsiest of nags,
      The wagon of the white man.
      Because oh the whites!
30   Things who entered this country of Phalo,
      The country of Phalo and Ndaba,
      They place God ahead of them,
      But they conceal cannon behind their backs.
      I love a white woman,
35   But I can't sleep with a white woman,
      For she's a thing of filth:
      When she's high on a plateau she runs all the way down just
         to sit in her house and shit!
      Let's go home, fair-skinned son of Mhlobo's wife,
      For your home at Nolukhoko's place is far;
40   Let's go home, lofty one of Tato's place,
      For your home is far indeed.
      Time is passing, and Ndaba's land is in trouble,
      In trouble then is the land of the Xhosa,
      For even as we expel the thugs they continue to plague us,
45   Even as we drive out the English they grind us in the dust,
      We turned our backs on the French and they just thumbed
         their noses.
      I disappear!

In this poem, Manisi expresses his impatience to depart. Even that simple impulse, however, is given darker overtones: The reason Manisi gives for urgency is the troubled state of Transkei (lines 17 and 42). Lines 6 and 7 are one of the praises of the Thembu chief Ngangelizwe and serve to locate Kaiser Matanzima in his genealogical context (as do line 5, with its reference to his great-grandfather Matanzima the brother of Ngangelizwe; lines 12, 18, and 38, with their references to his father, Mhlobo; and line 39, with its reference to his sister Nolukhoko); the bearded puff adder is the penis, and the couplet records a sexual scandal. Since leopard skins are traditionally reserved for the chief's garments, lines 22 and 23 mean that Matanzima is not quite worthy of chieftainship: Manisi offers as an additional gloss, "He is always insulted by critics for inefficiencies while other chiefs who have done little are praised for nothing." Lines 24 and 28 refer to Matanzima's relationship with his political opponent, the paramount chief of the Thembu, Sabata Dalindyebo, who has his great place at Bumbana: Because of their political rivalry and Sabata's seniority, Kaiser Matanzima feels insecure when he has to deal with Sabata, but he finds in Sabata an ineffectual enemy and returns in joy and pomp, riding in a white man's car. Having thus offered implied criticism of white support of his chief, Manisi proceeds to inveigh against the duplicity and destructiveness of Europeans in their treatment of the Xhosa before ending his poem.

The crowd, which had opened a small circle for Manisi during the performance of this izibongo, listened attentively, laughed at line 37, and greeted the conclusion with applause. Manisi wandered off in search of his chief.

5
EULOGY AND RITUAL

The Xhosa imbongi has the power through his poetic performances to sway emotions, to incite actions. Quite apart from aspects of performance such as voice and physical gesture that might arouse emotion in the audience, however, the poetry itself has power. We have noted that memorized izibongo are occasionally irrelevant to the persons to whom they are addressed, as if the recitation of a poem serves a function almost independent of its text. An old Mfengu once offered to bonga us as we were about to leave his location near Peddie in 1969, and claimed that his performance would ensure our safe journey home; when we asked if that end would be attained through the inspiration we would derive from hearing the poem, he asserted that the same effect would be achieved whether he recited the poem in our presence or not. The poem itself has power. In the previous chapters we were concerned with Xhosa poets; now we shift our emphasis to a consideration of Xhosa poetry and its role in society, to a consideration of what it *does*. This necessarily entails consideration of the content of the poetry, of what it *is*. Both aspects are essential to an appreciation of the distinctive qualities of the kind of poetry we have been discussing, to an appreciation of its genre. An understanding of what Xhosa oral poetry is can in turn be enhanced through a consideration of what it is not, of the qualities that distinguish it from epic or narrative poetry for example, and through a comparison of Xhosa eulogy with other examples of eulogy. The present chapter constitutes an attempt to locate Xhosa izibongo within the context of the genre of eulogy.

First we must examine a little more carefully some of the beliefs and rituals of the Cape Nguni, in particular the system of ancestor veneration, the concept of chieftainship, and the role of cattle. In the second chapter I set Xhosa poetry in three intersecting domains of social activity, considering poetry in the life of domestic man, in the life of man as a member of a clan, and in the life of man as a member of a chiefdom. If we sharpen slightly our focus on the first domain, we arrive at three nesting social and political contexts in which the ordinary tribesman operates: the lineage, the clan, and the chiefdom. A lineage consists "of all the descendants of a common ancestor in the male line" (M. Wilson, 1969b:116). In traditional society, usually three generations of a lineage live together in a group of dwellings called an umzi, a homestead. On a broader level of social organization, a number of such lineages descended ultimately from the same ancestor form a patrilineal clan, the members of which are not permitted to intermarry. A clan is thus "an exogamous group claiming common descent" (M. Wilson 1969b:118). Since members of a lineage are generally free to leave a district and seek settlement in another, and since in any case a wife cannot be a member of the same clan as her husband, any one location is generally inhabited by members of different clans. Such a location is subject to the jurisdiction of a chief, perhaps through the authority of subchiefs or headmen responsible for a number of locations that might constitute the chiefdom. "By chiefdom is meant a political unit occupying a defined area under an independent chief" (M. Wilson 1969b:118); independent chiefs may in turn acknowledge the seniority of a paramount chief. Thus in traditional society everyone is a member of a lineage, of a clan, and of a chiefdom; membership of a lineage and clan is determined by ancestry, whereas membership of a chiefdom is theoretically a matter of choice.

Michael Gelfand remarked of the beliefs of another Bantu-speaking group that "most Shona who have experience of western teachings maintain that it is more comforting and real to pray to their ancestral spirits than to a remote Creator. Only those who really loved them in this world can be relied upon to take an interest in their problems and intercede on their behalf with the mightier spirits" (1969:44). Henry Callaway's collection of testimonies on Zulu religious beliefs includes the following remarks by Umpengula Mbanda:

> Speaking generally, the head of each house is worshipped by the children of that house; for they do not know the ancients who are dead, nor their [izibongo], nor their names. But their father whom they knew is the head by whom they begin and end in their prayer, for they know him best, and his love for his children; they remember his kindness to them whilst he was living; they compare his treatment of them whilst he was living; support themselves by it, and say, "He will still treat us in the same way now he is dead. We do not know why he should regard others besides us; he will regard us only." [1870/1970:144–5]

And so it is too with the Cape Nguni: A man cares for his children during his life, demonstrating a paternal concern that endures after death. It may well be, as Hammond-Tooke asserts (1978), that the concept of mediation of the ancestral shades between the living and a Supreme Being derives from the missionaries; yet the belief of the Cape

Nguni in the continued interest of the departed spirits in the affairs of the living is not in dispute. These ancestral shades may be addressed, appealed to, and appeased through certain ritual actions generally involving beer, cattle, and izibongo. In times of trouble the lineage head appeals to his ancestors, especially his father, with whom he is most familiar, for assistance: The medium of communication is the ancestors' izibongo. Mbanda's testimony on Zulu practices affirms this:

> Their father is a great treasure to them even when he is dead. And those of his children who are already grown up know him thoroughly, his gentleness, and his bravery. And if there is illness in the village, the eldest son [bongas] him with the [izibongo] which he gained when fighting with the enemy, and at the same time [bongas] all the other Amatongo; the son reproves the father, saying, "We for our parts may just die. Who are you looking after? Let us die all of us, that we may see into whose house you will enter. You will eat grasshoppers; you will no longer be invited to go any where, if you destroy your own village."
>
> After that, because they have [bonga'd] him, they take courage saying, "He has heard; he will come and treat our diseases, and they will cease."
>
> Such, then, is the faith which children have in the Itongo which is their father. [Callaway 1870/1970:146]

One of the most detailed investigations of the religious beliefs of a Cape Nguni group is that undertaken by E. H. Bigalke (1969) among the Ndlambe in the East London district between October 1967 and September 1969. The area between the main hut in the umzi (which faces the gates of the cattle kraal) and the gates of the kraal, as well as the kraal itself, is held to be sacred to the ancestors of the lineage; it is in the cattle kraal that men are buried. This area is strictly out of bounds to wives, who as members of another clan are not members of the lineage. As Bigalke remarks, "The area between the doorways of the huts . . . and the gateway to the cattle kraal is the *inkundla*, the place of assembly, and, with the kraal, the abode of the ancestors who are believed to visit their descendants there . . . The owner and his children of both sexes walk freely within this area but wives, who are not full members of the lineage, must take care not to go too near the cattle kraal" (p. 26). Bigalke also comments on the continuing interaction between the ancestors and the members of the lineage:

> Like their descendants, ancestors are normally (and ideally) thought to be in and around the homesteads they once occu-

pied, especially towards evening, when the cattle have been herded into the kraal. Ancestors also assemble whenever there are many people at the homes of their descendants, not only when there is a sacrifice but also when a beer drink is held, for all the ancestors like conviviality, just as they did when they were alive on earth. Blood of sacrificial beasts and the *ubulawu* (a herbal decoction) brought into the kraal also attract them. In fact, every householder should make an effort to have beer brewed at least once a year, even if he cannot do it more often, for "ancestors say this house must not smell only of cowdung [with which the floor is smeared], it must smell of beer too" . . .

In general, however, informants are not concerned with the ancestors' personalities but with their influence on the lives of the living. Sometimes in dreams ancestors merely visit their descendants with friendly motives but they usually come to request sacrifices or the brewing of beer. If these requests are heeded, "ancestors protect you as you protect your own children. They reward you with maize, cattle, goats and sheep for your good conduct." Also, "If you do all the sacrifices, your ancestors will give you strength." If the living are tardy, they receive warning and "if you take heed they are pleased; if you do not they punish you with illness," "they can even punish by killing stock" or "your stock won't increase and your crops won't grow well." [Pp. 76–7]

Many ceremonies involve not only members of the lineage but also all members of the clan living in the neighborhood. Clan solidarity is a vital element in Nguni society, binding a man to his living relatives as belief in the spirit world binds him to the dead. Thus John Henderson Soga wrote:

There are two forces which bind all tribes of the Bantu into a racial unit. The first is spiritual as exemplified in their religion, and in the spirit world wherein dwell the spirits of their ancestral chiefs, and of each family's departed relatives. These spirits are alive, concerning themselves with the things which pertain to their unseen world, and, at the same time, keeping in touch with the living, and requiring the living to keep in touch with them through ritual acts and ceremonial rites.

The second force is relationship, which works through the kinship of a progenitor, and through a common blood stream reacting to the furthest off descendant; thus binding the progenitor to the family, clan and tribe which have their being in

him, and likewise binding family, clan and tribe to him.
[1931:7–8]

Bigalke notes that the shades "are invited to be present on all occasions when lineage members and their clansmen gather" (p. 95), at mortuary rituals, weddings, and female initiation celebrations. "At all rituals the clan name . . . and/or one or more clan praise names are called in the invocation. In addition, in the mortuary rituals the name of the deceased is mentioned . . . and sometimes the name of his father and grandfather" (p. 114). This invocation, isinqulo, and the sacrifice of an animal are the two most important elements in the rituals. In the invocation "the ancestors are called upon and informed why the beast is being offered. All clan ancestors are, by implication, addressed by the use of the clan name and, usually, one or other of the clan praise names (*izinqulo*). This reflects the important place of deceased members of the lineage and clan and of their living descendants who are present at the ritual" (p. 130). Bigalke provides examples of invocations. One, uttered at a ceremony (*ukukhapa*) performed shortly after death to offer a beast to accompany the deceased, runs: "Yes, son of Sigonyela who is named Ntulo, we mourn you with this black-and-white ox. We wish that you should appear to us in dreams we here at (the home of) Ncibana, at the (home of the) Cira people" (p. 81); here Cirha is a clan name and Ncibana a clan praise name. Another, uttered more than a year after the death at a ceremony (*ukubuyisa*) designed to bring the deceased back and "reintegrate him, on a higher level, in the life of his lineage" (p. 80), runs: "It is like that, son of Ngoje, we have done everything here at this home of yours, of Mtika, of Mazaleni. We are returning to you, Nangqoke of Tshali. Come amongst us" (p. 84). The ceremony's subject was Nangqoke the son of Ngoje the son of Tshali of the Jwarha clan; Mtika and Mazaleni are clan praise names.

P. A. McAllister (1979) studied the rituals associated with labor migration among the Gcaleka, in particular the beer-drink oratory on the departure or return of migrants. At these ceremonies the migrants always invoke (*nqula*) the ancestors. McAllister offers two examples of invocation on departure, the first by Ndlebezendja of the Cirha clan: "Cattle of Qhangqolo, of Hlomla. It is old, it has horns. Cattle of Nxibana, of the elephant's jawbone, of Gubela, of Sihabe, of the daughter of Mva's lover, who is from the place of the amaBamba. I hope I will travel and return again as before." Masilingane, a young man of a different Cirha lineage, says: "Sons of Gobozane, of Mhlantla, of Qhangqolo, of Cangci, of Siyo. I hope that my people (ancestors) will look after me, so that I will arrive there where I am going to, and also that I will return and enter these (cattlebyre) gates of ours. Sons of Gobozane, of Siyo, of Mhlantla, of Cangci" (pp. 121–2). McAllister comments:

> In these invocations the migrant uses the praises (*izibongo*) of the clan and lineage ancestors. He is addressing himself to the ancestral group as a whole, including the descendants of the clan ancestors, but the implication is that it is not the remote ancestors but their sons/descendants (spoken of as "cattle" by Ndlebezendja), i.e. more immediate ancestors, who will protect the invoker on his journey to work and ensure a safe return. The empty beaker is left in the cattlebyre for a number of days – the period that the journey to work lasts – after which it is taken out by a child. [P. 122]

McAllister recorded the testimony of Nothusile the wife of Mzilikazi concerning the ceremonies occasioned by his return from work on a platinum mine in the Transvaal in May 1976:

> On his arrival he slept and early the following morning sent children to call the amaCira to come to this homestead. When they arrived he said to them; "I have called you here, this is what I have got." The first bottle was for the amaCira and it was compulsory that they be called. The second bottle was for women, and it was given to me as the mother of the home (*umama wekhaya*). After this they (the amaCira) thanked him, using all the praise names (*izibongo*). They *nqula* (invoke, in using the praises) the ancestors so that he should be protected from any dangers. He has been to war and they have looked after him. [Pp. 280–1]

We should note from the testimony of Ndlebezendja that the immediate ancestors are addressed as cattle, from the testimony of Nothusile that the ancestors are invoked through a recitation of izibongo to protect their descendant Mzilikazi from dangers, and in general the crucial role played by izibongo in the ritual veneration of the ancestors of the lineage and of the clan.

In Jordan's *Ingqumbo yeminyanya,* during the debate following the killing of the snake, the Mfengu chief Dabula is addressed by the names of his clan ancestors, Tolo and Zulu; he in turn swears by Zulu (1980:207). Kuse confirmed that "when one uses one's *isiduko* as in 'MaRudulu!' or 'Ndifunga amaRudulu' (I swear by the Rudulu clan), one is giving or pledging his (her) honour and the reputation of his/her clan. He swears by all that is holy and sacred" (1973:8). Just as one may swear by the name of an ancestor, one may swear by the name of a

chief: Lichtenstein observed that "the Koossas, when they want to affirm anything very solemnly, or to utter any malediction, make use of
the name of their king, or of some of his ancestors" (1812/1928:310). By
birth, a man is a member of a certain lineage and a certain clan.
Theoretically, he is a member of a chiefdom by choice, since he may
remove to another chiefdom if he so wishes. A chief is a member of
the dominant lineage in the chiefdom, and usually the senior son of the
most important wife of a chief, but other members of the royal lineage
may and frequently do break away to establish new chiefdoms if they
can attract supporters (see Hammond-Tooke 1965): *Inkosi yinkosi
ngabantu,* "a chief is a chief by virtue of people." Lichtenstein observed that "the government is entirely monarchic; the king is absolute
sovereign. He makes laws, and executes them entirely according to his
sole will. Yet there is a power to balance his in the people; he governs
only as long as they choose to obey" (p. 352). In the rural areas,
everyone lives in a chiefdom, and the relationship between chief and
tribesman is of ritual significance, for the chief is a sacral chief: As
Bennie put it, "The head of the tribe was the Chief, the father and
protector of his people and the representative of the tribe, so that any
injury done to him was an injury to the whole tribe" (1939:24), and in
the words of John Henderson Soga, "The mystical idea that in the
chief resides the life and well-being of the tribe, that as the head of the
tribe, and as such the repository of wisdom, endowed with the power
to guide the collective members of the tribal body, and nourish the
body politic; all this surrounds him with a halo more enduring than any
outward symbol" (1931:30).

More fully, Monica Wilson has expressed as follows the traditional
and ritual relation between chief and people:

> Political and kinship structures interlocked as has been indi-
> cated, and both were expressed in and reinforced by ritual.
> The Nguni chief not only exercised practical authority but also
> partook of the nature of divinity. A chief was "born not
> made," and his position as senior kinsman of a senior lineage
> made him the mediator between his people and his ancestors,
> who were thought of as exercising power over the country they
> had once ruled. It has been shown how, among the Swazi, the
> strength and fertility of the nation were thought to be bound
> up with the strength and virility of the chief. Annually, at the
> summer solstice, a great ritual was celebrated at which the
> chief and his army were treated with medicines to make them
> strong, and the new green vegetables offered first to the ances-
> tors, then tasted by the chief, and each of his sub-chiefs in

order of rank. Only after that might the common people eat of the new crops. It was an occasion when criticism of the chief was openly expressed and the anger men felt against him confessed. This *incwala* (or *ingxwala*) ritual was at one time celebrated by all the Nguni chiefdoms. During a drought further rites were celebrated and sacrifices offered by the chief on behalf of his country.

Commoners sacrificed to their own ancestors, the descendants of a common great-grandfather, or occasionally a whole clan, gathering to partake of the sacrificial meat and beer . . .

The rituals reflect the preoccupation of the Nguni with cattle. These provided the most usual and most acceptable sacrifice, at puberty and at marriage, in sickness and at death. They were offered by a commoner to the shades of his lineage or a chief on behalf of his people. [Wilson 1969b:126–7]

And Hammond-Tooke writes, like Wilson, of the Nguni in general:

The centre of tribal life is the chief, the senior representative of the senior (royal) clan of the tribe. The office is hereditary in the male line and the chief is by far the most important man in the tribe. He is the chief priest of the tribe and sacrifices on its behalf to the most powerful ancestral spirits – those of his dead ancestors. He is supreme judge and lawgiver and the head of the administrative system of district headmen; his court is the final court of appeal for cases from the local courts. He controls the wealth of the tribe and leads the army in war. He is, in fact, the symbol of tribal unity; in his person all the complex emotions which go to form the solidarity of the tribe are centred – he *is* the tribe. His position, however, is not one of exclusive privilege. It also entails obligations. By sacrifice and magic he is responsible for the welfare of the tribe and the interests of all its members . . .

Much of the chief's power stems from mystical sources. He holds the position hallowed from time immemorial and is the direct descendant of the mythical founders of the tribe whose powerful spirits are ever watching over the fortunes of their children who are, say the Bantu, quick to take offence. [1954:34]

Finally, before we examine more closely the role of poetry in these systems of belief, we must consider the significance of cattle. Many writers have commented on the dominance of cattle in Cape Nguni thought. In the first chapter, for example, I quoted the testimonies of

Fritsch and Kropf and a passage from Jordan's *Ingqumbo yeminyanya* on the Mpondomise royal ox. Kropf observed that the Cape Nguni believe that "a special sympathy" exists between them and their cattle, "not only on earth but even after death." Further,

> the bull was formerly the property of the chief alone, and symbolized his power and strength: the cow represents wealth, luck and generosity. Each tribe has a tribal ox, after which it is also called in order to honor the tribe, just as each distinguished man has such an ox to which he accords all kinds of titles and honor, which is protected in battle and must not be killed, but has to be brought back home again. The illness and death of a beloved ox often occasions moaning and crying quite as loud as over a sick or dead person, and one might then hear from the mouth of the afflicted Kaffir: "Death has broken into our place with much greater might than when he wants merely to carry off a person. Our great ox is sick, and when he who is stronger than all others dies, what will become of us? We shall all perish!" And just as they do at the death of a person, the Kaffirs often abandon the place where the beloved great ox died. [1889a:108–9]

This passage suggests that cattle in some ways are treated like and identified with people, a suggestion that is supported by independent evidence. We have already seen that the Gcaleka Ndlebezendja addressed his immediate ancestors as cattle. Friedrich Müller, for many years a Moravian missionary at Bethesda, remarks that the Hlubi do not give names to their horses (an animal introduced to them by the white man), "but every calf, every cow, every ox has its name" (1926:38). Kropf records the testimony of one Kwitshi on his role in the disastrous cattle-killing episode of 1856 and 1857, when the Xhosa followed the instructions of the ancestors transmitted through the girl Nongqawuse to slaughter their cattle and destroy their grain in order to initiate a physical resurrection of the ancestors and the destruction of the whites: Kwitshi says that, on the orders of the chief Mhala, he "went to the pool and hid myself among the reeds and raised a pair of horns, which I had in my hands, high enough for Nonqaus to see. Thus I moved back and forth in the reeds bellowing and called: 'We will arise, we are people who were dead' " (1889b/1891:16). The Methodist pioneer missionary William Shaw himself observed the funeral obsequies of the chief Ndlambe, who died in February 1828. The hut in which the chief died was sealed and never used again. "A grave was dug, in which he was buried, and a circular enclosure, or cattle-fold, was formed over and around the spot where the grave was situate. In this fold were placed ten oxen, besides a number of milch cows, which stood at nights therein, and thus obliterated all trace of the grave itself" (1860:429–30). A watchman was appointed who for a year after Ndlambe's death had sole charge of the cattle in the kraal and alone milked the cows.

> He remained in charge for about a year; and then the cattle were removed to the ordinary cattle-fold, while the watchman was at liberty to return to his own dwelling; but from that time these cattle were considered as "devoted"; and they were not allowed to be killed and eaten, unless, in some time of sickness or calamity, the wise man or Priest consulted directed one of them to be slaughtered as an offering to the *umshologu* of the departed Chief. All the other cattle of the grave remained entirely unused till they died of age. [p. 430]

The cattle kraal is the usual burial place for the head of a household, and the kraal is thus a special abode of the ancestors, and the cattle are their living associates. Wives are not permitted to cross the space between the main hut and the entrance to the cattle kraal, nor to enter the kraal itself; wives are also not permitted ever to utter the names of their husbands' male progenitors and, in a practice known as *ukuhlonipha,* "to show respect," must master an elaborate alternative vocabulary in order not to violate this taboo (see Finlayson 1978).

Cattle, then, treated in many ways like people, constitute an integral element in the ancestor cult: In the sacred cattle kraal, the abode of the ancestors, the sacrifice of a beast and the recitation of the lineage or clan poems are media of communication with the ancestors. As Cope observed of cattle among the Zulu, "They have ritual value in religion, for it is only tne sacrifice of cattle to the accompaniment of the recital of praises that propitiates the ancestral spirits. This ritual value is also apparent in the fact that all family ceremonies are performed in the cattle-fold, and in the taboos relating to the cattle-fold, cattle, and milk" (1968:19). And Hammond-Tooke, writing on the Bhaca, Hlubi, and Xesibe, observed that "cattle loom far greater in importance than crops. For the Bantu have a cattle cult . . . Cattle are the door to sexual satisfaction (as *ikhazi*), social standing and for an approach to the ancestral spirits . . . Goats and cattle are the media for getting into touch with the *amathongo* spirits on the important occasions of birth, initiation, death, and in times of sickness" (1954:37). Among the Ndebele, a Nguni offshoot of the Zulu living in Transvaal, izibongo of people are introduced by the appeal *Thath' ikomo nasi,* "Take this head of cattle" (Van Warmelo 1930:66–95). It would appear that in Nguni ritual, cattle and people are related in a "symbolic equation" in which, writes Audrey Hayley, drawing on the work of Hana Segal, "the symbol-substitute is felt to *be* the original object, whereas the symbol proper is felt to *represent* the object" (1968:266).

It is evident that poetry plays a critical role in this system of belief and ritual. In the course of his life, a man composes a poem about himself, his boast, which consists of commemorative names and praises that he has coined or that others have composed about him. When he dies, his eldest son uses that poem in ritual invocations, just as he once used the poem about his father: The boasts, current during the lifetimes of their subjects, are used after their death as poems of the lineage. Where such individuals have in the course of time become ancestors of separate clans, phrases from their boasts enter a wider tradition as part of the clan praises, which are the names, praise names, and praises of common ancestors of the clan. These poems form part of the invocations in the course of rituals involving the clan. The senior male in the umzi recites the ritual poems of the lineage; the senior male in the clan recites the clan praises on behalf of the members of the clan. The senior member of the dominant clan is the chief; recitation of poetry about him and his ancestors is the function of the imbongi. The izibongo of an individual incorporates allusions to his qualities and his deeds; the izibongo of a clan alludes to the qualities and deeds of clan ancestors as well as to physical characteristics and the history of the clan as a whole; the izibongo of a chief similarly alludes to his qualities and deeds, to the qualities and deeds of his ancestors, and to significant events in the history of the chiefdom. In reciting izibongo of the chief, the imbongi is performing on behalf of the members of the chiefdom the same ritual function as is served by the senior member of the clan on behalf of the members of the clan when he uses clan izibongo to invoke the clan ancestors, the same ritual function as is served by the lineage head on behalf of the members of the lineage when he recites the izibongo of his forefathers. Merely to make this observation, however, to assert that izibongo have a ritual force, is to offer no comment on what izibongo are in essence and why they play the role that they do. To approach an appreciation of this aspect of izibongo, I believe, we must return to consider izibongo as naming poems.

In his definition of the Zulu word "izibongo," A. T. Bryant noted that "every Native, and especially chiefs, has a number of these praise-phrases coined for him by others, and which are often added to his name by way of a distinction" (1905:46). I have remarked on the underlying structure of izibongo that derives from this circumstance. A man earns or coins alternative names, and to these names might be added an extension of the metaphor, an explanation or an allusion to the circumstances from which they derive; a sequence of these names, followed by the descriptive or commemorative phrases (which, following Cope, I have called "praises") constitutes an izibongo, which only in that sense can be referred to as "the praises of" a person. Most of these names can be clearly recognized in a poem by their formulation in a nominal construction with a class prefix distinctive of persons. Thus, for example, in the Zengele clan izibongo quoted from Ndawo in the second chapter, the clan is said to have occupied the location where Thiyani is buried, Thiyani who was known as The Welcomer, because he welcomed the chief. The allusion is now obscure to us, but The Welcomer is clearly a name Thiyani earned because he once distinguished himself by welcoming a chief. Two lines of this izibongo are thus a praise built of a name, an alternative name, and an explanatory allusion to the circumstances that gave rise to the praise name. In Manisi's second izibongo about Chief Kaiser Matanzima quoted in the fourth chapter, Matanzima is said to be a descendant of "the bearded puff adder of Tato, which was seen by Mbanga's women on the way to work." This is a praise of the Thembu chief Ngangelizwe, who was involved in some sexual act witnessed by Mbanga's women. In the first poem, Manisi calls Matanzima by the names All blankets look alike, The stars who do not agree with the sun, and The powerful land, each of which is amplified in succeeding lines; he is also referred to without further elaboration as the paramount chief of the Thembu of Rhoda, the dignitary of the mountains of Mngqanga, the boy of Mhlobo, fair-skinned son of Mhlobo's wife, and fair-skinned son of Mhlobo. In his study of Southern Sotho oral poetry, D. P. Kunene called these praises that form the structural heart of the poetry "eulogues," which term he uses "generically to refer collectively to all types of eulogistic references used of the hero, whether they be praise names or associative references" (1971a:15).

Eulogues are names, and Kunene's analysis of Sotho oral poetry starts with a statement on the significance of Sotho names. He continues: "Against this background, it should not be difficult to understand the importance attached to names given to warriors and warrior-kings. The one significant difference is that warriors *earned* their names through distinction in battle or a similar situation. This means that a warrior could accumulate many names, directly or indirectly alluding to, or even describing, the various episodes in which he distinguished himself and, in particular, the *way* in which he distinguished himself" (p. 14). Kunene likens Southern Sotho poems that evolve from names in this way to Ulli Beier's description of Yoruba *oriki* in Nigeria, and quotes from Beier's article "The poetry of names" a passage which asserts that a person "may acquire more and more [*oriki*] during the course of his life. The *oriki* are descriptive phrases referring to the character or deeds of a person. They may be invented by relatives or neighbours or – most frequently – by the drummers, and they remain with the person and everybody in his surrounding will know them by heart. A collection of *oriki* is like a very loosely constructed poem having as its subject a simple individual or a chief, a town or even a god" (p. 14).

Zulu and Xhosa izibongo, like Southern Sotho *lithoko* and Yoruba *oriki*, are poems built on commemorative praises that function in society as alternative names. Edward Clodd, drawing on the work of Sir James Frazer, wrote a book entitled *Magic in names and in other things* (1920) in which he asserted that "to the civilized man, his name is only a necessary label: to the savage it is an integral part of himself" (p. 37). Clodd assembles examples of the power and magic that reside in names, which, using a word current in the Pacific, he terms *mana:* "*Mana* is the stuff through which magic works; it is not the trick itself, but the power whereby the sorcerer does the trick" (p. 3). Names have mana. Clodd offers as one example of the power held to reside in a name this extract from the diary of Cadwallader Colden:

> "The first time I was among the *Mohawks* I had this compliment from one of their old Sachems, which he did by giving me his own name, *Cayenderongue*. He had been a notable warrior, and he told me that now I had a right to assume all the acts of valour he had performed, and that now my name would echo from hill to hill over all the *Five Nations.*" When Colden went back into the same part ten or twelve years later, he found that he was still known by the name he had thus received, and that the old chief had taken another. [P. 50]

Through his deeds a man earns honorific names: The name *is* the person, and the bearer of the name is accordingly entitled to claim his deeds. It is intriguing to place this Mohawk anecdote against the Zulu testimony Stuart recorded from Dinya kaZokozwayo on 2 March 1905 concerning Shaka's actions before a battle with Zwide:

> Tshaka then took a stick and went with it into the council place where all the impi had assembled. He said, "See now, I thrust this stick into the ground. My praises, when I was with the chief Dingiswayo at Yengeni, were, 'Heavens that thunder in the open, where there is neither mimosa nor thorn tree; willow tree which overhangs the deep pools.' Let there come forward a warrior to pull out this stick. My praises will be

given to him as the first to attack in battle." Komfiya no sooner
heard this than he came in through the opening which Tshaka
used in going to the isigodhlo. He had been smearing the floor
in Tshaka's hut, being an inceku. He went and pulled out the
stick. Tshaka said, "I shall now watch and see how my dark
friend will conduct himself when it comes to the point to see if
he will deserve the praise 'The heavens that thunder' " . . . [In
the subsequent battle] Komfiya was stabbed in the upper left
arm between the shoulder blade and armbone. He killed a number and then got hurt. He thereupon earned Tshaka's praises.
[Webb and Wright 1976:102–3]

The editors of Stuart's papers do not provide us with the Zulu sentences that mingle with his English notes: If the council place was the
inkundla, the space between the principal hut and the cattle kraal that
is used for court cases and significant announcements and that is the
sacred abode of the ancestors, Shaka's offer, accompanied by a spear
thrust in the earth that holds the ancestors, is invested with ritual
significance.

Throughout Africa, words and names are held to have a particular
power (see Finnegan 1970:470–9). Philip Peek has recently claimed
that in Africa "human speech is frequently conceived of as a tangible
entity which defines individual presence and allows human interaction"
(1981:21). Peek cites Placide Tempels on African thought: "A living
man's words or his gesture are considered, more than any other manifestation, to be the formal expression or sign of his vital influence" (p.
23). Among the Cape Nguni, serious appeals to the ancestors are
uttered in the cattle kraal through the sacrifice of an ox in a ceremony
the generic term for which is *idini* (see Kropf 1899/1915:75–6 and
Mqhayi 1928). A spear is used to make an incision in the throat; the
officiant then reaches into the aperture, takes hold of the aorta, and
ruptures it by pulling sharply. The victim bellows; the izibongo are
recited and the ancestors addressed in a familiar manner as if they
were present in the kraal. The ox must bellow loudly; if it does not,
the sacrifice is held to be unacceptable to the ancestors. If a substitute
officiant cannot produce a bellow from the victim, the ceremony must
be abandoned. The victim is a familiar of the ancestors, living as it
does in the kraal that is the burial place and the abode of the ancestors. The bellow of the victim, in terms of the remarks of Tempels and
Peek, assures the celebrants of the vital presence of the ancestors. The
victim, moving during the ceremony between life and death, is a medium of communication between the living and the ancestral shades.
The izibongo too are such a medium. By uttering their names, using

the words they used in their boasts while alive, the officiant not only invokes them but conjures their presence. As Peek puts it, "Names do not simply describe; they *are* their referent . . . As the Dogon understand it 'to utter a name is to bring into existence a form and a habitation – the best form and the most suitable habitation to receive the life-force of the being invoked' " (p. 27). In her discussion of symbolic equations, Hayley cites Lucien Lévy-Bruhl's statement that "the symbol is felt as being, in some way, the very being or object that it represents, and to 'represent' has here the literal meaning of 'to make actually present' " (1968:269).

The recitation of the izibongo of a dead man, incorporating as it does the names of its subject, conjures his presence so that the living may commune with him; the recitation of the izibongo of a living man, incorporating as it does the names of its subject and reference to his lineage or clan ancestry, conjures the presence of his ancestors and ensures their sympathetic attention to his affairs. When the imbongi performs an izibongo in honor of his chief, he usually at least places the chief in a genealogical context by mentioning the names of his ancestors and frequently extends his performance by incorporating poems in honor of his chief's ancestors, poems based on their praises. In so doing, the imbongi performs on behalf of the chiefdom the role of the lineage or clan head reciting izibongo on behalf of the clan or the lineage: The chief's ancestral spirits, invoked through the imbongi's izibongo, will attend sympathetically to the well-being of the ruling chief, and thereby, since the chief *is* the chiefdom, the imbongi ensures the well-being of all the members of the chiefdom. Thus a Zulu poet who stumbled in recitation offered in explanation the comment "I have forgotten him" (not I have forgotten *it*, the poem); and the poet's chief, Gatsha Buthelezi, asserted that the izibongo of a person *is* the person, that every performance of an izibongo is a prayer (Opland 1980c:299). Thus the Zulu journalist H. I. E. Dhlomo could write: "The tribal man will tell you that the Izibongo are the wealth of our country, the soul of the state, the dignity and meaning of the Race – are God himself" (1948/1977:52). Izibongo have vitalizing power, a permanence – a continuing mana – that survives the transition of state that is death. Thus the Zulu izibongo of Shaka's brother, his murderer and successor, Dingana, contains the lines

> People will die but their izibongo remain
> These will remain to weep for them in their deserted homes.
> [Cope 1968:67]

Bennie cites a speech of consolation by a Thembu to the eldest son of his recently deceased brother that is dense with proverbial wisdom:

There is this to remember, son of my elder brother: nothing happens that has not happened before. Our brother has gone from us. A man dies even if he be praised, he disappears even if he be loved, and sinks out of sight even when we weep for him. It is not for a man to lick his wound – only a dog does so. Yes, "a fine eating-mat soon wears out with use." My father's son has gone – handsome man that he was. Be ye comforted; strengthen yourselves, and move about among people. [1939:41]

The proverb that starts the third sentence is cited by Kropf in his definition of "ukubonga": "Phr. *lento umntu iyemka noko ibongwayo,* man goes away, though he is celebrated, i.e., the most renowned must die" (1899/1915:42). I suggest that the proverb is stronger with ritual overtones: A man will die even if he is bonga'd; that is, the vitalizing power of izibongo will not be sufficient to prevent death. Dudley Kidd, writing in general terms about the Bantu-speaking peoples of South Africa, yet captures something of the essence of Nguni izibongo when he says, "The moment a man's praise-giving titles are forgotten it becomes impossible to worship him in any full sense, for wherewith shall the people praise him? He then drifts out of the sphere of practical politics, even though he may retain some vitality in the folk-lore of the people" (1904:95).

Basically, then, izibongo are names of individuals, and naming an individual and his ancestors in this particular form strengthens the living individual through ensuring the protective sympathy of his ancestors and promotes continuing intercourse between the living and the dead. The performance of an izibongo thus *does* something; uttering the words of the poem makes something happen. Sometimes the words may not be relevant to the subject, or the allusions may be elliptical and obscure; often, in the simplest form of a collection of praises, izibongo are used not to convey information so much as to express pride, or to encourage, thank, or strengthen the hearer(s). Izibongo always *do* things, regardless of what they say (which as we saw in Chapter 2, may not be relevant to the subject or indeed intelligible to the performer). In this sense, izibongo are performative utterances, illocutionary acts. These are terms coined by J. L. Austin, who draws a distinction between a locutionary act, which makes a statement, and an illocutionary act, which he defines as "performance of an act *in* saying something as opposed to performance of an act *of* saying something" (1962:99). Performative utterances achieve certain ends through their utterance. Austin presents as examples the utterances "I do" in a wedding ceremony, "I name this ship the *Queen Elizabeth*" at a dockyard ceremony, "I give and bequeath my watch to my brother" in a will, and "I bet you sixpence it will rain tomorrow," and observes: "In these examples it seems clear that to utter the sentence (in, of course, the appropriate circumstances) is not to *describe* my doing of what I should be said in so uttering to be doing or to state that I am doing it: it is to do it . . . To name the ship *is* to say (in the appropriate circumstances) the words 'I name, etc.' When I say, before the registrar or altar, etc., 'I do,' I am not reporting on a marriage: I am indulging in it" (p. 6). Recitation of izibongo in the cattle kraal during a ritual sacrifice helps to bring about the presence in the kraal of the ancestors so that they may be addressed. Consideration of izibongo as performative utterances helps us to understand an aspect of their force in society, but it does not offer us a complete explanation of the function of izibongo, for, as we have seen, the imbongi also comments in his poetry on current events, he molds public opinion, he offers criticism of excessive behavior.

If I knew more about comparative religion and about Xhosa philosophy, I might be tempted to locate izibongo within a framework such as Mircea Eliade constructs for the understanding of myth and ritual. Passages in Eliade's *Myth of the eternal return* seem to be suggestive of explanations of the phenomena and systems of belief I have been laboring to elucidate, for izibongo promote communication between the living and the dead and thus defy the passage of time; the imbongi, although concerned with history, in a way is more concerned with the continuing relevance of the past to the present, and his poetry thus serves to collapse history. Eliade's study bears on "the image of himself formed by the man of the archaic societies and on the place that he assumes in the Cosmos. The chief difference between the man of the archaic and traditional societies and the man of the modern societies with their strong imprint of Judaeo-Christianity lies in the fact that the former feels himself indissolubly connected with the Cosmos and the cosmic rhythms, whereas the latter insists that he is connected only with History" (1954:xiii–xiv). Profane time is a linear historical progression; in sacred time the past is constantly regenerated through myth and ritual. In his regular poetic performances, the imbongi might be seen to be holding up for emulation, to be recreating, an ideal just and moral society. The cattle kraal would be a sacred center in which ritual sacrifices involving poetry conjure the presence among the living of the dead. In the kraal, through repeated ritual, "the dead can come back now, for all barriers between the dead and the living are broken . . . , and they will come back because at this paradoxical instant time will be suspended, hence they can again be contemporaries of the living" (p. 62). The imbongi, the ecstatic spokesman for the ideal polis, might be held to participate through his performances in a sacred act that collapses time; "Insofar as an act (or an object) acquires a certain reality through the repetition of certain paradigmatic gestures, and acquires it through that alone, there is an implicit abolition of profane time, of duration, of 'history'; and he who reproduces the exemplary gesture thus finds himself transported into the mythical epoch in which its revelation took place" (p. 35). Eliade's framework is suggestive, and promises to be a guide to an appreciation of izibongo on a level that I am yet unable to attempt.

Recently Hammond-Tooke offered a construct of Cape Nguni cosmology (1975b). It might be informative to locate izibongo in this specific indigenous structure in lieu of a rigorous application of Eliade's universal schemes. Added interest is given to this exercise when we note that Charles Bird has related the actions of the heroes of Mandekan epic in west Africa to inherent forces in society symbolized by the bush on the one hand and the town on the other. The hero is "asocial," and considers "the social conventions for accommodation, conciliation and expression of respect as barriers to the quest for his true destiny" (1974:vii). The epic Bird edits was performed by a bard who specialized in the songs of hunters, whose heroes stand opposed to social values:

> The field of action in which the hunter operates is the bush, an area diametrically opposed to the town or village. These two areas symbolize opposing forces in the Maninka cosmos. The force that characterizes village life is one of stability, cohesion, accommodation, respect and cooperation. The force which characterizes life in the bush is oriented to the performance of deeds such that the performer's name is recorded in history. This is no mean task, since to gain a name sung for posterity means not only overcoming one's contemporaries, but also overcoming the deeds of one's predecessors. [P. vi]

Hammond-Tooke's Cape Nguni cosmology also sets wild nature (bad) against domestic culture (good), but allows for a marginal mediatory category. Hammond-Tooke proposes a scheme, which I have simplified in Table 1. I suspect that the imbongi belongs in a position of mediation. On the social level he enjoys the structural freedom to criticize those in authority; in his poetry he upholds the values of societas in praise and condemns individualism that acts contrary to the common good, but at the same time his poetry, like Maninka epic, praises the individual and his achievements. It must remain for future researchers to assess the validity of Hammond-Tooke's scheme; those concerned to give a place in such a scheme to izibongo might well care to examine the animal imagery that is so prominent a feature of izi-

Table 1.

	Nature	Mediation	Culture
	Wild	Marginal	Domestic
	Bad	Ambiguous	Good
Spirit beings	Familiars	River people	Shades
Spatial	Forest	Veld (river/grassland)	Homestead
Human	Witch	Diviner	Moral
Social	Individualism	Structural freedom	Societas
Animals	Ferocious wild animals	Animals of the River People	Cattle, goats

bongo and the significance of the imbongi's costume of animal skin. Schemes such as those proposed by Austin, Eliade, and Hammond-Tooke clearly promise to afford us great insight into aspects of izibongo, but I suspect that none of these schemes alone will be able to provide a complete explanation of eulogy as it operates throughout Cape Nguni society. In search of that goal, it might be more fruitful to return to African belief in the power of words. I have suggested in this chapter that izibongo have power because of their ritual character: In essence a series of names, an izibongo can conjure the presence of those named and ensure their sympathetic intervention in the affairs of the living. But in the third and fourth chapters I made much of the imbongi's political role as social commentator, of his freedom to use ribald or abusive language. We must reconcile these two tendencies and seek a resolution of the apparent contradiction: Are izibongo fixed (memorized) praises earned by an individual, or are they vehicles of (improvised) comment? I believe that we must conceive of the boast as the archetypal izibongo, the form that generates others. The poem that a man constructs of phrases he or others coin commemorating his qualities or deeds can be used by others to bonga him; it can be used by his son to communicate with him after death; it can form part of the izibongo of a clan if he is a clan ancestor; it can form part of the izibongo of a chief if he is a chief's ancestor. The head of a household or of a lineage recites his lineage or clan izibongo for the well-being of his relatives; the imbongi bongas the chief. Only the imbongi is a specialist poet; he performs the chief's izibongo on behalf of the chief for the well-being of the chiefdom. The chief is the senior member of the dominant royal lineage, but he does not recite his own izibongo or those of his ancestors; because of his sacral character, the imbongi does so for him, just as a counselor, known as *umlomo wenkosi,* "the mouth of the chief," speaks for him on certain occasions requiring public address. The imbongi's izibongo thus has the same ritual power as the izibongo recited by the head of a lineage or a clan. Ask him, out of context, to produce the izibongo of his chief, and he tends to produce the praises that form the stock of his regular performances; but in performance, in context, the imbongi produces poetry that is relevant to and that often refers to the social circumstances of the performance, at rare times to the exclusion of the relatively fixed praises of his chief.

However far it may move from a recital of the chief's praises, the imbongi's izibongo yet has power, the power it derives from being in essence a sequence of the names of his chief and his chief's ancestors. Throughout Africa the verbal artist enjoys the freedom to comment in performance on social circumstances and the license to criticize with impunity; he enjoys immunity from the consequences of his utterances. This has generally been held to be a measure of the artist's status, but Peek sees it as a consequence of the power of his words:

> While the special recognition granted the verbal artist by his community is frequently noted, the focus of attention has been on the role and status of the verbal artist, not his words. For example, Herskovits found that "the professional ahanjito (the singer, storyteller, and riddler) who wandered through the land . . . had sanctioned immunity against harm to his person and license to satirize without recrimination." But what is the meaning of this immunity? Why is it found so widely in Africa? Is it to protect the verbal artist from his own audience, the same community that supports him? In the sense that he is protected from direct reprisals for critical comments about members of the community, yes. But ultimately, the verbal artist is protected from his words at the time of their utterance. Olajubu writes that Yoruba verbal artists are protected because they "serve as the moral police of the people and are, therefore, free from arrests and punishment for offenses committed during the course of their performances. They are at liberty to say whatever they please in favor of or against anybody in the community" . . . Is the "setting apart" in order to make the words more powerful or *because* of the words' power? Is it that certain issues must be raised, certain words used, but due to the hazards of their use, their speaker, or creator, must be marked off from the community to prevent others from being harmed?
>
> This perspective is clearly relevant to the widespread custom in African societies that a person does not always speak for himself. A person may hire a professional singer to enter-

tain others on his behalf or have an appointed spokesman to make official speeches and announcements for him. The common interpretation is that these practices are only indications of wealth and status, whereas it may be closer to the mark to say that often one cannot afford *not* to have another speak for him. The dangers engendered by the words to be spoken necessitate the use of a surrogate speaker. [1981:39]

If this construct has validity, then the words of the imbongi have power not because of his freedom to criticize but because his izibongo in essence is the chief's boast, which he recites as a surrogate speaker for the chief; social commentary evolves from his public performances of the praises of the royal lineage.

If all izibongo are ritual, if they evolve from the boast, how are we to explain those izibongo that seem frivolous? Or are the poems about animals and birds also serious? Van Warmelo asserts that "as far as totemism is concerned, there appears to be little or no trace of it in Nguni culture. The Nguni neither call their tribes or clans by the names of animals, nor do they recognise any relationship between social groups and certain species of animals. In this respect also the Nguni are therefore very markedly distinct from their Sotho neighbours in the West, if not from the Tonga" (1939:16). Nonetheless, there are some indications of an identification of animal species with human groups among the Nguni. First, in the southeastern Bantu group, the Sotho peoples still support a totemic system; if one accepts a theory of a common ur-Bantu culture, it is quite as easy to conceive of the loss of totemism among the Nguni as it is to believe in its independent origin among the Sotho. Then there seems to be a connection between some Nguni groups and certain animals. On a mission for the Zulu chief Dingana, Charles Brownlee once encountered a python and ordered it to be killed; when he received opposition, he tried to kill it himself, but was prevented from doing so. "I afterwards ascertained that the reason of this was that it was thought the snake might have been the spirit of one of the original inhabitants of the country and some evil might have befallen us had we destroyed it" (Brownlee 1896/1977:59). Of course this says nothing about a totemic relation between the Zulu and the python, but travelers and would-be hunters record similar experiences among the Xhosa about the blue crane, whose feathers were worn as a distinguishing headdress by warriors, and we have seen from Jordan's *Ingqumbo yeminyanya* that the snake *nkwakhwa*, a brown cobra, was held by the Mpondomise to be the spirit of the chief's ancestors and was greeted on sight by reverence and a recital of the royal izibongo of the House of Majola.

Izibongo are filled with references to animals, of which cattle preponderate; these are usually considered metaphoric references (see D. P. Kunene 1972). One may consider reference to a chief as a black bull metaphoric, or one may note Hammond-Tooke's statement that among the Bhaca the animal sacrificed during the first-fruits festival, *ingcube,* was a black bull (1954:35) and suspect that the common poetic formula *inkunz' emnyama,* used for example by Mbutuma in the poem he uttered in Langa about the Joyi chief, has more than metaphoric import, or at least that the metaphor may originally have had ritual significance. What is remarkable about the animal imagery in the izibongo is not the dominance of references to cattle, but the selectivity, the absence of references to some animals that were common, animals such as the rhinoceros or the giraffe, and this selectivity suggests that those animals that are mentioned are mentioned because they hold or held some significance. It is possible too that izibongo of animals derive from the hunt, that those animals that were killed were the subjects of respectful or propitiatory izibongo before or at the killing. I do not care to belabor this point; clearly, further study is required. But I believe at this stage that it is at least possible that all izibongo were originally ritual, about people living or dead or about animals of ritual significance. As these beliefs waned, perhaps, the practice of performing izibongo about dogs or horses might have developed on the model of the ritual izibongo. If this be so, then the boast remains the archetypal izibongo, and specific other animals have poems composed about them because of their identification with people, as is evidently the case for cattle, or because of their status as quarry.

The kind of eulogy in honor of animals I am hypothesizing for the Cape Nguni can be found today among the Shona of Zimbabwe (see Hodza and Fortune 1979). The salient difference between the Xhosa and the Shona traditions of oral poetry is that among the Shona a figure comparable to the imbongi no longer exists, although he may once have been associated with a dynasty no longer dominant (Hodza and Fortune 1979:7), and the Shona clan praises refer to the qualities of the clan totems; in most other respects the two traditions share striking similarities, although Shona poetry displays more varieties. In 1971 Fortune offered a six-part typology for Shona spoken or intoned (as distinct from sung) poetry: praise poetry of clans, praise poetry of people, didactic poetry, critical or "blame" poetry, funeral elegies, and entertaining narrative poetry. In 1974 Fortune and Hodza focused on three types, clan praises, praises of persons (biographical), and boasts (autobiographical), a classification they maintain in their 1979 collection. Clan praises are traditional: "Fresh clan praises are no longer composed" (Hodza and Fortune 1979:31).

The praises of a clan are phrased, first of all, in terms of its totem. For example, the clan praises of the Tembo (Zebra) and Soko (Baboon and Monkey) clans and sub-clans are penetrated with imagery directly suggested by these animals . . . Next, the clan praises are full of ancestral references. Names of forefathers of the clan, and of their sisters, abound in the praises, together with the names of the places where they lie buried . . . When a clansman is thanked for a service, the real object of praise, to which the recital is addressed, is the lineage to which he belongs, of which he is a representative, and with which he is identified. It is the lineage, with all its members, which is praised. The members most in mind are those of the past. They are now ancestral spirits, and it is they who have prompted and made the service rendered by their descendants possible. Their life, active and beneficent, continues in the lives of their living descendants, and will extend into the future as the spirits come back to inspire progeny of the same blood as yet unborn. Clan pride in its ability to maintain this life by generation receives allusive references in all clan praises . . . Clan praises also make reference to special qualities on which the members pride themselves. [Pp. 28–30]

Biographical poems are composed in honor of third persons, a chief, for example, but especially a lover, and may become fixed and used over and again, especially if the composer and the subject remain in social contact; boasts are composed by young men or professional men about themselves. Both of the latter make extensive use of the fixed clan praises, so that they consist largely of lines from the poem about the subject's clan, with some original lines coined by the composer. Shona oral poems and in particular the clan praises, which dominate the tradition, emphasize flattering as well as unflattering characteristics (for example, p. 186); they may employ ribald language (for example, pp. 262–4); and they are built essentially from names, praise names, and praises (pp. 70–1). A member of the Zebra clan, Tembo, might be thanked as follows:

> You have done a service, Zebra;
>   Striped one;
>   Hornless beast of Renje;
>   Adorned with your own stripes.
> Thank you, Masters of Chirovarova,
>   who came from Marenje.
> You have done a service, people of Chirovarova where once
>   Mutasa lived,

Tembo,
The one who does good.
A service has been rendered, Muroro;
Weaver of lines;
Who wear your skin for display;
Masters of Mahemasimike.   [Pp. 132–3]

Among the Ọyọ Yoruba of western Nigeria a tradition of eulogistic chants, *ijala*, associated with the god Ogun is current especially among hunters (S. A. Babalọla 1966); again, there are striking similarities to Xhosa eulogy, although the Cape Nguni have no gods. Ijala can be in honor of gods, persons, clans, and animals. Chants in honor of gods contain lineage poems and comprise "(i) a multitude of alternative names for the progenitor being saluted; (ii) narratives (*ìtàn*) of several incidents connected with the progenitor and doing him either credit or discredit; (iii) remarks about the progenitor's claims to distinction, about his favourite sayings, and about his likes and dislikes" (Babalọla 1966:24). In an autobiographical chant the poet alludes to both his good and his bad qualities:

> The ijala-chanter chants about his own characteristic behaviour and his interesting experiences, about what he considers to be his past achievements and what he clings to as his principles of conduct . . . He mentions his most conspicuous physical defect, namely, his protruding teeth. He makes no secret of his shortcomings and he almost glories in his imperfections. He speaks of his achievements as a good huntsman skilled with bow and arrow in killing deer, antelopes, and bush pigs. He reveals his pedigree, referring to his father, his mother, his grandfather, and other forebears both by their personal names and by their attributive names. [P. 23]

A chant in honor of a bird or animal "usually gives a character-sketch of the said animal or bird. Such chant contains information about the physical appearance, the characteristic cry, the characteristic gait, and the characteristic habits of the animal or bird. Though the wording of the *oríkì* varies slightly from artist to artist, the kernel of the subject matter of the *oríkì* is the same in the repertoire of all the expert ijala-chanters" (p. 19). As in the Nguni and Shona traditions, ribaldry is permitted, although in his edition of texts Babalọla asserts that he "will exclude examples of those vulgar jokes which so many an ijala artist, in order to excite laughter, nonchalantly resorts to, especially when he is tipsy and is unashamed to chant lewd remarks and indecent narratives" (pp. 38–9). Ijala about individuals usually incorporate passages from the clan praises, and chants performed on specific occasions frequently incorporate established passages from traditional chants, although they might refer to the occasion; thus, at a thanksgiving feast, the chanter may say

> . . . I am physically sound and in great form.
> I have hit on the *odù* pattern called Ejiogbe, the stupor-inducer.
> Death the Waster shall not reduce your house to nought.
> Disease shall not reduce your house to nought.
> Ogun shall continually support you as he supported the Akálá of Ido Town
> As he supported Akálà who hailed from Ọwẹ.
> As he supported Gbọpa, offspring of Him who worshipped both Ogun and Ṣawele
> And also Digboluwọn, the renowned hunter of Inisa Town.
> Sorrow inflicted by Ogun is dreadful to behold.
> Ogun shall not afflict you with any sorrow, Ogun, king-size hump of raw iron metal, Chief of Iwọnran Town.
> Grass by the river-side sprouting into fresh verdure luxuri-antly.
> Ogun is lord of the earth, our father, Ogun is lord of heaven.
> [Pp. 226, 228]

Among the Hausa in northern Nigeria, specialized performance techniques distinguish the eulogies (*roka*) of the nobility, of male and female commoners, and of spirits. Praise singers, *maroka,* operating in troupes, perform in honor of chiefs and dignitaries, "praising the title, the virtues, and the lineage of the individual" (M. G. Smith 1957/1973:561). Royal maroka always work as a team praising the king and distinguished visitors; individual maroka roam the countryside. The king's maroka are court retainers, but the solo maroki must earn his own living wandering from village to village. He stations himself in a central location such as the market place, chooses prominent citizens about whom he has learned something in advance, and commences praising them on sight. His object is to secure from his targets a suitable reward; if his victim fails to satisfy the maroki, his praise turns to abuse.

> The content of a solo declamation consists in statements of the individual's ancestry, their notability, his prosperity and influence, the number of his dependents, his fame, and its range . . . If the declamation becomes hostile, the same themes recur, though with unfavorable emphases and connotations. Insinuations about the ancestry of the person addressed

are made at this time and, for many commoners at whom this type of declamation is directed, this may imply slavery. Unfavorable references to the individual's meanness, fortune (*arziki*), treatment of his dependents, occupation, reputation, and possible disloyalty to his community or political patrons are also liable to be made. The ultimate insult – imputation of ambiguous paternity – is never openly mentioned, but overshadows the process of increasing pressure. [P. 573]

Traditionally, Smith tells us, "no one has the right or power to silence the *maroki* while he addresses an individual with praise-songs" (p. 572). Among the Acoli of northern Uganda individuals compose *mwoc*, poems about themselves that consist of commemorative praise names. They are uttered in a shout as an expression of pride or belligerence; they are identified with individuals and can be used as a form of greeting. "There are two kinds of *mwoc*, one which belongs to a particular individual alone, and the other which belongs to the chiefdom. Every Acoli male has his own *mwoc*, and many but not all women have theirs too. It usually arises from some funny incident" (p'Bitek 1974:168). Southern Sotho eulogies are a dying art form in Lesotho. The poet, *seroki*, composes his poem, *lithoko*. "In the poet's absence, or after his death, the same *lithoko* would be chanted by others who had heard and memorized them, often with unintentional variations and omissions, but very rarely with deliberate additions" (Damane and Sanders 1974:24). Part of a tradition once as strong as the Zulu or Xhosa traditions, Sotho lithoko are a feature disappearing from Sotho life, and the seroki is no longer present at the court of the king:

> Today praises may still be heard at *lipitso* and *matsema*, though not very often, and fragments of them may still be quoted in ordinary conversation. But no *seroki* would think of waking up his neighbours in the early hours of the morning; no one would chant *lithoko* in order to announce his arrival; and any chief who recited his praises in an endeavour to put young boys to shame would be dismissed as an amiable eccentric. [P. 25]

> Today, as the traditional patterns of Sotho life are being steadily broken down, and as the powers and prestige of the chieftainship are being inexorably whittled away, the *lithoko*'s importance for the ordinary Sotho is rapidly declining. They are neither composed nor chanted as commonly as in the past. Very few men can remember more than a few lines, and fewer still can chant them effectively in public. Even at Matsieng, the home of the King, there is not a single *seroki*. [P. 33]

Examples of such poetry can be multiplied: Eulogy is widespread in Africa. In her magisterial survey of oral literature on the continent, Ruth Finnegan claimed that "in its specialised form panegyric is *the* type for court poetry and is one of the most developed and poetic genres in Africa" (1970:111) and devoted a chapter (the fifth) to eulogy. This, the most detailed exposition of the genre as it occurs in Africa, follows a general chapter on poetry and patronage, which concludes with a two-page note explaining the absence in the book of any treatment of epic on the grounds of its relative unimportance. "At least in the more obvious sense of a 'relatively long narrative poem,' epic hardly seems to occur in sub-Saharan Africa apart from forms like the (written) Swahili *utenzi* which are directly attributable to Arabic literary influence" (p. 108). Many examples of African oral literature published under the name of epics, Finnegan argued, are in fact produced in prose: "Many of these narratives seem quite clearly to be in prose merely interspersed with some sung pieces in the regular manner of African stories, and there is no reason to believe that they differ radically in form from such prose tales" (p. 109). Epics do exist in Africa, "but in general terms and apart from Islamic influences, epic seems to be of remarkably little significance in African oral literature, and the *a priori* assumption that epic is the natural form for many non-literate peoples turns out here to have little support" (p. 110). Although eulogy contains elements common to epic, eulogy is quite distinct from epic: "Many of the lengthy praise poems, particularly those in South Africa, do contain some epic elements and provide the nearest common parallel to this form in Africa. Nevertheless, as will emerge in the following chapter, panegyric poetry concentrates far more on the laudatory and apostrophic side than on the narrative and cannot really qualify as 'epic' poetry in the normal sense of the word" (p. 109).

Since the appearance of this brief note on epic ten years ago, a number of African epics have been published, and scholarly treatments of the genre have appeared; most scholars writing on the subject claim inaccurately that in her note Finnegan denied the existence of the epic in Africa. Daniel Biebuyck, himself the editor and author of studies on Nyanga epic in the Congo Republic (1972 and 1978a, Biebuyck and Mateene 1969), starts his survey of the African heroic epic with a rebuttal of Finnegan, but concludes that "the present evidence points to a strong occurrence of heroic epics in two major areas: the Mande-speakers (Mandeka, Bambara, Soninke) and groups closely interrelated with them (Fulani) in West Africa; several Bantu-speaking ethnic groups ranging from the Gabon Republic (Fang) to the Zaire Republic (Mongo, Lega, Nyanga, Mbole, and Tetela clusters)" (1978b:337). In spite of the fact that he allows prose narratives a place in his survey, Biebuyck's conclusion does little to undermine Finnegan's general point that epic is *relatively* unimportant in Africa, certainly when compared, say, to eulogy.

John William Johnson, an editor of the Mandekan epic of Sun-Jata from Mali (1979), also tilts at Finnegan in a recent article that attempts a general definition of the epic genre, which, Johnson avers, has much in common with eulogy, since "both praise-poetry and epic may be glossed together in the larger category of heroic poetry" (1980:310). Johnson proposes, on the basis of his work in Mali, eight defining characteristics of African epic, only two of which differentiate epic from eulogy. Four of these characteristics of the Sun-Jata epic Johnson labels primary "because these traits may be said to define heroic epic anywhere it occurs in the world" (p. 312); four further characteristics, which are specific to the epic in Mali but "may or may not be universal to this genre in other parts of the world" (p. 312), are labeled secondary. Johnson lists as primary those characteristics of epic that are *poetic,* by which he means features of performance that distinguish it from ordinary discourse; *narrative,* in that its plot comprises various episodes; *heroic,* by which he means that the pattern of the hero is stereotyped; and *legendary,* by which he means the incorporation of legendary material especially etiological. As secondary characteristics of the epic, Johnson lists its *length,* which he concedes is a relative concept, but he argues that epics are longer than eulogies; its *multifunctionality;* its *cultural and traditional transmission;* and, in that it draws on legend, genealogy, song, eulogy, proverbs, and other forms of folklore, its *multigeneric character.* Johnson claims that only two of these characteristics distinguish epic from eulogy:

> Panegyric abridges *narrative* to form *allusion,* a very subtle difference. This abridgement also affects the *length* of the poem; panegyrics are normally shorter than epics. The other six characteristics are not distinguishable in genre differentiation . . . It may also be noted that praise-poetry is often embedded inside epic poetry as an integral part of its whole. The praise-poem, with the proverb and a few other types of folklore, constitutes one of the standard modes of Mandekan epic . . . Observing both praise-poetry and epic concerning the same culture hero (Sun-Jata) in Mali aided me greatly in coming to the conclusion that allusion and narrative mark the difference between these genres. [p. 310]

Now this is a commendable effort to break free of the somewhat restrictive Western European and especially classical models and to attempt a universal definition that takes account of African evidence (see also Okpewho 1979) of a genre that has resisted easy definition: Paul Merchant's study of the epic starts with the disconcerting statement that "there would be no value in attempting a simple definition of a literary form which includes the *Iliad, The Prelude* and *War and Peace*" (1971:1). Yet Johnson's eight-part definition of epic, I suspect, poses more problems than it solves, however praiseworthy his effort might be to break free of the text-oriented approach that has dominated discussions of the genre and to accord due emphasis to qualities observable in performance. It is difficult to conceive of any item of folklore that is not subject to cultural and traditional transmission, for example, and it seems strange to propose as a defining characteristic of a genre the fact that it is composed of many genres; as to the multi-functionality of epic, Elliott Skinner has observed that "the most important characteristic of African aesthetics and recreational activities is their multifunctionality. It is possible, after diligent search, to find examples of 'art for art's sake' and the same for recreation in African societies, but on the whole, art and recreational activities are almost always related to other aspects of life" (1973:505). Since other genres of folklore can be long, in fact, all of Johnson's secondary characteristics do not seem to be especially distinctive of epic in Africa. Of his primary characteristics, Johnson claims that three are distinctive of eulogy as well as epic. That observation may well be valid for Mali, but, as we have seen, Xhosa izibongo, like other examples of eulogy in Africa, are based on commemorative names both flattering and unflattering associated with specific individuals and cannot be held accordingly to be either heroic or legendary in Johnson's senses of the words. Johnson notes, as does Biebuyck, that epic is confined to areas in western and central Africa. Given the tendency of epic in Mali and elsewhere in Africa to incorporate eulogy (and other genres), and the widespread occurrence of eulogy in sharp contrast with epic, I suspect that eulogy is primary (in the sense of original) in Africa and epic secondary, the product of cultural contact with Islamic or European civilizations. Apparently the introduction of epic among the Haya in Tanzania, who supported then and still support a tradition of eulogy, can be dated precisely to the beginning of the nineteenth century, a cultural innovation now commemorated in myth, and I hope to show in Chapter 7 that the Xhosa epic developed only as a result of familiarity with Western literary models. Johnson's observations that eulogy and epic are poetic, however, and that the former is allusive whereas the latter is narrative strike me as substantive.

Harold Scheub (1977b) has claimed that in 1975 he collected three "vast" epics totaling over three hundred hours in performance time

from a Gcaleka woman, but however impressive and significant they
might be, it is evident that they form part of a prose tradition of
folktale (Xhosa *intsomi:* see Scheub 1975) and do not participate in the
tradition of izibongo. In fact, oral epic poetry does not exist among the
Nguni peoples, and I doubt that it exists among the southeastern
Bantu either. Fortune (1971) notes the existence of entertaining narrative poetry (*ndyaringo*) among the Shona in Zimbabwe, but this is
distinct from the clan praises (*nhetembo*), praise poetry of individuals
(*madetembedzo*), blame poetry (*nheketerwa*), or elegies at funerals
(*nhembo*) (see also Fortune 1974). A long Zulu narrative on the history of the Ngwane frequently cites relevant snatches of izibongo and
assumes the character of an Icelandic heroic saga (Van Warmelo
1938), but this was a nonce performance dictated on request for transcription; the form seems to have no currency in the oral traditions of
either the Zulu- or the Xhosa-speaking peoples. The Xhosa imbongi
does occasionally in his izibongo offer explicit narrative, as Mbutuma
does in recounting his dreams or as Mqhayi did in his poem about the
Ndlambe chief Silimela (see Opland 1975), but such explicit narrative
whenever it appears is always subservient to the eulogistic purpose of
the poetry and in normal circumstances never expands to exclude eulogistic elements entirely: The imbongi, or for that matter any other
Xhosa oral poet, does not tell stories in poetic form. Since the praises
on which the poetry is based often commemorate events, however,
izibongo do refer to actions, but they allude to them elliptically rather
than narrate them explicitly in the manner of the epic, the lay, or the
ballad (see Richmond 1972). The praises commemorate physical and
moral qualities of the subject and events in which he participated, and
they locate the subject in a genealogical context.

Such are the stock of the memorized, traditional poems in honor of
lineage and clan ancestors, and such are the stock of the boasts. Such,
too, form the basis of the poems in honor of chiefs, although as we
have seen the Xhosa imbongi also feels free to comment in these
poems on current events. The praises – commemorative phrases, lines,
or groups of lines – are generally discrete and appear in variants of
poems on the same subject in differing order. In that sense the collection of praises that is an izibongo lacks coherence, since it does not
seem to matter if physical characteristics are mentioned after deeds or
before genealogical links, or indeed if those praises referring to physical characteristics (say) should not be distributed throughout any one
performance of a poem. It does not seem possible therefore to describe Xhosa izibongo in terms of the kind of structures proposed by
Vladimir Propp (1958/1968), in which a fixed order of elements is
essential, nor does it seem fruitful to me to seek pairs of elements in

izibongo in binary opposition according to the analytical lines proposed by Claude Lévi-Strauss, although both forms of structuralism have been widely employed by folklorists in recent years (see Ben-Amos 1972; Dundes 1975). Daniel Kunene's analysis of Sotho lithoko into various kinds of eulogues, incorporated by Damane and Sanders into their subsequent description of the same tradition, by Hodza and Fortune into their description of Shona oral poetry, and by Kuse into his thesis and dissertation on Xhosa izibongo, seems to me to be useful to a large extent for analyses of traditional texts, although explicitly narrative passages do not fit easily into the scheme of eulogues, and some categories proposed by Kunene and Kuse seem to be so vaguely defined as to be catchalls for various phrases that defy classification. The system of analysis of eulogy into eulogues seems less useful, however, when one is dealing with primarily improvised passages of social commentary such as the imbongi generally produces in performance.

I have found especially intriguing the similarities between Xhosa eulogies and funeral eulogies produced by Greek and especially Cretan women. The function of these essentially ritual laments has remained unaltered since classical times: "The living, by their offerings and passionate invocations, can enter into communion with the dead" (Alexiou 1974:46). Recently (1980), Anna Caraveli-Chaves has written of these laments as a "bridge between two worlds." The laments consist of six elements: a statement of intention, praise or invocation of the deceased, a history of the deceased, the plight of the mourner, the plight of the deceased, and an invitation to the audience to share the mourning. This is not a structural breakdown in the Proppian sense, since there seems to be no order or causal relation among the elements, which are not themselves discrete in any text (in other words, a number of lines scattered through the text might earn classification as one of the six elements). If we bear in mind that Cretan laments are produced as funeral obsequies, we may extend and generalize Caraveli-Chaves's elements and apply them to Xhosa eulogy in general and by way of example briefly to the first of the poems Manisi produced at Fort Hare.

1. *Intention.* Many Xhosa eulogies commence with a statement of intention to speak about a particular topic, or name the subject of the boast or izibongo; the formal salutation (isikhahlelo) of a chief who might be the subject of a poem or who might be referred to in the poem would serve the same purpose. When Manisi commences his poem with "Hail, Daliwonga!" he announces his intention to produce a poem concerning Chief Kaiser Matanzima, "the paramount chief of the Thembu of Rhoda" (line 3).

2. *Praise/invocation.* We have seen that Xhosa izibongo deal in praise as well as censure; they are generally frank assessments of the

subjects' virtues and failings. Manisi refers to Matanzima in praises that characterize him as tall and fair-skinned, but Matanzima also arouses debate in the community as a result of the controversial policies he follows at the dictates of the South African government. Matanzima's ancestors Mhlobo and Tato are mentioned; I have suggested that such genealogical references, in the poems of the imbongi as also in the poems recited during sacrifices in the cattle kraal, serve the function of invoking the ancestors, conjuring their presence, and ensuring their sympathetic attention to the affairs of the living; the praises of the dead are thus invocations.

3. *History of the deceased.* Xhosa eulogies in general refer not only to the physical and moral characteristics of the subject but also allusively to the significant events in which he participated or to his achievements, as Manisi refers to Matanzima's journey from his great place at Qamata to Fort Hare to seek education and now to receive his honorary doctorate (lines 21 to 26).

4. *Plight of the mourner.* Xhosa eulogies performed on ceremonial occasions are often spontaneous compositions and as such usually contain references to the context of the performance, the situation confronting the poet in the act of performance. The poet may also take the opportunity to comment on current situations of broader implication to his society, as Manisi comments on the need to reclaim land lost to the whites and to accord the ancestral heroes proper burial rites.

5. *Plight of the deceased.* In the Cretan laments the subject has recently joined the community of the dead. In the Xhosa system of ancestor veneration, the living and dead members of a lineage or a clan participate in one genealogical continuum, and the dead continue to show interest in and exert influence over the affairs of the living: The living members of a clan are addressed by the names of their ancestors. References to the ancestors of the subject of an izibongo are similar therefore to Cretan references to the deceased's connection with the dead. Manisi's first poem at Fort Hare refers to Matanzima's ancestors, and his second incorporates one of the praises of Matanzima's ancestor Ngangelizwe (lines 7 and 8); clan praises deal exclusively with ancestors, as do invocations of the lineage ancestors through izibongo.

6. *Invitation to share mourning.* A significant element in contemporary Xhosa eulogies is the poet's appeal to the audience in an effort to arouse emotion, to incite or prevent action; informants frequently refer to the role of the imbongi in exhorting warriors before battle. In his first poem Manisi urges Matanzima to lead his people to their destiny;

in his second poem Manisi appeals to Matanzima to leave for home as it is growing late.

Thus Caraveli-Chaves's six content categories for Cretan laments can be generalized and extended to Xhosa izibongo. The correspondence can be set out as follows:

Greek	Xhosa
Intention	Intention/salutation
Praise/invocation	Praises treating physical and moral qualities
History of the deceased	Praises treating achievements
Plight of the mourner	Social context
Plight of the deceased	Genealogical references
Invitation to share mourning	Exhortation

The physical or moral qualities may be flattering or unflattering to the subject; the achievements are not narrated but merely alluded to. These six elements will be reflected in the text of any performance with a degree of variation, in that not all elements will necessarily be present in every izibongo: For example, the izibongo of chiefs produced for early collectors invariably lack salutations (since no chief is present) and references to the social context of the performance or exhortations (since they are command performances for one man scribbling rapidly in a notebook). I believe that nothing will be found in Xhosa izibongo that cannot be classified under one of the six headings. Furthermore, the classification is not exclusively text-oriented; certain components of izibongo occur only because of the system of belief and ritual that informs Xhosa eulogy.

Further research might well show that this content analysis of Xhosa eulogy, itself an extension of Caraveli-Chaves's analysis of Cretan funeral laments, defines a structure for all eulogy. Certainly it bears a striking resemblance to the classical tradition transmitted in the West. The Greek rhetoricians Hermogenes (fl. A.D. 161–80) and Aphthonius (fl. A.D. 315) composed *progymnasmata,* school exercises for orations on set themes. Aphthonius was translated into Latin, and this version formed the basis of an English paraphrase with English examples produced in 1563 by an Oxford fellow, Richard Rainolde, under the title *The foundacion of rhetorike.* Walter Ong quotes a passage from this work in his discussion of Tudor writings on rhetoric:

> Rainolde lists Aphthonius' fourteen ways of "making" an oration as: fable (in the Aesopian sense), narration or tale, chria (praise or blame of a word or deed), sentence or gnomic saying, confutation or refutation, confirmation or proof, commonplace or amplification of a virtue or vice, praise or encomium,

dispraise or vituperation, comparison, ethopeia or character portrayal, visual description, thesis or generalization, and *legislatio* or a plea for or against a law. Schoolboys writing themes cast them in one or another of these molds or types. Each type had its subtypes and special formulary requirements. Thus:

This parte of Rhetorike called praise is either a particular praise of one, as of kyng Henry the fifte, Plato, Tullie, Demosthenes, Cyrus, Darius, Alexander the greate; or a generalle and universalle praise, as the praise of all the Britaines or of all the citezeins of London.

The order to make this Oracion is thus declared. First, for the enteryng of the matter, you shall place a *exordium,* or beginnyng. The seconde place, you shall bryng to his praise *Genus eius,* that is to saie, of what kinde he came of, which dooeth consiste in fower poinctes: of what nacion, of what countrie, of what auncetours, of what parentes. After that you shall declare his educacion. The educacion is conteined in three poinctes: in institucion, arte, lawes. Then put there to that, which is the chief grounde of al praise: his actes doen, which doe procede out of the giftes and excellencies of the minde, as the fortitude of the mynde, wisedome, and magnanimitee; of the bodie, as a beautifull face, amiable countenaunce, swiftnesse, the might and strength of the same; the excellencies of fortune, as his dignitée, power, aucthoritee, riches, substaunce, frendes. In the fifte place use a comparison, wherein that whiche you praise maie be advaunced to the uttermoste. Laste of all, use the *Epilogus* or conclusion.

The other thirteen kinds of thematic orations demanded procedures of comparable complexity. Of these themes, those of praise (*encomium*) and dispraise (*vituperatio*) were certainly the most important, since ancient, medieval, and Renaissance literary performance in practice and even more in theory hinged on these two activities to a degree quite incredible today. [1968/1971a:55–6]

Clearly, this tradition of eulogy, drawing on oral tradition though transmitted through the medium of writing and hence eliminating the need for references to social context, having separated praise from blame, yet encourages compositions based on a statement of intention, on references to physical and moral attributes, to achievements and to ancestry, and in Rainolde's fifth point, on exhortation.

Xhosa izibongo are not just poems of praise: They deal in both praise and censure as twin aspects of truth telling, or soothsaying.

Izibongo are eulogistic poems built from a system of commemorative phrases and general references that operate in society as alternative names; they are an expression of, and an integral part of, the veneration of the ancestors. Similar eulogistic traditions are common throughout Africa but are by no means unique to Africa: They can be found, for example, in early medieval Europe among the Celtic and Germanic peoples, in classical and in Old Testament times. (Among the ancient Scandinavians, Odin, whose name is etymologically connected with inspiration, frenzy, and eloquence, is the god of warriors, of beer, of poetry, and of runes that have power to resurrect the dead; the Moravian missionary Friedrich Müller observed that among the baptized Hlubi on his mission station the most popular passage in the Bible was Deborah's song of triumph in Judges 5.) Eulogies may be performed by individuals or by troupes of musicians and poets, for ritual or for mercenary purposes, to flatter or to offer a critical assessment of their subjects, by court retainers, by independent poets representing the people, by members of clans that may or may not be totemic, or by lineage heads, by specialist poets or by amateurs, in traditions that are flourishing, adapting, or dying; they seem generally to derive from a system of praise names and to be connected with a system of ancestor veneration. We will be able better to understand the genre of eulogy in Africa and elsewhere, in modern times as well as in the recent or ancient past, when a more detailed comparative study of its manifestations is undertaken. In such a comparative study, I believe, the living traditions of Africa and in particular the Xhosa tradition can play a critical role.

6

ORAL POETICS AND ORAL NOETICS

In the previous chapter passing reference was made to schemes established by Austin, Eliade, and Hammond-Tooke, schemes that promise to illuminate aspects of the Xhosa tradition of oral poetry. This chapter endeavors to examine the Xhosa material in greater detail in the light of schemes advanced by two other scholars who have contributed significantly to the academic debate on the theory of oral traditions, Albert B. Lord and Walter J. Ong, S. J. The intention in choosing these two theories for more rigorous comparison with the Xhosa tradition is to learn more thereby about aspects of the Xhosa tradition: The purpose is to learn about izibongo from a discussion of points raised by Lord and Ong rather than to establish what the Xhosa material can (or cannot) demonstrate to be weaknesses in their constructs. Reference to the theories of Lord and Ong should illuminate significant facets of the Xhosa tradition of oral poetry – how the imbongi composes his izibongo in performance, for example, the relation of oral izibongo to written, or izibongo as a manifestation of universal mental processes.

Lord himself stated simply that his study of South Slavic oral narrative poetry in Yugoslavia, *The singer of tales* (1960/1965), "set forth the processes of composition and transmission of that oral traditional poetry" (1974/1975:2). No scholar in this century has contributed more to our appreciation of what "oral" and "traditional" can mean in the study of ancient, medieval, and modern literatures. As Finnegan put it in her survey of the scholarly debate on oral poetry, "No-one who has read *The Singer of Tales* – surely one of the classics in the study of oral literature – can fail to be profoundly influenced by its findings and insights" (1977:69); she also says, commenting on the theory of oral poetry developed by Lord on the foundation of ideas advanced by his teacher Milman Parry,

> It would be hard to overestimate the importance of this approach. It has had a deep influence on Homeric studies; though not all scholars accept the theory *in toto*, few can ignore it, and many works have appeared which, in various ways, apply the approach to analysis of the Homeric epics . . . But the influence of this approach reaches far beyond Homeric studies . . . It is

not surprising [in view of Parry's comparative intentions] that his approach has been more widely extended, and that many scholars have tried to apply a similar oral-formulaic analysis to texts of all kinds, from Old Testament poetry, *Beowulf*, or medieval European epic to recent compositions like modern Greek ballads, Gaelic poetry or the formulaic intoned sermons of the Southern States of America. [P. 66]

As a classicist, Parry studied the epithets in the Homeric poems, came to the conclusion that they should be understood as the product of oral composition, and sought to substantiate his theory by studying at first hand the living tradition of oral narrative song in Yugoslavia. Parry was accompanied on his expedition to Yugoslavia in 1934 and 1935 by his pupil Albert Lord, who continued the lines of research established by Parry after his teacher's untimely death in 1935.

In *The singer of tales* Lord set out in detail his observations about the technique of Yugoslavian oral narrative song and applied his conclusions to the Homeric poems and to medieval epics. Perhaps the most revolutionary aspect of Lord's argument is his contention that the Yugoslavian epic singers do not memorize their tales but create them in the act of performance. For Lord, the word "oral" "does not mean merely oral presentation. Oral epics are performed orally, it is true, but so can any other poem be performed orally. What is important is not the oral performance but rather the composition *during* oral performance" (1960/1965:5). More fully expressed,

One of the most common misconceptions which has arisen from the use of the word "oral" is that the singer has memorized a song and is presenting it as he learned it word for word as exactly as possible. This is oral presentation of a fixed text. It implies that the singer sat at the feet of another singer and heard the song over and over again until he had memorized it, or that he had a manuscript from which he memorized the song. In neither of these cases would the term "oral composition" be applicable. Those who memorized the Homeric songs from a manuscript and then sang them were not bards, but mere reciters. It would be perfectly possible for a person aspiring to be a reciter to sit at the feet of such a one and by dint of memory finally learn the song. The reciter could learn from a manuscript or from another reciter orally. But it is quite impossible for the singer in an oral tradition, in the technical sense of the word, to memorize a song by sitting at the side of another singer. One can memorize only a fixed text, and in oral tradition a song is never sung twice word for word exactly the same. The differences between performances, however, are not mere lapses of memory. This again would be possible only if there were a fixed text to begin with. The key to understanding oral style lies in the fact that the singer and the generations of singers who preceded him are unlettered. They have no concept of a fixed text for epic song. Each performance represents a new composition of the song, and it is this method of composition among unlettered bards which we call "oral composition." It is a special technique which came into being long before the art of writing was invented by man. It is a technique of remembering rather than of memorization. [1962b:184–5]

To enable him to compose in performance in this manner, the singer masters through a period of conscious apprenticeship and training an elaborate grammar of words, phrases, and ideas that facilitates the spontaneous creation of his tale within the meter of his tradition. The basic unit of this grammar is the formula, a phrase that persists in the tradition because it has proved useful to the singer and/or to other singers, a phrase that helps the singer to verbalize within the meter of his tradition. On the basis of any of these formulas, the singer can construct similar phrases, so that the diction of any song can be termed formulaic: "If the oral poet is never at a loss for a word or group of words to express his idea, it is because the formulaic technique has provided him, not with the formula for every idea, but with a means of constantly recomposing the formulae for the less common ideas, with a sufficient variety of patterns so that the idea can take almost instantaneous form in the rhythm of his song" (1962b:188). The metrical lines of his song thus consist of formulas and formulaic expressions; his songs themselves consist of traditional narrative blocks called themes, set descriptions of a debate, for example, or the arrival of a message, or a battle. Thus,

> stated briefly, oral epic song is narrative poetry composed in a manner evolved over many generations by singers of tales who did not know how to write; it consists of the building of metrical lines and half lines by means of formulas and formulaic expressions and of the building of songs by the use of themes. This is the technical sense in which I shall use the word "oral" and "oral epic" in this book. By formula I mean "a group of words which is regularly employed under the same metrical conditions to express a given essential idea." This definition is Parry's. By formulaic expression I denote a line or half line constructed on the pattern of the formulas. By theme I refer to

the repeated incidents and descriptive passages in the songs. [1960/1965:4]

The oral singer *needs* the formulas, formulaic expressions, and themes to compose his tale in performance; the literate poet, free of the pressure to compose metrically adequate lines on the spur of the moment, does not depend on formulas and accordingly makes less use of them than the oral poet does. Thus an analysis of the formulaic content and the thematic structure of a text can reveal whether it was produced by an oral poet dictating his song for transcription or by a literate poet writing down his composition: "Formula analysis . . . is, therefore, able to indicate whether any given text is oral or 'literary.' An *oral* text will yield a predominance of clearly demonstrable formulas, with the bulk of the remainder 'formulaic,' and a small number of nonformulaic expressions. A *literary* text will show a predominance of nonformulaic expressions, with some formulaic expressions, and very few clear formulas" (1960/1965:130).

Thus the Yugoslavian singer draws from tradition a grammar of words, phrases, and narrative blocks, and by means of these he composes his metrical tales in performance. Although he is a traditional artist, however, he is responsible for shaping his creations:

He is the carrier of the tradition; he composes the songs. He must be sensible of both occasion and audience, but it is ultimately his skill or lack of it which will please, instruct, move to tears or laughter, or incite to action. The fate of the songs is in his hands. He may corrupt a good story, or he may enhance and set right a story which he received from the tradition in a corrupt state. He is no mere mouthpiece who repeats slavishly what he has learned. He is a creative artist. [1962b:184]

Lord has shown us more clearly than ever before the relation between a tradition and the creativity of an individual traditional artist: "The deeper our study of oral composition penetrates, the more we come to a realization that this traditional method of composition allows the individual singer some latitude and play for his original talents. The method aids the singer to tell his story; but even when the tradition furnishes the main outlines of the story, the resulting performance is the singer's own. He is not the mouthpiece of tradition; he is the tradition" (1962b:192).

From his detailed study of the Yugoslavian tradition of oral narrative song, Lord derived universal principles of oral technique that he and subsequent scholars then applied to other literatures (see Foley 1980 and Haymes 1973). The debate over the validity of the application has been heated (see Finnegan 1977:52–87 and Watts 1969). I do not intend here to *apply* Lord's theories to the Xhosa oral poetic tradition, still less to use his ideas to *prove* anything: The many differences between the two traditions vitiate a general application of Lord's oral theory. For example, Lord states that "epic is narrative song; it is a tale which is sung . . . Singing of tales which we call epics is almost everywhere accompanied by instrumental music" (1962b:180, 181); Xhosa izibongo are never accompanied by instrumental music. Epics may be performed by two singers, with or without additional instrumentalists; Xhosa izibongo are always solo performances. Epics are narratives the principal purpose of which is entertainment: "The oral epics which we have and the practice of epic poetry as we know it best fall rather into the category of entertainment. Even while epic is didactic, it is entertaining. It teaches by stories and it praises by telling a tale. Indeed, the moral is the more forceful, the praise the more vivid, by being cast in narrative form" (1962b:208). The social function of Xhosa eulogy is complex, as we have seen, but however amusing occasional comments may be, izibongo are never produced for entertainment. Furthermore, and perhaps most significantly, eulogy, as I argued in the last chapter, is distinct from narrative, a distinction that Lord himself drew attention to in commenting on D. P. Kunene's study of Sotho lithoko: "Kunene does not follow the formulaic and thematic type of analysis associated with Milman Parry, although he is well acquainted with it, but makes his own kind of investigation. This is perhaps as well, because the heroic poetry with which he is dealing is not narrative in our sense of the word, but eulogistic; it is praise poetry of a kind common, I believe, in Africa" (1974/1975:5); yet Lord welcomes the application of his theory to Chinese *lyric* poetry (1974/1975:6), and has himself undertaken an application of his theory to Angolan *prose* narratives (1962a).

　　Lord is sensitive to criticism, much of which has tended to be ill-informed comment by armchair textual critics with no firsthand experience of a living oral tradition, still less of the Yugoslavian tradition that they cite liberally in their polemics: "I am constantly amazed," Lord once wrote, "at the ease with which scholars, meticulous in their own field, make *ex cathedra* statements about poetries of whose language they know nothing" (1968:5). Even though the Yugoslavian poetry studied by Lord was narrative and the Xhosa poetry I encountered in the field was eulogistic, *The singer of tales* helped me considerably to understand the phenomena I observed and recorded. Without then wishing to embark on a detailed application of Lord's theories to the Xhosa tradition of oral poetry, without wishing to pass comment on the universal validity of his conclusions, I hope by concentrating on three aspects of Lord's theory to reveal something more of the art of the imbongi and his response to the introduction of writing: I shall here examine the Xhosa tradition in the light of Lord's observations on the formula, on the theme, and on the effect of writing on an oral tradition.

The formula is the crux of Lord's theory of oral poetry. The singer needs formulas and formulaic expressions to construct metrically correct lines in performance; a literate poet is freed from the constraints of public performance and does not use formulas for his compositions. Thus formulas are integral to Lord's revolutionary description of how a singer composes traditional songs in performance, to his assertion that an oral traditional performer must be illiterate, and to his analyses of formulaic density in a text in order to demonstrate its oral or lettered origin (whence the heroic epithet "oral-formulaic" often qualifying his theory). Parry's definition of a formula as "a group of words which is regularly employed under the same metrical conditions to express a given essential idea" embodies, as Edward R. Haymes has recently pointed out, the twin characteristics of repetition and usefulness. For the phrase (or, sometimes, one word) to be "regularly employed" it must be repeated. But repetition alone is not sufficient: It must also be useful. Haymes comments: "Both Parry and Lord have described the formula as a functional unit within the oral poet's language. It is only a formula if it is 'regularly employed' by the oral poet 'to express a given essential idea,' that is, if it has the function of making 'composition easier under the necessities of rapid composition in performance' " (1980:393). Haymes cites Parry's statements: "When the element of usefulness is lacking, one does not have a formula but a repeated phrase which has been knowingly brought into the verse for some special effect" (p. 393) and "It is important at this point to remember that the formula in Homer is not necessarily a repetition . . . It is the nature of an expression which makes it a formula" (p. 392). Lord has maintained Parry's twin emphases in his presentation of the formula.

In *The singer of tales* formulas were "repeated word groups" (1960/1965:30). In a major statement that refined and clarified concepts advanced in *The singer of tales,* Lord responded to a special issue of *Yale Classical Studies* (1966) on Homeric studies that contained a number of criticisms of his theory. He countered Joseph Russo's appeal for a structural definition of the formula independent of exact verbal repetition with the assertion that "to designate a phrase as formula only on the basis of the pattern is to invite disaster . . . It is only when the pattern is filled with specific words that it is usable by a singer, and it is the singer's art with which we are concerned. Without the exact words one has still only *patterns*" (1968:15). He announced an ongoing interest in the problem of texts produced by literate authors in imitation of traditional style and insisted that formula analysis could still reveal the distinction between such products and transcriptions of performances by "oral" poets. Lord produced statistical results of some analyses and concluded that "the imitator, it would seem from our experiment, usually shuns the exact repetition of true formulas, because that element in the style he does not need. To the oral poet there is a residue of exact repetitions, no matter how original he be, which he must have for composition. The imitator uses common phrases, as Parry long ago pointed out, but not formulas" (p. 29). The density in a text of "straight" formulas, that is, exact repetitions apart from formulaic expressions, is given greater prominence: "So far, I believe, we can conclude that a pattern of 50 to 60 per cent formula or formulaic, with 10 to perhaps 25 per cent straight formula, indicates clearly literary or written composition. I am still convinced that it is possible to determine orality by quantitative formulaic analysis, by the study of formula density" (p. 24). One of the major problems with such analysis, however, is the lack of proper material, since most medieval poems are anonymous, and ideally, for formula analysis, one needs a body of work by one poet: "In order to use this analysis one must have a fair amount of material for study, and it must be the right kind of material; that is, it must be at least presumably all from one person" (p. 25); "from the point of view of the purist, only the material from a single singer should be used in the analysis of oral poetry" (p. 28). Thus Lord came to distinguish between "two levels of formula": "One is that of the individual singer. Here, it seems to me, the formula is at its purest. It serves a need for a particular singer . . . The second level is that of the regional formula. It is one that is used by a majority of singers in a region" (pp. 29–30).

In a later survey of recent work on oral literature, Lord invoked once again the concept of usefulness in responding to Larry Benson (1966), who had demonstrated that a highly formulaic Anglo-Saxon poem was in fact a close translation of a Latin original by an obviously literate monk: "One cannot have *formulas* outside of oral traditional verse, because it is the function of formulas to make composition easier under the necessities of rapid composition in performance, and if that necessity no longer exists, one no longer has formulas. If one discovers repeated phrases in texts known not to be oral traditional texts, then they should be called repeated phrases rather than formulas. I do not believe that this is quibbling about terms, because the distinction is functional" (1974/1975: 18). Formulas are not marked as such by repetition alone.

To undertake a detailed cross-cultural comparison of Yugoslavian oral epic and Xhosa izibongo with regard to the formula as defined by Parry and Lord, therefore, one must take three aspects into consideration: meter, usefulness, and repetition. Now clearly, however much Parry and Lord may insist on it as a criterion in the recognition of a formula, usefulness is too subjective a concept to allow us to differentiate on its basis a repeated phrase from a formula: As Haymes expressed it, the weakness in Parry's method of formula recognition "is that it requires a large amount of intuition and judgment" (1980:393). If usefulness is a vague term, at least meter is more precise when dealing with the Greek hexameter or the Yugoslavian decasyllabic line. The meter of Xhosa izibongo awaits definition. It may, like Gregorian plainchant in the Middle Ages (see Bailey 1974 and Treitler 1981), be melodically based, as David Rycroft (1960) has demonstrated some Zulu izibongo to be. One of the most exciting developments in the study of southern Bantu meter has been Rycroft's recent recognition of the principle of extrinsic timing in Zulu song and his application of this principle to Shona and Zulu eulogy, with passing reference to plainchant. The metrical principle might thus be an aspect of performance that an examination of the text alone could not reveal: "The situation here is not altogether unlike the rendering of Anglican chants, where, in fitting unmetrical texts (like the Psalms and canticles) to metrical music, the device employed is to render only the *last* few syllables of each line metrically, while the varying number of syllables preceding these are rendered in free rhythm to a single prolonged initial note known as the 'reciting note' " (Rycroft 1980:304). It is too soon to know whether these suggestions will prove relevant to an apprehension of a metrical principle in the performance of Xhosa izibongo. Certainly, as Rycroft observes, even the concept of a "line" awaits definition. Illumination on this point might well come from a study of the transcriptions from tape recordings of their own oral performances by Manisi and Ncamashe, oral poets who have also written poetry for publication. The quest for meter in southeastern Bantu eulogy is not yet concluded, and this situation inhibits statements about Xhosa "formulas" (in Lord's sense of the term) at present. One can still, however, for our present purposes, beg the question of meter for the time being, and proceed to an examination of what might in the end pass for Xhosa formulas (when we have come to know more about the meter), using the criterion of repetition. We have already noted that the imbongi, like the Yugoslavian epic singer, composes his poetry in performance. To what extent are "repeated word groups" necessary to his art?

In conformity with Lord's ideal prescription of using for analysis the oral poems of one poet, I propose to examine for this purpose izibongo about Kaiser Matanzima produced by David Yali-Manisi. One of these was the first poem Manisi produced at the University of Fort Hare on 27 April 1974, a translation of which concluded the fourth chapter. Here is the Xhosa text, marked according to Lord's system of formula analysis: a solid underlining indicates exact verbal repetition elsewhere in Manisi's oral poetry (a "straight formula") and broken underlining indicates a phrase that can be classified as "formulaic."

```
      A Daliwonga
      A Daliwonga
      Yiyo leyo ke le nkumkani yabaThembu baseRhoda
      Yiyo leyo ke le nganga yeentaba zikaMngqanga
  5   NguBhayi nafelane kuyazalana
      Kuloko kwahlukana ngemigca ukubabanzi
      'Gusha ziyafana ngokuba mdaka
      Nabazaziyo bazahlula ngeempawu
      Yiyo leyo k' indwatyula yakwaTato
 10   Ngunkwenkwezi azivumani nelanga
      Kuba ziqhel' inyang' int' ezihamba nayo
      Ziyaloyik' ilanga ngokubashushu
      Umhlab' onamandla ndiwuqondile
      Nakub' unamandla woyisiwe lizulu
 15   Kuba lithob' imbalela kutsh' imilambo
      Nto zinolwini hay' iimbongi
      Kutsh' amatye kusal' iziziba
      Xa kulapho ke mabandla kaNtu
      Xa kulapho ke mabandl' akokwethu
      Mn' andithethi nto kuba niyibonil' inkwenkwe
      Iphumil' inkwenkwe kaMhlobo
      Yayicand' imilambo
      Ikhe yangangagunguluza kumahlathi kaHoho
      Kulokw' itwatyul' int' enkulu
 25   Yaza kungena phantsi koQelekequshe
      Induli yakuloSandile noDondashe
      Xa kulapho ke gwangqa lomkaMhlobo
      Wena ntonga zimnyama zisemlovulovini
      Esoza siziphuthume
 30   Mini siphuthum' amaxhob' akokwethu phantsi kwentab' eTa-
      file
      Siyinikiwe kambe loo ntonga
      Loo ntong' incikane
      Ngokuphath' imilanjan' asempumalanga
      Nkant' umhlaba kaXhosa uma phantsi kwentab' ooKhala
```

35   Intab' ooKhala nditheth' intab' eTafile
       Kuba kulaph' alele khon' amarwanq' akokwenu
       Kuba walal' aph' uMfant' ixhiba likaMtikrakra
       Walal' apho noMakan' into kaGwala
       Loo madoda k' afun' ukuphuthunywa
40   Asikuwaphuthuma ngezikhali
       Sesiya kuwaphuthuma ngokondel' akubinza kweenkwenkwezi
       Warhuqe ke gwangqa likaMhlobo
       Uwafundis' ukubinza kweenkwenkwezi
       Kuba lo mhlab' awusalifun' igazi
45   Koko siya kwalatha
       Kuba nathi salathisiwe
       Xa nditshoyo goduka nawo ngawakowenu
       Ndee bham dovalele ncincilili
       Ncincilili

On this count, fifteen of the forty-nine lines are not repeated elsewhere in my collection of Manisi's oral poetry. However, Manisi has been producing oral poetry since boyhood, and I have recorded only some of the poems he has produced during the last eleven years. Without stretching a point, I believe we can acknowledge additional phrases in this poem as "repeated." For example, though I have no other instance of it in Manisi's oral poetry, line 22 is a common phrase in the poetry of other iimbongi and in Rubusana's collection, what Lord terms a "regional" formula, and is likely to be a "formula" in Manisi's poetic vocabulary as well. Further, certain passages in this poem, such as lines 5 to 8 and lines 10 to 17, repeated verbatim elsewhere in Manisi's oral poetry, can also be found verbatim in his written poetry (see Yali-Manisi 1952:14 and 33, for example); such passages have been referred to as "praises" in previous chapters. It is likely, therefore, that Manisi incorporates these fixed praises into the poetry that he writes about Matanzima (and less likely that he composes such praises pen in hand for his written poetry, whence they enter subsequent oral performances). If that is in fact the case, then we could add to the list of probable "formulas" in this poem passages repeated verbatim in his written poetry, passages such as line 22 (confirming, perhaps, its status as a "formula"), lines 25 and 26, and line 30 (see respectively Yali-Manisi 1952:7, 26, and 35; 1952:59 and 1954:24; and 1954:22 and 24). On this count, twelve of the forty-nine lines are unmarked leaving roughly 75 percent of the poem repeated elsewhere in Manisi's poetry.

Now this analysis is undertaken somewhat tongue in cheek, since the statistics are clearly soft and imprecise, unclear as we are about the boundaries of a line or the principles of the meter. Yet the analysis is revealing. I have tried to be strict on admitting phrases as "formulas": I have not accepted *loo ntonga*, for example, in lines 31 and 32, since that repetition is the product of a stylistic trope, as is the repetition of the verbs *ukuphuthunywa* (line 39) and *siyakwalatha* (line 45) in the following lines with a change of voice; and, on the grounds that they are one word and not a phrase, I have not accepted distinctive verbs that recur in Manisi's poetry, like *yangangagunguluza* in line 23 and *itwatyul'* in line 24. Nonetheless, the analysis reveals that this poem contains a high proportion of phrases employed elsewhere by Manisi, a set of phrases that clearly constitutes part of Manisi's poetic vocabulary. One may or may not choose to call these repetitions formulas, following Lord's nomenclature, but it seems reasonable to ask whether these phrases operate in the same way as Lord's formulas: Are they *necessary* to the improvising imbongi, or are they substantially different from Lord's formulas?

The Yugoslavian singers usually perform in public coffeehouses, but Parry and Lord preferred to "take the singer aside and to have him dictate his song line for line, while the collector or his scribe writes. This method is beneficial even when collecting with a recording apparatus, because it removes the singer from the vagaries of a doubtful audience" (Lord 1962b:194). I suggested at the end of the last chapter that Xhosa poets who were asked to perform in this way (as early collectors must have asked them to do) would probably repeat the praises, those commemorative phrases that recur in their poems about the subject recording his deeds or referring to his physical and moral characteristics or to his genealogy; removed from the natural performance situation, dictating a poem for transcription, the imbongi would probably omit exhortations or references to the social context of the performance. At Fort Hare, Manisi performed in his traditional garb of animal skins, brandishing two spears, and I was merely one of the bystanders, who happened to have a tape recorder in operation. I had not engineered the occasion, and my presence or absence would not have affected the performance in any way; I was present only because I happened to hear the previous weekend that Manisi had been asked to accompany Matazima to the ceremony. It is worthy of note that of the lines unmarked in the text just quoted, most refer to the social context, either immediate (Matanzima's journey to Fort Hare [lines 23 and 24]) or more general (Transkei has been given too little land [lines 31 to 33]), or else they constitute exhortations (the dead heroes must be avenged [line 39], but not with violence [lines 40 and 44]; Matanzima should lead his people to their destiny [lines 41, 45, and 46], and it is time for him to return home [line 47]). It would appear that

Manisi's poem consists of lines that he generally repeats in his oral poems, especially those about Matanzima, and also of lines that are freely improvised in response to the particular social context; these latter seem not necessarily to be structured on the model of phrases that he has found useful or that he employs regularly.

Within the corpus of those phrases underlined in the above text, there is too a substantial difference not only, as Lord observed, between personal formulas that any one performer finds useful and regional formulas common to many performers, but also between full lines associated in the poet's mind with one and only one subject – the praises, such as lines 5 to 8 and lines 10 to 17, which occur only in Manisi's poems in reference to Kaiser Matanzima – and other phrases, such as *Yiyo leyo ke* and *Xa kulapho ke*, which occur at the beginnings of many of the lines of oral poems by Manisi and other poets in the tradition. The commemorative praises, as Ncamashe remarked, fix themselves imperceptibly in the poet's mind and recur time and again in performances about the same subject. After the subject's death, it is these recurrent phrases that will be remembered by his associates as "the praises of" the subject: He used to be bonga'd in those words. (It is probably such popular praises of many izimbongi current in folk memory that the Zulu poets collect to form the izibongo of a dead chief.) No other Xhosa imbongi that I know of uses what I have called Matanzima's praises in this poem; they recur regularly in Manisi's oral and written poetry about Matanzima, though not always in the same order (for example, in an oral poem produced on the occasion of Transkei's independence in 1976, Manisi uttered lines 7 and 8 of this poem followed immediately by lines 5 and 6). These are clearly fixed lines that are retained verbally unaltered from performance to performance, some of which the imbongi may use in varying order in any one performance: the second poem Manisi produced at Fort Hare contained more of the praises he has coined about Matanzima (lines 21 to 23, for example), and there are still others that he did not introduce in either of his poems on that particular day.

Such praises alone, I have suggested, with no additional material, constitute the memorized boasts, the lineage and clan izibongo. Clearly, as the basis of any poem about any one subject, they operate in an imbongi's verbalizations on a level different from the phrases of more general application: formulaic phrases indicating genealogical relation, such as *inkwenkwe kaMhlobo,* "the boy of Mhlobo" (which, if the subject were Sabata Dalindyebo, could be *inkwenkwe kaSampu*); or formulas indicating a thematic transition, such as *Xa kulapho ke,* "so then." Phrases referring to physical characteristics, such as *Ufaf' olumadolo lukaMatanzima,* "tall long-legged one of Matanzima," which Nelson Mabunu uses of Kaiser Matanzima (or possibly of any other tall person with a substitution of ancestral name), are obviously useful in this eulogistic tradition; such a phrase clearly forms part of a system represented in my collection by *uhlwath' olumadolo*, "sweet long-legged one," *ufaf' olundaba*, "tall chatty one," and *ufaf' oluntamo*, "tall long-necked one." Apart from the fixed praises of a person, then, Xhosa izibongo improvised by an imbongi also include phrases that seem to satisfy some of Lord's criteria for formulas and formulaic expressions. Certainly they are helpful to the imbongi in fashioning his poem in performance. But are they *necessary* to him?

On 20 December 1971, to test Manisi's ability to improvise poetry, I asked him to produce a poem about a subject I nominated. When he agreed, I suggested he do a poem about the cattle-killing episode; after twenty-two seconds' reflection, Manisi produced an 8½-minute poem that ran to 152 lines (see Opland 1975:200–2; the complete Xhosa text has appeared in Satyo 1980). These 152 lines contain the phrases *umhlaba kaPhalo*, "the land of Phalo" (repeated seven times), *intombi kaMhlakaza*, "the daughter of Mhlakaza" (four times), *(Xa) kulapho ke* (three times), and *Yiyo leyo ke* (once), and conclude with the word *Ncincilili* (twice). The proportionally overwhelming balance of the poem bears no phrasal resemblance to any other poem of Manisi's: It is a completely unpremeditated, spontaneous response to my request. Admittedly, this was hardly a normal performance, if only because I specifically asked for a narrative poem. There is a higher incidence of repeated phrases in eulogies (as distinct from narratives) that Manisi has produced about subjects he does not normally bonga (Rhodes University, for example, or me), but not nearly as high again as in eulogies about subjects he regularly bongas (his chief, Manzezulu Mtikrakra, for example, or Kaiser Matanzima). The point is not that the latter poems are typical or traditional and the others unusual; the point is that Manisi does not prepare *any* oral poem in advance, but composes all of them in performance as the situation inspires him, and if the incidence of repeated phrases varies widely in these oral poems (as it does) then clearly Manisi does not *need* the repeated phrases to compose his poetry in performance. He shares with many iimbongi the ability to respond poetically with no premeditation to situations or impulses however "normal" or "traditional." If he happens to bonga a typical subject there will be a high incidence of repeated phrases in his poetry, if not, there might well be a low incidence of such phrases. The repeated phrases thus cannot offer us an explanation of how the imbongi is able to perform his remarkable – though within his tradition not uncommon – feat.

Clearly, then, the repeated phrases help the imbongi to compose his poetry on the spur of the moment, they are useful to him, but they are not necessary to him. In his analysis of chanted sermons in the southern United States, Bruce Rosenberg accepted whole line repetitions as formulas (1970a:54–6; see also Rosenberg 1970b) since the sermons are "less rigid metrically" (1970a:5) than the Yugoslavian narrative songs. Rosenberg concluded that the preacher used formulas but was not dependent on them, enjoying the ability to fashion new "metrical" lines as he preached: "As concerns the formula, whatever implications this study may have for other oral literatures, of this fact one may be certain: the great individual talent of the American spiritual preacher lies not in his memorization of a special diction or of thousands of formulaic systems, but in his ability to compose spontaneously the vocabulary at his command to fit his metrical pattern" (1970a:102). Rosenberg commented on the ability of the preacher to convert a prose text into metrical phrases in the act of reading from the Bible: "The point is here that such ability is a further indication that formulas are the creations of the moment to a great extent, and that the spiritual preacher's genius lies in the ability to intuitively render metrical lines" (1970a:104).

Later, in seeking an explanation of the ability of the preacher to chant spontaneous metrical sermons, Rosenberg emphasized the criterion of usefulness in the repeated phrases of the sermons. Whatever repetitions helped the preacher to utter his metrical lines, to give him time to think ahead, Rosenberg termed "stall formulas" (1975:81). Repetitions served specific functions in advancing the sermon content (1970a:54–6); considered as "stalls" they helped the preacher structurally to move from line to line, and could take "manifold forms." "Quite often they are not simply techniques designed to gain some time, but are also mnemonic in that they help the performer retain the traditional aspects of his material. I wish to consider them together here as they are both techniques which function to simplify the performer's task. For this immediate purpose only, then, stalls may be seen to operate in several *aspects* of language: in 'memorized' formulas, in repetitive themes, in the use of appositives, in ideas or actions repeated in substantially different diction, and in certain enjambed lines which follow predictably" (1975:83). Thus sermon formulas could be merely stylistic, including for example the trait of retaining the same phrase at the start of successive lines, a trope the Greek rhetoricians termed "anaphora" (1975:87).

Ultimately, Rosenberg extended and weakened Lord's concept of the formula to such an extent that he had to arrive at a nonconclusion.

Now it is undoubtedly true that certain utterances are "formulaic" in Parry's sense and that their syntactical structure lends itself to variation by analogous composition . . . To cite just a few obvious examples, if . . . , then . . . ; neither . . . nor; as (adjective) as (noun). If these patterns are firmly ingrained in the performer's mind as would likely be the case in English, then we would probably be correct in saying that new "formulas" are created by adjusting one or two words according to this pattern.

But nearly every other phrase would be formed by this kind of analogy, unless the pattern underlying this utterance is in the deep structure of the language. If that is granted, as I think it must be, then our investigations into oral composition and the formula simply reveal some basic facts about all linguistics. [1975:100]

Here, however, I want merely in passing to draw attention to the many intriguing similarities of form between the southern sermons that Rosenberg described and Xhosa izibongo, and to dwell for a moment on Rosenberg's suggestion that certain stylistic traits assist the preacher in chanting his spontaneous sermon. Could similar traits help the imbongi to bonga?

Many commentators on African and southern African oral traditions have drawn attention to at least three recurrent stylistic tropes, termed by G. P. Lestrade (1935) linking, parallelism, and chiasmus (see, for example, Damane and Sanders 1974:54–9 and Fortune 1977); a number of commentators have noted similar features in Old Testament poetry, especially the Psalms (see Dhlomo 1939/1977 and Stefaniszyn 1951 on African and Old Testament similarities, and Kugel 1981 and apRoberts 1977 on Old Testament style). In the Manisi poem that has just been quoted, there are examples of parallelism in lines 4 and 5 and in lines 18 and 19, and of linking ("anadiplosis") in lines 31 and 32; an example of chiasmus occurs in Mqhayi's poem on Paramount Chief Archie Sandile (Opland 1975:31, lines 28 and 29):

Umacekis' ingcek' abuy' ayipthu-thume	He puts aside white clay and then reclaims it
Umaphuthum' ingcek' abuy' ayicekise	He reclaims white clay and then puts it aside.

Now there is no doubt that such stylistic traits are common in izibongo; the fact that they are also common in oral traditions throughout the world scarcely alters their significance in Xhosa izibongo. It is evident too that, like repeated phrases, these tropes help the imbongi to compose his poetry in performance; in other words, they are useful to him. Yet they are not so overwhelmingly dominant a feature of the poetry that of their own they explain how he does what he does, any more than the repeated phrases can explain the imbongi's ability to compose poetry in performance. The imbongi may use repeated lines or phrases, he may produce lines that exhibit parallelism, chiasmus, or linking; but then again he may not. Since none of these features seems *necessary*, however useful they may be to the poet, none satisfies Lord's definition of a formula, and we must then leave to other researchers qualified perhaps in linguistics and psychology the explanation of exactly how the imbongi performs. However, repeated phrases, similar in many ways to those phrases Lord terms formulas, as well as certain stylistic tropes, are common features of izibongo. In his survey of research on oral literature, Lord wrote: "In my attempts in the past to combat the idea of a fixed text that was memorized, I have apparently given the impression that not only is the text different at each singing by a given singer (which is true, of course), but that it is *radically* different, entirely improvised. This is not true. South Slavic oral epic is not, nor, to the best of my knowledge, is any oral traditional epic, the result of 'free improvisation' " (1974/1975:17); all that needs to be said here is that the eulogies of the Xhosa imbongi frequently are the result of free improvisation.

On the face of it, we should expect to find little in izibongo to compare with Lord's "themes," since these are stock narrative descriptions and izibongo are essentially eulogistic as distinct from narrative. Lord observed that a Yugoslavian singer composed lines with the aid of formulas and formulaic expressions, but his song as a whole comprised a concatenation of traditional narrative blocks. Any one tale could be expressed as a sequence of themes any one of which might well be employed in the narration of another tale. Descriptions of battles, debates, or journeys, in whatever song they occurred, tended to consist of a set of traditional elements. A singer knows a tale as an essential sequence of themes: "Singers boast that they sing a song word for word as they heard it; they mean essential theme for essential theme. They say that they always sing it in the same way and never change anything either by addition or subtraction; they are really talking about essential themes, because to them the story consists of those themes" (Lord 1962b:191). The imbongi does not tell stories in poetry; his izibongo generally present the subject, his genealogy, his qualities, and his deeds. As the living subject involves himself in significant events, the izibongo might alter from performance to performance to incorporate references to his latest deeds, or to events current at the time of the performance; but since the character of the subject, his qualities, and his ancestry do not change substantially, references to these will tend to be stable and will tend to recur. Is there a sense in which an improvised eulogy about a man is held by the Xhosa poet (consciously or subconsciously) to consist of references to specific aspects of his subject?

By way of example, let us examine relevant extracts from three poems Manisi produced about his chief, Ntshiza Manzezulu Mtikrakra. Manisi has been producing poems for Kaiser Matanzima for many years, but Manzezulu Mtikrakra, a relative of Matanzima, was installed as chief only in 1967, so although he lives in Manzezulu's chiefdom Manisi could not have bonga'd Manzezulu as a chief before then. In fact, Manzezulu's chiefdom in the Glen Grey district was reestablished by authority of the South African government only in 1965; the chieftainship had been dissolved at the end of the last frontier war in 1878 as punishment for the assistance Mfanta offered Gungubele against the whites. Mfanta, the great-great-grandfather of Manzezulu, was imprisoned for his role in the war and died on Robben Island. The fact that Mfanta's grave is not in ancestral territory, so that no sacrificial rites could be accorded the chief after his death (a rupture of Manzezulu's ritual connection with his ancestors), is a source of anguish that is echoed time and again in Manisi's poetry: He referred to Mfanta and the need to reclaim his bones from Robben Island in order to offer him due mortuary rites in lines 37 to 39 of the first poem that he produced at Fort Hare in 1974. Manzezulu's Glen Grey chiefdom is troubled. It has been manipulated by successive white governments in South Africa. Many inhabitants opposed the restoration of the chiefdom in 1965 as a protest against the treatment of Mfanta, and many opposed its incorporation into Transkei when that homeland was granted "independence" in 1976.

Such troubles were most explicitly alluded to in the first poem about Manzezulu I recorded from Manisi. In August 1976 I traveled with Morton W. Bloomfield of Harvard University, Caroline Bloomfield, and our assistant Sydney Zanemvula Zotwana to meet Manisi, and with him to meet Manzezulu. In the course of our conversation with the chief and the headman of the location, Manisi produced the following poem:

> Hail Manzezulu!
> My chief in reality.
> He is the one whose beauty invests his people
> For he tends the pastures and mountains of Ndaba;
> 5 Behold the mountain of Zingxondo
> Facing the mountain of Lukhanji,

The fair mountains of Ndaba's land.
Oh this chief of mine of the Xhiba house,
He's the one who strides in walking.
10   He's the one who paces in walking like a secretary bird;
He's the secretary bird of Tato's land who has opportunities,
For he's the one with extensive pasture,
Greater than the lands of other chiefs.
Hail Manzezulu!
15   Oh he's the essence of fertility,
He's the one who likes people who hate him,
He's the only who feeds people who spurn food,
Yet they are idlers,
They're the ones who starved with hollow stomachs,
20   For they grew hungry the day Mfanta was seized
By layabouts who laid into us,
Who troubled the Thembu already perplexed;
They seized the child of Mtikrakra of the Xhiba house.
Oh the matchstick-legged Englishmen!
25   They just dumped him on the Island!
This is the chief the object of great pride;
We've not yet given birth and led Manzezulu
To recover the bones of the paramount chief's son,
To retrieve them from the Island and sacrifice for the dead,
30   For all other paramount chiefs have received due sacrifice,
And all other subchiefs have received due sacrifice:
Oh how tragic are the bones of Mfanta!
It's Mfanta who leapt into action,
He seized his weapons and entered Gwatyu
35   To aid the troops of Gungubele of Bawana,
For trouble was initiated by the whites.
On the day the weapons clashed
Gungubele and the English were at loggerheads;
However, the English crushed us underfoot
40   But we'll rise again
For the black stick's kept in safety.
We'll speak on the day the bones tremble,
On the day we reclaim the bones of Mfanta.
So then, descendant of Mtikrakra of the Xhiba house,
45   Speak to the people of Tato so they seize their sticks,
But not the weapons of wood or spears,
Rather the sticks of knowledge and perception:
The people must be bound in a unified mass,
They must come together to be strong,

50   So that we take our forces and place them for all to see,
     So that we fight with perception to regain our rights;
     For way over there lie your outposts,
     Stretching from the mountains of Lukhanji,
     Extending far to the distance,
55   Way beyond the rivers of Hewu and Hewukile.
     I disappear!

In this poem we see an explicitly narrative passage (lines 33 to 39)
serving the ends of eulogy. We also observe some ideas common to
this poem and the two poems Manisi produced at Fort Hare: the need
to reclaim Mfanta's bones, the exhortation that the struggle for black
rights should be through negotiation rather than arms, the symbolic
black stick kept in safety, the ill-treatment of the blacks by white thugs
(*amagxagxa* in line 21, as well as in line 44 of the second Fort Hare
poem), especially the English who grind the blacks underfoot (*ayesi-
ganzinga* in line 39 and in line 45 of the second Fort Hare poem).

   There are greater similarities, however, between this performance
and the first of three oral poems Manisi produced in the stadium
before thousands of spectators during the celebration of Transkei's
"independence" in Umtata on 25 October 1976. Manisi started his first
poem by greeting and introducing his chief, Manzezulu, before passing
on to treat Kaiser Matanzima and Transkeian independence; only the
section referring to Manzezulu concerns us here:

     Hail Manzezulu!
     There then is this chief
     Of the Xhiba house of Mtikrakra,
     There then is Manzezulu,
5   The chief from under Lukhanji.
     He's so tall he must stoop, he looks hungry though he's eaten.
     He's slender, he's the hunter of the python.
     He cares for mountains of prominence,
     The mountain of Zingxondo and of Lukhanji,
10   Mountains of note in the Glen Grey district.
     He's the one who strides in walking like a secretary bird.
     He's a towering timber, a tree with no branches,
     For he's a chief of destitute people;
     In their daily life they're subject to layabouts.
15   Oh how the layabouts lay into them!
     Oh how the English crush them underfoot!
     To the extent that we're despised even by Coloureds,
     For in our daily lives we've nothing of our own:

When the paramount chief the son of Mhlobo was reclaiming
the land,
20   The Afrikaners just brushed us aside . . .

Manisi subsequently wrote a long poem about the independence of
Transkei, which was published in 1977; in it there is no reference to
Manzezulu or his Glen Grey chiefdom.
In 1979 Manisi submitted a volume of poetry that was published in
1980; one of the poems in this collection is *UNkosi Billy Ntshiza
Mthikrakra* (pp. 88 to 90), a poem about Manzezulu in traditional
form. It starts with a more detailed genealogy of the chief than is
offered in either of the two oral poems, and then passes on to urge the
Thembu to rejoice at the appearance of Manzezulu as chief:

Hail Manzezulu!
Peoples of Ndaba I comfort you.
Pluck the jealousy from the bull,
15   For summer has started,
Valleys large and small are roaring,
Rivers large and small are overflowing,
Hills and plains are garbed in green,
For Manzezulu has gone to tend the mountains.
20   He warmed himself on Dudumashe's and it nearly cried,
He supported himself at Zingxondo and walked with a stick,
He glared at Lukhanji and it trembled;
All nations screened their eyes,
Saying, what calf will be born of this?

30   Why do you cry so loudly?
Do you say Mfanta should not have fought?
It's Gungubele who led the contingent,
And royal Mfanta joined in
Rescuing his own from Thukwa's place.
35   Gungubele is the son of Mapasa the son of Mvanxeni,
Mvanxeni is the son of Xhoba of the Tshatshu.
When Gungubele attacked at Gwatyu,
When the English were taking booty,
Mfanta went out without consulting a soul,
40   And he led his own of the Xhiba,
And the whites were surrounded then,
And the dead dropped on both sides,
And because those thieves fight with lightning,
The royal sons of Nxeko jumped back,

45   And so Mfanta died on the Island.
Did you think he had no offspring, dignitaries?
Don't you see the herb with long legs?
A chief handsome as a water-snake,
A snake of rivers and pools.
50   He lumbers in walking like an elephant.

I say that to you, tall son of Mfanta,
Herdsman of the crippled cattle of Ndaba,
Who blazes in walking like the sun.
65   Bring down the rain, son of Mfanta, we are starving,
How long must we wait anxiously?
For the land and the rivers are dry,
And all the valleys are parched.
Point, cut meat, we're waiting for you,
70   My chief of Glen Grey and Lady Frere.
I disappear.

Now each of these three poems is very much influenced by its real or implied audience (on the effect of different audiences on the texts of Turkish and Indian performances, see Başgöz 1975 and Blackburn 1981; on implied readers see Iser 1978 and W. D. Wilson 1981). The written poem is tightly controlled and deliberately muted. The battle of Gwatyu and Mfanta's imprisonment are mentioned, but Mfanta's death on Robben Island is alluded to in only one elliptical line (line 45). The battle of Gwatyu and the destitution of Manzezulu's people are both referred to, but no connection between the two is established. The whites are the enemies at Gwatyu, but they do not abuse the Thembu and in no way are accountable for their present destitution: The whites do not even imprison Mfanta, he simply dies on Robben Island. In his oral performances Manisi is less circumspect than in his written poem, and exposes more openly the wounds in the Glen Grey body politic. In the Umtata poem, Manzezulu is again the chief of destitute people, but here their ill-treatment at the hands of the whites is explicit: The English abused them in defeat, the Afrikaners rejected their claim for ancestral land. There is no reference to Mfanta: The day belongs to Kaiser Matanzima the son of Mhlobo (line 19), and Manisi refers to his own chief, Manzezulu, only out of courtesy. In the first oral performance, produced before a small group of people, Manisi felt free to establish the connection among the destitution of Manzezulu's people, the death of Mfanta, and the detrimental interference of whites in black affairs.

In spite of their differences as distinct responses to specific audiences real or imagined, there are verbal similarities among the three poems.

Line 21 of the first poem and line 15 of the second is a recurrent phrase in Manisi's poetry (whether about Manzezulu or not) as is line 39 of the first poem and line 16 of the second; with reference to Manzezulu or to Mfanta, relation to the Xhiba house of Mtikrakra recurs, as in lines 8, 23, and 44 of the first poem, line 3 of the second, and line 40 of the third; with reference to Manzezulu, the two lines 9 and 10 of the first poem (*Ngumatwatyul' ukuhamba / Umagxanyaz' ukuhamb' axel' ingxangxosi*) are collapsed into one line of the second (*Ngumatwatyul' ukuhamb' axel' ingxangxosi,* line 11) and are clearly related to lines 50 (*Uwangxath' ukuhamba ngathi yindlovu*) and 64 (*Mavuth' ukuhamb' axel' ilanga*) of the third. On the whole, however, these verbal resemblances are statistically slight. If we bear in mind the different circumstances of production of the three poems, and especially the fact that the second oral poem actually runs to fifty-nine lines, only the first eighteen of which are quoted here as relevant to Manzezulu, then what is perhaps remarkable is that all three poems bear striking resemblances not in diction but in content. All three associate Manzezulu with mountains in the Glen Grey district, especially the culturally significant mountains of Zingxondo and Lukhanji; all three refer to Manzezulu's tall stature and the gait that is the consequence of his long legs; all three refer to the destitution of Manzezulu's people; and all three refer to the hostility of whites, muted perhaps in the third poem, explicit in the second, and in the first explicitly linked to the destitution of the people consequent upon the death of Mfanta on Robben Island as punishment for his participation in the battle of Gwatyu.

On this evidence, it would appear that Manisi does not prepare in advance the words of an izibongo about Manzezulu, and that he employs in these poems relatively few fixed praises, perhaps because Manzezulu has been a chief only since 1967 (curiously enough, there are more lines in the style of traditional praises in the written poem than in the two oral versions). It would also appear that Manisi's poems about Manzezulu are fairly consistent with regard to content, however much the exact verbalization might be influenced by the context. These recurrent elements of content would seem to operate in a manner similar to the operation of Lord's themes, in that Manisi apparently bears a relatively stable conception of what ought to be said in a poem about his troubled chief.

And finally, before we turn to the theories of Walter Ong, let us set the Xhosa tradition of eulogy against what Lord has to say about writing and oral poetry. One of Lord's most controversial assertions is that an oral poet cannot be literate; this conclusion depends on Lord's conception of the formula, and on it in turn depends the oral-formulaic theory. Lord put it this way in *The singer of tales:*

It is necessary for us to face squarely the problem of "transitional" texts. Is there in reality such a phenomenon as a text which is transitional between oral and written literary tradition? . . . It is worthy of emphasis that the question we have asked ourselves is whether there can be such a thing as a transitional *text;* not a *period* of transition between oral and written style, or between illiteracy and literacy, but a *text,* product of the creative brain of a single individual. When this emphasis is clear, it becomes possible to turn the question into whether there can be a single individual who in composing an epic would think now in one way and now in another, or, perhaps, in a manner that is a combination of two techniques. I believe that the answer must be in the negative, because the two techniques are, I submit, contradictory and mutually exclusive . . . The oral singer thinks in terms of these formulas and formula patterns. He *must* do so in order to compose. But when writing enters, the "must" is eliminated. The formulas and formula patterns can be broken, and a metrical line constructed that is regular and yet free of the old patterns . . . Formula analysis, providing, of course, that one has sufficient material for significant results, is, therefore, able to indicate whether any given text is oral or "literary." An *oral* text will yield a predominance of clearly demonstrable formulas, with the bulk of the remainder "formulaic," and a small number of nonformulaic expressions. A *literary* text will show a predominance of nonformulaic expressions, with some formulaic expressions, and very few clear formulas. [1960/1965:128–30]

In 1962 Lord stated that literate oral poets do exist, but that they lose the ability to compose orally as soon as they accept the concept of a fixed text – a "correct" version – that is a consequence of the introduction of writing. Oral poets may learn to write poetry, but formula analysis can still reveal the text to be the product of a literate poet:

What are the facts about literate oral poets? First, they are not rare; they can be found in Yugoslavia today. Second, most of them do not write very well, but have only an elementary knowledge of writing, which is for them only a means of recording, not a means of composition. Third, they are still basically oral singers, because they still follow the process of oral composition outlined above. They are in a dangerous position, because as soon as they come to the conclusion that the written text must be reproduced exactly, as soon as they have the concept of a fixed text, their singing days of oral songs are over. Their ability to compose orally is lost when this happens, and they become mere reciters. It is a demonstrable fact that when this point is reached, the singer cannot sing a song unless he has memorized it; and when he forgets a word or a line, he is no longer able to fill it in with the formulae.

There are singers who change from oral composition to written composition as well as to recitation. They know writing well enough and have read enough so that they can begin to compose in writing, not merely to record what they compose orally, but to "write" a song. What is significant, however, is that this is detectable in the style. One can tell when a song has been "written." The writer no longer has the necessity to abide by the formulaic style of oral composition; he has leisure which the singer lacks. [1962b:196]

This aspect of Lord's theory has been regularly assailed by scholars who produce contrary evidence from classical and medieval traditions, as well as from the Yugoslavian tradition itself (see, for example, Kirk 1976 and Adam Parry 1966 on classical data; Benson 1966, Miletich 1974, Shields 1980, and Spraycar 1976 on medieval data; and Haymes 1980 and Miletich 1978 on Yugoslavian data). Adam Parry, the son of Milman, raised doubts about whether the process of the introduction of literacy in Homer's Greece in any way resembles the process in Yugoslavia in the 1930s: In the latter situation the singer was introduced to "a whole literary culture, the culture of the cities of his own country and of what we call the civilized world . . . a culture of books and newspapers" (1966:213), whereas to Homer and his contemporaries writing was a novelty that was not yet associated with a manuscript – still less a print – culture. Lord responded to this and other criticism in 1968 with a number of clarifications. "I must plead 'not guilty' to the charge of entertaining the 'notion of the impossibility of a bard who cannot write' " (p. 2), he asserted; and

I know that there are oral poets who can write, that is to say, who are literate. I know also that they can, when asked, *write down* the poems that they know. But in the course of this study I have come to question the existence of such a category as that of the literate oral poet who "writes." Literate oral poets exist. Literary poets who imitate oral poetry exist. I have not found as yet a literate oral poet, that is to say a good oral poet who has learned to write, who has in fact written either imitations of oral poetry or oral poetry. [p. 13]

Imitations of oral style have been composed, but "they are written by people very familiar with the oral tradition, but not part of it" (p. 13).

Let us consider two poems by Chief S. M. Burns-Ncamashe, who

for many years before his installation as a chief practiced as an imbongi, and who still occasionally bongas in public. On 17 February
1977 the chief was invited to bonga at the installation of the new
chancellor of Rhodes University scheduled for 30 March. The organiz-
ing committee that issued the invitation asked Ncamashe to produce in
advance a text for inclusion in the program. He was provided with
biographical information about Dr. Ian Mackenzie, the chancellor-
elect. On 7 March the chief submitted a Xhosa izibongo he had written
that included references to Mackenzie's war record, his educational
career, his directorship of companies, and his active interest in the
preservation of historic buildings and in nature conservation; since
Ncamashe had never met Dr. Mackenzie, there are no references to
his physical characteristics, there are no references to the expected
social context except for Ncamashe's exhortation to Mackenzie to "as-
cend the stage" for his installation, and there are no references to
Mackenzie's genealogy. The Xhosa poem was printed with a translation as a supplement to "The Order for the Installation of Ian Mackenzie as Chancellor of Rhodes University," which was distributed to
members of the congregation who attended the ceremony. Here is the
translation, produced in consultation with Ncamashe:

> I've suddenly come upon an outstanding doctor!
> I've suddenly come upon a giant of the intellect,
> The bull who roars causing all Hitler's warriors to look round
>   about them
> In fear of the blows of the kilted Scotsman,
> 5   The bull who tosses the enemy fiercely with furious thunder,
> Who refuses to ignore a challenge, who refuses to be tossed
>   aside.
> Ascend the stage, man of sagacity!
> Ascend to eminence, man of experience,
> Whose chest is covered with medals of honour,
> 10   Whose learning has amassed, whose learning's piled up,
> Who has an M.A. through his own efforts,
> But who merited an honorary doctorate.
> That's why the great man has a tasseled cap,
> That's why the wizard wears a robe:
> 15   He's the man for whom the doctor's gown's not just the sun,
> Which lets grasshoppers and midges bask without effort –
> The one who wears it sweats hard to earn it,
> Perspiring so that others may benefit.
> His academic gown is a dignitary's swirling kaross,
> 20   Which he wears by virtue of labors widely manifest and
>   acknowledged.

He crossed rivers and oceans in quest of the key,
The key that would yield him wealth in money and mind.
We see him as a doctor although he took no medical courses,
We see him at the head of companies in the company of pre-
    stigious magnates,
25   We see him installed at the highest levels of education.
Oh the son of Mackenzie is a towering figure!
I speak of a veteran of war,
War which brings death to both country and man.
I speak in praise of the kilted Scotsman,
30   Who seized his weapons and rushed to the battlefront
During the second war, which overwhelmed all the world,
And he tracked down the Huns day and night.
His daring earned him war decorations,
And he was raised to the rank of Lieutenant-Colonel,
35   And he earned still more decorations,
And was invested with the rank of Commandant.
I speak of a leader in clear skies and in thunder:
When the world's at peace he's a leader of peace;
When the world's at war he's still fit to lead.
40   In a variety of subjects his interest is boundless.
Dilapidated houses interest him,
Especially houses with a story.
I'm amazed at this man,
Who's absorbed in shrubs and wild plants,
45   Because he sees they're the inheritance of our land;
He's a collector of mouldy books,
Because he sees they're rich with ancient knowledge.
He's renowned for his stature and able directorship,
Directing companies and august societies.
50   While at leisure at home he's often called in
And established in prominent positions
Fit for a man of distinction and honor.
He's the head through his high rank and ability,
The new Chancellor of Cecil's place.
55   I disappear!

The order also prints the text of the national anthem, which was sung at the ceremony, a prayer read by the dean of divinity, and a citation read by the public orator presenting Dr. Mackenzie to the congregation.

On the morning of 30 March, the day of the installation, I handed to Chief Ncamashe a copy of the poem he had written, which he had not seen since delivering it on 7 March. Before I did so, I asked the chief to produce an oral poem about Mackenzie. In response, with no hesitation, Ncamashe produced a fifty-two-line oral poem that bears only slight verbal resemblances to his written poem. During this morning meeting, Ncamashe told me that the poem he had written was his gift to the university, and that he intended to bonga it at the ceremony as written. That night, after the national anthem had been sung, after the dean of divinity had read his prayer and the public orator his citation, Ian Mackenzie was formally installed as chancellor. At this point Chief Ncamashe, wearing an academic gown and a headband of traditional Xhosa beads, moved to the podium with the text of his poem in his hand and produced the following izibongo about the newly installed chancellor, whom Ncamashe greeted in the manner of a chief with an isikhahlelo, *Zimwongile,* "They have honored him":

> Hail Zimwongile! Hail Zimwongile! Hail Zimwongile!
> The professors of his people have honored him,
>   And I too was there;
> The great men of his people have honored him,
> 5   And I too was there;
> People of high standing have honored him,
>   And I too was there;
> Eminent men have honored him, eminent men have honored
>   each other,
>   And I too was there.
> 10   Aho! Aho! Ahoho!
> Whoa, nations! Whoa, nations!
> Let the mind be alert and the ears listen:
> I'm going to talk about a real doctor!
> I've suddenly come upon an outstanding doctor!
> 15   I've suddenly come upon a giant of the intellect!
> The bull who roars causing Hitler's men to look round about
>   them
> In fear of the blows of the kilted Scotsman,
> The bull who tosses the enemy fiercely with furious thunder,
> Who refuses to ignore a challenge, who refuses to be tossed
>   aside.
> 20   Ahoho! Hoho!
>   Leliba!
> Ascend the stage, ascend the stage, man of sagacity!
> Ascend to eminence, man of experience!
> Whose chest is covered with medals of honor,
> 25   Whose learning has amassed,
> Whose learning's piled up,
> Who has an M.A. through his own efforts,

But who merited an honorary doctorate.
Aho! Ahoho!
30   Whoa, nations! I say whoa, and listen:
That's why the great man has a tasseled cap,
That's why the wizard wears a robe:
He's the man for whom the doctor's gown's not just the sun,
Which lets grasshoppers and midges bask without effort –
35   The one who wears it sweats hard to earn it,
Perspiring so that others may benefit.
His academic gown is a dignitary's swirling kaross,
Which he wears by virtue of labors widely manifest and
     acknowledged.
Leliba! Leliba!
40   I could go on, but let me leave some over.
When I speak of this homestead of Cecil,
This homestead of Cecil is Rhodes University.
You know him, you crowds of whites:
Cecil's the beast of Rhodes,
45   The thing who crossed the sea to come to this country
Carrying a trowel and a shovel;
He dug mines and money appeared,
Gold appeared and was refined;
He took the money and shut it in banks;
50   When he scooped it, he did so with bowls and buckets
And he built this village whose name we say:
          It is Rhodes University,
A deep river with deep waters.
There the children of the whites swim.
55   They go to it at the call of *gqoloma* and *chanti*
And they leave it wearing gowns and hoods,
And they leave it as experts and sages,
Knowing everything from top to bottom.
I plead for myself, then, homestead of the whites:
60   I plead also for the black peoples:
I say open the door, Zimwongile!
The son of Henderson has finished with you.
Open the door and let blacks enter,
Let them drink from this fountain!
65   Let them drink from this water!
I disappear!

After a prologue referring to the installation, Ncamashe starts reading
his text at line 14. He reads twenty lines exactly as written, except that

in line 16 he says *ezakuloHalitile* where his text has *imikhosi kaHitile* (line 3), he repeats *qabel' eqongeni* in line 22, and he inserts exclamations at lines 20–1, 29–30, and 39. He breaks off reading his text, announcing that he is doing so in line 40, and proceeds to a spontaneous exhortation to Mackenzie, newly installed as chancellor by Dr. Derek Henderson (line 62), to use his influence to have blacks admitted to the racially segregated university.

Now clearly this is an unusual set of texts. Nonetheless, Ncamashe is certainly an oral poet: No Xhosa-speaking member of the audience would hesitate in asserting that what he did was bonga Mackenzie just as the imbongi is accustomed to bonga a chief on his installation. (My collection, in fact, includes the izibongo produced on the occasion of Ncamashe's installation as a chief.) Just as the Yugoslavian singer of tales fashions his words in performance, so too Ncamashe produced an unpremeditated oral izibongo at my request earlier in the day, and the last twenty-seven lines of his izibongo that evening were the product of free improvisation. Ncamashe, then, is an improvising oral poet; yet he is also literate and capable of writing a poem that bears all the stylistic hallmarks of traditional Xhosa izibongo, part of which was in fact recited at the installation ceremony in a style indistinguishable from the improvised prologue and conclusion.

In 1974, in response to Benson's argument, Lord seemed to concede that "transitional" texts could be written in imitation of traditional oral performances:

> The fact of the matter is that the oral traditional style is easy to imitate by those who have heard much of it. Or, to put it another way, a person who has been brought up in an area, or lived long in one, in which he has listened to the singing and found an interest in it, can write verse using the general style and some of the formulas of the tradition. After all, the style was devised for rapid composition. If one wishes to compose rapidly in writing and comes from or has had much contact with an oral traditional poetry one not only can write in formulas, or something very like them, but normally does so. The style is natural to him. When the ideas are traditional the formulas may be those of the oral traditional poetry; when the ideas are not traditional, they will not. [1974/1975:18]

Yet Lord carefully shied away from conceding the possibility that an oral poet could be literate and could produce traditional poems in writing while retaining the ability to produce traditional oral (that is, improvised) poems in performance. On the evidence cited in this chapter alone, Manisi and Ncamashe can. Mbutuma can and Mqhayi clearly could, and none of these iimbongi are in this respect unusual. Whether or not they actually write izibongo, most iimbongi I have met are literate and all of them verbalize in performance; Ncamashe clearly had a concept of a fixed text on the installation of the chancellor – indeed, he held the fixed text in his hand – yet this in no way affected his ability to produce poetry in response to the specific context when he chose to lay aside his prepared text. Recently, from the perspective of his research on early medieval music, Leo Treitler offered the following comment on the debate in medieval studies over Lord's oral-formulaic theory: "It strikes me that the wrong question has been asked of the evidence. Formulaic style . . . is what Walter Ong has called a 'residual' of oral tradition. [It is] understandable in the light of a continuity from oral to written practice. That seems a fundamentally more important historical matter than the question of whether this or that production should be classified as 'oral' or 'literate' " (1981:481). And that brings us to the work of Walter Ong.

In his own words, the work of Walter J. Ong, S.J., has over the years "grown into its own kind of phenomenological history of culture and consciousness . . . elaborated in terms of noetic operations as these interrelate with primary oral verbalization and later with chirographic and typographic and electronic technologies that reorganize verbalization and thought" (1977b:10–11). Ong's studies are deeply influenced by the ideas of Milman Parry, Albert Lord, and Eric Havelock, and constitute a considerable extension of the work of Marshall McLuhan, whose concepts Ong exploits. Ong expresses his central thesis thus: "Major developments, and very likely even all major developments, in culture and consciousness are related, often in unexpected intimacy, to the evolution of the word from primary orality to its present state" (1977b:9–10). Ong's *The presence of the word: Some prolegomena for cultural and religious history* (1967/1970) "describes and interprets the evolution of modes of thought and verbal expression from primary oral culture, before the invention of script, through the subsequent technological transformations of the word – through writing, print, and the electronic devices of recent times (the so-called media) – and the resulting evolution of consciousness, of man's sense of presence in the human lifeworld, including the physical world and what man senses beyond" (1977b:9).

Ong pursued this line of investigation in a set of short essays gathered under the title *Rhetoric, romance, and technology: Studies in the interaction of expression and culture* (1971a), which sought "to show how the history of rhetoric in the West has mirrored the evolution of society, variously ordering knowledge, guiding thought, focusing perception, and shaping culture for over two thousand years until the ancient rhetorical economy of thought and expression was finally swamped by the effects of print and the advent of the Age of Romanticism" (1977b:9). Recently another collection of essays, many of them previously published, has been assembled in *Interfaces of the word: Studies in the evolution of consciousness and culture* (1977b). These essays "have to do with the alienation and subsequent transformations which have come about in the technological development of the word and the concomitant evolution of consciousness" (p. 47). Citing D. P. Kunene (1971a) and Opland (1975) as examples, Ong has asserted that the "noetic processes" examined by Havelock, the modes of thought of ancient Greeks before the introduction of writing, "can be readily recognized in the heroic poetry of other cultures" (p. 18); it seems profitable, therefore, to set the Xhosa tradition of oral poetry against the scheme Ong establishes as characteristic of oral cultures. I shall take as my text Ong's "African talking drums and oral noetics" (1977a/1977b).

In his essay on drum language and oral noetics, Ong notes that drum languages in Africa have been developed within primary oral cultures, that "the talking drum is not merely an element in some primary oral cultures but is also in fact a kind of paradigm of primary orality" (p. 97). Ong draws on a description of Lokele drum language in Zaire by John F. Carrington, setting it alongside the characteristics of the thought processes of primary oral cultures:

> Recent studies have shown how oral noetic processes – ways of acquiring, formulating, storing, and retrieving knowledge in cultures unfamiliar with writing or print – have certain distinctive features as compared to the noetic processes of cultures possessed of writing and, a fortiori, of print, and how these distinctive features are related to what can be called an oral lifestyle. Because Dr. Carrington's book re-creates, informally but quite substantially and circumstantially, the drum-language world as a whole, a reader of the book who is familiar with oral noetics can hardly avoid being struck by the way in which the drums exemplify and often informingly exaggerate the characteristics of the oral lifeworld, or of primary orality (oral culture untouched by writing or print, as contrasted with secondary orality, the electronic orality of present-day technological cultures, implemented by telephone, radio, television, and other instruments dependent for their existence and use on writing and print). My intent here is to bring together what we know about oral noetics and about concomitant oral lifestyles on the one hand and, on the

other hand, what is now known about the talking drums as explained by Dr. Carrington. [Pp. 96–7]

We are concerned here with "what we know about oral noetics" rather than with drum talk in Zaire: My intent is to bring together Ong's paradigm for primary oral cultures on the one hand, and, on the other hand, what we know about Xhosa oral poetry, hoping thereby to reveal more about Xhosa izibongo. Ong lists seven salient features of a primary oral culture: I shall take them one by one.

1. *Stereotyped or formulaic expression.* At first blush this would seem to be no different from claims for oral poetry advanced by Lord, whom Ong cites. Ong goes further than Lord, however. Not only do oral poets express themselves in formulas, but, as Havelock has argued, *everyone* in an oral culture expresses himself in formulas; and, further still, not only does everyone talk in formulas, everyone in an oral culture also *thinks* in formulas. These oral thought patterns change only with the introduction of new script technologies, writing, printing, or electronic media: As Ong observes in an essay entitled "Transformations of the word and alienation," "The mind does not enter into the alphabet or the printed book or the computer so much as the alphabet or print or the computer enters the mind, producing new states of awareness there" (Ong 1977c/1977b:47). Lord's concept of the formula is intimately associated with a theory of oral poetry, and his definition incorporates as a significant element the traditional meter of the poetry; Ong is concerned with oral thought patterns in general, with the way people think before they come into contact with writing. Lord insists that oral poetry is formulaic; Ong makes similar claims for preliterate discourse in general, asserting that "primary orality is radically formulary" (Ong 1971b/ 1971a:291). But if Ong has broadened the domain of the formula, he has also broadened its conception.

Ong's conception of the oral formula, characteristic not simply of poetry but of all verbalizations and mental processes in a primary oral culture, emerges more clearly from a number of studies over the years, especially "The literate orality of popular culture today," which seeks to study "popular literature in its relationship to the history of the media" (Ong 1971b/1971a:285). For Ong, as for Lord, the formula is recognized through repetition; the nebulous and subjective concept of "usefulness" is not often invoked, and of course there is no reference to meter. Ong's formulas or formulary devices, "which are well known to occur in great quantity at least in primary oral culture and which, as will be explained, have their place in secondary oral culture, too, and in particular in our popular arts, including literature" (1971b/1971a: 285), include Lord's formulas and much else besides:

By formulary device I mean here any set or standardized verbal expression, "set" and "standardized" implying, of course, that the expression is used more than once, and generally quite often. The term "formulary device" thus understood is rather expansive. It includes all manner of proverbs, adages, apothegms, proverbial phrases, and the like, the "old said saws" that weave through and support virtually all early writing, keeping even learned writing close to oral performance for centuries, from antiquity through the productions of Renaissance humanists such as St. Thomas More and Erasmus, affecting the very substance of Shakespeare and Pope, and to a diminishing extent later writings, as well as the speech of residually oral folk everywhere still today. In addition to proverbs and the like, the formulary device will include programmatically mnemonic verses such as the familiar "Thirty days hath September" . . . It also includes formulas of the Homeric sort, such as "rosy-fingered dawn" or "tamer of horses" . . . Among formulary devices must be included, moreover, . . . the "cumulative commonplaces" as we have styled them, prefabricated purple patches on some standard subject such as loyalty or mother love or dishonesty or general civic corruption or one's own incompetence ("unaccustomed as I am to public speaking") . . . Other kinds of standardization can be formulary devices in a larger but related sense, insofar as they are matrices for set or standardized verbal expressions. Such for example are standardized narrative themes which epic poets have used (the arming of the hero, the hero's shield, the message, the summoning of the council, and so on). [1971b/1971a:286–8]

Ong sees these devices, especially the commonplaces, as originating in oral style, but subsequently permeating writing after its introduction; their manipulation assists the orator to speak, just as Lord claims that formulas and themes help the oral poet to compose:

> The Greeks, and, following them, Cicero and Quintilian, advocated that the orator get up in advance a repertory of *loci communes* or commonplaces – little purple patches on loyalty or treachery or friendship or decadence ("O tempora! O mores!") or other themes "common" to any number of cases or occasions for insertion into an oration as opportunity offered. As has been seen, the classical oration was the product of a situation, typically an oral performance . . . For such a performance a stock of commonplaces was the equivalent of the epic singer's stock of formulas and themes . . . The com-

monplaces were an answer to the need for fluency which the orator, like the epic singer, felt much more acutely than the writer, since, as has been seen, oral performance, once begun, cannot be interrupted with impunity as written composition can. [1965/1971a:36–7]

We have seen that something very like Lord's formulas exist in Xhosa izibongo: These repeated phrases, however, do not seem to be *necessary* to the imbongi, as Lord claims formulas are to the Yugoslavian singers. The repeated phrases would seem to be useful to the imbongi, in that they help him to compose his lines, but so too are a number of stylistic devices useful to the imbongi. These stylistic devices are found in many oral traditions throughout the world, and the existence of Greek terms for them demonstrates that they were current too among the ancient Greek orators and their successors. We have seen that they also exist in the southern folk sermons described by Bruce Rosenberg, who broadened Lord's conception of the formula to include them in his definition of a sermon formula. It is clear that these rhetorical tropes, as well as the repeated phrases, are all embraced by Ong's conception of a formula or formulary device; we could also find a place under Ong's rubric for the relatively fixed sections of the izibongo, the praises that tend to recur in poems by any one imbongi about the same chief, even though we might not choose to term these "purple passages." If it is difficult to see Lord's formula, in the strict understanding of the term, in izibongo, it is easy to concede that to a large extent Xhosa oral poems consist of what Ong understands by formulary devices.

2. *Standardization of themes.* Here Ong means something quite distinct from Lord's themes, which are recurrent narrative blocks and would be included by Ong in his category of formulary devices. For Ong the themes that are standardized are topics that recur in oral discourse because of their significance in the way of life of the people: "Oral noetics, as manifested in poetry and narration of primary oral cultures, organizes thought largely around a controlled set of themes, more or less central to the human lifeworld: birth, marriage, death, celebration, struggle (ceremonial or ludic, and polemic or martial), initiation rites, dance and other ceremonies, arrivals and departures, descriptions or manipulations of implements (shields, swords, plows, boats, looms), and so on" (1977a/1977b:196).

In former days, when Nguni life was more settled, the imbongi might well produce a poem at the start or at the end of the day, greeting his chief and commenting on the day's happenings: Kropf's definition of "ukubonga" mentions that "old men of the chief's clan,

though distant, creep out of their huts at daybreak and loudly celebrate his praises" (1899/1915:42); and Shaw heard Hintsa's imbongi at
sunset calling out "his usual public announcement of the events of the
day" (1860:480). Nowadays the imbongi tends to perform when people
are gathered, at meetings, feasts, weddings, even–contrary to custom–at funerals: The modern imbongi's performances form part of
the kinds of ceremonies Ong refers to, and since their spontaneous
poetry is related to the context one may say that allusions to such
ceremonies recur in izibongo. Izibongo are produced on the arrival of
visiting dignitaries, or as an expression of pride in cattle or favorite
possessions (Mbutuma once produced a poem in praise of the vehicle
he runs as a taxi). Izibongo thus tend to refer to a set of themes more
or less central to the Nguni lifeworld. But this is only natural. The
essence of Ong's observation is that the set of themes should be limited: "It is true, of course, that all knowledge is organized in some way
around themes in the large sense of subject matters–there is no other
way to organize it. But the themes that govern oral discourse tend to
be relatively limited and bound to the human lifeworld, if only because, as Havelock has explained, elaboration of scientific categories
or of quasi-scientific categories (such as are used, for example, in the
modern writing of history) depends on the development of writing"
(1977a/1977b:106). Is there any indication that izibongo tend to be
organized around a limited set of topics?

Certainly, as we saw at the end of the last chapter, izibongo are
organized around broad subject categories: Izibongo tend to incorporate reference to physical and moral attributes, deeds, and genealogies, as well as exhortations to the audience or commentary on social
circumstances. Clearly, appeals to the audience or references to context are uttered under the inspiration of the unique moment of performance. So too, actions and personal qualities will be specific to the
particular subject: Not everyone is tall like Manzezulu or Kaiser Matanzima, or fat like Archie Sandile; not everyone has seen military
service as Ian Mackenzie has. Yet when that is granted, there are
certain qualities whose presence or absence tend to be commented on
by Xhosa poets: In the izibongo of chiefs, for example, the quality of
firm leadership is praised or encouraged, and its antithesis is decried.
Certain categories of action recur in izibongo, such as sexual exploits
or, recently, the ability to earn money; travels are constantly referred
to. Perhaps the existence of such topics of organization can best be
demonstrated by noting that achievements in battle loom large in
early izibongo, and continue to do so even though the last war between the Cape Nguni and the whites ended over a century ago:
Migrant laborers refer to their journey to work as an entry into

battle, and Manisi constantly exploits battle imagery and allusions in his exhortations to his audiences to fight for their rights, as in the following extract from a poem produced for a group of sixty-four black schoolchildren in Grahamstown on 13 June 1979:

> So then, beautiful girls of Phalo's homestead,
> So then, handsome fellows of Rharhabe's land,
> Sons of those who scorned flight,
> Sons of those who wear ivory arm-rings,
> 35   Sons of heroes:
> This land of Phalo is in trouble,
> For the English grabbed it with cannon and breechloader,
> While your fathers fought with spear and assegai.
> That's why we're vagabonds and refugees
> 40   In the land of our ancestors.
> Gone is the time for wriggling on our rumps,
> Dropping into rivers, scaling outcrops,
> Traversing rocky inclines,
> Running in futility and hiding under grass
> 45   In clefts that are the haunt of pythons,
> As we flee familiarity with the cannon
> Which shatters and scatters us,
> Which rips and hacks us.
> So today we say the time's at hand
> 50   To seize your weapons, men,
> To take the road we must tread,
> Which will yield us that power
> Which other nations have gained,
> Especially the nation of the English,
> 55   Who violated the land of Phalo and of Tshiwo.

It would seem then that in spite of the fact that much of Xhosa eulogy is specific to the subject, the kinds of topics that merit reference in izibongo tend to be a selection of qualities and activities of significance in Cape Nguni society.

3. *Epithetic identification for "disambiguation" of classes or of individuals.* By disambiguation, Ong means processes designed to make references less ambiguous or general. These processes may take the form of epithets or qualifiers: Odysseus is "wily Odysseus" in Homer, and on the Lokele drums a banana is a "pole-supported banana." "Epithets are a specific manifestation of formulaic techniques," Ong writes, "but common and distinctive enough to warrant separate mention" (1977a/1977b:108). My own impression is that epithets as such are far less significant in izibongo than qualificatory phrases that are

nominally based: Thus, for example, Mqhayi referred to Archie Sandile as *imbishi-mbishi,* "a corpulent person," a noun drawn from the
poetic tradition that came to be used as an alternative name for Archie
Sandile and that was incorporated by other iimbongi into their izibongo about him (see Opland 1974:21–3). Metaphoric expressions and
personification, both nominally based, predominate in izibongo; epithets as "disambiguating" identifiers seem not to have the significance
in izibongo that they have in other cultures.

    4. *Generation of "heavy" or ceremonial characters.* I am afraid that
I find Ong's brief discussion of this point a trifle confusing. On the one
hand, he talks of stock characters; on the other hand he acknowledges
that individuals merit special names. On the one hand, "heavy" characters are generated: "Havelock has shown how, in the absence of the
elaborate categorizations with which writing makes it possible to rack
up knowledge more 'abstractly,' oral cultures commonly organize their
knowledge in thematic narrative, peopled with impressive or 'heavy'
figures, often type characters (wise Nestor, clever Odysseus, faithful
Penelope). Around such heavily accoutered figures (and themes associated with them) the lore of the culture is focused" (1977a/1977b:108).
On the other hand (or so it seems to me) "ceremonial" characters are
generated, characters who are accorded elaborate names like the Lokele man Boyele, whose drum name is "The Always Poisonous Cobra,
Son of the Evil Spirit with the Lance, Nephew of the Men of Ya-
gonde" (where "The Always Poisonous Cobra" is Boyele's grandfather's drum name, "Evil Spirit with the Lance" his father's): "Any
name, even in ordinary parlance, is to some degree ceremonial: it fixes
a person ritually or conventionally in a relationship to his fellows,
though in patterns which of course vary from culture to culture. When
the name is massive, as it has to be on the drums, and is used in its
entirety every time the individual is mentioned, as it usually is on the
drums, the ceremonial weight of discourse becomes exceedingly heavy.
Primary oral culture commonly encourages very formal discourse" (p.
109). My problem with this discussion is that "heavy" characters seem
to be generalized, whereas "ceremonial" characters seem to be indi-
vidualized, and the two tendencies seem to be in opposition.

    "Heavy" characters are generated in Nguni discourse. Stories about
the precocious but wayward youth in exile who returns to assume
power, bearing striking resemblances to heroic biographies the world
over (see for example Campbell 1957 and Raglan 1936/1956), can be
shown to have developed about Zulu leaders, contrary to historical
fact (Argyle 1978). In the izibongo, fat people (for example) will tend
to be alluded to in stock expressions. But the izibongo are not narrative, and exploits are rarely explicitly narrated, so there is little room
for the generation of stock characters. In any event, the whole impulse

of eulogy is toward the depiction of the subject, his specific characteristics (in the case of Manzezulu the strutting gait that reminds Manisi
of a secretary bird, or in the case of the portly Archie Sandile the
sound of trousers swishing together as he walks that attracts Mqhayi's
notice), those defining qualities that mark him as an individual and
distinguish him from others. His praise names, however ceremonial,
are generally his alone, merited through some particular exploit, although as we have seen, like Boyele, any man may for ritual reasons
be referred to by the names of his ancestors, his clan's ancestors, or his
chief and his chief's ancestors. The Nguni naming system in general
would seem to fall happily within the ambit of Ong's fifth characteristic
of primary orality.

5. *Formulary, ceremonial appropriation of history.* Here Ong is concerned with how a society organizes its history, selecting relevant
events for record. Since history concerns deeds, names that derive
from deeds, what we have called praise names, serve as pegs for mental recall:

> Whereas highly developed writing and print cultures tend to
> appropriate the past analytically when they verbalize it, oral
> cultures tend to appropriate the past ceremonially, which is to
> say in stylized, formulary fashion. How this is so can be seen in
> part from their handling of names. In an oral culture, as we
> have seen, knowledge in its entirety tends to be organized
> around the action of individuals. Hence names, which distin-
> guish individuals from one another, can serve as especially
> important foci for noetic organization in oral cultures, and in
> particular for the organization of history . . .
> In all cultures, names come from history in one way or
> another. They refer the individual to his own history, and in
> doing so help constitute that history in a formulary fashion that
> confers on it a certain ceremonial weight. An individual may
> be named "after" an ancestor or another person older than
> himself, being assigned a "given" name which is or was that of
> the other person. In addition, he may at the same time auto-
> matically bear his father's and grandfather's and/or mother's
> name as well, thus acquiring more anchorages in history. In
> another pattern, names may derive directly from a historical
> event in an individual's own life, that of another, or that of a
> group. [1977a/1977b: 109–10]

Not only Lokele persons but also villages have ceremonial drum
names.

We have discussed at some length the Nguni naming system (on this
term, see McDowell 1981:1) and its relevance to izibongo. Xhosa and

Zulu eulogies are in essence names of people living and dead; cattle and other animals may also have praise names. So too may places: In the poem Manisi produced for the Grahamstown schoolchildren on 13 June 1979, he referred to Algoa Bay, where Port Elizabeth is now situated, as *IGqum' eliselwandle*, "it roars in the sea," and to Grahamstown as *iGqum' eliphezulu*, "it roars on high," although both places are now commonly referred to as *eBhayi* (literally "at the bay," from Afrikaans *baai*) and *eRhini* respectively. There is no doubt that the history of a chiefdom is encapsulated in the ceremonial names of the chiefs as incorporated into izibongo, derived as these names are from the chiefs' actions and qualities, and the same comment would hold good for the history of clans and lineages.

The intimate relation between history and izibongo is perhaps best reflected in a remarkable oral history dictated by Msebenzi (born about 1850) and edited and published by Van Warmelo (1938). Msebenzi was a Ngwane, and his language is Zulu. The Ngwan fled south from Shaka early in the nineteenth century, forming one wave of that surge of destructive incursions into Xhosa-speaking territory known as the Mfecane, and many of them came to settle among the Cape Nguni as Mfengu. Msebenzi recites the izibongo of the Ngwane chiefs, but apart from those set pieces, his narrative is peppered with snatches of izibongo, sometimes more praises used as alternative names, sometimes quoted in context to account for their origin. Thus a man is summoned, and referred to by his praise name: "And he, Zulu the son of Mafu, said, 'Let there be sent, two young men to fetch him, the "Angry talker like the heavens above" ' " (p. 32); or

> Mabhengwane had barely made this admission when the order was given to the Mhlungwini to beat those people of Ndungu-nya (Mabhengwane and his brothers) and they beat them all and drove Mabhengwane away, and set up Masumpa,
> "who stood behind him like a wizard"
> and they chased them with their sticks and they fled streaking for safety as hard as they could go. And then they smashed the pots containing the bad beer, leaving only that which was good, so that they might be praised in the line:–
> "they are the pot-smashers of Tshani"
> namely those men of the Ndaba clan. Masumpa thus became
> "the broad track on one side at Mkhabelweni"
> that is, the village of Mabhengwane. [P. 12]

At times mention of a person will occasion the recitation of a few lines from his izibongo:

The chief [Matiwane] flew into a terrible rage at this. "To whom do you say a thing like this? Was it not I that mustered the amaNgwane, to fight against Mthimkhulu, son of Bhungane Hadebe, when I thought to attack Mpangazitha? He was too strong for you, was Mpangazitha, and repeatedly you ran away.

The Angry-talker who frightens, like the heavens above
The bushbuck of Mayi and Dlomo, which stabs as it dashes
    along.
The cattle that rush down a dangerous place
Mahogwe is bitter (i.e. fierce in battle) like the shongwe
    plant
He, the river full of grinding stones that are slippery
The young reebuck of Mashiyi.

To whom do you say that I have eaten the lung of a sheep; when have I done such a thing? [Pp. 30, 32]

The second line of Mpangazitha's izibongo can be found in Ndawo's version of the izibongo (1928:16), the first and second lines can be found at separate points in the version translated by Jordan (1957–60/1973:24–5), and the entire six lines are incorporated into the extended izibongo of Matiwane that Msebenzi later recites (Van Warmelo 1938:66), except that the second line has *Mashiyi* for *Mayi* and the fourth *Hogo* for *Mahogwe*). To quite a remarkable degree, the style of this Zulu narrative resembles that of the medieval Icelandic sagas, which also intersperse authenticating verse in the prose narrative. It is perhaps not surprising then to find a passage that reflects a typically Germanic ethic:

Thereupon Mgovu, son of Ndindane, replied,
"Mazongwe, why are you silent?"
"Sir, we were afraid that these might be Swazis, we thought perhaps they might have killed the prince, and now they had come to slay us also."
Then said Mgovu son of Ndindane,
"If they had killed you, what would it have mattered if you had lost your chief?" [Van Warmelo 1938:96; cf. the Xhosa phrase for the chief's comrades-in-arms, *amafanenkosi,* "those who die with the chief," and Woolf 1976]

We may conclude that izibongo reflect, especially through their concatenation of commemorative praise names, a "ceremonial appropriation of history."

6. *Cultivation of praise and vituperation.* Ong claims that an oral noetic economy "is sure to carry a heavy load of praise and vitupera-

tion. Indeed, the preoccupation with praise and vituperation, characteristic of primary oral culture generally, remains long after writing in the West, so long as orality is actively fostered by the concerted study of rhetoric (that is, basically, public speaking). Such study continues until the Romantic movement finally matures" (1977a/1977b:112). There seems to be little more that need be said under this heading except to reiterate that izibongo deal in praise and blame as twin aspects of the imbongi's truth telling; the praises referring to physical and moral qualities may be both flattering and critical.

7. *Copiousness.* Here, finally, Ong is concerned with repetitions and verbal redundancies that are acceptable in oral discourse but out of place in modern writing. These features may well be the same as some of those earlier labeled "formulary devices" by Ong, but here he makes a different point. To concoct a crude example, if Manisi addressed his young audience through the medium of writing, he could call them the sons of heroes wearing ivory arm-rings who scorned flight, but in performance it is acceptable – indeed appealing – to invoke the "handsome fellows of Rharhabe's land" as

> Sons of those who scorned flight,
> Sons of those who wear ivory arm-rings,
> Sons of heroes.

As Ong puts it,

> Oral cultures need repetition, redundancy, verbosity for several reasons. First, . . . *verba volant:* spoken words fly away. A reader can pause over a point he wants to reflect on, or go back a few pages to return it. The inscribed word is still there. The spoken word is gone. So the orator repeats himself, to help his hearers think it over. Second, words do not infallibly carry equally well to everyone in an audience: synonyms, parallelisms, repetitions, neat oppositions give the individual hearer a second chance if he did not hear well the first time. If he missed the "not only," he can probably reconstruct it from the "but also." Third and finally, the orator's thoughts do not always come as fast as he would wish, and even the best orator is at times inclined to repeat what he has just said in order to "mark time" while he is undertaking to find what move to make next. [1977a/1977b:114–15; see Finnegan 1970: chap.1 and 1977:16–24; and Opland 1980b on differences between oral and written productions]

Xhosa izibongo, then, seems to satify far more happily Ong's criteria for primary oral noetic processes than Lord's criteria for oral poetry. With minor exceptions, Ong's paradigm can be seen to encompass the observable phenomena of the Xhosa tradition, providing an acceptable account of repeated phrases in the poetry, where Lord's definition of the formula proves too restrictive. If Ong's seven characteristics are necessary and sufficient for defining a primary oral culture, then we would have to conclude that Xhosa izibongo appears to be a manifestation of such a culture. In arriving at such a tentative conclusion, however, we must be careful to avoid any ethnocentric judgment of the sort many early travelers and missionaries in the eastern Cape were susceptible to: Such a conclusion carries with it no possibility of contention that Xhosa culture is in any way "primitive" or backward. Ong is concerned with alterations in human patterns of thought as the mind encounters developments in script technology: "For human thought structures are tied in with verbalization and must fit available media of communication: there is no way for persons with no experience of writing to put their minds through the continuous linear sequence of thought such as goes, for example, into an encyclopedia article. Lengthy verbal performances in oral cultures are never analytic but formulaic" (1977b:2). But Manisi, Mbutuma, Ncamashe, and other contemporary iimbongi are literate; they are not members of a primary oral culture. If their oral poetry satisfies Ong's paradigm, then that is what is worthy of note: The oral tradition seems to have been sufficiently assertive to resist influence from print.

This does not mean that the tradition has not changed, as we shall see in the final chapter; nor does it mean that the oral tradition has not achieved its accommodation with writing and printing. In the Western tradition, such an accommodation was slow in coming:

> After the invention of script (around 3500 B.C.) the central verbal activity to which systematic attention was at first given was the art of public speaking, not the art of written composition. Scribes learned how to commit discourse to writing, but basically composition as such remained an oral matter. Early written prose is more or less like a transcribed oration, and early poetry is even more oral in its economy. This fixation on the oral diminished only slowly. From antiquity through the Renaissance and to the beginnings of romanticism, under all teaching about the art of verbal expression there lies the more or less dominant supposition that the paradigm of all expression is the oration. [Ong 1971a:2–3]

Unlike the situation in ancient Greece (see Harelock 1982), in the eastern Cape writing was not evolved but introduced to the Xhosa-speaking peoples by representatives of a foreign culture. The introduction of writing and some of the consequences for Xhosa izibongo are treated in the next chapter.

7
POETRY IN PRINT

The Cape Nguni skipped the long process of script evolution under-gone by Western European societies, and from the start of the nine-teenth century were brought into contact – often violent – with bearers of a culture familiar with the printed book. In order to examine a little more carefully some of the effects on traditional Xhosa poetry of the introduction of writing and printing and of the spread of literacy, we must dip into the early history of mission education on the eastern frontier, the attitude of missionary institutions to vernacular literature, and the development of Xhosa journalism as a vehicle of vernacular literature. The balance of this chapter will then be given over to a consideration of the Xhosa epic, which evolved only as a result of literate contact with Western European models.

Two hundred years ago writing was unknown to the Cape Nguni; they lived, in Ong's terms, in a primary oral state. To a large extent the education of the Cape Nguni, and hence their introduction to literacy, rested initially in the hands of Christian missionaries. Literacy came slowly, although the actual literacy rate in any given period is difficult to determine. In 1951, official sources claimed that 23.8% of the black population of South Africa was literate (defined as capable of reading and writing English, Afrikaans, or an African language). By this time the present Nationalist government had been in power for three years; since their election, they have continued to assert univer-sal control over education, segregating it at all levels on racial lines, so that teaching of blacks soon passed to the authority of a Department of Bantu Education. In 1958 this department estimated that 35% of blacks in South Africa were literate. The 1970 census revealed that the population of South Africa included 3.7 million whites (17.5% of the total population) and 15.1 million blacks (70.2%), 49.5% of whom were literate (literacy figures from Switzer and Switzer 1979:14); the black population included 3.9 million Xhosa (18.3% of the total popu-lation). The literacy rate among these "Xhosa," with whom we are concerned, is difficult to determine from these figures, and becomes more difficult to determine from the 1980 census, at which time Trans-kei was "independent" and its "citizens," whether living in Transkei or in South Africa, were excluded from South African statistics.

The story of the spread of literacy and its effect on traditional Xhosa literature initially follows the course of missionary education, for "mission schools created literate communities on mission stations and out-stations and, especially after 1850, mission presses gradually produced a literature in the vernacular among the Zulu in Natal/Zululand, the Xhosa and Tswana in the Cape, and the Sotho in what is now Lesotho and the southern Orange Free State" (Switzer and Switzer 1979:2; see also D. P. Kunene and Kirsch 1967). Mission presses were established by the Methodists, the Anglicans, and the Scottish Presbyterians among the Xhosa-speaking peoples (the Cape Nguni). The Anglicans enthusiastically established presses on their stations, but by the early twentieth century they had stopped producing vernacular publications. The "first serial publication aimed at a black audience in Southern Africa" (Switzer and Switzer 1979:1), *Umshumayeli wendaba,* was published irregularly as a quarterly by the Methodists between 1837 and 1841, but shortly after 1876 they stopped their printing operations. The greatest success in Xhosa education, and certainly in vernacular publications, can be credited to the representatives of the Glasgow Missionary Society, especially through the agency of the Lovedale Mission. It is largely their story that I follow here (on Mpondo reactions to missionary activity, see Etherington 1978).

The first missionary to work in Xhosa territory was Dr. J. T. van der Kemp, representing the London Missionary Society, who moved about between the Keiskamma and Buffalo rivers from September 1799 to December 1800 before withdrawing to establish a mission station at Bethelsdorp near what is now Port Elizabeth. Van der Kemp took with him to Bethelsdorp as a pupil the young son of the Ntinde chief Tshatshu. The boy was baptized at Bethelsdorp by Van der Kemp in 1811 and given the name Jan; he may well have been, as Basil Holt claims, "the first of his race to be baptized" (1976:64). Jan Tshatshu served as interpreter and loyal assistant to Van der Kemp's missionary successors, Joseph Williams and John Brownlee, and traveled to England with John Philip in 1836 to give evidence in the House of Commons before the Aborigines Committee. After his return, he assumed the Ntinde chieftainship in his father's infirmity and, much to the disappointed disgust of his former mentor, reverted to a traditional way of life: On 14 February 1839 Brownlee wrote to London, "The concerns of the tribe devolve on Jan, and bad counsellors from among his friends seem to have a bad influence on his mind; and, instead of Jan being a bright example to the Kafirs of Christian virtue, he seems greatly behind the native converts, and in several instances his conduct has been rather matter of grief to them than a cause of encouragement" (Holt 1976:101). Joseph Williams, also representing the London Missionary Society, established the first mission station in Xhosa territory on the Kat River near present-day Fort Beaufort in 1816, but the station closed on Williams's death in 1818.

In 1820 John Brownlee, formerly associated with the London Missionary Society but at that time temporarily a "government" missionary, settled on an outstation named Chumie established by Williams on the Gwali stream in the Tyhume Valley. Here, in 1821, Brownlee was joined by William Ritchie Thomson and John Bennie, sent through the influence of John Love as agents of the Glasgow Missionary Society; in the course of 1823 the first baptismal and communion services were held at Chumie, and John Ross, also sent out by the Glasgow Missionary Society, joined the three missionaries. In November 1824 Ross and Bennie opened a new station some twelve miles to the southeast on the River Incerha, and in 1825 Brownlee moved to establish a station on the Buffalo River where King William's Town now stands. The station established by Ross and Bennie on the Incerha, named Lovedale after Dr. Love, was destroyed in the war that broke out in 1834. After the war the new Lovedale station was built not far from the old site; its buildings still stand today, just outside the town of Alice (for a history of Lovedale, see Shepherd 1971).

As R. H. W. Shepherd, himself principal of Lovedale from 1942 to 1955, tells the story, Bennie established a school immediately on his arrival at Chumie in 1821.

> Within four months the school had an attendance of between fifty and sixty.
>
> Some of the tribesmen as well as the Hottentots in the vicinity had been in touch with Dutch settlers, and it is noteworthy that the missionaries in consequence found it necessary to learn not only Xhosa, but the Dutch language also. In a few months Bennie – a gifted linguist – was so proficient in the latter that he was able to converse and teach in it. The Xhosa language which, of course, had never been reduced to writing – he found more difficult, but within a year he had the children repeating in their native tongue the Lord's Prayer and other items . . . Bennie indeed was soon engaged in preparing a large vocabulary and in "reducing to form and rule this language which hitherto floated in the wind." [1971:4]

Bennie was assisted in his task as teacher by the arrival in 1823 of John Ross, who brought with him a printing press. Within days of his arrival, Ross ran off copies of a one-page reading sheet written by Bennie with a picture of a bull at the top of the page and a text that starts *Inkomo zonke zezikaTixo: ungumninizo yena,* "All cattle belong to God: he alone is the owner"; the Xhosa language had been printed for the first time.

In 1825, when Brownlee moved to the Buffalo River, the Chumie school had 70 pupils and old Lovedale on the Incerha had 30. By 1828 Thomson was being helped at Chumie by a Xhosa teacher named Robert Balfour, who had been among the first baptized in 1823, and Bennie was helped at Lovedale by Charles Henry, another Xhosa from among those baptized in 1823. Bennie opened the school at New Lovedale on 5 September 1838; by 3 April 1839 he was teaching 132 pupils, 94 girls and 38 boys. Of these 132 children, Shepherd remarks, "19 were dressed in European clothes" (1971:10). The first ordained Xhosa missionary, Tiyo Soga, established a station at Mgwali in 1857. Two years later 108 children were attending weekday school and 80 attended Sunday school. "Of these 145 could read (25 English, 120 Kaffir); 21 were learning to write and 50 were 'arithmeticians' " (D. Williams 1978:69). In 1886, as part of an aggressive justification of its existence, the Lovedale mission published *Lovedale Past and Present,* listing details of the careers of over 2,000 former pupils.

Against this chronicle of apparent progress must be balanced the difficulties encountered by the missionary educators through Xhosa resistance to Christianity. In 1846 John Philip of the London Missionary Society admitted that "such has been the want of success in the Kaffirland Mission, that some of our Missionary societies have for years been on the point of abandoning it wholly" (D. Williams 1978:47), and William McDiarmid of the Glasgow Missionary Society stated in 1849 that he had "been twenty years in Kaffirland, and could not name more than two or three real converts in all that time" (D. Williams 1978:67). In 1856 J. C. Warner, government agent among the Thembu, drafted a memorandum on native custom; in passing, he criticized preachers who assumed that their black audiences shared their own Christian system of belief, ascribing their failure to the persistence of the native system of belief:

> And then, after years of labour, suffering and privation, on perceiving that they have almost laboured in vain, and spent their strength for nought, they despairingly exclaim, *Why* is it that the Gospel is comparatively powerless when preached to the Kafirs? The answer to this question is, Because in addition to these *ordinary* obstacles, there is most assuredly a *system of superstition* to be denounced and overturned, before they can possibly embrace Christianity; and which is none the less powerfully pernicious because it has (apparently) reference to the blessings and calamities incident to this life only. [Maclean 1858/1968:79–80]

The despairing cry of the preacher is often heard in the early years of the Christian mission to the Cape Nguni.

How can missionary claims of burgeoning school attendance be reconciled with such cries of failure? There is evidence that missionary successes were achieved among marginals in Xhosa society: Those who attended schools were largely dropouts, undesirables, Khoi, Mfengu (those Natal Nguni refugees from Shaka who sought refuge among the Xhosa and who sided with the whites against the Xhosa in the frontier wars), and ,Gqunukhwebe (a group of mixed descent led by commoner chiefs with white sympathies). According to Michael Ashley, "The mission educational effort, for the first half of the century, was directed largely towards the Mfengu, the Gqunukhwebe and refugees from tribal society such as people accused of witchcraft" (1974:202).

The Xhosa chiefs themselves recognized the missionaries as agents of the white government and the Christianity they preached as a threat to traditional custom, and sanctions were brought to bear on those who attended school. One chief remarked to a missionary, "When my people become Christians, they cease to be my people" (D. Williams 1978:82), and in 1867 Tiyo Soga wrote of Sarhili and his Gcaleka that "the prevalent opinion of that tribe is, that missionaries are emissaries of Government, to act upon the minds and feelings of the people, with an instrument which they call '*the Word*,' and that those who become affected by the Word, and exchange Kafir customs for those of the white men become subjects of the English Government" (D. Williams 1978:79–80). In this belief, the Xhosa chiefs were certainly correct, as we have seen from Warner's comment on the need for missionaries to eradicate native beliefs. Not only was Xhosa custom a target, the institution of the chieftainship came to be marked: Donovan Williams remarks that "already by the forties, certain disillusioned missionaries were calling for an end by force to the power of the chiefs. John Cumming was one of those who considered that if the chiefs were deprived of their authority by the British Government the Gospel would spread in Caffraria" (1978:93). Mission education became an agent of pacification:

> Education was seen as indispensable to the work of conversion. Schools were necessary to teach Africans to read the Bible. Thus functional literacy both in the vernacular, as translations became available, and English, was the initial aim. As the cultural obstacle to conversion became apparent, education was to be a means whereby pupils were weaned away from the tribal way of life . . . Schools were focal points for the missionary pressure on those aspects of traditional culture which were seen to be obstructing the advance of Christian civilisation. The Cape Nguni rejected the education that was

offered. It was rejected as part of the attempt to change their way of life, their national customs and their identity . . . After the war of 1847 and the subsequent annexation of British Kaffraria . . . government saw education as an instrument for the pacification and incorporation of the tribesmen into colonial society. As African political and military resistance sprang from an intact tribal structure, the aim became one of "civilisation." Missionary activities fitted well into this programme. [Ashley 1974:201–3]

For the first half of the century, then, education to a large extent affected only those living on the fringes of Xhosa society, those like the Mfengu and Gqunukhwebe without a strong line of chiefs, or those cripples or victims of witchcraft accusations who were outcasts from the mainstream; the Cape Nguni chiefs and their people presented a solid front of resistance to mission education. Thus, in this early period, literacy could have but little effect on Xhosa poetic practices. The book itself became a symbol of the corrupting values of Christianity, as it still is today in Manisi's oral poetry: In July 1977, a poem Manisi produced at the 1820 Settlers Monument in Grahamstown included the lines

> We thank you tribes of the Settler people
> For you entered carrying the Bible,
> 25   Saying we should take up the tome
> And lay down custom and tradition.
> We took the Bible and followed you.
> The minister turned into a soldier.
> He shouldered his rifle and fired his cannon:
> 30   The mountains of Rharhabe roared,
> Dust rose up and the land was aflame.

But conditions and attitudes soon changed.

The second half of the nineteenth century started with a long frontier war, and was followed in the same decade by the cattle-killing episode. When in 1856 the Gcaleka girl Nongqawuse claimed that the ancestral spirits had appealed to her to urge the destruction of crops and cattle in order to repulse white encroachment, most of the chiefs supported her call. The self-inflicted disaster of 1857, the so-called national suicide of the Xhosa, undermined confidence in the chiefs and led to widespread starvation and migration to white territory in search of succor. The Cape Nguni sought work on white farms, and when gold and diamonds were discovered in the following decades, blacks became a permanent feature of white economic enterprise. With the power of the chiefs broken and the pacification of those living beyond the eastern frontier in large measure secured, the doors to the mission schools stood open; the lines formed readily enough, but those now seeking entrance to the schools found an altered attitude among the white teachers. Ashley notes that for Sir George Grey, who assumed office as governor at the Cape in 1854 after a period of service in New Zealand,

> education was fitted into an overall policy aimed at undermin-
> ing the power of chiefs, encouragement of African peasant
> agriculture and mixed patchwork landholding in the Ciskei.
> The combined effect of these policies, the war of 1850–3, and
> the disastrous cattle-killing of 1857 was the serious disruption
> of tribal society. Numbers of individuals became detached
> from the tribal social matrices and ready to enter into new
> relationships. This process was accelerated by the decisive eco-
> nomic changes resulting from the discovery of diamonds and,
> later, gold. Africans were sucked into the developing economy
> and racial inter-dependence became characteristic of South Af-
> rican economic life everywhere . . . Whereas the missionary
> and government aim had hitherto been the cultural conversion
> of Africans, now that the latter were ready for change Europe-
> ans no longer wanted it, at least along the lines worked for by
> the early missionaries. Growing racial competition in South
> African society was one important factor, and the society that
> was emerging saw Europeans stressing the subordinate posi-
> tion of Africans. [1974:203–4]

The altered white attitude to black education is reflected in the clash between William Govan, the first principal of Lovedale, from 1841 until 1870, and James Stewart, who succeeded him, serving from 1870 until his death in 1905. Briefly, "Govan was sacrificed because of his conviction that a primitive people could best be elevated first by the highest education of the few and Stewart took his place as Principal because he advocated first the elementary education of the many" (Shepherd 1971:32). Govan offered Lovedale students of whatever color a European education; Stewart, with the support of the Foreign Mission Committee of the Free Church of Scotland, favored a less academic and more practical education for blacks.

> Govan, catering both for the children of European missionaries
> and Africans, aimed for European standards and curricula, pro-
> viding what the Rev. H. Calderwood described as "a very supe-
> rior English classical and mathematical education" at the higher

levels . . . He saw the African future in an integrated society and maintained that they needed the highest form of European education they could cope with . . . Thus Africans, following the Tiyo Soga model, were to be given a European education which would assimilate them fully into European society. There were no considerations of a racial nature in the matter of the individual's achievement of status. The Foreign Mission Committee, however, wished to stop the teaching of Latin and Greek to Africans, having English as the only "classical" language . . . This in effect cut Africans off from the core of Victorian education, as the study of the dead languages was seen as preparing the whole person for a higher life of fine taste and judgement. The education Stewart planned was broad and practical and designed to begin the long task of general uplift, also of fitting Africans for the realities of colonial society. Thus Lovedale should turn out men who had had a practical education and who would work industriously, under European supervision if necessary. [Ashley 1974:205–6]

By the end of the century, when Africans were turning to education to equip them to compete on equal terms in white society, they were offered an education inferior to that of the whites, who feared the social, political, and economic implications of educated black masses. "Thus the nineteenth century closed with strong African demands for the adequate provision of a Western education which would equip Africans to compete in a South Africa offering increasing economic and social opportunities. This demand met strong resistance from the entrenched whites who feared the consequences of anything other than a carefully controlled expansion of African education. The pattern which persists to the present had been set" (Ashley 1974:210). For the Cape Nguni, then, education became integral to their political aspirations, and the ideal of education they upheld – but came to be denied – was that of Victorian England. In such a system the classical languages offered the only literature worthy of study, and Victorian poetry became for them the model for imitation; but by the turn of the century no volume of Xhosa poetry had yet been published.

The printing press brought by John Ross to the Tyhume Valley in 1823 was destroyed with Old Lovedale in the war that started in 1834; a replacement arrived in 1839, and was set up at New Lovedale. In 1844 the Lovedale Mission produced its first serial publication in Xhosa, *Ikwezi*. The first issue appeared in August 1844, the second in December of the same year, the third in February 1845, and the fourth and final in December 1845; in total, the four issues of *Ikwezi* amounted to less than sixty pages. The content was heavily Christian in character, and included contributions in English: The second issue carried an article on George Washington entitled "I cannot lie" and a "Hymn for the New Year"; the third issue's English passage was called "Is the word of God good news to me?" The third issue contained an article in Xhosa, completed in the fourth issue, on Ntsikana, fascinating in its effort to demythologize the stories that must already have sprung up claiming that Ntsikana prophesied the advent of Christianity; this anonymous account of the life of Ntsikana is the earliest vernacular record of Ntsikana that I know of. *Ikwezi* was clearly designed to provide suitable reading material for the products of mission schools. As R. H. W. Shepherd, principal of Lovedale from 1942 to 1955 and director of the press from 1927 to 1958, explained it,

> In all its efforts for the spread of literature Lovedale recognized that there was a danger lest the missionary agencies, having in their schools taught vast numbers to read, should leave non-Christian and even anti-religious elements to supply the reading matter. Not only so, but it recognized that the tribes of South Africa were facing a new and perplexing world. Their old life was passing because of the inrush of western civilisation. Old sanctions no longer held. Great numbers were being taught to read. While in school and when they left it it was imperative that they find within their reach literature suited to their every need, in order that they might have an understanding grasp of Christian life and morals. Only thus could they be equipped for the demands of the day. Only thus could they find a substitute of a satisfying kind to take the place of so much that had passed from them. No individual and no nation will reach their highest development without a thoughtful and reverent love for good literature. [1971:104]

It is clear that for Shepherd and Lovedale "good literature" was equivalent to "Christian literature."

From August 1862 until February 1865, the Lovedale Press produced thirty-one monthly issues of *Indaba*, which "was probably the first newspaper to be published in English as well as a vernacular language, establishing a trend that would characterize a major portion of the Black Press within little more than a generation" (Switzer and Switzer 1979:1). The first issue carried an extract from the prospectus, dated 19 November 1861, setting out the aims of the newspaper:

> The *Indaba* is designed specially for those speaking the Kafir language. But, as it is of manifest importance, in order to their

intellectual advancement, that the study of English should be encouraged and stimulated among them, it is intended that about a-third of each Number shall be in that language.

The *Indaba*, it is intended, shall contain a Digest of Home and Foreign News, especially as they bear on the interests of the Native Tribes; brief notices of Missionary operations and successes, in this as well as in other lands: and Articles, and, above all, Spiritual Enlightenment of those for whom it is specially designed. In every department, local and party politics will, as far as possible, be avoided.

The English section of *Indaba* was edited by William Govan, the principal of Lovedale, and the Xhosa by Bryce Ross, a teacher at Lovedale and the son of John Ross. *Indaba* enjoyed a circulation of five to six hundred. In its pages one may find William Kobe Ntsikana's account of his father (reprinted in Bennie 1935:9–12; cf. Jordan 1957–60/1973:44–5) and a number of letters and articles by Tiyo Soga written under the pseudonym UNonjiba waseluhlangeni, "the dove of the nation" (see Jordan 1957–60/1973:84–7). In the first issue, in August 1862, Soga wrote in Xhosa with high hopes for the role of *Indaba* in the preservation of folklore: "Had we no chiefs in days gone by? Where are the anecdotes of their periods? Were these things buried with them in their graves? Is there no one to unearth these things from the graves? Were there no national poets in the days of yore? Whose praises did they sing? Is there no one to emulate this eloquence?" *Indaba*, Soga wrote, could be

> a beautiful vessel for preserving the stories, fables, legends, customs, anecdotes and history of the tribes . . . Our veterans of the Xhosa and Embo [Mfengu] people must disgorge all they know. Everything must be imparted to the nation as a whole . . . We should revive and bring to light all this great wealth of information. Let us bring to life our ancestors: Ngconde, Togu, Tshiwo, Phalo, Rharhabe, Mlawu, Ngqika and Ndlambe. Let us resurrect our ancestral forebears who bequeathed to us a rich heritage. All anecdotes connected with the life of the nation should be brought to this big cornpit, our national newspaper *Indaba*. [Trans. D. Williams 1978:98–9]

By the time *Indaba* ceased publication in February 1865, it could hardly be held to have fulfilled Soga's hopes for it.

Soga's classic translation of the first part of Bunyan's *Pilgrim's progress, Uhambo lomhambi*, was published by the Lovedale Press in 1867 and became an immediate success. The Cory Library for Historical

Research at Rhodes University holds a Lovedale statement of "Kaffir Books on hand and probable number of each Sold during *this year* ending Der/67" (MS 8839), which notes that three thousand copies of *Pilgrim's progress* had been printed. All the other stock in hand listed is Christian and didactic (607 hymnbooks on hand, about 236 sold; 4,000 shorter catechisms on hand, about 250 sold; 7,000 Gospel of St. Mark on hand, about 300 sold; Kaffir tracts "Dead Stock as usual." By 1870 Lovedale was ready to launch another serial publication; this one proved more long-lived than its predecessors. The first issue of the *Kaffir express* appeared on 1 October 1870; much of the material in this English monthly was repeated in the Xhosa version, *Isigidimi sa-maXosa*. In 1876 the *Kaffir express* changed its name to the *Christian express*, and in 1922 to the *South African outlook*, under which name it still appears. *Isigidimi* parted company from the *Christian express* in 1876, and ceased publication in 1888. *Isigidimi* was "the first African newspaper edited by Africans in Southern Africa" (Switzer and Switzer 1979:3); it was also the vehicle for the first publication of original poetry in Xhosa.

For the first six years of its existence, *Isigidimi* was part of the *Kaffir express;* the two were bound together, the *Kaffir express* first and *Isigidimi* next, and the pagination was consecutive. In this period the material for *Isigidimi* was assembled by Elijah Makiwane and John Knox Bokwe. From January 1876 until its closure, *Isigidimi* appeared separately from the *Christian express;* in this latter independent period, John Tengo Jabavu was appointed editor from 1881 to 1883 and was succeeded by W. W. Gqoba. It is difficult to follow the evolving editorial policy accurately, since the issues from 1875 to early 1882 are no longer extant. It is clear, however, that initially the editorial policy was as narrow as that of *Indaba* had been. The fifth issue (4 February 1871), for example, carried a number of responses to a letter from "Kokela" that had appeared in the previous issue, echoing Soga's appeal for the preservation of traditional material. The responses were printed in both the *Kaffir express* and *Isigidimi,* but the *Kaffir express* included an editorial on the controversy that had arisen. One letter in particular, written by "Fundani Makowetu" ("Become educated, my countrymen") in English, was printed complete in English and Xhosa except for the deletion by the editor of "an unneccessarcy paragraph"; Fundani Makowetu ended his letter, "I am not myself averse to the writing of a Kaffir history, but at the same time I think that to send the *Amavo* to the *Isigidimi Samaxosa* will tend to make the paper a receptacle for all sorts of miscellaneous rubbish. I would therefore propose a certain person to undertake the task of writing it. For this, I would heartily propose Kokela." The editor's comment is revealing:

It is very plain, that there are two parties even among the natives – the one progressive, and the other conservative of the old customs and non-progressive – to whom the times gone by are the brave days of old, – far better than the present. Our sympathies are entirely with the party of progress. There is very little in old Kaffirdom worth preserving – and we think it will be the wisdom of the natives as soon as possible to move forward into day – and secure the blessings which the present time brings to them. We make this statement even while we intend if possible to publish from time to time brief notices of Kaffir Laws and Customs. These possess a value, as enabling us to understand the native people better – and have an interest as belonging to a certain state of society. But this is a very different thing from holding up that state as worthy of imitation or preservation. There is a portion of every nation's history which must be forgotten: and to this, that of the Kaffir people is no exception. "Nature brings not back the mastodon," nor need we try to bring back the sentiments and the rude inspiration of barbarous times and a savage state. There is surely quite enough happening in the world at the present day to occupy men's minds, and give them food for grave reflection or profound study, without going back into a poor and meagre past. But let the controversy be conducted with good temper. [P. 3]

The editor was James Stewart, who had succeeded William Govan as principal of Lovedale after a bitter clash over educational principles.

With this editorial attitude, it would be rash to expect traditional Xhosa poetry in the early issues of *Isigidimi*. In fact, in the very next number, a traditional poem was explicitly rejected for publication. The third issue of the *Kaffir express* carried a letter appealing for the production of songs in Xhosa. In the issue of 3 March 1871 "Umlungu" ("White man") wrote in support of the proposal and encouraged the production of Xhosa poetry.

The *raw* Kaffirs, as is well known by all who have lived amongst them, are passionately fond of singing and dancing. They have splendid ears for music. They are poetical as well as oratorical. They, in their uncivilized state, are a fine, active, and intelligent race of people. Their modes of amusements tend to bring out the fine qualities they possess both mental and physical. But, by our manner of trying to civilize them and making them religious, we not only deprive them of their national amusements, but we *convert* them into a dull, idle, melancholy, and discontented set of people. While professing Christianity, and having assumed civilized habits, they themselves feel something wanting, and that something is their amusements . . .

A word to the Kaffir youths themselves who are being educated at Lovedale and other institutions. Let them bestir themselves and show us what they can do in carrying out your correspondent's suggestion. I know they can do much. As an example of what can be done I enclose a portion of an *Umbongo* which (besides many others) was composed and recited, or rather chanted, in a rich, clear voice by a young Kaffir named "Tshota" at the circumcision dance of "Nonqane," Kreli's son by his principal wife. I do not at all pretend to any correctness in my style of writing Kaffir. If you think the enclosure worthy of publication I trust you will have what is faulty corrected. The *umbongo* may interest and amuse your native readers, and may be an inducement to the youths to make an attempt to carry out the suggestion of your correspondent. The *Umbongo* is very long. I send you only the part addressed to "Nonqane." Should you wish to have the remainder I shall gladly furnish it in parts. [P. 4]

The izibongo Umlungu enclosed may have been written down during performance, or dictated subsequently: Clearly the poet did not write it, since Umlungu apologized for his faulty Xhosa. The *"umbongo"* was part of a poem produced during a Gcaleka initiation ceremony to tshayelela or encourage the dancers; Umlungu submitted the section referring to Nonqane the son of Sarhili the Gcaleka paramount. Stewart as editor rejected the invitation to publish the poem on the grounds that it

is not suited to our purpose. The inducements to young men to forsake their education, and to leave their employments, for the ceremonies of circumcision are so many, that we cannot afford to place an additional one before them by throwing the halo of song and romance about the practice. We have this day heard of a case where all the young lads have lately left a mission and the missionary's care to have this rite performed. Some of them he had been educating for years.

Circumcision as at present practised, is a great barrier to the progress of civilization and Christianity. Though we have not been able to publish the *Umbongo,* we should esteem it a favour if the writer of the letter given above would send us further communications. From his long and intimate acquaintance with the natives he is well able to do so. [P. 4]

There were no further letters from Umlungu in subsequent issues. The tenth issue contained the first poem published in the newspaper, giving a clear indication of the kind of poetry Stewart considered suitable: It was a long, allegorical poem in English filling two columns written by "Broad Church" and entitled "No sect: a dream by the river" (1 August 1871, p. 4). The twelfth issue, dated 1 September 1871, assessed the situation after the first year of publication, professed a circulation of 800 ("500 native"), and appealed to missionaries to assist sales in an editorial headed "Without printing the mass of the people must remain barbarous." The same issue carried obituaries of Tiyo Soga, who died on 12 August. On 1 January 1872, after a long correspondence on the need to produce Xhosa songs, the *Kaffir express* printed a translation into Xhosa of an English song, and followed this in the next month with a translation of "God save the Queen." Issue 20, 1 May 1872, carried a translation of the English song "Speak the truth," as well as an English poem by the missionary C. H. Malan entitled "A few words for the Kaffir by a British soldier." The next issue carried another translation of "God save the Queen," and the following issue contained an original Xhosa song in ten rhyming stanzas entitled "Ingcingane ngeRomans I.14" ("Thoughts on Romans I.14") and set by the anonymous composer to the tune of "Greenland's icy mountains." On 1 August 1872, in the twenty-third issue, there appeared the first original Xhosa poem published as a poem, "NgaseLwandle" ("Near the sea"), in ten rhyming stanzas. Issue 30 carried a remarkable original Xhosa poem written in hexameters, "the first attempt of the same length, to adapt Kaffir to hexameter verse. The subject is – The Past and Present – or the state of the natives of this country before the introduction of Christianity, compared with what it is now. The writer is a veteran missionary whose name is widely known and respected in South Africa" (p. 3). Under the editorship of Stewart, then, the *Kaffir express* and *Isigidimi samaXosa* published the first poems in the vernacular, but their style and sentiment were uniformly Western and Christian; traditional poetry was not to be encouraged. Xhosa verse was informed by the strains of "Greenland's icy mountains."

Under the editorship of John Tengo Jabavu, *Isigidimi*, then separated from the *Kaffir express*, published much traditional material of the sort Tiyo Soga and Kokela had pleaded for. Jabavu, however, came to feel the restrictions of editing a newspaper published by a mission press; in Shepherd's words, he "was anxious for more journalistic freedom and to deal with political questions" (1955:37). He resigned to found the first independent newspaper under black control, *Imvo zabantsundu*, in King William's Town. The first weekly issue of *Imvo* appeared in November 1884, and it is still appearing today, although since 1963 it has been owned by Perskor, so that "the oldest, continuous newspaper found by an African in South African now promotes the ideology of *apartheid*" (Switzer and Switzer 1979:40). Jabavu's successor as editor of *Isigidimi*, William Wellington Gqoba, continued and indeed expanded the policy of printing traditional material, but Gqoba died in 1888 and, in the face of the escalating popularity of *Imvo*, the last issue of *Isigidimi*, number 294, appeared on 1 December 1888.

Under Jabavu and Gqoba, *Isigidimi* carried traditional histories of ethnic groups that often included snatches of traditional izibongo in the style of the Zulu history of the Ngwane dictated by Msebenzi and edited by Van Warmelo (1938). Articles and poems written by Jonas Ntsiko under the pseudonym Uhadi waseluhlangeni, "The harp of the nation," and poems by M. K. Mtakati and Silwangangubo-nye were regularly featured; the most frequent contributor of poetry, however, was Gqoba himself, whose two extended poems published serially will be mentioned later. Apart from traditional izibongo quoted in usually historical prose articles or a few lines of izibongo following a man's name in a report, all this early poetry was generally written in Western systems of meter, stanzaic structure, or rhyme, all of which are foreign to traditional izibongo. Although *Isigidimi*, in the freedom after its severance from its yokemate the *Kaffir express*, did publish poetry and traditional material, with one exception no original poem written in traditional Xhosa style seems ever to have appeared in its pages. The sole exception was appended to a letter published in the issue of 1 October 1884 and written by Thomas Mqanda, who complained of the adverse effect of Christianity on social cohesion. Mqanda's letter was followed by an eight-line poem in traditional style using two traditional metaphors addressed to the editor and warning him of the destructive consequences of collaboration with the whites: "Go, black snake that cleaves pools, return to that homestead where we're being killed. Look at the white man's ways and you're looked at by a breechloader." Mqanda's remarkable little izibongo was the first original poem in Xhosa written for publication in traditional style, exploiting traditional imagery, and serving the same function (exhortation) as the oral performances of the imbongi, but this pioneering literary effort seems to have inspired no imitators in subsequent issues of *Isigidimi*. However, the seed had been sown, and it was nurtured and brought to full flower in the pages of *Izwi labantu*.

After the demise of *Isigidimi*, *Imvo* ruled the roost, until in November 1897 a rival weekly appeared under the editorship of Chief Nathaniel Cyril Mhala, *Izwi labantu*. Mhala had as his subeditor the young Samuel Mqhayi, who contributed to *Izwi* poetry under the pseudonym Imbongi yakwaGompo; W. B. Rubusana contributed political articles. In April 1909 *Izwi* went the way of so many of its predecessors and ceased publication. The rivalry between *Imvo* and *Izwi* is essential to an understanding of the black political debate in the critical years preceding the formation of the Union of South Africa in 1910; *Imvo* under Jabavu supported the Afrikaner Bond, whereas *Izwi* was established with the financial support of Cecil John Rhodes. The exchanges between *Imvo* and *Izwi* are also critical for an understanding of the development of Xhosa poetry. Unfortunately, *Izwi* is extant only from June 1901 to December 1902 and from January 1906 to April 1909, so the details of the rivalry can never be finally known. What is apparent from the extant issues of *Izwi*, however, is that Mqhayi was a remarkably prolific poet: The pages of *Izwi* are filled with his poetry, much of it, but by no means all, subsequently reprinted in Bennie (1935) and Rubusana (1906/1911) as well as in some of Mqhayi's published works. What was not subsequently reprinted seems largely to have been ephemeral (Mqhayi often wrote poetry on the deaths of individuals or at the start of a new year) or inflammatory (on Xhosa-Mfengu relations, for example).

The poetic guru of *Imvo* was Jonas Ntsiko, a frequent contributor to *Isigidimi*, and we have already discussed Ntsiko's attack on Mqhayi in 1900 for producing an original poem that incorporated praises of Sarhili coined by the late chief's imbongi. Ntsiko's poetic diatribe, which appeared in *Imvo* on 26 November 1900, was couched in eighty-six stanzas, each consisting of two rhyming octosyllabic couplets. Ntsiko wrote Xhosa poetry within a Western tradition, the kind of poetry established as ideal by the mission schools and amply represented in the pages of *Isigidimi;* Mqhayi and those contributors to *Izwi* who supported him in the sharp exchange with *Imvo* produced poetry traditional in form, free of classical meters and rhyme (see Kuse 1978:chap. 1). The spirit of nationalism that flowed from black suspicions of white political intentions was reflected perhaps in the appearance in *Izwi labantu* of poetry that rejected Western models in its return to traditional roots.

At the turn of the century, then, Xhosa poets had started using the print media to express themselves creatively in the form of their traditional oral poetry. No book had as yet appeared that included original Xhosa poems. In 1906 the first edition of W. B. Rubusana's *Zemk' inkomo magwalandini* was published in London; in it Rubusana assembled traditional poetry and history, including much material culled from journals and newspapers. The Lovedale Press published in 1907 Mqhayi's booklet on Samson, and in 1914 his novel *Ityala lamawele*, which is set in the Gcaleka court of Hintsa the father of Sarhili, and includes izibongo that Mqhayi put in the mouth of Hintsa's imbongi.

As far as I know, this is the first book published in South Africa that incorporates original Xhosa poetry written in traditional style. In 1927 the Sheldon Press in London published the first volume of original poetry in Xhosa, Mqhayi's *Imihobe nemibongo,* which was written specifically for schoolchildren. In the years that followed, Lovedale in particular published a host of books that have become classics of Xhosa literature, especially between 1927 and 1955, when Shepherd served as director of the press. Shepherd observes that during the ten-year principalship of Arthur Wilkie

> the aim of the Press was, as always, to provide the ministry of the printed word to the African people . . . Two subsidiary principles guided Lovedale in the years under review. One was that books which were to be paid for and used by the African people of South Africa should, as far as possible, be printed and bound by African workmen. The other principle was that African authors should be encouraged as much as possible. During the period 1932–42 Lovedale accepted for publication at its own risk and cost the books of some fifteen authors and some eight composers of music. The difficulty that African authors and composers had in financing the publication of their work was met by the Lovedale Press bearing all the costs of publication and paying royalties on sales to the authors or composers. [1971:102]

No longer did the Lovedale Press reject traditional poetry; it encouraged vernacular literature (see Shepherd 1945, but see also Peires 1980) and committed to print volumes of poetry, novels, drama, translations, biographies, and histories. Other publishers and some mission presses also printed Xhosa literature, and gradually altruistic motives retreated, giving way to commercial considerations. Whereas in the nineteenth century the mission presses would produce only what was suitable for Christian readers, in the latter part of the twentieth century the commercial presses will produce only what is certain to earn a reasonable return on investment. With very few exceptions, this in fact means that what has been published in recent years in Xhosa has been what is suitable for prescription in schools. Since this in turn is likely to be bland and uncontentious in content, written poetry has once again diverged from the oral tradition, as it did for most of the nineteenth century: Contemporary Xhosa poets are in general encouraged to write for readers who are still at school.

Newspapers have often printed vernacular poems in traditional style on contemporary events or personalities, but these are rarely reproduced in book form, although D. D. T. Jabavu, John Tengo Jabavu's son, assembled thirty-one izibongo that had been written about him between 1917 and 1954 and paid for their printing by the Lovedale Press under the title *Izithuko*. Iimbongi like Mqhayi or Manisi have composed volumes of poetry that have been published; though most of the poems are traditional in form, all these collections contain some poems written in Western style, often on abstract topics like love and humanity, often on religious topics or on nature. The late Reverend St. John Page Yako once told me that he had submitted for publication a collection of his poems in traditional style and had been informed that they could be published only if he added to them others in Western style; Yako, who published two volumes of poetry before his death in 1977, was not an imbongi, although he liked to bonga occasionally. Thus, with very few exceptions, Xhosa poetry in print is a weak reflection of the tradition of oral poetry, designed as it is primarily for school consumption.

Outside the schools, there is a very restricted reading populace (no novels or popular books are produced for mass consumption). In a survey conducted in the Ciskeian city of Mdantsane in 1975 and 1976, Les Switzer found that 85.9% of household heads read newspapers and magazines and 87% listened to the radio regularly. But, like urban blacks elsewhere in South Africa, they tended to read English-language newspapers and magazines and listen to the Xhosa radio station; 35.6% claimed the ability to read Afrikaans, but "virtually no one read publications in this language" (1979:9). Only two newspapers cited by respondents catered to a black audience: *Imvo zabantsundu* in Xhosa was read by 39.8% and *Weekend world* in English by 33.7%. The most popular newspaper, however, was neighboring East London's English-language *Daily dispatch*, read by 76.1% of the respondents. The most popular magazines were two aimed at a black audience, *Drum* in English, read by 45.3%, and *Bona* in both Xhosa and English, by 17.3%. In this Mdantsane survey, "87.5% of the household heads claimed an educational level beyond standard 2 – UNESCO's minimum criterion for 'literacy' in any language" (p. 10). In 1976 a similar survey was undertaken in two rural villages in the Ciskei: 78% of the respondents "did not read newspapers, 95% did not read magazines, 91% did not have relatives, friends or acquaintances read to them, and 64% did not listen to the radio. *Imvo zabantsundu* was read occasionally by 19% of the rural respondents and 36% listened to the Xhosa-language service of Radio Bantu" (Switzer 1979:11). Commercial publishers are faced with the stark fact that there is no market for their vernacular books unless they are prescribed in school, and Xhosa poets are faced with the stark fact they are unlikely to see their work published in book form unless it is considered suitable for prescription by educational authorities.

In the nineteenth century, the products of mission schools wrote poetry in Western form in the belief that that was the proper form for poetry; in the twentieth century Xhosa poets seeking publication of their work write poetry in Western style or inoffensive poetry in traditional style in an effort to please educational authorities. Few poets have succeeded in expressing themselves more than competently in Western style: The metrical restrictions are alien to the spirit of oral improvisation in poetry and song, and the structure of the language resists the imposition of rhyme and classical meter. As the *Kaffir express* noted in 1874 in an editorial entitled "Kaffir poetry: Its accentuation in relation to sacred music," setting Xhosa to Western meter and hymn tunes led to a "misaccentuation" that discouraged congregational enthusiasm. Only Ntsikana's hymn provided an exception: "We have heard only one Kaffir hymn, which deeply moved the Congregation of worshippers. It was composed by a chief named Tsikana, who died in the faith. It is sung to a wild, plaintive air – irregular like the words, but without misaccentuation – and the Kaffirs from the circumstances of its composition, look on it with a kind of national feeling, especially now that they droop their heads from the loss of national freedom, and the dominance of the white man" (1 August 1874, p. 1). The words of Ntsikana's hymn are composed in the style of a traditional izibongo, and hence would be free of the misaccentuation of Xhosa forced unnaturally into a matrix of Western meter.

The Christian mission to the Cape Nguni brought with it education and the book; the literate products of the mission schools came to write poetry in imitation of Western models. But imitation expressed itself not only on the level of outward forms such as meter, stanzaic structure, and rhyme; it also expressed itself on the level of genre. Writing provided the means for extended composition, and the model of the Western epic lay before Xhosa poets, even though it might be absent from the tradition of oral eulogy. In now proceeding to trace the development of the epic in Xhosa, I do not wish to imply necessarily that there was a development in the sense of consistent extension of the efforts of one's predecessors. The epic has developed in Xhosa largely as a result of independent creative impulses, since as we have seen there is a very limited circulation of Xhosa books outside the schools, Xhosa books are rarely bought by adults from stores for leisure reading, and in any case some of the poems referred to went quickly out of print. Nonetheless, the Xhosa epic has developed, and it has done so only as a result of contact with a Western system of education. We start with the earliest poetic response to Christianity, the earliest Xhosa poem we have, Ntsikana's hymn.

Ntsikana might have heard the preaching of the missionary Johannes van der Kemp at the end of the eighteenth century; certainly Ntsikana associated himself with Williams's Kat River mission station (see Bokwe 1900/1914 and Holt 1954). After the death of Williams he tried to lead his followers to Brownlee's new mission station in the Tyhume Valley, but died before he reached Gwali, probably in 1821. At some indeterminate time, Ntsikana had a conversion experience that led him to abjure certain traditional customs. He gathered about him a band of disciples who met for regular worship that included some songs and a hymn of his own composition. Makaphela Noyi Balfour, the son of Ntsikana's principal disciple and successor, described Ntsikana's services as follows:

> At divine service he used to sit near the doorway, while the rest of the hut was filled completely with people, men and women. His kaross of male leopard skins covered his body entirely, that body that he would not reveal even to himself.
> The prelude to the service was the hymn, *That Great Cloak That Covereth Us.* And when his disciples had thus acknowledged his entry, he would then preach this thing that had entered him, this thing that hated sin. And he would name what was sinful in their daily lives, pointing out whatever in them was hateful to God . . . This man preached Christ, saying, "Repent ye! Repent ye from your sins!" He preached the Son of God, the only begotten of His Father, the Great Cloak, the true Refuge, the Stronghold and Rock of Truth. [Trans. Jordan 1957–60/1973:46 from Bennie 1935:7]

Ntsikana's hymn has become the most popular of Xhosa hymns, appearing on the first page of the standard hymnbook, *Amaculo ase-Rabe,* since its first publication in 1835. The hymn itself must have passed through a period of oral memorial transmission until it was first published in the hymnbook in a version sanctioned by John Knox Bokwe, a widespread printed version that has now tended to stabilize the text. Before this version was published, however, other observers quoted it in whole or in part, so that it is possible to trace the development of the text in transmission (see Hodgson 1980). John Bennie, who arrived at Gwali after Ntsikana's death, reports sending a transcript to the Glasgow Missionary Society in 1822, and Brownlee's version was published in London in 1827. In the following year John Philip published his *Researches in South Africa,* which includes a version of Ntsikana's hymn identical to Brownlee's except for the addition of four lines. Here is part of Philip's account with his translation of the hymn:

Sicana was a poet, as well as a Christian, and though he could
neither read nor write, he composed hymns, which he repeated to his people, till they could retain them upon their
memories. The following may be considered as a specimen of
his poetical abilities, and which the people are still accustomed
to sing in a low monotonous native air.

Ulin guba inkulu siambata tina	He who is our mantle of comfort,
Ulodali bom' uadali pezula,	The giver of life, ancient, on high,
Umdala uadala idala izula,	He is the creator of the heavens
Yebinza inquinquis zixeliela.	And the ever-burning stars.
Utika umkula gozizuline,	God is mighty in the heavens,
Yebinza inquinquis nozilimele.	And whirls the stars around the
Umze uakonana subiziele,	sky.
Umkokeli ua sikokeli tina,	We call on him in his dwelling-
Uenza infama zenza go bomi;	place,
Imali inkula subiziele,	That he may be our mighty leader,
Wena wena q'aba inyaniza,	For he maketh the blind to see;
Wena wena kaka linyaniza,	We adore him as the only good,
Wena wena klati linyaniza;	For he alone is a sure defence,
Invena inh'inani sibiziele,	He alone is a trusty shield,
Ugaze laku ziman'heba wena,	He alone is our bush of refuge;
Usanhla zaku ziman'heba wena,	We supplicate the Holy Lamb,
Umkokili ua, sikokeli tina:	Whose blood for us was shed,
Ulodali bom' uadali pezula,	Whose feet for us were torn,
Umdala uadala idala izula.	Whose hands for us were pierced:
	Even He, the giver of life on high,
	Who is the creator of the heavens.

[*South African outlook*, 1 January 1937, pp. 15–16]

A. C. Jordan has assessed thus the significance of Ntsikana:

The fact that his Hymn of Praise is the first literary composition ever to be assigned to individual formulation – thus constituting a bridge between the traditional and the post-traditional
period – is of great historical significance. But even more important than this is the fact that, through his influence, a few
young disciples were introduced to the arts of reading and
writing, and that, inspired by his exemplary life and teaching,
these men became the harbingers of the dawn of literacy
among the indigenous peoples of Southern Africa. [1957–
60/1973:50–1]

Ntsikana's hymn adopts the form of traditional Xhosa izibongo for its
Christian material (on the Christian exploitation of Zulu royal izi-

bongo, see Gunner 1982). The hymn is a Xhosa eulogy in praise of God, displaying stylistic traits characteristic of izibongo. Clearly it is not in any way narrative, and merely alludes to the achievements and qualities of God, exhorting the congregation to loyalty for him. We have no record that the poem, however recognizably traditional in form, has ever been performed as a poem. It has apparently always been sung as a hymn: The text alone suggests it is an izibongo. As a hymn, it performs a function in Christian society similar in some ways to that of an izibongo in Nguni society, though its mode of performance is quite distinct.

William Wellington Gqoba was born in 1840 and studied at Lovedale; like Tiyo Soga he participated in the missionary enterprise. In 1884 Gqoba succeeded Jabavu as editor of *Isigidimi*. In its issue published on 1 January 1885, *Isigidimi* carried the first installment of Gqoba's poem *Ingxoxo enkulu ngemfundo*, "The great discussion on education"; no installment appeared in the February issue, but from March to August six further installments came out. When it was finished, the poem had run to 1,150 lines, the longest Xhosa poem yet published (reprinted in Rubusana 1906/1911:63–130). The discussion is held in a homestead between six young model scholars with names like Lover of Education, He Dies for Truth, and Open-eyes, six reluctant young scholars with names like Gossip, Scorched by Fire, and Dim-wit, and seven other men and nine women with similar names (Sharp Tongue, Thankless, Vagabond, Gently, Upright, and so on). All these youngsters discuss contemporary educational practices from varying points of view in octosyllabic lines with irregular rhyme. Gqoba's writing, poetic and historical, spiced *Isigidimi*'s pages in the months that followed. Then on 1 December 1887 *Isigidimi* carried the first installment of his *Ingxoxo enkulu yomginwa nomkristu*, "The great discussion between pagan and Christian." The next four issues carried further installments of this discussion between Present-world and World-to-come on educational, social, and political issues in lines of twelve syllables arranged in four-line stanzas with an irregular rhyme scheme. By the time the fifth installment appeared on 2 April 1888, 850 lines had been printed; the next issue of *Isigidimi* carried news of Gqoba's death on 26 April. Jordan attributes the symbolic characters in the poems to the influence of Soga's translation of *Pilgrim's progress*, which had appeared in 1867. Although Gqoba refers often in these poems to folk customs, beliefs, and lore, his point of view is didactically and doggedly Christian, and the form of the poems is clearly Western. These are the earliest poems of significant length in Xhosa, but they are not narrative and cannot qualify as epics.

We must wait some fifty years before the appearance of the next long poem in Xhosa, Mqhayi's eleven-page poem on the Gcaleka chief Hintsa, *Umhlekazi uHintsa,* which was entered for and won a literary competition in 1936 and was published by the Lovedale Press in 1937. Mqhayi's poem on Hintsa has long been out of print, though it has recently been reprinted in L. L. Sebe (1980) with the omission of one line. The poem is divided into eight sections: A thirty-five-line introduction is followed by seven sections ranging in length from twenty-one to sixty-five lines addressed to the British, the Ngwane, the Thembu, the Bomvana, the Zulu, the Mfengu, and the royal Xhosa house. There are no stanzaic divisions within the sections; there is no end-rhyme; and the form of the poem is that of traditional izibongo. The mode is allusive, to the extent that Mqhayi appends one-and-a-half pages of notes (omitted in Sebe) to make his local references explicit. The introductory lines explain the purpose of the poem:

Zifikil' iimini! zifikil' iimini!
Zifikil' iimini zokukhunjulwa
kuka Hintsa.
U Hintsa lo ngoka Khawuta ka
Gcaleka,
UGcaleka lo ngoka Phalo ka
Tshiwo.
UTshiwo lo ngoka Ngconde ka
Togu.
Ulifincil' ikhulu leminyaka
wafayo,
Kok' usatheth' iint' ezinkul' eziz-
weni zomhlaba
. . . .
Zifikil' iimini zesikrokro so No-
butho;
U Gangath' ilizwe libe ngumgan-
gatho,
UMamkeli wezizwe ngezizwe,
Ikhaya leentlanga ngeentlanga;
Uyise weendwadunge ngeendwa-
dunge.
Mbongen' uHintsa zizwe zomh-
laba!
MaBilitani nithe cwaka nganina?
Hinani na nina ma Mfengu!

The days have come! The days
have come!
The days of the remembrance of
Hintsa have come.
This Hintsa belongs to Khawuta
of Gcaleka,
This Gcaleka belongs to Phalo of
Tshiwo,
This Tshiwo belongs to Ngconde
of Togu.
One hundred years have passed
since he died,
But he is still saying great things
to the nations of the world
. . . .
The days of the The Grumbling
of Nobutho have come;
The Treader of the land till it be-
comes a floor.
The Welcomer of different na-
tions,
The Home of different races,
The Father of different homeless
wanderers.
Praise Hintsa, nations of the
world!
You British, why are you so
silent?
What is it, you Mfengu?

MaBomvana ningabi niyalibala,
Nani be Suthu base Qhudeni,
Ningathi cwaka na mhla ngo
  Hintsa?
Mhla kuthethwa ngaye mhla
  ngeemini zakhe?
. . . .
Nina bakwa Ntsinga ka Nomag-
  wayi wase Mbo;
Nina ma Bandla asekuNene,
Zifikil' iimini zomfo ka Khawuta,
Zifikil' iimini zesi kroko soNobu-
tho.   [Mqhayi 1937:5–6]

Bomvana, I hope you are not
  forgetting,
Even you Sotho of Qhudeni,
Can you be so silent on Hintsa's
  day?
When we are talking about his
  prime?
. . . .
You of the family of Ntsinga of
  Nomagwayi in eMbo;
You divisions of the Right-hand
  house,
The days of Khawuta's son have
  come,
The days of The Grumbling of
  Nobutho have come.

Mqhayi proceeds to appeal to seven different groups in turn to remember Hintsa as the centenary anniversary of his shocking death at the hands of British soldiers in 1835 approaches. The British, a nation of conquering soldiers, are urged to speak well of Hintsa, against whom they should bear no grudges:

> Is it not he who bowed down like a lamb?
> The lamb of sacrifice for the nation?   [P. 6]

In turn the Ngwane, the Thembu, the Bomvana, the Zulu, and the Mfengu are urged to remember Hintsa for his interventions in their history. Finally the Xhosa chiefs are urged to act on the suggestion of Brownlee John Ross, whose isikhahlelo was Zam' ukulungisa, "Bringer of reform," and W. T. Brownlee (Busobengwe, "Leopard's face") to erect a memorial to Hintsa:

> Ross's son says you should build a Memorial,
> I say Ross's son Bringer of Reform!
> Leopard's Face was saying it himself, –
> The white chief of Gcalekaland.
> They said Mfengu and Xhosa unite!
> And organize Hintsa's Memorial Service.
> And organize a great ceremonial feast,
> So that he should never be forgotten in Xhosaland,
> So that his good Name should remain forever,
> Which is also inscribed in European books.
> Peace, European gentlemen!
> You're trying to incite us though we be old men,

Old Xhosa men who need to be cooled down.
Peace, nations, for mentioning you!
It's not spite but glorification.
Khawuta's son should have his own day, –
He should be acknowledged by the whole of Africa,
    Because they have learned about the white man from him, –
The nations benefited, he was blunted.   [P. 14]

The form of this poem is that of traditional izibongo. Mqhayi inter-sperses lines from the traditional poems of chiefs; this is the traditional way of Xhosa poetry. In recounting the historical connections between Hintsa's Gcaleka and the ethnic groups Mqhayi addresses, Mqhayi occasionally falls into a coherent narrative mode, notably in the pas-sage addressed to the Ngwane. This narrative is itself allusive: To it are appended three explanatory footnotes, although presumably Ngwane readers at that time might not have needed an explanation of the historical references; also, this narrative passage is followed by an appeal to the Ngwane people to praise Hintsa and stands parallel to passages in succeeding sections that provide reason for the people addressed to be grateful to or to remember Hintsa. The narrative passage is designed to serve the overall purpose of the poem, to pro-vide support for the appeal for a memorial to Hintsa. Mqhayi functions as a traditional imbongi in incorporating into his poem genealogical, historical, and ethnographic data, and in attempting to sway public opinion. The last line of his poem is *Ncincilili*, "I disappear," the traditional closure used by iimbongi.

Traditional izibongo, as we have noted, are not explicit narratives, though they may incorporate explicitly narrative sections. Jordan is sensitive to the distinction between eulogy and narrative in this obser-vation of Mqhayi: "If he had been able to write narrative poetry, we can almost be sure that the poem entitled *UmHlekazi uHintsa,* instead of consisting of eight cantos disappointingly lacking in unity, should have been an epic" (1945/1973:111). This assumes, however, that Mqhayi tried but failed to write an epic; I do not believe that to be the case. The poem does have unity: Hintsa is praised and each of eight groups is reminded of its obligation to preserve his memory. This is a long poem in Xhosa, but it is not an epic. It consists of eight separate eulogies, linked by the common purpose Mqhayi reveals in the closing lines of his poem. As such, *Umlekazi uHintsa* bears comparison with the early Celtic battle poem *The Gododdin,* which is not a narrative of the battle so much as a concatenation of eulogies of the warriors who participated in it (see K. H. Jackson 1969).

The Reverend James James Ranisi Jolobe (1902–76) was, like

Mqhayi, a prolific writer, the author of poetry, novels, essays, drama, and translations (see Mahlasela 1973b, Scheub 1970b, and Scott 1973). Unlike Mqhayi's, however, Jolobe's talent expressed itself not in traditional Xhosa forms but in Western forms; unlike Mqhayi, Jolobe as poet distanced himself from the imbongi. An ordained minister, Jolobe rose to serve as moderator of the Presbyterian Church in South Africa. He composed some strong protest poems (one is translated in Kavanagh and Qangule 1971), lyrical evocations of domestic life, and a number of historical narratives; sensitive as Jolobe was to Xhosa beliefs and values, the moral center of his work is Christian. One of his narrative poems, *UThuthula*, published in *Umyezo*, "The orchard," in 1936, can by virtue of its length and content lay claim to being the first epic poem in Xhosa. (Mahlasela 1973b:33–4 comments on a shorter narrative poem in *Umyezo*, and Kuse 1978:287–301 translates an epic on Nongqawuse that appeared in 1959.) In 1946 the Lovedale Press published Jolobe's own translations of *UThuthula* and three others from *Umyezo* in a volume entitled *Poems of an African*. This translation, like the original, has decasyllabic lines with enjambment common, and as such clearly displays its distinction from traditional izibongo and its Western source of inspiration. Consider, for example, the opening lines:

Ewe siyawuvula umlomo	Oh yes, in sooth I open now my mouth
Sivuma ngabantwana begazi	
Inyange lomhobe libe nathi	To sing and tell of men of royal blood;
Lisikhaphe kwingoma yandulo,	
Lisikhusele zesingaphandlwa	And may the Muse with me along the way,
Sakujong' ilanga umhlekazi	
Sinqul' izinyanya zamabali	Keep company in this my song of yore,
Zisiphe amazwi olu daba.	
[1936/1957:85–6]	Vouchsafe protection to my common eyes
	As I look up to face the sun – the king.
	Indeed, I pray the spirits of the old
	To give me words befitting this my theme. [1946:9]

The poem is divided into five numbered sections. In the first Jolobe describes the chance meeting at a forest pool between Thuthula the daughter of Mthunzana and Ngqika the son of Mlawu in the Xhosa royal line. Ngqika and Thuthula fall instantly in love. In the following commentary, Jolobe displays his romantic as well as his Christian sympathies:

Their tender souls had shaken hands that hour,
For love is old as this gaunt world of ours.
Our souls were made in twos like unto twins.
In life there is a search, a quest, a hunt –
One twin goes out to seek for its twin mate,
For long ago it was proclaimed and said,
"It is not good that man should be alone.
Now let us make a helping mate for him."
The twin mate, we believe was meant by this.   [P. 12]

After this first encounter, years pass before the two meet again:

The flame however, kindled at that spring
In neither of them was allowed to die.   [P. 14]

In the second section Ngqika succeeds to the kingship, and his uncle Ndlambe, regent in Ngqika's minority, departs with his followers, among them Mthunzana and his daughter. Ndlambe, who has at least ten wives, desires a young wife for his old age, and he sues successfully for the hand of Thuthula. They are married according to traditional custom.

Such was the marriage of Thuthula sweet.
She thus became the wife of Ndlambe bold.
With life around she seemed to be in death;
To her life seemed an empty honeycomb,
Because of her soul-twin, the man she loved.   [P. 17]

The third section recounts Ntsikana's vision and conversion, and incorporates his hymn. Ngqika is impressed by Ntsikana's preaching and invites him to settle in his chiefdom. The chief's counselors resent Ntsikana:

Amaphakathi staid were moved with fear
When they beheld the Gospel's power at work.
They were not ready yet for any change
In ancient order, custom, life and faith.
For counsel fresh in secret some did meet
To find a way to kill this strange new thing.
Alas! this Truth for ever dogged by hate
Though muffled it shall never be by man.
At Babylon was not a furnace made?
And yet amid its flames it stalked unharmed.
To kill it Herod, too, at Palestine
By Massacre of Innocents did try.
At Calvary did they not once exult

With hope of triumph over this same Truth?
And yet it rose victorious over death.   [Pp. 20–1]

The counselors plot to separate Ntsikana and Ngqika:

They said: "They must be punished, as is fit,
By one of blood, by Ndlambe regent chief.
The cause of war, his wife, the favourite –
The beautiful Thuthula – we must steal.
Be sure a war will break as ne'er was seen,
For by our custom this is evil base."   [P. 21]

And so they speak to Ngqika of Thuthula and revive in him

the fire
Of love, which was well-nigh extinguished then,
The forest spark enkindled long ago.   [P. 21]

Ngqika consents to Thuthula's abduction.
    The fourth section tells of two messengers who travel from Ngqika
to Ndlambe's kraal to put Ngqika's secret invitation to Thuthula.

A battle grim raged in the woman's heart.
This day, this night, her life entire was raised
From its deep grave where buried long it was.
The lover of her heart, her twin, her mate,
At last had come to claim her into life.
But woe is she! So tightly was she bound
In bonds of strength which were unbreakable.
She had to choose between this sacred vow
Of marriage called *umdudo,* and her love;
Between her pleasure and this holy thing.   [Pp. 23–4]

At first Thuthula, duty bound, refuses, but after brief reflection she
changes her mind and flees with the messengers by night.

And as she crossed the court of royal kraal
The cock did crow.

Jolobe leaves the reader in no doubt about his attitude to Thuthula's
decision and the spiritual source of his moral judgment:

Alas! Thuthula, thou didst bring disgrace
And shame on marriage vows. Thy conscience, too,
Did witness to the violation made.
In man's association wedlock's pure.
Thou didst lose the crown of womanhood,
And see the charm and beauty's dignity
Seem to depart from thee, and there is left

Thine outward glitter, dazzling still to eye,
But now a husk without a character.
And all the women folk this day are shamed,
For marriage vows are precious far beyond
All other pleasures that may win the heart.
Perhaps 'twas love that tempted thee, poor dame,
The pain of being weaned from thy soul twin,
On altar of *lobola* [bridewealth] sacrificed.
Forsooth, that was a death in life, but this
Is death, and yea, a death seven times o'er.   [P. 25]

Ngqika and Thuthula are reunited, happy for the moment: The plot ("The aim supreme it was to bring to naught the Word of God") has succeeded.

In the final section Thuthula's absence is noted and Ndlambe gathers his forces for a just war. The armies of Ndlambe and Ngqika meet in internecine battle, and Ndlambe holds the day. Ngqika and Ntsikana escape, the plotters die on the battlefield, and Thuthula is returned to Ndlambe.

Henceforth, however, was Lwaganda [Ngqika] weaned
From Word of God. His people were appeased.
But often he was heard to sigh with grief,
And pained at heart, he would confess and say,
"Had I a friend, he would report my state
In heaven." A heavenly vision never dies,
Take note from Mlawu's son, Chief Ngqika great.   [Pp. 30–1]

Jolobe concludes his poem with a vision of the sun of Christianity shining over Africa:

Until the gloomy shadows of our land
Of darkness and of ignorance are gone,
Such as did bring about the bitter wars
Like this great war for dame Thuthula sweet.   [P. 30]

Jolobe takes as his subject a traumatic and divisive episode in Xhosa history, investing his narrative with his own Christian view of the events: The villainous counselors oppose the Word of God, Thuthula is condemned for breaking her sacred vows of marriage, and paganism is but a dark prelude to the light of Christianity. Apart from the story itself, the poem incorporates references to Xhosa customs and practices, as in the extended description of the traditional wedding of Thuthula and Ndlambe. Although the form and conception distinguish this poem from traditional Xhosa izibongo, Jolobe, like Mqhayi, on occasion quotes from traditional poems of chiefs like Rharhabe and Ngqika; at one point he has the imbongi exhorting the forces of Ndlambe before battle:

Imbongi too a string of praises sang,
As he did strut around the royal folds.
In course of speech he said, "What seek ye more,
Chief Ndlambe great his charge has given out:
  Who is the topic of the day,
  The hoer of the weeds of land,
  The heeder not of timely word,
  The grower of the forest thorn,
  The cruel thorn which pricks him now
  The Basho of Xukashe land."   [P. 28]

The form of the traditional izibongo of Ndlambe clearly distinguishes it from that of the Western narrative poem in which it is embedded.

In 1952 the Lovedale Press published David Yali-Manisi's first volume of poetry, *Izibongo zeenkosi zamaXhosa,* "Izibongo of Xhosa chiefs," now out of print. In conversation in December 1970, Manisi described the genesis of the book in these words: "When I started writing it, I was at Lovedale. Then I thought of writing a poem. Then I went towards the river called Tyhume. Then I got among the trees there. I slept on my stomach. Then I started writing. The first poem I wrote there." In this book the poems are arranged in eight sections. The first three sections are respectively poems concerning the chiefs of the Thembu, the Gcaleka, and the Rharhabe peoples. All are traditional in form, and display aspects of diction characteristic of the oral poetry of the imbongi. By the time he wrote these poems, Manisi had not yet encountered Rubusana's *Zemk' inkomo magwalandini,* with its invaluable collection of traditional izibongo of the Cape Nguni chiefs; Manisi's poems are all of his own composition. Where did he get the historical, genealogical, and ethnographic lore that informs them?

MANISI: I got the knowledge from my grandfather, Jim Mcinziba, and my father's elder brother, Mdubane Manisi, and other old men. Then I visited many places after that and I met old people, including chiefs and old counselors, and I got stories about chiefs. They related to me histories of our nation. Then I started then collecting the names of the old chiefs and their generations.

OPLAND: So you didn't get all your information from books?

MANISI: No, not at all. There's a little I got from the books, but most of the information I got is from the old people.

OPLAND: From the old people?
MANISI: Yes.
OPLAND: You didn't get from the old people praises, you just got the information, the histories?
MANISI: The history.

The fourth section is a group of lyrical or religious poems on topics such as peace, humanity, custom, Satan, and the moon; only one of these eighteen poems does not display strictly regular stanzaic structure, and most have end rhyme. The next section consists of poems about people of past generations, including Rubusana and Mqhayi. None of these poems is end rhymed, although three of the fifteen have regular stanzaic structure. There follows a short section of three poems on missionaries, all divided into short stanzas, and then a group of seven laments for the dead in traditional form including again poems on Rubusana and Mqhayi. The last section is labeled "Izibongo-mbaliso," a compound of izibongo and *imbaliso,* history. It includes short narrative poems on Ntsikana and on the Ngwane invasion. A similar range of concerns is reflected in the twenty-three poems that make up *Inguqu,* "A return to the attack," Manisi's second book, published in 1954 by the Khundulu Methodist School and long since out of print. Three of the poems are narrative in traditional form about historic battles.

Manisi has the ability as an imbongi to produce spontaneous oral poems, and his publications display an interest in explicit historical narrative. Accordingly, in the course of our first interview in 1970, I asked him to produce a spontaneous narrative poem on a topic of my choice, and he complied with a magnificent 8½-minute 152-line account of the cattle-killing episode of 1857 (see Opland 1975 and Satyo 1980). On our next meeting, Manisi produced at my request oral narrative poems on the abduction of Thuthula and on the battle of Amalinde that followed between the forces of Ngqika and Ndlambe. In 1974 I asked Manisi to perform a very long poem for me. At first he was reluctant because the gruffly articulated style would tax his voice, but I invited him to speak the poem rather than bonga it. He called for a subject and I nominated the history of his own people, the Thembu. With little pause he started speaking his poem, but soon broke into the traditional style and rhythm. He continued to bonga for thirty-four minutes, producing a poem of 504 lines, the longest Xhosa izibongo I have recorded.

In October 1976, Manisi attended the celebration of the "independence" of Transkei in Umtata. In the stadium in the course of the festivities and ceremonies, Manisi produced three spontaneous oral izibongo, one (quoted in Chapter 6) starting with reference to his local chief, Manzezulu Mtikrakra (fifty-nine lines); one on Chief K. D. Matanzima, Manisi's paramount chief and Transkei's first prime minister (sixty-six lines); and one on Chief Botha Sigcawu, the first president of Transkei (ninety-two lines). Shortly after this event, Manisi sent me a poem he had subsequently written about Transkei's independence, and asked me to see to its publication. This thirty-nine-page poem, written in traditional form as a typical though long izibongo, was published in 1977 under the title *Inkululeko: Uzimele-geqe eTranskayi,* "Freedom: Independence in Transkei."

In 1979 Manisi spent five weeks at the Institute of Social and Economic Research at Rhodes University. While he was at the institute, Manisi produced eight oral poems, all of them spontaneous and clearly related to the context in which they were produced. Six weeks after he left the institute to return to work in Transkei, I received from him in the mail an eleven-page poem that he had written about his experiences at Rhodes University. Although the bulk of this poem is in traditional form, a five-line refrain recurs irregularly.

David Manisi is a traditional Xhosa imbongi imbued with a feeling for the history of his people. On his own impulse he has written in traditional style short narrative poems about incidents in that history. He has the imbongi's ability to produce spontaneous eulogies, and at my request has produced spontaneous oral narrative izibongo. One of these extended to 504 lines and could accordingly be considered an epic; it was, however, produced in response to an exoteric impulse (my specific request). A poem of such length would not normally be performed orally by an imbongi, just as Manisi's explicitly narrative written poetry would not normally be produced by an imbongi in performance. As a literate author, Manisi has on his own impulse written extended poems such as those on Transkei's independence or on Rhodes University; these are long eulogies in traditional form and style, much longer than those he normally performs orally.

Unlike Manisi, Michael Huna is not an imbongi: He has never donned the skins of the imbongi or performed oral poetry. Yet Huna is the most accomplished author of Xhosa epics. His first book, *Ukutya kweendlebe,* is a collection of poetry all Western in form. His next book, *Ulindipasi,* is a forty-one-page poem on the rinderpest, a cattle sickness that struck in 1897. In 1973 his 2,650-line Xhosa epic *UNtsikana* was first published. In 1979 I read the manuscript of Huna's epic poem in English, entitled *Havoc!* which treats the assassination of Julius Caesar and for which he is trying to raise funds for private publication; he hopes subsequently to publish his Xhosa translation of the epic.

Ulindipasi is divided into four sections (see Mundell 1975, from whom I quote translations with occasional modifications). The first, entitled *Mandulo*, "Olden times," describes the abundance before the rinderpest. The following stanza is typical:

Bek' indlebe, mntwanam!	Lend me your ears, my child!
Ndikutyel' iindaba zamandulo,	Let me tell you tales of days
Mandul' umhlaba uselinqatha,	gone by,
Iinkomo zityebile zimbumba	In the days gone by earth was a
zithandeka.	choice bit of fatty meat,
Amathol' ayedloba phay' emad-	The fat cattle were shapely and
lelweni,	desirable.
Mandulo phambi kwesibetho:	Calves gamboled yonder in the
ULindipasi! [P. 13]	pastures,
	In the olden days before the dis-
	aster:
	Rinderpest!
	[Based on Mundell 1975:44]

Fourteen of the twenty stanzas in this section start with the word *mandulo* or *mhlamnene* (identical in meaning), all twenty end with the word *Ulindipasi!* all but one preceded by the line (*A-a!* or *Ewe!*) *Mandulo phambi kwesibetho*, ("Ah!" or "Yes!") "In olden times before the disaster."

The second section bears the title *Isihelegu*, "Disaster," and offers four examples of the impact of the rinderpest: on a party of Arabs on pilgrimage to Mecca through the Sahara, on a red hartebeest fighting a buck for a doe, on a suitor with cattle for his bride's dowry, and on a white couple trekking in an ox wagon. All of the forty-five stanzas in this section end with the line *Eso sihelegu!* (or *Sihelegu!* or *Sihelegundini!*) *ULindipasi, Isihelegu!* "That disaster!" (or "You disaster!") "Rinderpest! Disaster!" thirty-eight of them preceded by the line *Kwowu! Hayi ke khon' eso sihelegu!* "Indeed! Oh no, that disaster!"

The third section is entitled *Iindatyana namare ngentsusa yesibeth' uLindipasi*, "News and rumors about the origin of the pestilence Rinderpest," and recounts the consequences in Malawi of the violation of an injunction against hunting after the "sighing" of a wild cat has been heard at night.

The final section, *Emva kwesibeth' uLindipasi*, "After the pestilence Rinderpest," announces the passing of the plague in three stanzas that are followed by eight stanzas each referring to a social ill that came in its wake: migration, poverty, vagabonds, fraud, assassination, thieves, antisocial people, drunkenness. The penultimate stanza treats the joy occasioned by the actions of the veterinarians at Onderstepoort mentioned in the final stanza of the poem who put the rinderpest to flight with their knowledge. Except for the last, all thirteen stanzas end with the line *Awu! Ewe!* (or *Kwowu!*) *Isibeth' uLindipasi!* "Oh! Yes!" (or "Indeed!") "The pestilence Rinderpest!" The first three stanzas start with the line *Sadlula! Sadlula! Sadlula!* "It passed!" The following eight stanzas each start with the word for the social ill repeated three times: *Imfuduko! Imfuduko! Imfuduko!, Ubuhlwempu! Ubuhlwempu! Ubuhlwempu!* and so on. The penultimate stanza starts with the line *Uvuyo! Uvuyo! Uvuyo!* "Joy! Joy! Joy!"

All the stanzas in the poem are of irregular length, and there is no end rhyme. The form is thus characteristic of traditional izibongo except for the extreme stylization of the repetitions that mark stanzaic divisions. The poem is not so much a coherent narrative as a set of narrative pieces and passages commenting on the impact of the cattle sickness. The subject is hardly the stuff of heroic epics: There are no leading characters, no admirable exploits. Felicia Mundell attempts the following generic classification:

> The poem "Ulindipasi" is a long epic poem written in Xhosa about the Rinderpest of 1897, and can, on the gounds of content and style, be classified as an historic narrative poem. Although one may be tempted to classify it as a traditional Xhosa praise-poem, I think that such a classification would be incorrect.
>
> The poem certainly makes use of many elements commonly found in praise-poetry, but the content of the poem is of such a nature that it can hardly be qualified as praise-poetry. [1975:43]

In her concluding remark, she notes the unusual character of Huna's poem in relation to the literary tradition that precedes it: "Let us . . . see Huna standing on the threshold of an exciting new genre in Xhosa literature that he and other poets will hopefully develop in the near future" (p. 47).

Huna's other long poem, *UNtsikana,* is divided into five sections. The first, *Umnombo wakhe,* "His lineage," starts, in the manner of izibongo, with Ntsikana's genealogy, and proceeds to recount conditions imediately prior to Ntsikana's birth. His father, Gabha, lives in Ndlambe's chiefdom with his two wives, Noyiki the senior wife and Nonabe the junior wife. Noyiki hatches many unsuccessful plots to discredit Nonabe; Nonabe finds solace in prayer to God. Nonabe falls pregnant and requests leave to return home to Zingqayi in Ngqika's chiefdom for the birth. Before she leaves, Gabha prophetically (since he cannot know the sex of the child) names the unborn boy Ntsikana,

"Little pillar." After the birth the boy flourishes, and Gabha is so pleased with him when he arrives with his mother that he presents to Ntsikana his favorite ox, Hulushe, and, to Noyiki's chagrin, makes Nonabe his senior wife.

The second section, *Intlalo yakhe,* "His way of life," has Ntsikana growing up, involved in boyish pastimes. He is particularly gifted as an imbongi; he meditates alone on nature and composes poems in praise of God with the ox Hulushe as audience. He is a peacemaker, calming a boys' quarrel by quoting from the Beatitudes and, by uttering one of his memorized poems, stopping in its tracks an irate badger in murderous pursuit of a boy who had stolen its honeycomb; the boy, delivered, abjures theft:

Wath' akutsho lathi xhwenen' ichelesi!	The hurtling badger froze in its tracks!
Lajika labuyela kwisizwe sak- waChelesi.	Its steps it retraced to Badger- burgh.
Ngenene likhul' igama lOphezu- konke!	How great is the Highest and all his works!
Ngokuba lizukiswa yindalo yonke;	All Nature praises him;
Nezilo zasendle ziyalizukisa zonke	All the wood-denizens praise him.
Yen' uDelihlazo wabuyek' ubu- sela bonke.	Delihlazo swore to mend his ways.

[Huna 1973/1981:17]

Ntsikana saves a suicide from drowning. He fights a leopard while searching for the missing Hulushe, and catches sight of the ox at the very moment that he kills the wild animal: He skins the leopard and chants his poem in praise of God as he and Hulushe make their way home. According to custom, the skin is dispatched to the chief, who returns it to Ntsikana for him to wear on attaining manhood. Ntsikana undergoes initiation and learns traditional crafts and skills: He carves pipes second to none and joins his peers in the hunt. After his initiation, Ntsikana must prove his innocence of a malicious accusation that he plotted to abduct the chief's daughter by hunting a rogue lion reputed to be the devil incarnate. He succeeds, and repeating and expanding on the prayer he learned from his mother he returns to his village in triumph; his false accuser hangs himself. Ntsikana marries Nontsonta, who produces a son named Khophe; he takes a second wife, Nomanto, who gives birth to another boy, Dukwana. Gabha dies; Noyiki successfully begs Nonabe's forgiveness for her hostility, and then dies; Nonabe dies.

The third section, *Imibono yakhe,* "His visions," describes at length Ntsikana's withdrawal into the seclusion of the wilderness to meditate.

He is tempted by the devil, but rejects him. An angel appears to announce the devil's defeat, and then a succession of visions appears to Ntsikana. He sees a Bible and the consequences for those sinners who reject it; he sees the advent of money, Europeans, the railway, aircraft. The imbongi Ncamashe goes in search of Ntsikana, sees him in his meditations, and returns without disturbing him. After many days, Ntsikana returns home. An ox-racing contest is held, and Ntsikana's Hulushe wins, with Ncamashe's ox second, but Ntsikana does not attend. After the race a feast is held. At dawn on the day of the feast Ntsikana sees a light shining through Hulushe's horns and hears a voice calling on him to prophesy about the Bible. His friends summon Ntsikana to the dance, but as he joins the dancers a strong wind arises to dispel the dance. When the dance resumes, the wind rises again to prevent Ntsikana's participation. A third time Ntsikana is invited to the dance, but in response he now sings his song of praise to God and preaches about his vision.

The fourth section, *Izililo zakhe,* "His anguish," consists of Ntsikana's prophetic sermon concerning imminent moral and social degradation. The final section, *Ukufa kwakhe,* "His death," briefly alludes to the acceptance of his message by some people, who learn his songs, and after thirty lines proceeds to an account of Ntsikana's last hours. Ntsikana talks of death, and urges his sons, Khophe and Dukwana, to continue praying for each other; the gathering sings Ntsikana's song of praise.

> Then the people burst into song:
> "Hail, Thou shield of truth,
> Hail, Thou fort of truth,
> Hail, Thou forest of truth,
> Hail, Thou joy of truth,
> Hail, Thou lover of truth,
> Hail, Thou peace of truth,
> Hail, Thou God of truth,
> Hail, Thou Lord Above,
> Thou art the maker of life and heaven!"   [P. 80]

Ntsikana responds with his bell song. After he has made his will, he orders his grave to be dug, and assists the task by measuring himself in his grave. Ntsikana dies and the nation mourns.

> Ntsikana died and was buried at Thwathwa.
> The nation entered a long mourning period;
> The nation entered a long fasting period;
> His song was sung as they laid Ntsikana to rest.

Even today the nations still sing *Ntsikana's bell:*
"Listen! Listen!
We are summoned to heaven.
Respond! Respond!
We are summoned to heaven.
Ahom! Ahom! Ahom!
Ahom! Ah-o-o-om!"   [P. 81]

Huna's *UNtsikana* represents a marked technical improvement on his *Ulindipasi.* In the latter poem the narrative is not coherent, and such characters as there are appear only in discrete sketches; within the sections the stanzas are clearly marked by repeated lines at the beginning or end, and at times whole stanzas are repeated with little variation. In the later poem, the narrative is coherent and the character of Ntsikana is clearly conceived; within the sections there are no stanzaic divisions. The line *Akukho nt' ingaphezulu kokuthandaza,* "Nothing is greater than prayer," uttered first by Ntsikana's mother and then by Ntsikana, and finally taken up by Huna in authorial comment, serves as a unifying leitmotiv throughout the poem, as do the various citations of Ntsikana's songs, not always identical.

Huna has taken as his subject probably the most popular and revered figure in Xhosa history, but he has not followed the received historical account: He marks his independence by providing versions of Ntsikana's hymn and his bell song that differ from the received versions. He makes careful selections from the historical account and alters that account to apply his own emphasis. He omits, for example, all reference to Ntsikana's relationship with Ngqika and his critical rivalry with Ndlambe's adviser Makhanda. Huna also underplays the difference between Christianity and traditional religious beliefs by omitting all references to traditional religion and by having Ntsikana's mother and her generation praying to the One God. Ntsikana's role is thus not to introduce worship of a Christian God but to prophesy, to prepare for the advent of the Bible, and to teach his hymns; Ntsikana is marked as exceptional by his meditations, his outstanding skills, and his prophetic visions. The poem is unified by its Christian vision: Jolobe as Christian author passes negative comment on his pagan characters, but Huna's authorial comments are entirely consonant with the feelings expressed by his main characters, Ntsikana and his mother. Michael Huna's *UNtsikana* is the most accomplished epic yet to be published in Xhosa (on the epic in North Sotho, see Groenewald 1981).

Literacy was introduced to the Xhosa-speaking peoples by European missionaries in the second decade of the nineteenth century.

Their oral traditions, predating the arrival of those missionaries, have persisted, but literacy provided the opportunity for an extension of the range of literary endeavors; such an extension can either draw on native tradition for its inspiration or take as its starting point the literary models introduced by those representatives of Western culture who brought with them the Bible and the printing press.

Ntsikana's hymn demonstrates the earliest poetic response from within the native tradition to the foreign concepts introduced by the missionaries. Izibongo of the iimbongi customarily refer to chiefs and dignitaries; when the tradition of eulogy is extended to refer not to a chief but to Jesus, it is a matter essentially of cultural rather than literary significance. The form and technique remain the same, and no great violence is done to the oral literary tradition.

As education and literacy spread, Xhosa speakers are introduced to publication for literary purposes and to Western literary models. In the oral tradition, the length of a poem is very much a function of the performer's stamina and control of voice in a taxing style of articulation; writing offers the opportunity to extend the limits of the literary composition. Gqoba writes two long poems, in Western form and under Western inspiration. This is clearly a literary development, though it is not a development of the native oral tradition. The long poems are written in Xhosa, they have Xhosa characters and reflect Xhosa beliefs and concerns, but their length alone does not make them epics.

Mqhayi introduces innovations in the history of written literature in Xhosa. Himself a traditional imbongi, he writes poetry as an imbongi. His written izibongo sometimes incorporate the praises of past chiefs; they are written in the form, style, and diction of traditional oral izibongo; and they are clearly intended to be read as if uttered in performance by an oral poet. Mqhayi writes prose biographies and novels, but no epics. His longest poem, *Umhlekazi uHintsa,* is no more than a long izibongo comprising eulogistic units concerning the same theme addressed to separate groups.

With Jolobe we have the first true epic in Xhosa. *UThuthula* is a long narrative poem set in the historic past. Although it is romantic and didactic rather than heroic, it refers to a period of warfare and the great migration of peoples, and concerns an incident that led to war. The literary inspiration of the poem is clearly European, the moral impetus is Christian, and the form is doggedly Western: The strictly decasyllabic line is frequently enjambed, and the first of two juxtaposed vowels is either elided or not according to the dictates of the meter. Such techniques are foreign to traditional izibongo.

Manisi, like Mqhayi an imbongi, has of his own impulse written short historical poems in traditional form and style, thereby exploiting and extending the tradition of izibongo for explicit narrative. He has, also of his own impulse, written long traditional izibongo about the independence of Transkei or his experiences at Rhodes University. These poems, however, remain long eulogies, characteristic in form and style of traditional izibongo. At my suggestion, Manisi has produced oral narratives in traditional form and has responded to my request for a long izibongo by producing a poetic history of the Thembu people over five hundred lines long. That performance could be classified as an epic, although it treats not so much the exploits of one hero as the deeds of a succession of warrior chiefs. Were I to ask Manisi to write a long epic, I believe he could and would; but his own impulse is to produce short narrative poems or long extensions of traditional eulogy.

Huna, like Jolobe, is conscious of the epic as a Western form, but unlike Jolobe he has turned to his own native tradition for all but the idea of the epic. Huna, not himself an imbongi, yet employs the stylistic techniques of oral izibongo: The first of all juxtaposed vowels is always elided, and there are extended passages exhibiting parallelism. Huna feels confident in the epic mode to the extent that he has written a historical epic in English. The crucial significance of Huna resides in the fact that he is the first poet to exploit naturally the native tradition of oral eulogistic izibongo to write a Xhosa epic. With Michael Huna, 150 years after the arrival of the printing press in the Tyhume River Valley, an indigenous Xhosa epic can be seen to have developed. However dependent it may be on native tradition for style and content, however, *UNtsikana* is a literary epic; the epic continues to absent itself from the oral tradition of izibongo, in which eulogy remains the exclusive form.

The Xhosa epic does not exist in oral tradition; it depends on writing for its gestation. It develops only through familiarity with Western models. Early Xhosa poems adopt Western form, but from about the turn of the century, as the poetry of Mqhayi appears in *Izwi labantu*, poets feel free to return to traditional style and rhythm. The traditional poetry of Mqhayi and Manisi demonstrates that allusive eulogy occasionally turns to explicit narrative; Manisi and Huna demonstrate that this incipient tendency can be exploited to produce purely narrative poetry traditional in form. The traditional diction, designed to refer often metaphorically to personality traits, physical characteristics, or actions, is less useful for detailed description and a coherent plot, but Manisi's oral narratives and Huna's written epics remain unfettered by European meter and rhyme. The advent of writing, literacy, and printing does not in itself entail the death of the oral poetic tradition; on the contrary, the oral tradition has persisted for over 150 years and has eventually come to be exploited and extended in the evolution of a new poetic genre that exists only in print.

Empirical evidence demonstrates that among the Cape Nguni the ability to write does not operate in opposition to the ability to produce oral poetry; literacy is only one of an array of forces contributing to the interaction between Xhosa and European culture on the eastern Cape frontier. As Jack Goody and Ian Watt observed, "The rise of Greek civilization, then, is the prime historical example of the transition to a really literate society. In all subsequent cases where the widespread introduction of an alphabetic script occurred, as in Rome for example, other cultural features were inevitably imported from the loan country along with the writing system" (1963/1968:42). Many political and economic factors are proving to be far more powerful agents of change than mass education and literacy. In the final chapter I shall consider some of those agents of change operating on the Xhosa tradition of oral poetry.

8
CHANGE IN THE TRADITION

At first blush there might seem to be as much of a contradiction inherent in the title of this chapter as there might be in a consideration of the traditional artist as an individual. Every Yugoslavian guslar or Xhosa imbongi has attributes that are both traditional and individual – Mbutuma and Manisi are both "traditional" iimbongi, but Manisi's oral poetry is more historical than Mbutuma's – so that the bearer of a tradition is an individual creative artist even though he shares attributes with other participants in the tradition. But how can one consider change in a tradition: Once a tradition changes, does it not cease to be a tradition? "Tradition" is conceived of in varying ways by anthropologists, historians, sociologists, or students of religion and literature; like "epic," it is a term used far more frequently than it is defined. In general, the concept conveys ideas of fixity and uniformity over a length of time. Lord, for example, conceives of formulas as the product of development in a tradition over a course of years; his definition of oral epic song as "narrative poetry composed in a manner evolved over many generations by singers of tales who did not know how to write" (1960/1965:4) incorporates as an element an extended period of time. But exactly how many generations does a feature have to exist in order to quality as traditional? If the revolutionary music of the Beatles is so popular that it immediately spawns a host of imitators, at what stage does the music of these groups become traditional? Time is an elusive element in the definition of tradition. Recently the sociologist S. N. Eisenstadt criticized the tendency in his colleagues to consider fixity and uniformity as elements in the definition of tradition. In these earlier writings, "traditional society was viewed as a static one with little differentiation or specialization as well as low levels of urbanization and literacy. Modern society, in contrast, was characterized as having thorough differentiation, urbanization, literacy, and exposure to mass media" (1972:1). Few Xhosa iimbongi today are untouched by urbanization, literacy, and exposure to mass media. How have these forces affected the tradition? To what extent can modern iimbongi be considered traditional?

In the nineteenth century, anthropologists and philologists held folklore to be modern remnants or "survivals" from a primitive or savage past (see Dorson 1968). Recently, American folklorists in particular have added to a concern for the text that dominated earlier folklore studies a concern for the context, a concern not only for what is said but also for how and in what circumstances it is said. Aided by the development of modern recording and filming media, many scholars today view folklore essentially as performance, as a communicative event. Thus in the introduction to his collection of Afro-American worksongs recorded in Texas prisons, Bruce Jackson writes

> There is an important difference in our approach to art song and folk song. Art song requires that we perceive the nature of the art involved; folk song requires not only perception of the art but also the generating or supporting musical, social, and historical contexts. Folk song is not simply textual, but *con-textual*: it does not exist – save for historians and scholars – on pages in books, or even on shiny black discs. It exists in a specific place at a specific time, it is sung by specific people for whom it has specific meanings and functions. [1972:xvi–xvii; on the effect of context on performance, see Başgöz 1975 and Blackburn 1981]

Alan Dundes traces this altered emphasis in American folklore to the influence of Franz Boas: "Boas considered folklore to be a kind of a mirror for a culture and he suggested that a people's folklore was that people's autobiographical ethnography. This meant that although folklore might be a key to the past, it likewise reflected the present culture and thus was also a key to the present. The importance of this shift in the American concept of folklore cannot be exaggerated" (1975:13). Now if folklore is a people's autobiographical ethnography, then a tradition of folklore is likely to change and adapt as the folk changes and adapts. Traditions do die, of course: The tradition of the improvising guslar is no longer extant in Yugoslavia; Damane and Sanders testify to the waning of the tradition of eulogy in Lesotho; and throughout Africa traditions of court music and poetry have died as the traditional rulers have become redundant in modern states. But the Xhosa tradition of eulogy is alive today, over 150 years after our earliest records of its existence, and it must have changed in some ways over the course of time.

Our approach to Xhosa tradition, then, cannot be static; it must be dynamic. It must also be differentiated. Eisenstadt reacted against earlier sociological analyses in which "tradition was seen or defined as some general reservoir of experience that, although it contained a great variety of components – such as patterns of habitual behaviour, symbols of social and cultural identity, patterns of legitimation of the social order – constituted a rather general undifferentiated whole. The growing accumulation of research has indicated the inadequacy of these 'historicist' emphases as well as of the rather general definition of tradition implied in some of them" (p. 3). His response was to seek a model of tradition both differentiated and dynamic:

> Thus, instead of talking in a general way about "tradition" and its unfolding, one must attempt to distinguish systematically between different aspects of what has often been called "tradition" and to analyze their relation to social structure and organization. Only insofar as one takes into account the interaction between the various aspects of "tradition," as they influence the activities of different groups and societies in the new modern settings, can one analyze the dynamics of the construction of post-traditional orders in their social, political, and cultural dimensions. [P. 4]

The dynamic element is necessary in our approach since the tradition of Xhosa oral poetry has clearly changed and is continuing to change with changes in Cape Nguni society. Tradition is not a lifeless thing; It alters and adapts to new social circumstances. A differentiated approach is also called for, since a tradition is not any one thing but is made up of many things, each of which responds differently to new social forces or environments. Tradition, in this differentiated and dynamic view, is an aggregate of elements held together by a centripetal force operating on the individual bearer of the tradition, a force that conduces to conformity with other bearers of the tradition. In the course of time the bearers of the tradition might relinquish some elements in favor of new elements, with different elements altering at different points in time; thus aspects of the tradition might change, and the tradition would yet retain an identifiable character. At one point, the tradition might consist of elements 1 to 10, say; when next viewed, the tradition might be seen to consist of elements 3 to 14, say, and at another point in time, perhaps of elements 7 to 18 (and possibly at a later point 11 to 24, so that it could have nothing in common with its existence at the first point of observation and yet by virtue of continuities and changes still be the same tradition) (see M. Wilson 1978 on continuity and change in Nguni ritual; and, on sociological approaches to tradition and to change in tradition, see Eisenstadt 1973 and Shils 1981, esp. pp. 12–21).

Stratified observations over a vertical time axis will reveal continuity and change in a tradition, but they are in practice difficult to engineer. Clearly, too, time is not essential to the definition of a tradition; the tradition may change rapidly at some periods, slowly at others, and recognizing this, we are still left with the problem of what it *is* that changes over time. To define a tradition we need to observe it along a horizontal axis, synchronically, at one point in time (and in practice most descriptions of traditions are of this order); thus defined, the tradition may, if there is sufficient evidence, be compared diachronically with its earlier manifestations in order to determine how it has reacted to internal or external impulses. If we are concerned with folklore as it is performed in context, then the age of the tradition is not a factor in its definition. Dan Ben-Amos has dismissed the relevance of tradition, in the (traditional) sense of existence over time, for the definition of folklore in context. Folklore, he concludes, is "artistic communication in small groups" and

> the traditional character of folklore is an accidental quality, associated with it in some cases, rather than an objectively intrinsic feature of it. In fact, some groups specifically divorce the notion of antiquity from certain folklore forms and present them as novelty instead. Thus, for example, the lore of children derives its efficacy from its supposed newness. Often children consider their rhymes as fresh creations of their own invention. Similarly, riddles have to be unfamiliar to the audience. A known riddle is a contradiction in terms and cannot fulfill its rhetorical function any more. In fact, riddles may disappear from circulation exactly because they are traditional and recognized as such by the members of the group.
>   In both cases the traditional character of folklore is an analytical construct. It is a scholarly and not a cultural fact. The antiquity of the material has been established after laborious research, and the tellers themselves are completely ignorant of it. Therefore, tradition should not be a criterion for the definition of folklore in its context. [1971/1972:13; but see Joyner 1975:261–2]

How then do we recognize the elements that are significant for a definition of the tradition at any given point? If we observed Manisi, for example, we might note that his oral poetry is mainly eulogistic, but sometimes he produces oral poems that are explicitly narrative; on the basis of this observation, we might conclude that Xhosa izibongo can be both eulogistic and narrative. But if we observe other poets, we come to realize that Manisi is in this respect highly unusual; I have in fact met only one other imbongi – the late E. G. Sihele – who has produced for me an explicitly narrative oral izibongo. If we compare Manisi with other poets, then, we conclude that Xhosa izibongo is eulogistic; Manisi's narrative oral poetry can accordingly be seen to be not traditional. (This does not mean that izibongo do not have explicitly narrative passages; as we have seen, they do. It is extraordinarily rare, however, for an imbongi to bonga an explicit narrative.) Again, if we observed only Ncamashe, we might conclude that an imbongi is a chief; when we compare him to other iimbongi today we realize that status or clan or occupation are elements insignificant in the definition of the tradition because Ncamashe is the only imbongi who has become a chief and other iimbongi come from different clans and may work as butchers, teachers, clerks, laborers, or agricultural consultants. Those elements that we incorporate into the definition of a tradition are those elements of significance common to bearers of the tradition at any one point. If Mabunu carries two metal-shafted spears when he performs, and Manisi carries two wooden-shafted spears, we may conclude that it is traditional for iimbongi to carry two spears (irrespective of the material of construction); when we observe Mbutuma with two knobbed sticks, however, we would have to modify our conclusion and say that it is traditional for iimbongi to carry two long-shafted weapons, whether sticks or spears, and wider observation bears out the accuracy of this level of generalization (on Greek and Germanic warriors carrying pairs of spears, see Hatto 1980:xii–xiii). Having arrived at this conclusion, we might, if there were sufficient evidence, seek to understand the meaning of this traditional element by tracing its origin or evolution over time.

Which elements common to performances are significant for the definition of a tradition? American folklorists have recently urged that folklore is not merely a text; the text is only one aspect of the performance, of the act of communication between performer and audience. Dundes proposed that a definition of any folklore tradition should incorporate considerations of the text, the texture, and the context of the performance. Textual concerns are opening and closing formulas and the internal structure; textural concerns are rhythm of delivery or vocal effects that would not be apparent from an examination of the verbal text of the performance; and "the context of an item of folklore is the specific social situation in which that particular item is actually employed" (1964/1980:23). Ben-Amos subsequently offered a tripartite approach to the definition of folklore in Africa:

> The attempts to discover the principles of folklore communication in each culture in Africa must begin with the identification and analysis of the cognitive, expressive and social distinctive features of folklore forms. The cognitive features consist of the names, taxonomy and commentary by which a society labels, categorizes and interprets its forms of folklore within a wider system of discourse; the expressive features are the styles, the

contents and the structures which characterize each genre, and the social features are the constituents of the situational contexts of each folklore performance. [1975/1977:166]

We are concerned here with only one form of folklore in Cape Nguni society, what is called izibongo, a form of eulogy produced when people bonga. Relevant for our definition of this poetic tradition are expressive elements (which conflate Dundes's textual and textural considerations) and social elements (equivalent to Dundes's contextual considerations). I should like to isolate here a number of elements distinctive of the tradition of Xhosa oral poetry and to attempt an examination of how these elements might have been affected over time. I shall concern myself with textual, textural, and contextual considerations, by which I mean respectively aspects revealed by a study of the words, nonverbal aspects audible and visible to audiences, and social aspects concerning the situation of the performance; I shall also be concerned, fourthly, with what I see as the function of Xhosa izibongo in society (on function as distinct from context, see Dundes 1964/1980:23–4).

The method adopted is an identification of a number of elements under each of the four categories that are common to most poetic performers and performances I have encountered in the course of my fieldwork since 1969. These elements are called traditional. Thus it is relatively simple to identify as traditional aspects the iimbongi's garb of animal skins or reference in izibongo to people or animals, because such elements can readily be seen to be common to iimbongi and izibongo. We face a slight problem, however, when we attempt to trace the evolution (if any) of those elements over time: We have to rely on extant references, analyses of extant texts, or the recollections of persons interviewed. Specifically, there might be no way of determining, because of a lack of satisfactory evidence, whether a traditional element has been traditional for any length of time; also, we might have to try to hypothesize the existence of elements once traditional that have in the course of time ceased to enjoy currency. Further, the tradition of Xhosa izibongo, as I argued in the second chapter, is complex, and a full treatment of change in the tradition would have to follow the fortunes of the traditions of domestic and clan poetry as well as of poetry connected with chiefs and dignitaries; out of practical considerations – length, simplicity of presentation, and lack of information – I shall confine my comments on domestic and clan izibongo to brief remarks in passing, and concentrate on the imbongi and his tradition.

Whereas it might be relatively easy to define the tradition propagated by the Xhosa imbongi through a selection of salient observable elements common to contemporary iimbongi and their performances, the attempt to trace changes in those elements over time is considerably bedeviled by inadequate evidence. We have observations by travelers, European intimates, and the Cape Nguni themselves, such as were presented in the first chapter. Often these documentary sources do not afford testimony on aspects we would wish to learn more of, and often we must make allowances for the (ethnocentric) bias of the authors. The earliest extant Xhosa poem traditional in form is Ntsikana's hymn, but that is preserved for us, precisely like the analogous seventh-century English Cadmon's Hymn (see Opland 1978), because it exploits the tradition to encompass the new ideas introduced by Christian missionaries; in some respects it is traditional, but in other critical respects it represents a departure from tradition. As a result of the didactic principles of the Christian missionaries who controlled the printing presses, traditional poems were not published for the first three-quarters of the nineteenth century. As far as I can determine, the first traditional izibongo ever to have been printed is a four-line snatch of a boast that appeared in *Isigidimi samaXosa* on 1 January 1883; the first published original izibongo in traditional style using traditional imagery seems to have been an eight-line poem written by Thomas Mqanda that appeared in *Isigidimi* (1 October 1884, p. 6). Subsequent issues of *Isigidimi* carried traditional poems about Mfengu chiefs and prominent men (notably a thirty-one-line izibongo of Radebe on 1 August 1887, p. 62); the front-page editorial on 1 August 1887 included a seven-line izibongo of Charles Brownlee. *Imvo* and *Izwi* carried traditional poetry, but our holdings of *Isigidimi* and *Izwi* are incomplete, so the precise chronology must remain obscure. The earliest publication of poems collected from oral tradition is Rubusana's *Zemk' inkomo magwalandini*, the first edition of which appeared in 1906. Various publications in the twentieth century contain traditional Xhosa izibongo or original izibongo written for publication in traditional style.

The earliest recordings of Xhosa izibongo are those made by Hugh Tracey of Mqhayi in a recording studio in the early thirties (see Opland 1977b); in 1957 Tracey recorded and subsequently published on four of the "Sound of Africa" discs issued by the International Library of African Music izibongo by an Mpondo imbongi and by Mpondo women bongaing the chief's wife (AMA TR-31), boasts by Hlubi men (AMA TR-49), izibongo of a chief produced by three Thembu schoolchildren (AMA TR-50), and "praise cries" uttered by Bhaca men during a headman's speech (AMA TR-64). The International Library of African Music also houses in its archives an unpublished recording made by Tracey in 1948 of two izibongo performed by Wellington Ngunga of Brakpan that were apparently written by Mqhayi. The first publication of oral izibongo transcribed from tape recordings of performances seems to be in Mafeje's 1967 article. The evidence for tracing developments in the traditions of Xhosa oral poetry, then, is hardly ideal.

Let us start with textual elements common to contemporary oral izibongo. In this category we can identify opening and closing formulas and interjections; the six features of content identified at the close of Chapter 5; parallelism and other stylistic traits, including what Kunene terms eulogues; animal imagery; and repeated phrases. When we start searching the material at our disposal to determine the existence of these elements in the past, we are immediately confronted with the limitations of that material. One of these limitations can perhaps most readily be appreciated through a consideration of the two poems Chief Ncamashe produced about the new chancellor of Rhodes University, cited in Chapter 6. The first poem was written by Ncamashe three weeks before the performance of the second, in the course of which performance the first twenty lines of the written poem were read from a printed text. If we compare the written twenty lines to their oral performance, we note that Ncamashe prefaced his reading of the text with a prologue consisting of an introductory salutation (isikhahlelo) to Mackenzie as to a chief and eight lines referring to the context of the academic ceremony Ncamashe was witnessing, and he interspersed in his reading of the text from time to time interjections like "Aho," "Whoa, nations," and "Leliba." The written text, prepared in advance and out of context, lacks the salutation and interjections and reference to the context; in performance, Ncamashe laid aside the written text to appeal extemporaneously to the new chancellor to admit black students to the university. At the end of Chapter 5 I noted that poems produced out of context, perhaps at dictation speed for a collector, tended to lack salutations, references to context, and exhortations to the audience. These features of performance, readily discernible to the contemporary observer, might be absent from early texts because of the manner of their transcription or production, and we might not be in a position to determine whether their absence in the texts reflects their absence in the oral tradition at the time.

Xhosa izibongo produced by an imbongi in the presence of a chief generally start with or include at some point a salutation in the form of the exclamation *A!* followed by the chief's isikhahlelo. In the first decade of the nineteenth century Lichtenstein noted that chiefs are greeted by their name "with the syllable *Ann* before it" (1812/1928:353). It is likely that the imbongi incorporated this general form of salutation into his poetry about the chief in the presence of the chief, but the earliest incorporation of an isikhahlelo in an izibongo that I can find is in the seventh line of the izibongo of Tini son of Maqoma published in Rubusana (1906/1911:265). Mqhayi starts both the poems recorded by Tracey in about 1934 with izikhahlelo. The chief's isikhahlelo is likely to have served as an opening formula in izibongo for some time, as it still does. There are other opening formulas current in the tradition, many of them now lacking specific meaning and used also as interjections in the course of the poem. As opening formulas, they often serve to attract attention and secure a measure of silence for the ensuing performance: Manisi coined the nonce word *letshitshiba* for just this purpose at the start of his narrative izibongo on the cattle killing (see Opland 1975). Mqhayi starts his izibongo on Christmas 1906 with the call *Ta-ta-la-ho-o-te-e-e-e-ee!!!* (*Izwi labantu,* 11 December 1906), and two poems in his novel *Ityala lamawele* put in the mouth of an imbongi start with *Hoyina! Hoyina! Hoyina!!* (p. 30) and *Ho-o-o-o-o-o-yini! Ho-o-o-o-yini!* (p. 60), the latter call recurring twice in the course of the same poem and also occurring in a poem by Mqhayi published in *Izwi* on 4 September 1906. Ncamashe's *Aho!* and *Leliba!* in his poem at the installation of the chancellor are of this order; the earliest use of *leliba* that I can find is as the title of a stanzaic poem published in *Izwi* on 17 September 1884 and reprinted in Rubusana's anthology. Such interjections sometimes used as opening formulas are still current in the tradition and are often heard in performances by iimbongi.

Perhaps more regular than opening formulas or interjections is the occurrence of a concluding formula at the end of a performance. By far the most common formula today is *Ncincilili!* "I disappear," but others are current, such as *Ndee ncom, Ndee ncekelele!* (Mbutuma's favorite), *Bham dovalele!* (used by Mqhayi on occasion), *Itshw' imbongi,* "The imbongi has spoken," or *Ndentsho-ntshobololo.* None of the traditional izibongo that appeared in *Isigidimi* has a concluding formula, though the inclusion in Rubusana (1906/1911:363) of a poem in traditional style by Bryce Ross that ends with *Ncincilili* suggests that it was a traditional formula; three other poems in Rubusana end with *Ncincilili* (including one by Mqhayi on the year 1900), and one ends with *Cicilili.* *Izwi* carries many poems in the first decade of the twentieth century ending with *Ncincilili,* and one written by "Imbongi" ending with *Ndentsho-ntshobololo* (27 August 1901); occasionally one finds variations of *Mvula mayine!* "May the rain fall," at the end of poems, a formula Deakin heard from the imbongi (Mqhayi) in King William's Town in 1925. The presence of concluding formulas in the oral tradition can perhaps be gauged by Lewis Soha's attempt to coin a

Christian conclusion for his poem *Ibala lembongi,* published in *Izwi* on 23 October 1906, which ends *Ewe Ameni!* "Yes, amen"; the early occurrence of *Ncincilili* as a traditional concluding formula can perhaps be gauged not only by Bryce Ross's use of it but also by the fact that, at least in the extant pages of *Izwi, Ncincilili* is never used at the end of a poem with Western rhyme, meter, or stanzaic structure but only at the conclusion of poems in traditional style.

At the end of the fifth chapter I claimed that everything found in Xhosa izibongo can be classified under one of six content categories: a statement of intention or a salutation; praises treating physical and moral qualities of the subject; praises treating his achievements; genealogical information; references to the social context of the performance; and exhortation of the audience. Performances removed from their natural setting, I suggested, would tend to lack salutations, exhortations, and references to the immediate context. Izibongo of early chiefs printed in Rubusana's anthology are generally, like the Zulu izibongo in Cope's anthology, a collection of praises referring to physical or moral attributes, to deeds or to ancestry, and occasionally to current events and their implications. The earliest Xhosa poem we have, Ntsikana's hymn, which must have been composed in the first two decades of the nineteenth century, praises God as powerful creator, healer, and defender who died for us, referring thus to his qualities and achievements and alluding to his physical suffering and death and according him praise names like those Makaphela Noyi Balfour incorporates into his comment that Ntsikana "preached the Son of God, the only begotton of his Father, the Great Cloak, the true Refuge, the Stronghold and Rock of Truth" (Jordan 1957–60/1973:46); in content, then, Ntsikana's hymn is wholly traditional. Ntsikana merely used the tradition of izibongo to praise a new chief. Mbutuma exploited the tradition of izibongo to a greater extent when he responded to a nutritionist's talk at All Saints Hospital near Engcobo with a spontaneous poem in praise of the fortified breakfast cereal Pronutro, greeting it like a chief with a nonce isikhahlelo, *A! Polonutolo!* The performance was recorded and is now used by a mobile clinic on its rounds in the rural district.

The praises that form the basis of an izibongo would have been coined during his lifetime by the subject or by his contemporaries, or, in the case of a chief, the praises would evolve from performances by his iimbongi; since individual praises could serve as alternative names, many early izibongo of chiefs comprise a sequence of praises starting with the copulative "He is." Sarhili the son of Hintsa, for example, is "the black one of Nomsa," "the big python that encircles the Hohita," "ships that surrounded soldiers," and so on (Rubusana 1906/1911:228–

9). The praises of God in Ntsikana's hymn would not have had their origin as commemorative phrases current in the community during the lifetime on the subject, but they refer to the same topics, metaphorically to God's qualities and elliptically to the passion of Jesus. So too Ncamashe's poem about Dr. Mackenzie refers to his qualities and achievements in praises traditional in structure, albeit praises that are coined by the poet for a one-time performance. Normally, a chief's imbongi coins praises about his chief that recur in his izibongo about the chief, as we have seen from Manisi's oral poems about Kaiser Matanzima or Manzezulu Mtikrakra.

The modern imbongi might be aware of happenings in the global village rather than merely in the isolated rural village that was the ambit of his early predecessors, so that his izibongo might contain a relatively greater incidence of allusions to the immediate or the wider context of the performance or a higher proportion of such allusions in relation to the relatively fixed praises he has assembled about his chief. On the other hand, the izibongo of early chiefs might contain a comparatively higher proportion of praises because they were dictated to a collector out of context. The texts in Rubusana's collection might seem to suggest that early izibongo of chiefs consisted largely of cryptically allusive praises. Did early izibongo indeed consist exclusively of relatively fixed praises? Are references to context accordingly a modern development? Fortunately, Shaw's testimony provides evidence that as early as 1825 performances by the chief's imbongi mixed references to current events with the chief's praises: Hintsa's imbongi produced toward sunset on the day of their arrival "his usual public announcement of the events of the day. Mixed up with many highly complimentary praises of his master, he said 'Our Chief is a great Chief, &c. When the white men came to see him, he received them. He looked at them. He shook hands, and gave them an ox to eat.' This was followed by another long rigmarole, consisting of the recital of the pedigree, titles, virtues, and glorious deeds of the Chief" (1860:480). It would seem from this evidence that the traditional content of Xhosa izibongo has changed little in the past 160 years.

In the sixth chapter I referred to stylistic traits described by Lestrade, who writes that "the chief structural features of Bantu verse, like those of Hebrew poetry, are balance of ideas and balance of metrical form. This notional and metrical balance takes various shapes: it is found as *parallelism* . . . as *cross-parallelism* or *chiasmus* . . . [and] also as a form for which we have elsewhere provisionally coined the term *linking*" (1937:307). These traits are a marked feature of contemporary izibongo (see Opland 1975:195–6); Ntsikana's hymn demonstrates a penchant for parallelism. Daniel Kunene (1971a) offered an advance on Lestrade's observations in his analysis of the structure of Sotho praises, which he termed eulogues, and Kuse (1973) applied Kunene's method of analysis to some Xhosa izibongo. There is no doubt that one can recognize Kunene's structures in the praises that constitute most of the izibongo of nineteenth-century chiefs in Rubusana's collection: Thus, for example, Kunene's structures can be seen in the three praises of Sarhili referred to a few paragraphs back, which continue as follows.

> He is The black one of Nomsa, A bag with legs
> In which to stuff the great men of Pato and Sandile.
> He is The big python that encircles the Hohita:
> He who wakes late has missed something,
> For he has not seen the python uncoiling
> . . . .
> He is Ships that surrounded soldiers
> And let them loose at Shepstone's place;
> Hence the Bhaca fought with the Ngutyana.
> [Rubusana 1906/1911:229]

Such structures persist in the tradition of Xhosa izibongo, since iimbongi seem to allude in this manner to qualities and deeds whether the subjects are chiefs whom they regularly bonga or visiting dignitaries honored in only one poem. Thus Manisi refers to Kaiser Matanzima in the following two praises:

> He is The stars who do not agree with the sun,
> Because they are used to travelling with the moon:
> They fear the sun because of its heat.
> I understand that he is The powerful land;
> Though it is powerful it has been defeated by the heavens,
> Because they brought drought and the rivers dried up

and Ncamashe refers to Ian Mackenzie as

> The bull who roars causing all Hitler's warriors to look round
>   about them
> In fear of the blows of the kilted Scotsman,
> The bull who tosses the enemy fiercely with furious thunder,
> Who refuses to ignore a challenge, who refuses to be tossed
>   aside

and exploits the same structures to allude to Mackenzie's interests:

> I am amazed at this man,
> Who is absorbed in shrubs and wild plants,

Because he sees they are the inheritance of our land;
He is a collector of mouldy books,
Because he sees they are rich with the knowledge of past
days.

Contemporary iimbongi are expressing themselves poetically within
the same structures exhibiting the same stylistic traits as characterize
the earliest izibongo we have.

The izibongo of nineteenth-century chiefs collected by Rubusana
are filled with structures termed eulogues by Kunene. Especially striking is the metaphorical eulogue (see D. Kunene 1972) and in particular
metaphors identifying the subjects as animals. Of these, in turn, by far
the most prominent are cattle metaphors: Dozens of Rubusana's
poems about chiefs contain metaphors involving *inkunzi*, "a bull,"
imazi, "a cow," *ithole*, "a calf," or *inkomo*, "a head of cattle." To
take three examples of the use of metaphors, in the fifty-line izibongo
of Sarhili the son of Hintsa, the chief is a bag with legs, a big fortress,
ships that surround soldiers, the world that died because of Mbune's
pots, letters that were mixed up, and also, from the animal world, a
big python that encircles the Hohita, a just cuckoo, an animal whose
hole is hidden, and the hypnotic snake Mamlambo (1906/1911:231–2);
in the nineteen-line izibongo of Ngqika the son of Mlawu, the chief is a
thornless aloe and a wooden bar, and also a little monkey, a black
snake that cleaves a pool, a brown-winged vulture, an Egyptian kite, a
hartebeest doe, and a beast of prey (pp. 245–6); and in the seventy-
seven-line izibongo of Ngqika's son Sandile, the chief is shade for all
his people (twice), a red wall, a fallen branch, the ruined country, a
pool, an arm, and a tree, and also a parrot, a bird, a honeysucker, a
big python the encircles the Ngcuka (cf. Sarhili's izibongo), an elephant, an ox, and a horse (pp. 247–9). Rubusana's izibongo also display animal metaphors involving birds, dogs, mice, swallows, buffa-
loes, lions, monitors, hyenas, owls, and puff adders, among others.

The metaphoric eulogue was clearly traditional: It is a feature of
Ntsikana's nineteen-line hymn (although perhaps understandably animal metaphors are absent), in which God is our mantle of comfort, a
sure defense, a trusty shield, and our bush of refuge. Animal imagery,
and in particular cattle imagery, is frequently remarked on as a feature
of poetry by early observers of the Cape Nguni. Fritsch notes that the
praise songs of the chief refer to cattle; Kropf prints an eight-line
izibongo that refers to Rharhabe as a small moon, a raven, a hawk,
and grass and observes that "ox," "bull," and "cow" have become
titles of honor for people; Scully talks of being compared to the lion
for bravery and to the serpent for subtlety; and Bokwe says that Ntsi-

kana was addressed as "cow that conceals her udder." Strikingly absent from these popular poetic metaphors are any references to the cannibals, rabbits, wolves, and jackals that feature prominently in Xhosa folktales.

One searches for metaphors in contemporary izibongo with far less success. For example, in the two izibongo Mqhayi put on disc in the early thirties (Opland 1977b), Velile in a seventy-two-line poem is a supple thong and a bag with legs (cf. Sarhili's izibongo), and the sixty-two-line poem on Silimela has no metaphors. Of the oral poems by contemporary iimbongi I have quoted, Manisi at Fort Hare refers to Kaiser Matanzima as All blankets look alike, as The stars who disagree with the sun, and as The powerful land but uses no metaphors in his second poem produced minutes later; Manisi refers to Manzezulu Mtikrakra in his presence as a secretary bird and the essence of fertility, at the Transkei independence celebrations as a towering timber, a tree without branches, and in the seventy-one-line poem he wrote for *Yaphum' ingqina* as *udwarh' olumadolo,* "a long-legged plant" (*Senecio latifolius*) (twice), a spear, a spearthrust that breaks the shaft, and a cattleherd; and Ncamashe in the poem he wrote in advance of the installation ceremony calls Dr. Mackenzie a bull who roars and a bull who tosses the enemy and in his extemporaneous additions uses no metaphors for Mackenzie, although Cecil is the *inkomo* of Rhodes and Rhodes University is a deep river with deep waters.

Although my examination of texts for this feature is far from exhaustive, I suspect that the metaphor and in particular the animal metaphor is no longer as widespread in izibongo as it once was, that it is a feature that is passing from the tradition though by no means obsolete yet. The decline in popularity of the animal metaphor might be ascribed to the fact that wild animals no longer roam freely and hence are less useful as poetic metaphors; or, if the animal imagery derived from totemic beliefs, the imagery might disappear from poetry in a society that no longer supported such beliefs. But these explanations would not account for the apparent decline of the metaphoric eulogue itself. What Daniel Kunene terms a deverbative eulogue, a praise whose "structural core is a verb" (1972:296), seems to remain popular, imbuing contemporary poetry with an air of greater realism, a more matter-of-fact tone. I suspect that an explanation might well lie in the decreasing currency of the praises that formed the basis of earlier izibongo and that now seem to be but a vestige; however, that hypothesis is only suggestive, as suggestive indeed as the evidence for the apparent decline of the metaphoric eulogue. A more definitive solution must await the products of further research in more conservative rural areas, especially on boasts and the currency of commemorative praises.

Finally, among the textual considerations, there are the repeated phrases. In earlier izibongo these tended often to be metaphoric eulogues like *inamb' enkul' ejikel* . . . , "the large python encircling . . . ," *inamb' icombuluka,* "the python uncoiling," or *inyok' emnyam' ecand' isiziba,* "the black snake cleaving a pool." To a limited extent metaphors like *inkunz' emnyama,* "the black bull," are still current today (Mafeje records Mbutuma using this particular metaphor in Langa in his poem about Joyi: see Chapter 3), but as I have just observed, they seem to be less prominent now. There are, however, other phrases that recur in the izibongo of many iimbongi today, and a number of these can be found too in earlier izibongo. Phrases like *usapho lukaNtu,* "the family of Ntu" (= the black people), *mabandl' akowethu,* "fellow countrymen," and *amadun' akowabo,* "dignitaries of his people," are encountered frequently in Rubusana's anthology and in the poetry of contemporary iimbongi, and are also common in formal oratory. Phrases like *igwangq' elibomvu,* "a light-brown person," *ufaf' olumadolo,* "a long-legged person," *umhlaba kaPhalo,* "the country of Phalo" (= Xhosa territory), and *thath' intonga,* "take a stick," are also found in Rubusana and in modern izibongo, but are confined to poetry. Phrases like *isikizi nenyala,* "a disgrace and an abomination," *xa kulapho ke,* "so then," and *yiyo loo nto,* "that is why," are common in Mqhayi's poetry, and may be current among the iimbongi today because Mqhayi's poetry is widely read in schools. Whether or not one wishes to call such repeated phrases "formulas," after Lord, it seems clear that traditional poets have continued to use phrases that their predecessors or contemporaries have also found useful, although the stock of phrases current throughout the tradition would continually incorporate new phrases that achieve popularity, and the popular phrase of yesterday might no longer enjoy currency today.

I turn next to consider textural elements common to the performances of contemporary iimbongi, those features that an audience can see and hear but that would not be evident from an examination of the transcribed text of the performance (see Scheub 1971 and Tedlock 1971/1972). By their very nature, it will be most difficult to trace the evolution of such elements over time, since the texts of early izibongo will not yield information about them; we must rely on chance remarks from early observers. None of these testify to the rhythm or intonation of the performance, beyond Theal's reference to "rude chants" (1882:14) and Deakin's statement that the imbongi in King William's Town in 1925 "half-recited, half-chanted the Prince's praises" (p. 92). Iimbongi today produce their izibongo with a characteristically gruff style of articulation readily noticeable in the low-pitched growl that boys adopt when they imitate the imbongi. The rhythm and intonation of Xhosa izibongo are clearly related to those of Zulu izibongo – there is the same tendency as in Zulu performances to hold a high tone until a stretched and lowered penultimate syllable is uttered (see Rycroft 1960) – but they are just as clearly distinct. This distinction might rest in the primarily memorized nature of Zulu performances; it is possible to hear a difference in the izibongo produced in 1957 by an Mpondo imbongi about Chief Botha Sigcau at Qaukeni, which sounds like a Zulu izibongo, and the izibongo produced by an Mpondo woman about the chief's wife, which might be more freely improvised and sounds like a Xhosa izibongo (both performances can be found on the "Sound of Africa" disc TR-31 published by the International Library of African Music). The rhythm, intonation, and meter of Xhosa izibongo await definition; Rycroft's significant findings about Zulu and Shona poetry (1980) might well show the way to future researchers.

If they have nothing to say about the rhythm or intonation of Xhosa poetry, the early observers sing in chorus on the volume of the performance. Shaw notes that Hintsa's imbongi "cried aloud" (1860:480); Kropf says that individual women at dances "shout out (*ruft*)" praises of their men (1889a:111), and in his dictionary he defines "ukubonga" as "to praise, extol loudly and impromptu by songs or orations" and goes on to mention that "old men of the chief's clan, though distant, creep out of their huts at daybreak and loudly celebrate his praises" (1899/1915:42). Scully claims to be embarrassed by the izibongo of an imbongi, whom he describes as "a man of strong lungs declaiming" about him, and who is eventually fobbed off and withdraws "rending the heavens with the clamour of his poetic eulogy" (1913:270–2). In our earliest reference to izibongo, Alberti talks of a hunter praising his successful colleague in "a screaming voice, accompanied by a variety of leaps" (1968:77) and Jordan describes an imbongi who "broke forth into ecstatic song" (1980:134). Clearly izibongo must have been shouted out if, as Kropf asserts, cattle were incited by their izibongo during races. Alberti's testimony makes it clear that the performance was accompanied by vigorous gesticulations, and this evidence of a histrionic performance is confirmed by Kropf, who says that the owner of the victorious ox would bonga it after the race while imitating its movements. The high volume that characterizes the performance of some izibongo – though not the ritual izibongo reverently recited in the cattle kraal during idini – accounts perhaps for the fact that performances are rarely long in endurance, although, performing intermittently, the imbongi may bonga throughout a ceremony; Max Khamile observed that one advantage the modern imbongi enjoys over his predecessors is that he can readily find medication to soothe an overtaxed throat.

The modern imbongi in general still performs in a loud voice, since he must often be heard by a milling throng; frequently he rushes about among the crowd or paces back and forth brandishing his spears. Modern technology, however, is changing this aspect of performance. Nowadays the imbongi often performs on official occasions to which crowds are bused from afar: The greater size of the crowds entails the use of public address systems, and when the modern imbongi performs before a microphone he does not have to raise his voice to be heard and must stand rooted in one spot. When Mqhayi put on record his two izibongo about Velile and Silimela in a studio in the early thirties, he spoke his poetry rather than uttering it in characteristic style. (I have heard descriptions of Mqhayi's oral performances from observers who remark on the ability of his voice to carry clearly and on his dramatic gestures and casts with spears, though Ncamashe recalls that he rarely moved about much during a performance.) Perhaps a "civilized" sensibility also inhibits the modern imbongi from gesticulations too unrestrained.

Finally, the imbongi's spears and animal-skin garb call for comment. Only Deakin mentions an imbongi dressed in a "vermilion cape"; we have no other early description of an imbongi. A photograph published by the *Cape times* in 1925 (reproduced in Chapter 4) identifies Mqhayi as the imbongi who performed before the Prince of Wales in King William's Town: He is shown wearing a leopard-skin cloak and a hat trimmed with leopard skin, holding a spear in one hand. Under his cloak he appears to be wearing a dark suit with a white shirt; Mqhayi wears the same dress (with a clearly visible bow tie) in an illustration opposite page 5 of the eighth printing of *Ityala lamawele*, in which he sits on a chair holding a spear across his lap. A younger Mqhayi is shown in the frontispiece to *Idini* (1928), in which he wears the same leopard-skin cloak and hat but holds across his lap a spear and a beaded knobbed stick, with another knobbed stick leaning against the wall behind him; an illustration in *USoGqumahashe* (1921) opposite page 21 again depicts him in the same outfit but carrying two spears stuck under his left arm. These are the earliest pictures of an imbongi that I can find, some predating the earliest reference to an imbongi's dress but all (the pictures and the earliest description) depicting Mqhayi, who, an individualist in so many respects, might well have established a mode of dress that influenced his successors. This is possible, but unlikely, since Zulu izimbongi also wear animal skins, suggesting a common tradition on this point. When the imbongi performs on official occasions nowadays, he invariably wears animal skins and carries weapons – two spears, two knobbed sticks, or one of each. Manisi's cloak is of springbok skin and his hat of leopard skin. Mbutuma carries a document prepared by a local magistrate explaining that he carries spears not with hostile intent but in exercising his function as imbongi to the paramount chief of the Thembu.

With such fragmentary evidence of the history of the imbongi's traditional dress and accoutrements, it might be rash to inquire after their origin and significance. Nonetheless, certain provocative circumstances in this connection entice me to rush in, scattering fearful angels in the process. The animal skin, and especially that of the leopard, is clearly supposed to be worn by chiefs only. After postulating his symbolic structure of Cape Nguni cosmology, cited at the end of my fifth chapter, Hammond-Tooke returns to the problem of the animal skin:

> In conclusion I should like to return to the use of the tail of elephant and leopard (and also the leopard-skin) as symbols of chieftainship. Why should it be that chiefs are associated with wild animals, with all their associations of evil and witchcraft?
>
> It may be, of course, that sympathetic magic is at work here: the powerful and fierce wild animals convey courage and power. But it is interesting to reflect that chiefs occupy a special place in Cape Nguni social structure. They are individuals, but they also represent in their persons society itself. Chiefs are, in a sense, the tribe made concrete: tribes are called by the very names of chiefs. These animal pelts are royal insignia and represent essentially the mystical aspects of chieftainship rather than the executive, for, while Cape Nguni chiefs play little active part in decision-making, they possess the quality of *isithunzi* (shadow), an aura of fearsomeness and malevolent charisma, that sets them apart from ordinary people. [1975b:32]

He suggests that chiefs, like diviners, who also wear animal skins but whose role is distinct from that of the chief, should assume in his scheme a position of mediation between nature and culture. I have already suggested that the imbongi should be located in such a mediatory position: Perhaps his animal-skin garb identifies him symbolically with the chief, since his poetry about the chief and his ancestors is analogous in function to the poetry that the head of a household recites about his ancestors or that a clan head recites about the clan's ancestors. In the poetic scheme of things, the imbongi serves as a surrogate for the chief, wearing the animal skins that identify the chief.

No modern imbongi can offer me an explanation of why he wears skins or why he carries spears. Performing before a microphone, Manisi brandishes his spears; performing free of the physical restriction imposed on him by a microphone, Manisi uses his spears in a greater variety of positions, on occasion hurling one into the earth before him. Ncamashe observed that such a gesture would call the attention of the ancestors to the point made, since the earth was the abode of the ancestors, but Manisi himself denied such a significance to his actions in performance. The spears the imbongi carries might well signify the connection between his poetry and the cult of the ancestors: O'Connell observes that Xesibe initiates, suffering from *ukuthwasa,* in a school for diviners "carry a spear which is 'like a ring for a married woman.' It represents the marriage between the patient and the ancestors . . . The spear, then, symbolizes the ancestors" (1982:35). The imbongi's spears are curious, if only because the Ugandan *omwevugi* holds a spear during the recitation of his boast. According to Henry F. Morris, the Bahima, a Bantu-speaking people in Uganda, support two forms of poetry, *ebyevugo* in praise of oneself and *ebirahiro* in praise of one's cattle. These eulogies are built of praise names and commemorative praises (*enkome*) recited in a style the description of which is strikingly reminiscent of Rycroft's description of the intonation of Zulu izibongo: "At the beginning of the *enkome,* the high tones in the early part of the line are accentuated, thus keeping up the pitch of the *omwevugi*'s voice until near the end. Towards the end, and very markedly during the last part of the line, the pitch of the *omwevugi*'s voice trails away" (1980:357). A spear is held or brandished during the performance: "In delivering an *ekyevugo,* the *omwevugi* stands with a spear in his right hand held horizontal above the shoulder or with the spear planted in the ground and his right arm outstretched. As he recites, he takes small paces backwards and forwards and marks the stresses with his heel and small forward movements with his outstretched arm or spear" (p. 357; cf. Morris 1964:21). Hugh Tracey's field notes for a recording of an ekyevugo made in Uganda on 16 August 1950 read: "It is customary for a praise reciter to hold a spear upright in one hand resting its butt on the ground, gesticulating with the other. At the end of the chant he stabs the butt of the spear into the ground. This can be heard in the recording. At the end he stuck the spear into the ground and went off, hence the noise."

The similarities between aspects of the Nguni and Bahima traditions of oral poetry are curious, but they become provocative when we read Monica Wilson's theory of Nguni origins:

> I conclude then that the ancestors of the Nguni people arrived between the Drakensberg and the sea in the eleventh century when archaeologists note the change in settlement pattern from valley to hill, and a break in the pottery patterns . . . The Nguni language was formed in the fusion through marriage of

the new settlers with Khoikhoi and San, and earlier iron-age people who spoke a Bantu language. Because of characteristics of Nguni law, symbolism, and structure, and their preoccupation with cattle, I think they came from the cattle people of East Africa. [1981:154–5]

Further comparative research into the traditions of eulogy from South Africa up to East Africa might establish whether the spears of the Xhosa imbongi and the Hima omwevugi are related.

When we pass from textural to contextual concerns, we have to consider the male imbongi's rural performances usually before his chief and often in association with battle. All early references to the im-bongi – by Shaw, Scully, Deakin, and Soga, and in the novels of Mqhayi and Jordan – are to a male performer. Men, women, and children, as we have seen, may all bonga, but only a man dresses in the traditional garb of the imbongi and performs on ceremonial occasions; only Scheub refers to "a female *imbongi*" (1970/1977:120), and I suspect he is referring to a woman bongaing. It is clear from the testimony of Shaw and Soga that the imbongi was closely associated with the chief's residence, the great place, and from the testimony of Deakin and Jordan that the imbongi performed before his chief on festive occasions such as installations or welcomes accorded to visiting dignitaries. After the settlement of whites to the west of the Fish River, even after the settlement of whites in Xhosa territory and the settlement of blacks in white territory subsequent to the cattle killing of 1857 and the discovery of gold and diamonds, iimbongi might attach themselves to whites in authority, as a Bhaca imbongi attached himself to Scully, but this extension of tradition could never become a permanent departure, since black and white society have remained separate in South Africa, and as we can see from Scully's attitude white society would not easily tolerate a histrionic black performer in its midst. It is somewhat easier for an imbongi to extend the tradition of performing before visiting dignitaries or at installations of chiefs when the visitors or the "chiefs" are white: Mqhayi welcomed the Prince of Wales in 1925, and Ncamashe offered an izibongo on Ian Mackenzie's installation as chancellor of Rhodes University in 1977. In its issue of 8 January 1923, the *Methodist churchman* carried a thirty-five-line poem under the heading "The president through the eyes of the imbongi":

> The President of the Conference has a variety of experiences as he journeys about the Connexion. At a large gathering of Native people held in our Molteno Native Church, many tribes were represented, and after the *Imbongi* had given praise for the various South African Chiefs, the President's turn came.

We give a free rendering of the ascription of praise – with apologies to the President for the publication.

We greet thee. O ye Head of the Wesleyans!
Thou honourable grey head,
And on whose chin hangs,
Graceful beards like those of a he-goat;
A man of good brains thou art.
A man of commanding voice to all nations;
Whose voice is heard by the
Mpondomises Fingos and Indians;
Thou art called "Life," live,
For thou giveth promise of everlasting life
To all nations that believe God's Words . . .

Cory Library MS 13632 is a translation of a forty-five-line poem in honor of Senator F. S. Malan, the respected minister of education whose sympathies with the cause of African higher education enabled the University College of Fort Hare to be opened in 1916. The poem was "composed and given in Xhosa by Pumelele M. Mpumlwana" at the Fort Hare graduation ceremony in 1939:

Go out April and let in May,
Star that ruleth our Rulers,
The month that closed the breach thirty years ago,
This May that gave our Land its banner,
That gave us the language Afrikaans;
In England too thou are praised.
In May do we initiate the young men;
Today makes graduates of the young men of Fort Hare.

Awake, Chief Maqoma, and cry out in wonder.
Awake, Chief Tyhala, beat thy breast in wonder.
Awake, Chief Sandile, and stare in wonder
To see this army growing from thy bones;
Their assegais by no enemy can be taken.
Behold the fruit of the War of the Axe;
Behold the fruit of the War of Umlanjeni –
War that began with the snatching of the Court-skin
Shared between Sutu and Brownlee.
Awake Mlanjeni; behold the new doctors who wot not of
  ancestors,
But look with a glass and hear with a stethoscope
· ·

Greet, all ye, greet Malan, the gray-head, the Closer of the
  Breach,

For his name is writ on the foundation-stones of No-College;
For thou, Malan, won for us the smiles of our Government,
Stroked it gently and made it kind so that it gave liberally.
Thou art Senator of Senators among the Bantu people.
Thou art our voice. Hail! Thou Closer of the Breach.
Thou did sift out our thoughts and chose wisely,
    Val'umsantsa.
To-day thou dost initiate our young men,
And a maiden also, my sister, Nothungabasele.
Copiously we pour forth our thanks;
Greatly we appreciate the counsel of experience.
Again we cry:
We thank thee and thank thee, thou Closer of the Breach,
Hail, thou, Val'umsantsa!
Val'umsantsa!

The imbongi who produced izibongo in honor of his chief before members of the chiefdom, or in honor of a visiting chief or dignitary before his entourage and members of the host chiefdom, has come to produce izibongo in honor of white dignitaries in black or white contexts. The traditional situation has been extended to accommodate a wider range of subjects and contexts. So too Ntsikana exploited traditional imagery in order to bonga God, and Mabunu in December 1970 referred to the crucifixion in traditional style and imagery:

Because the beast was sacrificed on the mountain of Calvary,
He was sacrificed as you know on the mountain of bones,
And all the nation said, "Camagu,"
"Camagu" because the sins of the earth have been forgiven,
And all the nations said, "Camagu,"
Because God and the people have been united.

The tradition can be extended to refer to whites, as we can see already in Shaw's statement that the izibongo at the end of their first day at Hintsa's great place incorporated reference to Hintsa's generous treatment of his missionary visitors. Whites have even become the subject of phrases that are current throughout the tradition: The deception of the whites is often depicted in their carrying the Bible before them and a breechloader behind them, or the vast difference between black and white sensibility in white women's filthy practice of defecating in their own houses. But something critical is lost when whites become the subjects of izibongo. Whites are necessarily outsiders and generally transitory visitors from another world; although officials like Charles Brownlee or missionaries might live in Xhosa territory, they are never fully absorbed into Xhosa society. Accordingly, they would not grow up earning praises, shaping their poetic

boasts that feed the izibongo of amateur poet or imbongi; their ancestors are not relevant to the black world, physical or spiritual. In the
izibongo about whites, therefore, the arcane and compact allusions
that characterize the praises referring to deeds or to physical and moral
qualities tend to be absent; there are few genealogical references,
there is little ethnographic detail. The imbongi cannot readily incorporate into his poetry about whites relatively fixed phrases that have
been coined by members of the community to commemorate an action
or a trait; he must rely more on the physical appearance of his subject
as it impresses him on the day of his performance, on the fame that has
preceded his subject.

I have suggested that part of the imbongi's izibongo – especially the
praises – was relatively fixed, part of it – reference to the context, appeals to the audience – was improvised during performance; Hintsa's
imbongi, in Shaw's account, produced a "long rigmarole, consisting of
a recital of the pedigree, titles, virtues, and glorious deeds of the
Chief" as well as a poetic account of "the events of the day"
(1860:480). In the poems about Malan or the Methodist president,
about the Prince of Wales or Ian Mackenzie, there are no references to
pedigree and limited references to titles, virtues, and deeds. The immediate context of the occasion and the broader context of black–
white interaction receive greater emphasis. There is one other salient
distinction between the imbongi's performance before chief and tribesmen and his performance before white visitors or perhaps even white
audiences: Mqhayi's eloquent appeal to the Prince of Wales about the
adverse circumstances of his black subjects or Ncamashe's appeal to
Mackenzie to open Rhodes University to black students would not
have been understood by the prince, by Mackenzie, or by a large
proportion of their audiences. It often happens that the modern imbongi must perform before white officials, that he might have to express in his poetry criticism on behalf of his people knowing full well
that the person bearing authority to whom he addresses his poem will
not understand what he is saying. He must at times perform orally in
dislocation, as a writer does, for an imagined or theoretical audience
that understands his poetry (see Clark 1966/1970 and Ong 1975/1977b),
even if his actual audience present before him during his performance
might not.

The imbongi seems never to have been a professional retainer of the
chief in the sense that he was paid for his services; prominent chiefs
attracted iimbongi by means of an informal process. Before the coming
of the white man, Nguni chiefdoms were relatively homogeneous and
isolated, rarely coming into contact with each other. As Hammond-
Tooke describes the situation, "There was little or no trade between

these small-scale subsistence economies apart from limited barter in salt, iron and ochre, and the only diplomatic links between chiefdoms, apart from cluster ties, were those forged by royal intermarriage" (1975a:39). Since they have become economically integrated into white society, the Cape Nguni have been obliged to acquire money to buy necessities and to pay rents and taxes. The wage earners have generally been the men, who have traveled to urban centers as participants in a system of migrant labor that has left the rural areas to women, children, and old people and that has accordingly had a devastating effect on the rural economy and on family life (see Manona 1980). Efficient means of transport and communication keep members of the rural chiefdoms better informed about events of national and international significance and afford them greater mobility.

One effect of these socioeconomic changes is that few men today follow their life cycle exclusively in the rural areas. This means in turn that the modern imbongi is not nurtured exclusively in the shadow of the great place. He is technologically sophisticated, likely to have lived at least part of his life in a city and probably holding down a full-time job as a wage earner. Few indeed are the modern iimbongi who live near the great place, though Mabunu enjoys proximity to his chief since he serves not only as Kaiser Matanzima's imbongi but also as his bodyguard, having spent many years in the police force before his retirement. As a consequence, iimbongi today are rarely involved in the day-to-day affairs of the great place; if they are free, they are generally available to perform only over weekends. If a chief wishes to have an imbongi as a member of his entourage when he travels, he must find one who is free of commitments. Thus the services of a few iimbongi are often required by many chiefs; the late Benjamin Hoza of King William's Town was often fetched by Ciskeian chiefs to perform at ceremonies or to accompany them on their travels. The imbongi thus perforce tends to grow distant physically and spiritually from his chief's great place, and an imbongi at a local ceremony might well be an invited guest who is not a member of the chiefdom.

The distance between imbongi and great place extends to hundreds of miles when the imbongi seeks work in an urban area. In an urban location, men are subject to a harsh system of influx control that tries to bar admission to wives and children and deny permanent residence to blacks; in this detribalized environment there are no chiefs and little interest in home politics (see M. Wilson and Mafeje 1963). Occasionally an urban imbongi may exercise his talent, especially when chiefs or dignitaries visit the locations. Waraya Ranuka of Grahamstown and Mase Bhuti of Langa talk of performing in their urban locations when chiefs come to call. Thus the able-bodied rural imbongi in a chiefdom

lives at a distance from the heart of the chiefdom and often has commitments that prevent him from attending ceremonies except perhaps
over a weekend; the rural imbongi without commitments is often
called upon to serve many different chiefs; and the urban imbongi
invariably produces izibongo when his location is visited by chiefs
other than the one he nominally serves. A good modern imbongi must
know the genealogies of many chiefs in order to make himself more
versatile. The inevitable consequence of these altered residential patterns is that the imbongi frequently produces izibongo about chiefs
other than his own at ceremonies in chiefdoms other than his own. Just
as if he were to bonga a white visitor, the imbongi's izibongo about
chiefs who are strangers to him tend to lose the intimacy and familiarity that inform the izibongo of chiefs he knows and serves. Again, the
result is a lesser reliance on fixed praises, a deemphasis on genealogical and ethnographical material, and a growing attention to immediate
physical impressions, to context, and to current affairs not circum-
scribed by the geographical limits of the chiefdom.

It might well be in considerations such as these that we are to seek
an explanation for the striking difference between the Xhosa and Zulu
traditions of izibongo. Zulu izibongo about chiefs are primarily memorial; a Zulu imbongi feels that his izibongo about a chief should be the
same as that of another imbongi. Xhosa izibongo about chiefs are
today primarily improvisational (on the terms "primarily memorial"
and "primarily improvisational" see Jabbour 1969:178); contemporary
Xhosa iimbongi draw sharp distinctions between memorizers who can
produce only what they have prepared in advance and poets like themselves who are free to comment poetically on events in the course of
those events. I am conscious of the Zulu influence that might have
been introduced to the Cape Nguni by the Mfengu, but I suspect that
the Xhosa and Zulu traditions were once more similar in this respect
than they now are. When iimbongi grew up and lived in the neighborhood of the great place, when they performed regularly (Shaw and
Kropf suggest daily performances) in honor of a chief who lived his life
with his followers in a relatively homogeneous and isolated chiefdom,
their izibongo of their chief would tend to rely on the fixed praises
earned by the chief in the course of his career. The centralization of
power in the Zulu kingdom from the time of Shaka would have tended
to preserve this aspect of the Zulu tradition; the Cape Nguni were
never united under one ruler, and social developments over the past
century have tended to distance the imbongi from the great place, so
that, free of the centralizing restraint operating in the Zulu tradition,
Xhosa izibongo has responded more to context and become more improvisational. It is possible that Mqhayi, at one time the imbongi of

the East London area and later the imbongi of the whole nation, might himself have given the tradition an impetus toward improvisation, but it is perhaps doubtful that one man alone could have wrought such a change on urban and rural Xhosa iimbongi.

Mqhayi alone, however, might have had a profound influence on the development of the tradition not only if we accord to him the significance of being the first imbongi successfully to bridge the gap between oral and written productions, a poet whose preeminence influenced and invigorated the oral tradition, but also if we assign to him the role of invigorator of a flagging tradition. There is no evidence yet for this belief, but a reasonable hypothesis would run somewhat as follows. The imbongi is intimately connected with a chief and gravitates toward a focus of power; a strong chief will attract iimbongi, but a chief without authority is unlikely to elicit eulogies. If the chieftainship is strong, the tradition transmitted by the imbongi will flourish; when the chieftainship is weak, the imbongi will disappear. In his study of local government, Hammond-Tooke observed that the Transkeian chiefdoms lacked political unity and operated independently until a period of annexation between 1879 and 1894. After annexation, the formerly independent chiefdoms were merged for purposes of administration:

> This process saw radical changes in the nature of the political units and involved chiefs and headmen in a drastic redefinition of their roles. From self-governing communities the chiefdoms became, in effect, units of local government, and even here, as we shall see, they tended to be by-passed in favour of the locations into which the Transkei as a whole was divided. Rule by chiefs gave way to a system of direct rule through magistrates who relied on the location headmen as their main means of liaison with the tribespeople . . . In 1951 the Bantu Authorities Act was passed, and introduced what approximates to a form of indirect rule, endeavouring to re-establish the power of the chiefs and the integrity of the old chiefdoms, and in 1963 a "self-governing" Legislative Assembly came into being. [1975:2]

We have seen that early missionaries and some colonial administrators like Sir George Grey wished to break the power of the chiefs in the interests of peace, and we have remarked on the mutual hostility between chiefs and missionary educators and the opposition of missionaries to what they held to be pagan practices, which included the production of traditional poetry. In a period when Christianity was spreading while the power of the chiefs was waning, what was happening to the imbongi? If (and the hypothetical character of this paragraph must

again be stressed) the tradition propagated by the imbongi was undermined as the power of the chiefs was undermined by political and
religious forces, then Mqhayi the traditionalist growing up in the conservative Centane district and drawing perhaps on the traditions of
personal and clan poetry (which would not be linked to the fortunes of
the chieftainship) might well have served to resurrect a moribund institution. If Mqhayi, the imbongi of the whole nation, was primarily an
improviser, his preeminence might well have served to redirect the
current of tradition in this regard. The evidence for such a scenario is
at the moment entirely lacking, but the hypothesis might well repay
further investigation.

To retreat slightly from the airy realms of hypothesis, there is some
evidence that the imbongi was a prominent figure in times of war.
Although there are descriptions of poetry and song in the context of
battle, we have no descriptions of iimbongi exhorting troops. However, Soga remarks that the imbongi "praised when there was no war
in preparation for a time when war broke out" (Cory MS 16369), and
many modern iimbongi assert that their predecessors were prominent
in times of war. Of course, the last war fought between the Cape
Nguni and the whites on the eastern frontier ended in 1878, so these
(consistent) assertions of contemporary iimbongi can at best be based
on oral tradition transmitted over a century. A black contingent was
sent to the Mediterranean in World War I, and we do have two poems
by Mqhayi inciting the troops through the medium of print and commemorating their tragic end in the troopship *Mendi* ("Umkhosi wemi-
daka" and "Ukutshona kukaMendi" both reprinted in *Ityala lamawele;*
see Bennie 1936 for translations).

The evidence for the imbongi's poetic participation in battle is
slight, but the idea itself is plausible in view of the imbongi's general
role as inciter and the use of izibongo, especially when women tshayelela, to encourage men in dancing or stick fighting. Battle on a large
scale is no longer a feature of Cape Nguni life, although faction fights
between men or youths armed with two sticks (one held in the left
hand used like a shield for blocking and the other a striking stick
wielded by the right hand) are still common and frequently lead to
fatalities. One might then remark that izibongo in the context of
battle, like izibongo in the context of the hunt clearly attested to by
Alberti and Kropf, or in the context of cattle racing (see Kropf), are
no longer as common as in former times because hunting and armed
combat and cattle racing are no longer current pastimes. I have suggested that contemporary izibongo are not as densely populated by
animal metaphors as in the past; if the presence of those images in fact
derived from or was nourished by the production of izibongo in the

contexts of the hunt and cattle races, their relative absence in izibongo today might be ascribed to the disappearance of hunting and cattle racing. Nonetheless, just as animal and especially cattle imagery still persists, so too the modern imbongi occasionally exploits battle imagery in his poetry. Mpumlwana at the Fort Hare graduation ceremony in 1939 exhorts the warrior chiefs Maqoma, Tyhali, and Sandile to awake and witness the invincible army of graduands who are the fruit of the frontier wars; Manisi incites black schoolchildren in Grahamstown in 1979 to take up arms in the struggle for their rights as their heroic ancestors did, although this time their weapon must be not a spear but education. It might well be, then, that though certain pastimes are no longer part of the Cape Nguni way of life, the former production of izibongo in the context of those obsolete pastimes has left its traces in the battle and animal imagery of modern izibongo.

Finally, we turn to the many functions of the imbongi. There is no reason why some of these functions should change over time: A nineteenth-century imbongi may act as a herald for his chief just as a twentieth-century imbongi may do, even if the latter might now sit on the hood of his chief's car declaiming his izibongo as he rides through an urban location. The fullest study of Xhosa oral poetry in an urban setting is that undertaken by Wainwright, who collected over 250 izibongo from migrant laborers working on gold and platinum mines in the Transvaal, and interviewed the poets' colleagues on the interpretation and significance of the poetry. Few of the poets interviewed by Wainright served as iimbongi at home; most of the poems were on subjects of the poets' own choice produced at Wainright's request. One by Victor Thubeni lamented the erosion of traditional custom and the assimilation of European ways:

No! No! men,
Modernization has finished me off!
Because I once saw miracles.
I once saw a man wearing a table napkin
Sitting at a table eating with a panga and a fork.
Let us leave it at that, men.
Because were I to tell women to change their ways
And wear traditional leather skirts
They would be able to outrun us!
But they flaunt themselves perching atop of high heels
Oh! No! Men!
I once saw a woman wearing a "double" on her head
This hat was called a wig.
What is it called by Xhosa men?

Alas! Gone are the nations while I watch!
No! Your preaching amazes me,
Child of the White man
Boy of Verwoerd, you have power
Because you destroy nations
While just sitting in Pretoria!
Are the Xhosa aware
That people are still betrothed?
Are we still aware that circumcision is still practised?
(Today) those who are circumcised head for the hospitals to
    consult doctors.
Leave me alone, child of overseas girls.
I too have left you.
Ndee-vovo-lo-lo-o-o-!   [1979:57]

So too Mqhayi in a recording studio lamented the fact that Velile's
subjects in urban centers had sent him on his initiation cash in place of
the traditional gift of cattle:

Men of Port Elizabeth, you have given good presents,
You have given fine presents to your chief.
A small matter still puzzles us:
We do not see the colours of your cattle.
People of Grahamstown and Cape Town, we thank you too,
Although we do not see the colours of your cattle.
                                        [Opland 1977b:33]

Mbutuma also commented on the erosion of custom in Langa. How
have urbanization and the strange life-style on the mines and in the
urban locations affected the function of Xhosa izibongo?

Wainwright notes that the imbongi on the mines (like the imbongi in
any urban location, as we have seen) has limited opportunity to practice his craft, and because of his commitments, his poetry becomes as
informal and unofficial as that of any other Xhosa poet:

Of the small number of *iimbongi* on the mines who operate as
official *iimbongi* when at home, only a few had their traditional robes of office with them on the mines. One such *imbongi* who did, Victor Thubeni, would wear his traditional
attire and praise visiting Black dignitaries when they came to
the mine or when they arrived at Jan Smuts airport.

However, the mine *imbongi* like any other worker, has a
full-time job to do. Thus the extent to which he can operate as
an *imbongi* while at work is naturally limited by his working
commitments. He is thus not often in the public eye and,

moreover, having come to the mine to earn money he may, unlike at home, keep a low profile. The migratory nature of the labour force also contributes to the lack of opportunity to encounter many true *iimbongi* on mines.

A further distinction that may be drawn between "home" and "mine" *iimbongi* is that the mine *imbongi*'s status is primarily that of a worker and thus his activities are largely unofficial and informal. This factor affects the official *imbongi* rather than the amateur whose praise poetry at home is also largely informal. [1979:15]

One effect of this withdrawal of the imbongi from a position of prominence and the collapsing of the distinction between him and other poets is that the poetry of ordinary men who are not iimbongi at home tends to assume some of the functions of the rural imbongi's poetry. Using the term "imbongi" now to refer to all poets he has interviewed, whether everyday poets or iimbongi, Wainwright finds that miners perceive the role of the poet on the mines to be

> as a mobilizer of public opinion and as a judge or moral guardian. These two aspects are distinct. On the one hand the *imbongi* seeks, in his praises, to reflect what others feel and think, whereas on the other he reminds them of "good" and "moral" behaviour. In the words of the respondents "he speaks of satisfactory things in the hostel" and also "praises the good things in life." It was pointed out by men interviewed that the *imbongi* reinforced the *imithetho* (rules) of the mine, that he discouraged crime, violence and excessive materialism. In this way the *imbongi* acted as a force for social harmony and consensus by verbalizing and thus reinforcing norms and values. One man likened the *imbongi* to a minister of religion, saying that praise poetry was akin to "the work of a priest who prays at the beginning of every meeting. He brings peace among people." Another theme that emerged was the role of the *imbongi* in reinforcing traditionalist norms in keeping with his association with Xhosa traditions. [Pp. 23–4]

Two aspects of mine poetry that exaggerate tendencies in rural poetry are probably a product of the tense, all-male society: Wainwright observes that the mine poet serves to relieve social pressures by amusing or entertaining his audiences, with poetry often far more boldly obscene than seems to be customary in rural areas (pp. 138–63); obscenity is found in rural poetry, as we have seen (for sexual explicitness in Zulu poetry see Gunner 1979), and the imbongi does on occasion amuse his audiences, but entertainment is not as marked a feature of his role in the rural areas as on the mines, and rural poetic obscenity is perhaps not as concentrated or scatological as mine poetry seems to be, although we have limited information on which to base such a comparison.

By and large, then, Wainwright's investigations lead to the conclusion that poetry on the mines serves much the same functions as poetry of the rural imbongi. Poets on the mines are all everyday poets, since none is officially recognized by a management lacking in understanding of the poetic tradition, and they produce boasts and poems about their friends and colleagues; apparently many poets assume to themselves the roles of the rural imbongi, praising or citicizing those in authority, inciting, upholding the norm of traditional behavior, mediating, and expressing public opinion (on continuities and discontinuities between rural and urban religious beliefs, see Pauw 1975 and West 1975).

Strangely enough, it is in the rural areas and the homelands of Ciskei and Transkei that the function of the imbongi's poetry seems subject to greatest pressures for change. I argued in the fifth chapter that izibongo served a ritual function in communicating with the ancestors, and that the imbongi's poetry about a sacral chief ensured the well-being of the chiefdom by ensuring the protective sympathy of the chief's ancestors. That Xhosa izibongo of ancestors or clans have a ritual function few would deny; however, only Ncamashe is prepared to attribute such a dimension to the Xhosa imbongi's izibongo. The system I sketched in Chapter 5 for the poetry of the Xhosa imbongi drew on Zulu evidence, including Chief Gatsha Buthelezi's assertion that all Zulu izibongo are ritual, and on the role of Xhosa clan and personal poetry in ancestor veneration. I suspect that the Cape Nguni imbongi was once, like the Zulu imbongi, a ritual figure, though with the spread of Christianity this function might now have been usurped.

Izibongo of chiefs in Rubusana's anthology often contain criticism as well as praise, and commentary on current events. The imbongi's function as truth teller or soothsayer, his freedom to speak his mind, seems long to have been a constituent element in his tradition. So powerful is the imbongi's license to speak his mind with impunity that, as we have seen, Manisi felt free to express criticism of Kaiser Matanzima and the assumption of independence for Transkei in front of Matanzima at the independence celebration in Umtata in 1976. In 1977 the new republic of Transkei issued the Public Security Act with ominous implications: Section 12 made it an offense for any person "to make any statement, verbally or in writing or perform any act which is intended or likely to have the effect of subverting or interfering with the authority of any chief or headman." It also became an offense to treat any chief or headman "with disrespect, contempt or ridicule or fail or neglect to show that respect and obedience and to render such services to such chief or headman as should be shown or rendered in accordance with customary law" (quoted from Streek and Wicksteed 1981:42). Free speech was threatened and the imbongi's role as fearless soothsayer with it, but would action ever be taken against an imbongi in violation of custom and precedent? Perhaps not in a traditional society, but in a traditional society unhappily wedded to a Westminster system of politics, where political power can override the customary authority of chiefs, especially in a political system derived from that of South Africa, with its punitive security legislation, anything can happen, and in 1979 something unheard of did happen.

Kaiser Matanzima, first prime minister of Transkei and now its president, who was himself created a "paramount chief" of the emigrant Thembu by Pretoria in violation of custom (since the Thembu willingly offered loyalty to their legitimate paramount, Sabata Dalindyebo), had long been troubled by Sabata's political opposition to him and his policies. Sabata, according to custom Kaiser's senior, was a member of the opposition party, refused Kaiser's invitation to become Transkei's first president, had his parliamentary allowance removed by Kaiser, and by 1979 had become leader of the opposition. On 19 July 1979 the head of Transkei's security police announced that Sabata had been charged under the Public Security Act and the Constitution Act, which made it an offense to violate the dignity or injure the reputation of the state president (by that time Kaiser Matanzima himself). The paramount chief of the Thembu was imprisoned and released a few days later. Testifying at his trial the following year, Sabata said that he had written a letter to Kaiser following a dream in prison: "In the dream I saw my ancestors looked very angry and they told me to go to Kaiser and tell him the place I was in was not suitable for a man of my status. I visualised that, as my ancestors had said, the prison in which the government had placed me was unsuitable. I said in the letter I was remorseful because as a King of a nation, the place was unfit for me. The ancestors of Daliwonga Kaiser Matanzima and mine are the same" (*Daily dispatch*, 21 March 1980). Chief Sabata was found guilty and fined R700 or eighteen months' imprisonment. In August 1980 Prime Minister George Matanzima announced that the cabinet had asked his brother, President Kaiser Matanzima, to depose Sabata as paramount chief as a consequence of his conviction. Later that month Sabata Dalindyebo left his great place, Bumbane, and his country as an exile. Tensions persist. In January 1981 a fifty-six-year-old vegetable vendor was detained for twenty-two days by the security police and charged under section 12 of the Public Security Act for insulting Sabata's successor. Evidence was produced at her trial that she left Paramount Chief Bambilanga Dalindyebo's offices "shouting: 'Bambilanga will defecate, this is not his great place, Bumbane' " (*Daily dispatch* 12 January 1982).

This narrative demonstrates the defenselessness of custom in the face of a powerful antagonistic state, but the story is also told because it involves an imbongi. On 30 July 1979, crowds gathered outside the Umtata magistrate's court to protest the arrest of Sabata and to demand his release.

> The police did not act immediately against the crowd, but as more and more Thembus, attracted by Sabata's mbongi (praise singer), Mncedisi Qangule – who was singing about Sabata's arrest and detention – interrupted court proceedings, they came up and told him to stop praise-singing and leave the area. Meanwhile, members of Sabata's family were singing and waving clenched fists in the air and the crowd was swelling as Thembu workers, now on their lunch-hour, began to join the angry crowd. The police eventually dispersed the crowd peacefully. [Streek and Wicksteed 1981:314]

The following day, 31 July, the East London *Daily dispatch* carried a story of the incident alongside a picture of Qangule, wearing a hat and cloak of animal skin and carrying a beaded knobbed stick, performing before the crowd at the magistrate's offices; the report gave fuller details of Qangule's role in the proceedings.

> The Thembus who thronged the main entrance of the court building listened to Chief Sabata's praise singer, Mr Mncedisi Qangule, sing about the arrest.
>
> When the Prime Minister, Chief George Matanzima, descended the steps of the Palace of Justice after a meeting with Transkei magistrates, one of Chief Sabata's wives, Mrs NoCanada Dalindyebo, caught hold of his hand, knelt and said: "Umzimvubu [Chief George's isikhahlelo], where is my husband, Jonguhlanga [Chief Sabata's isikhahlelo]?
>
> "We demand his release. We spent sleepless nights not knowing where our paramount chief is."
>
> Chief Matanzima replied: "This is not a place where we should discuss this matter."
>
> "I will not go to you," said Mrs Dalindyebo.
>
> Chief Matanzima, who was with the Minister of Justice, Mr Digby Koyana, left in his official car.

Mr Qangule said at the top of his voice: "All is not well in Transkei. We call upon the ancestors to come and arbitrate." The crowd of Tembus chorused: "Ah, Jonguhlanga!" Tembu workers swelled the crowd during the lunch hour . . .

The Umtata police station commander, Captain C. M. Vuke, made his way through the crowd and warned Mr Qangule to be quiet because he was disturbing people in their offices.

Captain Vuke told the crowd to disperse or face action. The Tembus dispersed and formed groups.

The following day Qangule was back with the crowds outside the courthouse, where he "ran a commentary of the circumstances of the King's arrest, saying the incident marked the beginning of the end for peace in Transkei" (Streek and Wicksteed 1981:315, quoting *Post*, 1 August 1979). The police continued to harass Qangule: In October he was interrupted during a performance. The *Daily dispatch* carried the story under the heading "Sabata's praise singer told to stop singing":

UMTATA–The praise singer of Paramount Chief Sabata Dalindyebo was detained by Security Police on Saturday when he was invited to sing praises at the centenary celebrations of St John's College here.

He was released on Monday after questioning.

Mr Professor Mncedisi Qangule said he was taken at the school premises by two members of the Security Police to the offices at Botha Sigcau and from there to Umtata Prison where he was detained incommunicado.

Colonel Martin Ngceba, Acting Commissioner of Police and head of Security Police, yesterday confirmed Mr Qangule was detained for questioning on Saturday and released on Monday.

"All that I know is that Mr Qangule was missing in Transkei and his whereabouts were not known. When the Security Police found him they took him for questioning," Colonel Ngceba said.

Mr Qangule said he was invited to sing praises on the educational achievements of the school for the past hundred years.

"At the offices of the security police I was warned not to sing praises anymore. When I was locked into my cell at the Wellington Prison, I continued singing praises about my detention.

"This precious talent is bestowed on me by God. Nobody can arrogate to himself the dubious authority of telling me not to use it," Mr Qangule said. [24 October 1979]

Nor is Qangule the only imbongi whose performance has been interrupted by police action in the newly independent Transkei; curiously
enough, Nelson Mabunu, Kaiser Matanzima's bodyguard and at one
time a sergeant in the South African security police, was interrupted at
this sensitive time for attracting an audience during an izibongo praising
Matanzima's claim for more land from the South African government:

> UMTATA – The praise singer of President Kaiser Matanzima
> of Transkei, Mr Nelson Mabunu, was stopped singing praises
> yesterday at the Palace of Justice, after he was inspired by a
> story in the Daily Dispatch that Transkei might get East Gri-
> qualand, and crowds milled around him.
>
> "Where there is smoke there is fire. Prophets of doom said
> Paramount Chief Kaiser Matanzima was day-dreaming when
> he claimed East Griqualand," Mr Mabunu said.
>
> Dressed in his traditional regalia he sang:
>
> "Paramount Chief Matanzima used ink and a pen as a weap-
> on to get Port St Johns and the same thing has happened to
> East Griqualand [note the battle imagery]. Some Whites in
> East Griqualand said Chief Matanzima's claim was a pipe-
> dream but this will be a reality."
>
> When the crowds swelled around Mr Mabunu the branch
> commander of the Security Police here, Lieutenant D. Lavisa,
> arrived. Mr Mabunu was told to stop singing and left in a car.
>
> Later Mr Mabunu said Lieutenant Lavisa ordered him to
> stop because he was disturbing officials working.
>
> "I was inspired by the headlines in the Daily Dispatch."
>
> Lieutenant Lavisa said he was not in a position to comment.
> [*Daily dispatch*, 25 September 1979]

Mabunu's izibongo proved to be a trifle premature: South Africa has
to date refused to cede East Griqualand to Transkei.

I have in this book preferred the term "eulogy" to "praise poetry"
because the imbongi traffics in censure as well as praise; the izibongo
in Rubusana's anthology confirm that the imbongi has performed this
critical social function for some time. I have suggested that the imbongi in past days enacted a ritual of rebellion through his poetry,
voicing on behalf of the chiefdom disapproval of any behavior beyond
the norm, whether among the people or in the chief himself. Evidence
suggests that the imbongi has always enjoyed a degree of license to
criticize with impunity; there is no record of action ever being taken
against any imbongi by a chief, and Chief Mabandla, in an interview
quoted in the third chapter, asserted that he could not take action
against an imbongi who criticized him. The imbongi must be free to

express his views poetically before the people and before the chief in order to exercise his social function as critic. When the individual chiefdoms form part of a wider polity, however, one that enacts legislation and authorizes officials to act in the interests of the state, when, as in Transkei, it becomes an offense to criticize a chief or to impugn the sovereignty of the state, then the imbongi speaks his mind at considerable personal risk.

The modern state is learning to control the imbongi's access to his public. At the Transkei independence celebrations, only Mabunu and Manisi were granted access to the microphones on the dais; Mbutuma, Qangule, and Edgar Dontsa, all of whom sought access, were prevented physically from mounting the steps of the dais. At Ciskei's independence celebrations in December 1981, only one imbongi, Nkosinathi Payi, was allowed to perform. Payi is a powerful imbongi. On 31 May 1974, at the Fingo Day celebrations near Peddie, he produced a poem in his absence about Lennox Sebe, a commoner who had just defeated Chief Mabandla and won election as chief minister of the Ciskeian Territorial Authority by means of a vote that at the time of Payi's performance was being contested in a judicial dispute; Payi's poem included the following lines:

> Go back overseas, child of Sebe:
> Here I heard a clamor.
> They said over and again, "Africa must return"
> Till I asked "Who are you?"
> To this day I've had no answer.
> This is no game, it's serious.
> Oh the calf of the animal of Langa was angered
> Among the Bhele of Krwakrwa in Alice
> By men whose hearts are hidden:
> The one who asks questions will get burnt.
> The days for voting will come round again,
> There will be great changes and an uproar,
> And I too will speak out then.
> Farewell, my dear people.
> Farewell, leaders each and every one.

Seven years later, with Lennox Sebe firmly entrenched as the leader of a one-party state in which his brother serves as head of the security police, Payi was the only imbongi allowed to bonga Sebe, now holder of an honorary doctorate from the University of Fort Hare and installed as a Gqunukhwebe chief, as the first president of independent Ciskei. Payi's izibongo of Sebe reflects the altered structure of power in Ciskei:

Hail Ngweyesizwe [Leopard of the nation]!
Hail Ngweyesizwe!
That is the son of Sebe,
That is the chief of the Gqunukhwebe,
Of the Gqunukhwebe of Khwane.
That is the bull who challenges bulls far away
Beyond the rivers and beyond the sea.
That is the most honored man in Ciskei.
That is the most honored man in Ciskei.
Hail Ngweyesizwe!
. . . .

The whites have spoken of him,
People say he has done it.
He did well not to force this issue
While other chiefs force issues,
But he did well because he used his brains.
That is why we prefer brains, men.

I have heard masters of ceremonies complain about iimbongi because, given a chance, they will dominate proceedings to the detriment of other items on an agenda. The iimbongi have always before been free to comment, but through tight control of the platform a number of iimbongi at both the Transkei and the Ciskei celebrations were denied access to their public through the microphone.

The modern imbongi, then, is growing more and more isolated from his chief's great place. Compelled to enter the labor force, he tends to perform only when he is free from work, and he tends to perform more generally for many chiefs or dignitaries on occasions that transcend local significance. Informed by newspapers and radio about the world at large, the imbongi is becoming a universal freelance poet. He is losing the intimate contact with his chief's great place that informed the izibongo of his predecessors. His izibongo has lost its ritual connotation, and his freedom to comment independently, to voice the protests of the ruled against the excesses of their rulers, is being undermined. Thus his public stature is threatened. The imbongi of old served a chief but preserved his independence because he was never a retainer of the chief; Mabunu, retired from the police force and now in Kaiser Matanzima's employ as his personal bodyguard, produced izibongo immediately prior to Transkeian independence in 1976 that sounded like summaries of Matanzima's political speeches. Under present circumstances the role of the imbongi as respected soothsayer faces its gravest threat, and the way is opening for the imbongi to become a mere sycophant or, as with the Hausa maroki, an itinerant professional; as real power passes from the chiefs to the politicians, he may follow the path of the seroki in Lesotho and gradually disappear from the great place.

Now I have no romantic notions about the death of customs. Traditions must change if they are living traditions: Hilda Ellis Davidson writes of "the very nature of folklore, which draws its life from its powers of adaption to circumstances and changing environment, and its ability to reshape itself to fill a new need, like the shape-changing wizards in the old tales" (1978:ix). What I have argued for here is the prospect of change in aspects of the Xhosa imbongi's tradition, especially in his role in society, but I have tried to show that the social forces that might threaten this aspect of the imbongi's tradition do not necessarily threaten other aspects, whether textual, textural, or contextual. So too, if aspects of the imbongi's tradition change, as we would expect them to do in the course of time and especially now when social change is radical, the other traditions of izibongo are not necessarily threatened. When Wainwright invited miners to bonga on topics of their own choice, many of them produced boasts or biographical or clan praises. Where they are relatively fixed, as the clan praises are, izibongo might become shorter, more fragmentary, and obscure with transmission over time; but personal or clan praises still flatter or incite a man when uttered by his wife or friend, whether or not the imbongi is a universally respected figure in society. Rather than lament the passing of an old order, we should view change as one aspect of the complex tradition of Xhosa oral poetry, quite as rewarding of study as any of the other aspects presented for consideration in the course of this book.

REFERENCES

This bibliography conflates three lists: first, a list of all works specifically cited or referred to in the text; second, a selective list of works relevant to points raised in the text, with special emphasis on studies of Nguni poetic traditions (Zulu, Swazi, Ndebele, Ngoni, etc.) and to a lesser extent of other southeastern Bantu poetic traditions (Southern Sotho, Northern Sotho, Tswana, etc.); and third, a comprehensive list of works on Xhosa oral poetry. Spellings of titles in the text are generally modernized; here they are given in the forms that appear on title pages. The date assigned is generally the date of earliest publication of the work; in spite of that date, page references in the text are always to the most recent publication of the work.

Ainslie, Jill. 1981. *Archibald Campbell Jordan: A bibliography.* Working paper 6. Grahamstown: Department of African Languages, Rhodes University.

Alberti, Ludwig. 1968. *Ludwig Alberti's account of the tribal life and customs of the Xhosa in 1807.* Trans. William Fehr. Cape Town: Balkema.

Alexiou, Margaret. 1974. *The ritual lament in Greek tradition.* Cambridge: Cambridge University Press.

Argyle, John. 1978. Dingiswayo discovered: An interpretation of his legendary origins. In Argyle and Preston-Whyte, pp. 1–18.

Argyle, John, and Preston-Whyte, Eleanor (eds.). 1978. *Social system and tradition in southern Africa: Essays in honour of Eileen Krige.* Cape Town: Oxford University Press.

Ashley, Michael. 1974. African education and society in the nineteenth century eastern Cape. In Saunders and Derricourt, pp. 199–211.

Austin, J. L. 1962. *How to do things with words.* The William James Lectures delivered at Harvard University in 1955. Oxford: Oxford University Press (Clarendon Press).

Awe, Bolanle. 1974. Praise poems as historical data: The example of the Yoruba oríkì. *Africa,* 44:331–49.

Axelson, Eric. 1938. Discovery of the farthest pillar erected by Bartholomew Dias. *South African Journal of Science,* 35:417–29.

Ayliff, John, and Whiteside, Joseph. 1912. *History of the abaMbo generally known as the Fingos.* Butterworth: The Gazette. Reprinted 1962. Cape Town: Struik.

Babalọla, S. A. 1966. *The content and form of Yoruba ijala.* Oxford: Oxford University Press (Clarendon Press).

Bailey, Terence. 1974. *The intonation formulas of western chant.* Toronto: Pontifical Institute of Mediaeval Studies.

Bascom, William R. (ed.). 1977. *Frontiers of folklore.* AAAS Selected Symposium 5. Boulder, Colo.: Westview Press.

Başgöz, Ilhan. 1975. The tale-singer and his audience. In Ben-Amos and Goldstein, pp. 143–203.

Ben-Amos, Dan. 1971. Toward a definition of folklore in context. *Journal of American folklore,* 84:3–15. Reprinted 1972 in Paredes and Bauman, pp. 3–15.

  1972. Review of Bertel Nathhorst, *Formal or structural studies of traditional tales. Journal of American Folklore,* 85:82–4.

  1975. Folklore in African society. *Research in African Literatures,* 6:165–98. Reprinted 1977 in Lindfors, pp. 1–34.

  1977. The context of folklore: Implications and prospects. In Bascom, pp. 36–53.

Ben-Amos, Dan, and Goldstein, Kenneth S. (eds.). 1975. *Folklore: Performance and communication.* The Hague: Mouton.

Bennie, W. G. 1936. Two Xhosa poems in English renderings. *Critic,* 4:99–104.

  1939. The Ciskei and southern Transkei tribes (Xhosa and Thembu). In Duggan-Cronin, pp. 21–42.

Bennie, W. G. (ed.). 1935. *Imibengo.* Lovedale: Lovedale Press.

Benson, Larry D. 1966. The literary character of Anglo-Saxon formulaic poetry. *PMLA,* 81:334–41.

Biebuyck, Daniel. 1972. The epic as a genre in Congo oral literature. In Dorson, pp. 257–93.

  1978a. *Hero and chief: Epic literature from the Banyanga (Zaire Republic).* Berkeley: University of California Press.

  1978b. The African heroic epic. In *Heroic epic and saga,* ed. Felix J. Oinas, pp. 336–67. Bloomington: Indiana University Press.

Biebuyck, Daniel, and Mateene, Kahombo C. (eds. and trans.). 1969. *The Mwindo epic.* Berkeley: University of California Press.

Bigalke, E. H. 1969. The religious system of the Ndlambe of East London district. M. A. thesis, Rhodes University.

Bilen, Max. 1965. The African poet as bard of his people. *Présence Africaine,* 26:141–5.

Bird, Charles (ed. and trans.). 1974. *The songs of Seydou Camara I. Kambili.* Bloomington: African Studies Center, Indiana University.

Blackburn, Stuart H. 1981. Oral performance: Narrative and ritual in a Tamil tradition. *Journal of American Folklore,* 94:207–27.

Blohm, W. 1933. Das Opfer und dessen Sinn bei den Xosa in Südafrika. *Archiv für Anthropologie,* N.F. 23:150–3.

Bokwe, John Knox. 1900. *Ntsikana: The story of an African convert.* 2nd ed. 1914. Lovedale: Lovedale Press.

Bowra, C. M. 1952. *Heroic poetry.* London: Macmillan.

Brownlee, Charles Pacalt. 1896. *Reminiscences of Kafir life and history and*

other papers. 2nd ed. 1916. Reprinted 1977, ed. Christopher
Saunders. Pietermaritzburg and Durban: University of Natal Press
and Killie Campbell Africana Library.

Brownlee, John. 1827. Account of the AmaKosæ, or southern Caffers. In
George Thompson, *Travels and adventures in southern Africa*, pts. 2
and 3, pp. 191–219. London: Henry Colburn. Reprinted 1968. Cape
Town: Van Riebeeck Society.

Bryant, Alfred T. 1905. *A Zulu-English dictionary.* Marianhill, Natal: Marianhill Mission Press.

Bulane, Joseph Mofolo. 1966. Jack Cope on Bantu oral poetic tradition. *African Communist*, 24:60–6.

1968. Then and now: The praise poem in Southern Sotho. *New African*,
7:40–3.

Bulwer, C. E. Earle. 1957. Xhosa language and literature: The contribution of
the Church of the Province of South Africa. *South African Outlook*,
87:44–5, 77–9, 90–1.

1971. History of the Xhosa language and its literature: The contribution
of the Church of the Province of South Africa. *Coelacanth*, 9:31–6,
37–44.

Burns-Ncamashe, S. M. 1961. *Masibaliselane.* Cape Town: Oxford University
Press.

1979. *Izibongo zakwaSesile (Rhodes University).* ISER Xhosa texts 4.
Grahamstown: Institute of Social and Economic Research, Rhodes
University.

Bynum, David E. 1969. The generic nature of oral epic poetry. *Genre*, 2:236–
58. Reprinted 1976 in *Folklore genres*, ed. Dan Ben-Amos, pp. 35–
58. Austin: University of Texas Press.

Callaway, H. 1870. *The religious system of the amaZulu.* Pietermaritzburg:
Davis. Reprinted 1970. Cape Town: Struik.

Campbell, Joseph. 1956. *The hero with a thousand faces.* New York: Meridian
Books.

Caraveli-Chaves, Anna. 1980. Bridge between two worlds: The Greek
women's lament as communicative event. *Journal of American Folklore*, 93:129–57.

Carter, Gwendolen M., Karis, Thomas, and Stultz, Newell M. 1967. *South
Africa's Transkei: The politics of domestic colonialism.* London: Heinemann Educational Books.

Chadwick, H. M., and Chadwick, N. K. 1932, 1936, 1940. *The growth of
literature.* 3 vols. Cambridge: Cambridge University Press.

Charton, Nancy (ed.). 1980. *Ciskei: Economics and politics of dependence in a
South African homeland.* London: Croom Helm.

Cingo, W. D. 1925. *Ibali lama Mpondo nama Bhaca, Xesibe, Mpondomise:
Intlalo namasiko ka Ntu.* Palmerton: Palmerton Mission Press.

1927. *Ibali laba Tembu.* Emfundisweni: n.p.

Clark, John Pepper. 1966. The communication line between poet and public.
Reprinted 1970 in Clark, *The example of Shakespeare*, pp. 61–75.
London: Longman.

Clodd, Edward. 1920. *Magic in names and in other things.* London: Chapman & Hall.

Collingwood, August (trans.). 1966. The case of the twins. *New African,* 5:5–8, 41–4, 74–6.

Conquergood, Dwight. 1981. Boasting in Anglo-Saxon England: Performance and the heroic ethos. *Literature in Performance,* 1:24–35.

Cook, P. A. W. 1931a. History and izibongo of the Swazi chiefs. *Bantu Studies,* 5:181–201.

1931b. *Social organisation and ceremonial institutions of the Bomvana.* Cape Town: Juta.

Cope, Trevor. 1974. *The Zulu people: A select bibliography.* Durban: Department of Bantu Languages, University of Natal.

Cope, Trevor (ed.). 1968. *Izibongo: Zulu praise poems.* Oxford: Oxford University Press (Clarendon Press).

Damane, M., and Sanders, P. B. (eds. and trans.). 1974. *Lithoko: Sotho praise-poems.* Oxford: Oxford University Press (Clarendon Press).

Davidson, Hilda Ellis. 1978. *Patterns of folklore.* Ipswich and Totowa, N.J.: Brewer and Rowman & Littlefield.

Davis, R. H. 1969. Nineteenth century African education in the Cape Colony: A historical analysis. Ph.D. diss., University of Wisconsin.

Deakin, Ralph. 1925. *Southward ho! With the prince in Africa and South America.* London: Methuen.

De Vries, Jan. 1963. *Heroic song and heroic legend.* Trans. B. J. Timmer. London: Oxford University Press.

Dhlomo, H. I. E. 1939. African drama and poetry. *South African Outlook,* 69:88–90. Reprinted 1977 in *English in Africa,* 4:13–17.

1948. Zulu folk poetry. *Native Teachers' Journal* (April), pp. 84–7. Reprinted 1977 in *English in Africa,* 4:43–59.

Doke, C. M. 1933. A preliminary investigation into the state of the native languages of South Africa with suggestions as to research and the development of literature. *Bantu Studies,* 7:1–98.

1935. Vernacular text-books in South African native schools. *Africa,* 7:183–209.

1936. The future of Bantu literature. *African Observer,* 6:18–22.

1948. The basis of Bantu literature. *Africa,* 18:284–301.

Dorson, Richard M. 1968. *The British folklorists: A history.* London, Routledge & Kegan Paul.

Dorson, Richard M. (ed.). 1972. *African folklore.* Garden City, N.J.: Doubleday.

Dubb, A. A. 1966. Red and school: A quantitative approach. *Africa,* 36:292–302.

Duggan-Cronin, A. M. 1939. *The Bantu tribes of South Africa: Reproductions of photographic studies.* Vol. 3, sec. 1. Cambridge and Kimberley: Deighton, Bell and Alexander McGregor Memorial Museum.

1954. *The Bantu tribes of South Africa: Reproductions of photographic studies.* Vol. 3, sec. 5. Cambridge and Kimberley: Deighton, Bell and Alexander McGregor Memorial Museum.

Dugmore, Henry Hare. 1958. *The reminiscences of an Albany settler.* Ed. F. G. van der Riet and L. A. Hewson. Grahamstown: Grocott & Sherry.

Dundes, Alan. 1964. Texture, text, and context. *Southern Folklore Quarterly,* 28:251–65. Reprinted 1980 in Dundes, pp. 20–32.

1966. The American concept of folklore. *Journal of the Folklore Institute,* 3:226–49. Reprinted 1975 in Dundes, pp. 3–16.

1975. *Analytic essays in folklore.* The Hague: Mouton.

1980. *Interpreting folklore.* Bloomington: Indiana University Press.

Durand, Ralph A. 1907. Christian influence on African folk-lore. *Anthropos,* 2:976–80.

Eisenstadt, S. N. 1972. Post-traditional societies and the continuity and reconstruction of tradition. In *Post-traditional societies,* ed. S. N. Eisenstadt, pp. 1–27. New York: Norton.

1973. The construction and dynamics of tradition in traditional societies. In Eisenstadt, *Tradition, change, and modernity,* pp. 151–67. New York: Wiley.

Eliade, Mircea. 1954. *The myth of the eternal return or, cosmos and history.* Trans. Willard R. Trask. Princeton, N.J.: Princeton University Press.

1957. *Shamanism: Archaic techniques of ecstasy.* Reprinted 1964. New York: Pantheon.

Elliott, Ralph C. 1960. *The power of satire.* Princeton, N.J.: Princeton University Press.

El-Miskin, Tijani. 1981. The *Kayawar* in the context of the epic tradition. *Research in African Literatures,* 12:285–308.

Elphick, Richard, and Giliomee, Hermann (eds.). 1979. *The shaping of South African society, 1652–1820.* Cape Town: Longman.

Emmett, Tony. 1979. Oral, political and communal aspects of township poetry in the mid-seventies. *English in Africa,* 6:72–81.

Etherington, Norman. 1978. *Preachers, peasants and politics in southeast African Christian communities in Natal, Pondoland and Zululand.* London: Royal Historical Society.

Ewels, Allison. 1981. Is there a voice of protest in Xhosa poetry? In *Essays in Bantu language studies,* ed. D. Fivaz, pp. 10–33. Working paper 7. Grahamstown: Department of African Languages, Rhodes University.

Finlayson, R. 1978. A preliminary survey of hlonipha among the Xhosa. *Taalafsette,* 24:48–63.

Finnegan, Ruth. 1969. How to do things with words: Performative utterances among the Limba of Sierra Leone. *Man,* 4:537–52.

1970. *Oral literature in Africa.* Oxford: Oxford University Press (Clarendon Press).

1977. *Oral poetry: Its nature, significance and social context.* Cambridge: Cambridge University Press.

Foley, John Miles. 1980. Oral literature: Premises and problems. *Choice* (December), pp. 487–96.

Foley, John Miles, and Halpern, Barbara Kerewsky. 1978. The power of the word: Healing charms as an oral genre. *Journal of American Folklore*, 91:903–24.

Fortune, G. 1971. Shona traditional poetry. *Zambezia*, 2:41–60.

1974. *Nhango* and *ndyaringo:* Two complementary poetic genres. *Zambezia*, 3:27–49.

1977. Frames for comparison and contrast in Shona poetry. *Limi*, 5:67–74.

Fortune, G., and Hodza, A. C. 1974. Shona praise-poetry. *Bulletin of the School of Oriental and African Studies, University of London*, 37:65–75.

Fritsch, Gustav. 1872. *Die Eingeborenen Süd Afrika's: Ethnographisch und anatomisch beschrieben*. Breslau: Ferdinand Hirt.

Garrison, James D. 1976. *Dryden and the tradition of panegyric*. Berkeley: University of California Press.

Gelfand, M. 1969. The Shona religion. *Zambezia*, 1:37–45.

George, Katharine. 1958. The civilized west looks at primitive Africa: 1400–1800, a study in ethnocentrism. *Isis*, 49:62–72. Reprinted 1968 in *Every man his way: Readings in cultural anthropology*, ed. Alan Dundes, pp. 23–35. Englewood Cliffs, N.J.: Prentice-Hall.

Gérard, Albert S. 1971. *Four African literatures: Xhosa, Sotho, Zulu, Amharic*. Berkeley: University of California Press.

Gidley, C. G. B. 1975. *Roko:* A Hausa praise crier's account of his craft. *African Language Studies*, 16:93–115.

Gluckman, Max. 1938. Social aspects of first fruits ceremonies among the south-eastern Bantu. *Africa*, 11:25–41.

1954. *Rituals of rebellion in south-east Africa*. The Frazer Lecture, 1952. Manchester: Manchester University Press.

Godfrey, Robert. 1934. Rev. John Bennie, the father of Kafir literature. *Bantu Studies*, 8:123–34.

1941. *Bird-lore of the eastern Cape Province*. Johannesburg: Witwatersrand University Press.

Goldstein, Kenneth S. 1971. On the application of the concepts of active and inactive traditions to the study of repertory. *Journal of American Folklore*, 84:62–7. Reprinted 1972 in Paredes and Bauman, pp. 62–7.

Goody, Jack. 1977. *The domestication of the savage mind*. Cambridge: Cambridge University Press.

Goody, Jack (ed.). 1968. *Literacy in traditional societies*. Cambridge: Cambridge University Press.

Goody, Jack, and Watt, Ian. 1963. The consequences of literacy. *Comparative Studies in Society and History*, 5:304–45. Reprinted 1968 in Goody, pp. 27–68.

Grant, E. W. 1927–9. The *izibongo* of the Zulu chiefs. *Bantu Studies*, 3:205–44.

Greene, William Chase. 1951. The spoken and the written word. *Harvard Studies in Classical Philology*, 60:23–59.

Groenwald, P. S. 1980. Die pryslied, prysgedig, prysdig, prysvers. *Studies in Bantoetale*, 7:16–38.

1981. Die epiese gedig. *Studies in Bantoetale*, 8:1–25.

Guma, S. M. 1967. *The form, content and technique of traditional literature in Southern Sotho*. Pretoria: J. L. van Schaik.

Gunner, Elizabeth. 1976. Forgotten men: Zulu bards and praising at the time of the Zulu kings. *African Languages/Langues Africaines*, 2:71–89.

1979. Songs of innocence and experience: Women as composers and performers of *izibongo*, Zulu praise poetry. *Research in African Literatures*, 10:239–67.

1982. New wine in old bottles: Imagery in the izibongo of the Zulu Zionist prophet, Isaiah Shembe. *Journal of the Anthropological Society of Oxford*, 13:99–108.

Hammond-Tooke, W. D. 1954. The Baca, Hlubi and Xesibe. In Duggan-Cronin, pp. 9–40.

1962. *Bhaca society: A people of the Transkeian uplands South Africa*. Cape Town: Oxford University Press.

1965. Segmentation and fission in Cape Nguni political units. *Africa*, 35:143–66.

1968. The morphology of Mpondomise descent groups. *Africa*, 38:26–46.

1969. The "other side" of frontier history: A model of Cape Nguni political progress. In *African societies in southern Africa*, ed. Leonard Thompson, pp. 230–58. London: Heinemann Educational Books.

1975a. *Command or consensus: The development of Transkeian local government*. Cape Town: David Philip.

1975b. The symbolic structure of Cape Nguni cosmology. In Whisson and West, pp. 15–33.

1978. Do the south eastern Bantu worship their ancestors? In Argyle and Preston-Whyte, pp. 134–49.

Hammond-Tooke, W. D. (ed.). 1974. *The Bantu-speaking peoples of southern Africa*. London: Routledge & Kegan Paul.

Hatto, A. T. (ed.). 1980. *Traditions of heroic and epic poetry I: The traditions*. London: Modern Humanities Research Association.

Havelock, Eric A. 1963. *Preface to Plato*. Oxford: Blackwell.

1982. *The literate revolution in Greece and its consequences*. Princeton, N.J.: Princeton University Press.

Hayley, Audrey. 1968. Symbolic equations: The ox and the cucumber. *Man*, 3:262–71.

Haymes, Edward R. 1973. *A bibliography of studies relating to Parry's and Lord's oral theory*. Cambridge, Mass.: Center for the Study of Oral Literature, Harvard University.

1980. Formulaic density and Bishop Njegoš. *Comparative Literature*, 32:390–401.

Hemans, T. J. 1971. Praises given to the kings of the amaNdebele. *Nada*, 10:94–6.

Hodgson, Janet. 1980. *Ntsikana's "Great Hymn": A Xhosa expression of Christianity in the early 19th century eastern Cape*. Communications 4. Cape Town: Centre for African Studies, University of Cape Town.

Hodza, Aaron C., and Fortune, George (eds. and trans.). 1979. *Shona praise poetry*. Oxford: Oxford University Press (Clarendon Press).

Hollander, Lee M. 1945. *The skalds: A selection of their poems with introduction and notes.* Reprinted 1968. Ann Arbor: The University of Michigan Press.

Holt, Basil. 1954. *Joseph Williams and the pioneer mission to the south-eastern Bantu.* Lovedale: Lovedale Press.

1976. *Greatheart of the border: A life of John Brownlee, pioneer missionary in South Africa.* King William's Town: South African Missionary Museum.

Huna, Michael. n.d. *Ukutya kweendlebe.* Johannesburg: A. P. B.

1966. *Ulindipasi.* Elsies River: Via Afrika.

1973. *UNtsikana.* Umtata: Paul's Mission Press. 3rd ed. 1981. ISER Xhosa texts 5. Grahamstown: Institute of Social and Economic Research, Rhodes University.

Hunter, Monica. 1936. *Reaction to conquest: Effects of contact with Europeans on the Pondo of South Africa.* 2nd ed. 1961. Oxford: Oxford University Press.

Hutchinson, Bertram. 1957. Some social consequences of nineteenth century missionary activity among the South African Bantu. *Africa,* 27:160–75.

Iser, Wolfgang. 1978. *The act of reading: A theory of aesthetic response.* Baltimore: Johns Hopkins University Press.

Izevbaye, D. S. 1981. Naming and the character of African fiction. *Research in African Literatures,* 12:162–84.

Jabavu, D. D. T. 1921. *Bantu literature: Classification and reviews.* Lovedale: Lovedale Press.

1934. The origin of "Nkosi sikelel' i Afrika." In Enoch Sontonga, *Nkosi sikelel' i Afrika (the Bantu national anthem).* Lovedale Sol-fa Leaflets 17. Lovedale: Lovedale Press. Reprinted 1975 in *South African Outlook,* 109:192.

1943. *The influence of English on Bantu literature.* Lovedale: Lovedale Press.

Jabavu, D. D. T. (ed.). 1954. *Izithuko.* Lovedale: The Author.

Jabbour, Alan. 1969. Memorial transmission in Old English poetry. *Chaucer Review,* 3:174–90.

Jackson, Bruce. 1972. *Wake up dead man: Afro-American worksongs from Texas prisons.* Cambridge, Mass.: Harvard University Press.

Jackson, Kenneth H. (trans.). 1969. *The Gododdin: The oldest Scottish poem.* Edinburgh: University of Edinburgh Press.

Jahn, Janheinz. 1967. The tragedy of southern Bantu literature. Trans. W. Fenser. *Black Orpheus,* 21:44–52.

Johnson, Aubrey R. 1944. *The cultic prophet in ancient Israel.* Reprinted 1962. Cardiff: University of Wales Press.

Johnson, John William. 1980. Yes, Virginia, there is an epic in Africa. *Research in African Literatures,* 11:308–26.

Johnson, John William (ed. and trans.). 1979. *The epic of Sun-Jata according to Magan Sisòkò.* 2 vols. Bloomington, Ind.: Folklore Publications Group.

Jolobe, James J. R. 1936. *Umyezo.* 3rd. ed. 1957. Bantu treasury 2. Johannesburg: Witwatersrand University Press.

Jolobe, James J. R. (trans.). 1946. *Poems of an African.* Lovedale: Lovedale Press.

Jordan, A. C. 1940. *Ingqumbo yeminyanya.* Lovedale: Lovedale Press.

———— 1945. Samuel Edward Krune Mqhayi. *South African Outlook,* 75:135–8. Reprinted 1973 in Jordan, pp. 103–16.

———— 1957–60. Towards an African literature. *Africa South,* vol. 1, no. 4–vol. 4, no. 3. Reprinted 1973 in Jordan, pp. 1–102.

———— 1973. *Towards an African literature: The emergence of literary form in Xhosa.* Berkeley: University of California Press.

Jordan, A. C. (trans.). 1980. *The wrath of the ancestors.* Lovedale: Lovedale Press.

Joyner, Charles W. 1975. A model for the analysis of folklore performance in historical context. *Journal of American Folklore,* 88:254–65.

Jubase, J. 1967. Samuel Edward Krune Mqhayi. *Limi,* 4:23–6.

Jungraithmayr, Herrmann. 1981. *Gedächtniskultur und Schriftlichkeit in Afrika.* Wiesbaden: Steiner Verlag.

Kavanagh, R., and Qangule, Z. S. (trans.). 1971. *The making of a servant, and other poems.* Pretoria: Ophir.

Kawa, Richard Tainton. 1929. *I-bali lama Mfengu.* Lovedale: Lovedale Press.

Kidd, Dudley. 1904. *The essential Kafir.* London: Adam and Charles Black.

Kirk, G. S. 1976. *Homer and the oral tradition.* Cambridge: Cambridge University Press.

Knappert, Jan. 1964. The first Christian utenzi: A new development in Swahili literature. *Afrika and Ubersee,* 47:221–32.

———— 1967. The epic in Africa. *Journal of the Folklore Institute,* 4:171–90.

Koopman, Adrian. 1976. A study of Zulu names with special reference to the structural aspect. Honors thesis in Bantu Languages, University of Natal, Durban.

Kropf, A. 1888. Die religiösen Anschauungen der Kaffern und die damit zusammenhängenden Gebräuche. *Verhandlungen der Berliner Gesellschaft für Anthropologie, Ethnologie and Urgeschichte,* 20:42–7.

———— 1889a. *Das Volk der Xosa-Kaffern im östlichen Süd-Afrika nach seiner Geschichte, Eigenart, Verfassung und Religion.* Berlin: Verlag des Missionshauses.

———— 1889b. *Die Lügenpropheten Kafferlandes.* 2nd ed. 1891. Berlin: Verlag des Missionshauses.

———— 1891a. Die Lebensweise der Xosa-Kaffern I. *Mitteilungen der Geographischen Gesellschaft (für Thüringen) zu Jena,* 9:7–16.

———— 1891b. Die Lebensweise der Xosa-Kaffern II. *Mitteilungen der Geographischen Gesellschaft (für Thüringen) zu Jena,* 10:14–21.

———— 1899. *A Kafir-English dictionary.* 2nd ed. 1915, rev. Robert Godfrey. Lovedale: Lovedale Press.

Kugel, James L. 1981. *The idea of biblical poetry: Parallelism and its history.* New Haven: Yale University Press.

Kunene, Daniel P. 1967. Background to the South African vernacular author and his writings. In D. P. Kunene and Kirsch, pp. 1–13.

1970. African vernacular writing: An essay on self-devaluation. *African Social Research (Lusaka)*, 9:639–59.

1971a. *Heroic poetry of the Basotho.* Oxford: Oxford University Press (Clarendon Press).

1971b. Problems in creating creative writing: The example of southern Africa. *Review of National Literatures*, 2:81–103.

1972. Metaphor and symbolism in the heroic poetry of southern Africa. In Dorson, pp. 295–318.

1979. Levels of communication in the heroic poetry of southern Africa. In *Artist and audience: African literature as a shared experience*, ed. Richard K. Priebe and Thomas A. Hale, pp. 60–76. Washington, D.C.: Three Continents Press.

Kunene, Daniel P., and Kirsch, Randal A. 1967. *The beginning of South African vernacular literature.* Los Angeles: African Studies Association.

Kunene, Mazisi. 1967. Portrait of Magolwane, the great Zulu poet. *Cultural Events in Africa*, 32:1–4.

1968. Background to African literature. *Afro-Asian Writings*, 1:35–40.

1976. South African oral traditions. In *Aspects of South African literature*, ed. Christopher Heywood, pp. 24–41. London: Heinemann Educational Books.

1980. The relevance of African cosmological systems to African literature today. *African Literature Today*, 11:190–205.

Kunene, Mazisi, Kunene, Daniel, and Awoonor, Kofi. 1976. Panel on South African oral traditions. *Issue*, 6:5–13.

Kunene, Raymond. 1961. An analytical survey of Zulu poetry both traditional and modern. M.A. thesis, University of Natal, Durban.

Kuse, Wandile F. 1973. The traditional praise poetry of Xhosa: Iziduko and izibongo. M.A. thesis, University of Wisconsin.

1975a. Mqhayi: Oral bard and author. *South African Outlook*, 109:183–4.

1975b. Mqhayi through the eyes of his contemporaries. *South African Outlook*, 109:185–8.

1978. The form and themes of Mqhayi's poetry and prose. Ph.D. diss., University of Wisconsin.

1979. *Izibongo zeenkosi* (the praises of kings): Aspects of Xhosa heroic poetry. *Research in African Literatures*, 10:208–38.

Lamar, Howard, and Thompson, Leonard (eds.). 1981. *The frontier in history: North America and southern Africa compared.* New Haven: Yale University Press.

Lange, Werner J. 1979–80. Status and functions of Kafa bards in feudal Ethiopia. *Northeast African Studies*, 1:85–90.

Laydevant, Father F. 1933. The praises of the divining bones among the Basotho. *Bantu Studies*, 7:341–73.

Lefkowitz, Mary R. 1977. *The victory ode: An introduction.* Park Ridge, N.J.: Noyes Press.

Lestrade, G. P. 1934. European influence upon the development of Bantu languages and literature. In *Western civilization and the natives of South Africa: Studies in culture contact,* ed. I. Schapera, pp. 105–27. London: Routledge.

1935. Bantu praise-poems. *Critic,* 4:1–10.

1937. Traditional literature. In Schapera, pp. 291–308, 443–4.

Lewis, I. M. 1971. *Ecstatic religion: An anthropological study of spirit possession and shamanism.* Harmondsworth: Penguin.

Lichtenstein, Henry. 1812. *Travels in southern Africa in the years 1803, 1804, 1805, and 1806.* Reprinted 1928, trans. Anne Plumptre, vol. 1. Publications 10. Cape Town: Van Riebeeck Society.

Lindfors, Bernth (ed.). 1977. *Forms of folklore in Africa: Narrative, poetic, gnomic, dramatic.* Austin: University of Texas Press.

Lord, Albert B. 1960. *The singer of tales.* Cambridge, Mass.: Harvard University Press. Reprinted 1965. New York: Atheneum.

1962a. A comparative analysis. In *Umbundu: Folk tales from Angola,* ed. and trans. Merlin Ennis, pp. xiii–xxix. Boston: Beacon Press.

1962b. Homer and other epic poetry. In *A companion to Homer,* ed. Alan J. B. Wace and Frank H. Stubbings, pp. 179–214. London: Macmillan.

1968. Homer as oral poet. *Harvard Studies in Classical Philology,* 72:1–46.

1974. Perspectives on recent work on oral literature. *Forum for Modern Language Studies,* 10:187–210. Reprinted 1975 in *Oral literature: Seven essays,* ed. Joseph J. Duggan, pp. 1–24. Edinburgh: Scottish Academic Press.

McAllister, Patrick Alister. 1979. The rituals of labour migration among the Gcaleka. M.A. thesis, Rhodes University.

1981. *Umsindleko: A Gcaleka ritual of incorporation.* Occasional paper 26. Grahamstown: Institute of Social and Economic Research, Rhodes University.

McDowell, John H. 1981. Toward a semiotics of nicknaming: The Kamsá example. *Journal of American Folklore,* 94:1–18.

McGregor, Andrew Murray. 1977. *Butterworth, first Christian mission in Transkei: The story of one hundred and fifty years (1827–1977).* King William's Town: South African Missionary Museum.

Maclean, John. 1858. *A compendium of Kafir laws and customs including genealogical tables of Kafir chiefs and various tribal census returns.* Mount Coke: Wesleyan Mission Press. Reprinted 1968. Pretoria: State Library.

Mafeje, Archie. 1963. A chief visits town. *Journal of Local Administration Overseas,* 2:88–99.

1967. The role of the bard in a contemporary African community. *Journal of African Languages,* 6:193–223.

Mahlasela, B. E. N. 1973a. *A general survey of Xhosa literature from its early beginnings in the 1800s to the present.* Working paper 2. Grahamstown: Department of African Languages, Rhodes University.

1973b. *Jolobe: Xhosa poet and writer.* Working paper 3. Grahamstown: Department of African Languages, Rhodes University.

Makalima, R. G. S. 1975a. Interview with Herbert Mqhayi. *South African Outlook*, 109:189–90.

1975b. Rambling thoughts about Mqhayi the writer. *South African Outlook*, 109:190–1.

Makaula, David Z. 1966. *UMadzikane okanye imbali yamaBhaca.* Cape Town: Oxford University Press.

Manisi. *See* Yali-Manisi.

Manona, C. W. 1980. Marriage, family life and migrancy in a Ciskei village. In *Black villagers in an industrial society: Anthropological perspectives on labour migration in South Africa*, ed. Philip Mayer, pp. 169–214. Cape Town: Oxford University Press.

Marivate, C. T. D. 1978. Clan praises in Tsonga. *Limi*, 6:31–43.

Marquard, Jean. 1978. W. C. Scully: South African pioneer. *English in Africa*, 5:28–43.

Masiea, J. R. 1971. The symbolical element as found in Mangwaela's collection of the war praise-poems. *Limi*, 12:66–86.

Matonis, A. T. E. 1978. Traditions of panegyric in Welsh poetry: The heroic and the chivalric. *Speculum*, 53:667–87.

Mayer, Philip. 1961. *Townsmen or tribesmen: Conservatism and the process of urbanization in a South African city.* 2nd ed. 1971. Cape Town: Oxford University Press.

Mbebe, Adolphus Z. T. 1951. Ngomfi S. E. Krune Mqhayi. In *Indyebo ka-Xhosa*, ed. G. Soya Mama, pp. 27–8. Johannesburg: Bona Press.

Mbutuma, Melikaya. 1977. *Isife somzi.* ISER Xhosa texts 3. Grahamstown: Institute of Social and Economic Research, Rhodes University.

Mdiya, Wilson M. 1929–30. Isibongo in *Xosa*-language. Trans. W. Blohm. *Zeitschrift für Eingeborenen-Sprachen*, 20:148–50.

Merchant, Paul. 1971. *The epic.* The critical idiom 17. London: Methuen.

Miletich, John. 1974. Narrative style in Spanish and Slavic traditional narrative poetry: Implications for the study of the Romance epic. *Olifant*, 2:109–28.

1976. The quest for the "formula": A comparative reappraisal. *Modern Philology*, 74:111–23.

1977–8. Medieval Spanish epic and European narrative traditions. *La Corónica*, 6:90–6.

1978. Oral-traditional style and learned literature: A new perspective, *PTL*, 3:345–56.

Mofokeng, S. M. 1945. Notes and annotations of the praise-poems of certain chiefs and the structure of praise-poems in southern Sotho. Honors thesis, University of the Witwatersrand.

Moloto, Ernest Sedumedi. 1970. The growth and tendencies of Tswana poetry. D.Litt. diss., University of South Africa.

Morris, Henry F. 1964. *The heroic recitations of the Bahima of Ankole.* Oxford: Oxford University Press (Clarendon Press).

1980. East African (the Bahima praise poems). In Hatto, pp. 345–76.

Moyer, Richard A. 1976. A history of the Mfengu of the eastern Cape, 1815–1865. Ph.D. diss., University of London.

Mqhayi, S. E. K. 1907. *U-Samson*. Lovedale: Lovedale Press.

1914. *Ityala lama-wele*. Lovedale: Lovedale Press.

1921. *USo-Gqumahashe*. Lovedale: Lovedale Press.

1923. *I-bandla laBantu*. Lovedale: Lovedale Press.

1925. *U-bomi bom-fundisi u-John Knox Bokwe*. Lovedale: Lovedale Press.

1926. *Isikumbuzo zom Polofiti u-Ntsikana*. Johannesburg: Caluza.

1927. *Imihobe nemibongo yokufundwa ezikolweni*. London: Sheldon Press.

1928. *Idini*. Johannesburg: Caluza.

1929. *UDon Jadu*. Lovedale: Lovedale Press.

1935. *U-Aggrey um-Afrika*. London: Sheldon Press.

1937. *U-mhlekazi u-Hintsa*. Lovedale: Lovedale Press.

1939. *U-Mqhayi wase-Ntab'ozuko*. Lovedale: Lovedale Press.

1943. *Inzuzo*. Bantu treasury 7. Rev. ed. 1957. Johannesburg: Witwatersrand University Press.

1949. *U-adonisi wasentlango*. Lovedale: Lovedale Press.

Msimang, C. T. 1980. Factors that influence the composition of a praise poem in Zulu. In Wentzel, pp. 220–38.

1981. Imagery in Zulu praise-poetry. *Limi*, 9:51–76.

Müller, Friedrich. 1926. *Die Hlubikaffern: Land und Leben*. Herrnhut: Verlag der Missionsbuchhandlung.

Mundell, Felicia. 1975. A critical analysis of the poem "Ulindipasi." *Limi*, 3:43–7.

Mzolo, Douglas. 1977. A study of Nguni clan praises in Natal and Zululand. M.A. thesis, University of Natal, Durban.

1978. Zulu clan praises. In Argyle and Preston-Whyte, pp. 206–21.

1980. Zulu clan praises: Structural and functional aspects. In Wentzel, pp. 239–53.

Nagy, Gregory. 1976. Iambos: Typologies of invective and praise. *Arethusa*, 9:191–205.

1979. *The best of the Achaeans: Concepts of the hero in archaic Greek poetry*. Baltimore: Johns Hopkins University Press.

Ncamashe. *See* Burns-Ncamashe.

Ncwana, K. K. 1953. *Amanqakwana ngeminombo yezizwe zase-Mbo*. Lovedale: Lovedale Press.

Ndabanda. 1966. Die Bantoepryslied. *Bantu*, 13:196–8.

Ndamase, Victor Poto. n.d. *Ama-Mpondo: Ibali ne-ntlalo*. Lovedale: Lovedale Press.

Ndawo, Henry Masila. 1928. *Izibongo zenkosi zama-Hlubi nezama-Bàca*. Marianhill, Natal: Marianhill Mission Press.

1939. *Iziduko zama-Hlubi*. Lovedale: Lovedale Press.

Ngani, Alfred Z. 1947a. *Ibali lamaGqunukhwebe*. Lovedale: Lovedale Press.

1947b. Utyelelo lokumkani nokumkanikazi kuMzantsi weAfrika: The visit of the king and queen to South Africa. *African Studies,* 6:121–3.

Norbeck, Edward. 1963. African rituals of conflict. *American Anthropologist,* 65:1254–79. Reprinted 1967 in *Gods and rituals: Readings in religious beliefs and practices,* ed. John Middleton, pp. 197–226. Garden City, N.Y.: Natural History Press.

Notopoulos, J. A. 1938. Mnemosyne in oral literature. *Transactions of the American Philological Association,* 69:465–93.

Ntantala, Phyllis P. 1971. The writer and his social responsibility: The Xhosa writer. Paper presented at the fourteenth annual meeting of the African Studies Association, Denver, 3–6 November.

Ntuli, D. B. 1971. Imitation in Zulu poetry. *Limi,* 12:1–28.

Nurse, G. T. 1966–7. The installation of inkosi ya makosi Gomani III. *African Music,* 4:56–63.

Nwoga, D. I. 1971. The concept and practice of satire among the Igbo. *Conch,* 3:30–45.

Nyembezi, C. L. S. 1948. The historical background to the izibongo of the Zulu military age. *African Studies,* 7:110–25, 157–74.

Nyembezi, C. L. S. (ed.). 1958. *Izibongo zamakhosi.* Pietermaritzburg: Shuter & Shooter.

Obiechina, E. N. 1967. Transition from oral to literary tradition. *Présence Africaine,* 63:140–61.

O'Connell, M. C. 1982. Spirit possession and role stress among the Xesibe of eastern Transkei. *Ethnology,* 21:21–37.

Oettlé, Alison. 1973. A survey of oral poetry in selected southern Bantu languages. Honors thesis in African Languages, Rhodes University.

Okpewho, Isidore. 1977. Does the epic exist in Africa? Some formal considerations. *Research in African Literatures,* 8:171–200.

1979. *The epic in Africa: Towards a poetics of the oral performance.* New York: Columbia University Press.

Ong, Walter J., S. J. 1965. Oral residue in Tudor prose style. *PMLA,* 80:145–54. Reprinted in Ong 1971a, pp. 23–47.

1967. *The presence of the word: Some prolegomena for cultural and religious history.* Reprinted 1970. New York: Simon & Schuster.

1968. Tudor writings on rhetoric, poetic and literary theory. *Studies in the Renaissance,* 15:36–69. Reprinted in Ong 1971a, pp. 48–103.

1971a. *Rhetoric, romance, and technology: Studies in the interaction of expression and culture.* Ithaca, N.Y.: Cornell University Press.

1971b. The literate orality of popular culture today. In Ong 1971a, pp. 284–303.

1975. The writer's audience is always a fiction. *PMLA,* 90:9–21. Reprinted in Ong 1977b, pp. 53–81.

1977a. African talking drums and oral noetics. *New Literary History,* 8:411–29. Reprinted in Ong 1977b, pp. 92–120.

1977b. *Interfaces of the word: Studies in the evolution of consciousness and culture.* Ithaca, N.Y.: Cornell University Press.

1977c. Transformations of the word and alienation. In Ong 1977b, pp. 17–49.

Opie, Iona, and Opie, Peter. 1978. Tradition and transmission. *Times Literary Supplement* (14 July), pp. 799–80.

Opland, Jeff. 1970. Two Xhosa oral poems. *Papers in African Languages, 1970* (School of African Studies, University of Cape Town), pp. 86–98.

1971. *Scop* and *imbongi:* Anglo-Saxon and Bantu oral poets. *English Studies in Africa,* 14:161–78.

1973. African phenomena relevant to a study of the European middle ages: Oral tradition. *English Studies in Africa,* 16:87–90.

1974. Praise poems as historical sources. In Saunders and Derricourt, pp. 1–38.

1975. *Imbongi nezibongo:* The Xhosa tribal poet and the contemporary poetic tradition. *PMLA,* 90:185–208.

1977a. On Anglo-Saxon poetry and the comparative study of oral poetic traditions. *Acta Germanica,* 10:49–62.

1977b. Two unpublished poems by S. E. K. Mqhayi. *Research in African Literatures,* 8:27–53.

1978. Cædmon and Ntsikana: Anglo-Saxon and Xhosa transitional poets. *Annals of the Grahamstown Historical Society, 1977,* 2, no. 3:56–65.

1980a. *Anglo-Saxon oral poetry: A study of the traditions.* New Haven: Yale University Press.

1980b. From horseback to monastic cell: The impact on English literature of the introduction of writing. In *Old English literature in context: Ten essays,* ed. John D. Niles, pp. 30–43, 161–3. Oxford and Totowa, N.J.: Brewer and Rowman & Littlefield.

1980c. Southeastern Bantu eulogy and early Indo-European poetry. *Research in African Literatures,* 11:295–307.

Oxenham, John. 1981. *Literacy: Writing, reading and social organisation.* London: Routledge & Kegan Paul.

Pahl, H. W., Jafta, D. N., and Jolobe, J. J. R. 1971. *Xhosa literature: Its past and future.* Lovedale: Lovedale Press.

Paredes, Américo, and Bauman, Richard (eds.). 1972. *Toward new perspectives in folklore.* Austin: University of Texas Press.

Parry, Adam. 1966. Have we Homer's *Iliad? Yale Classical Studies,* 20:177–216.

Parry, Adam (ed.). 1971. *The making of Homeric verse: The collected papers of Milman Parry.* Oxford: Oxford University Press (Clarendon Press).

Pauw, B. A. 1965. Patterns of Christianization among the Tswana and the Xhosa-speaking peoples. In *African systems of thought,* ed. M. Fortes and G. Dieterlen, pp. 240–53. London: Oxford University Press.

1975. *Christianity and Xhosa tradition: Belief and ritual among Xhosa-speaking Christians.* Cape Town: Oxford University Press.

p'Bitek, Okot. 1974. *Horn of my love.* London: Heinemann Educational Books.

Peek, Philip M. 1981. The power of words in African verbal arts. *Journal of American Folklore,* 94:19–43.

Peires, Jeffrey Brian. 1976. A history of the Xhosa c1700–1835. M.A. thesis, Rhodes University.
1980. Lovedale Press: Literature for the Bantu revisited. *English in Africa*, 7:71–85.
1981a. Chiefs and commoners in precolonial Xhosa society. In Peires 1981c, pp. 125–44.
1981b. *The house of Phalo: A history of the Xhosa people in the days of their independence.* Johannesburg: Ravan Press.
Peires, J. B. (ed.). 1981c. *Before and after Shaka: Papers in Nguni history.* Grahamstown: Institute of Social and Economic Research, Rhodes University.
Perham, Margery (ed.). 1936. *Ten Africans.* 2nd ed. 1963. London: Faber.
Pettersson, Olof. 1953. *Chiefs and gods: Religious and social elements in the south eastern Bantu kingship.* Studie theologica Lundensia 3. Lund: Gleerup.
Propp, V. 1958. *Morphology of the folktale.* Trans. Laurence Scott. 2nd ed. 1968. Austin: University of Texas Press.
Qangule, Z. S. 1968. A brief survey of modern literature in the South African Bantu languages: Xhosa. *Limi*, 6:14–28.
1979. A study of theme and technique in the creative works of S.E.K.L.N. Mqhayi. Ph.D. diss., University of Cape Town.
Raglan, F. R. S. 1936. *The hero: A study in tradition, myth, and drama.* Reprinted 1956. New York: Vintage Books.
Raum, O. F., and De Jager, E. J. 1972. *Transition and change in a rural community: A survey of acculturation in the Ciskei, South Africa.* Alice: University of Fort Hare Press.
Read, Margaret. 1937. Songs of the Ngoni people. *Bantu Studies*, 11:1–35.
1866? *Recollections of a visit to British Kaffraria.* Oxford: Clarendon Press for SPCK.
Richmond, W. Edson. 1972. Narrative folk poetry. In *Folklore and Folklife: An introduction*, ed. Richard M. Dorson, pp. 85–98. Chicago: University of Chicago Press.
Riordan, J. 1961. The wrath of the ancestors. *African Studies*, 20:53–60.
apRoberts, Ruth. 1977. Old Testament poetry: The translatable structure. *PMLA*, 92:987–1004.
Rose, Cowper. 1829. *Four years in southern Africa.* London: Henry Colburn and Richard Bentley.
Rosenberg, Bruce. 1970a. *The art of the American folk preacher.* Oxford: Oxford University Press.
1970b. The formulaic quality of spontaneous sermons. *Journal of American Folklore*, 83:3–20.
1975. Oral sermons and oral narrative. In Ben-Amos and Goldstein, pp. 75–101.
Ross, B. J. n.d. *Amabali emfazwe zakwa-Xosa.* 2nd ed. Lovedale: Lovedale Press.
Rubusana, W. B. (ed.). 1906. *Zemk'inkomo magwalandini.* 2nd ed. 1911. Frome and London: Butler and Tanner.

Rycroft, David K. 1960. Melodic features in Zulu eulogistic recitation. *African Language Studies*, 1:60–78.

1962. Zulu and Xhosa praise-poetry and song. *African Music*, 3:79–85.

1980. The question of metre in southern African praise poetry. In Wentzel, pp. 289–312.

Satyo, S. C. (ed.). 1980. *Elugayini*. Pretoria: J. L. van Schaik.

Saunders, Christopher, and Derricourt, Robin (eds.). 1974. *Beyond the Cape frontier: Studies in the history of the Transkei and Ciskei*. London: Longman.

Schapera, Isaac. 1956. *Government and politics in tribal societies*. London: C. A. Watts.

Schapera, Isaac (ed.). 1937. *The Bantu-speaking tribes of South Africa*. Cape Town: Maskew Miller.

1965. *Praise poems of Tswana chiefs*. Oxford: Oxford University Press (Clarendon Press).

Scheub, Harold. 1970a. Approach to a Xhosa novel. *Contrast*, 23:77–91.

1970b. Interviews at New Brighton. *African Arts*, 3:58–63, 80.

1970c. The technique of the expansible image in Xhosa *ntsomi*-performances. *Research in African Literatures*, 1:119–46. Reprinted 1977 in Lindfors, pp. 37–63.

1971. Translation of African oral narrative-performances to the written word. *Yearbook of Comparative and General Literature*, 20:28–36.

1975. *The Xhosa "ntsomi."* Oxford: Oxford University Press (Clarendon Press).

1977a. Body and image in oral narrative performance. *New Literary History*, 8:345–67.

1977b. Performance of oral narrative. In Bascom, pp. 54–78.

Schutte, P. J. 1969. Sendingdrukperse in Suid-Afrika. Ph.D. diss., Potchefstroom Universiteit vir Christelike Hoër Onderwys.

Scott, Patricia E. 1973. *James James Ranisi Jolobe: An annotated bibliography*. Communication 1. Grahamstown: Department of African Languages, Rhodes University.

1975. Mqhayi: His work – a bibliography. *South African Outlook*, 109:193.

1976a. *Samuel Edward Krune Mqhayi, 1875–1945: A bibliographic survey*. Communication 5. Grahamstown: Department of African languages, Rhodes University.

1977a. *South African Bantu language theses, 1919–76: A preliminary bibliography*. Working paper 4. Grahamstown: Department of African Languages, Rhodes University.

1977b. *Southern Bantu literature: A preliminary bibliography of some secondary sources*. Working paper 5. Grahamstown: Department of African Languages, Rhodes University.

Scott, Patricia E. (ed.). 1976b. *Mqhayi in translation*. Communication 6. Grahamstown: Department of African Languages, Rhodes University.

Scully, William Charles. 1913. *Further reminiscences of a South African pioneer*. London: Unwin.

Sebe, Lennox L. 1973. Some aspects of African literature. *South African*

Outlook, 103:97–8, 107. Reprinted 1978 in *African perspectives on South Africa*, ed. Hendrik W. van der Merwe, Nancy C. J. Charton, D. A. Kotzé, and Åke Magnusson, pp. 29–33. Stanford, Calif.: Cape Town, and London: Hoover Institution Press, David Philip, and Rex Collings.

1980. *Ucamngco*. Goodwood: Via Afrika.

Shaw, William. 1860. *The story of my mission in south-eastern Africa*. London: Hamilton, Adams.

Shepherd, R. H. W. 1945. *Lovedale and literature for the Bantu: A brief history and a forecast*. Lovedale: Lovedale Press.

1953. The evolution of an African press: Lovedale's outstanding contribution to Bantu literacy. *African World* (November), pp. 7–8.

1955. *Bantu literature and life*. Lovedale: Lovedale Press.

1971. *Lovedale, South Africa, 1824–1955*. Lovedale: Lovedale Press.

1975. S. E. K. Mqhayi: His life. *South African Outlook*, 109:191.

Shepherd, R. H. W. (ed.). 1948. *Brownlee J. Ross: His ancestry and some writings*. Lovedale: Lovedale Press.

Shields, Hugh. 1980. Oral techniques in written verse: Philippe de Thaon's *Livre de Sibile*. *Medium Ævum*, 49:194–206.

Shils, Edward. 1981. *Tradition*. London: Faber.

Silinga, J. 1938–9. Dankreden für die religiösen Zusammenkünfte in Baziya und Umgegend 1934: Izibongo zemvuselelo ka 1934 e-Baziya nasemmandleni. Trans. W. Blohm. *Zeitschrift für Eingeborenen-Sprachen*, 29:287–93.

Skinner, Elliott P. (ed.). 1973. *Peoples and cultures of Africa: An anthropological reader*. Garden City, N.Y.: Natural History Press.

Smith, Esther Y. 1975. Apaeε: Praise poetry of the Akan kings. *Southern Folklore Quarterly*, 39:171–86.

Smith, M. G. 1957. The social functions and meaning of Hausa praise-singing. *Africa*, 27:26–43. Reprinted 1973 in Skinner, pp. 554–79.

Soga, John Henderson. 1930. *The south-eastern Bantu (abe-Nguni, aba-Mbo, ama-Lala)*. Johannesburg: Witwatersrand University Press.

1931. *The ama-Xosa: Life and customs*. Lovedale and London: Lovedale Press and Kegan Paul, Trench, Trubner.

Spraycar, Rudy. 1976. *La Chanson de Roland*: An oral poem? *Olifant*, 4:63–74.

Stefaniszyn, B. 1951. The hunting songs of the Ambo. *African Studies*, 10:1–12.

Streek, Barry, and Wicksteed, Richard. 1981. *Render unto Kaiser: A Transkei dossier*. Johannesburg: Ravan Press.

Stultz, Newell M. 1979. *Transkei's half loaf: Race separatism in South Africa*. New Haven: Yale University Press.

Switzer, Les. 1979. *Politics and communication in the Ciskei, an African "homeland" in South Africa*. Occasional paper 23. Grahamstown: Institute of Social and Economic Research, Rhodes University.

Switzer, Les, and Switzer, Donna. 1979. *The black press in South Africa and Lesotho: A descriptive bibliographic guide to African, coloured and Indian newspapers, newsletters and magazines, 1836–1976*. Boston: G. K. Hall.

Tayedzerhwa, Lettie G. N. 1951. Umbengo: A Xhosa poem on the death of
    S. E. K. Mqhayi. Trans. F. S. M. Mncube. *African Studies*, 10:125–9.
Tedlock, Dennis. 1971. On the translation of style in oral narrative. *Journal of
    American Folklore*, 84:114–33. Reprinted 1972 in Paredes and Bau-
    man, pp. 114–33.
Theal, George McCall. 1882. *Kaffir folklore; or, a selection from the traditional
    tales current among the people living on the eastern border of the Cape
    Colony*. London: W. Swan Sonnenschein.
Tonjeni, E. V. M. 1959. *Sihambele ubulawu*. Johannesburg: Bona Press.
Treitler, Leo. 1981. Oral, written, and literate process in the transmission of
    medieval music. *Speculum*, 56:471–91.
Underhill, Ruth Murray. 1938. *Singing for power: The song magic of the
    Papago Indians of southern Arizona*. Reprinted 1976. Berkeley: Uni-
    versity of California Press.
Van Warmelo, N. J. 1939. The Nguni. In Duggan-Cronin, pp. 9–18.
Van Warmelo, N. J. (ed.). 1930. *Transvaal Ndebele texts*. Ethnological publi-
    cations 1. Pretoria: Department of Native Affairs.
    1938. *History of Matiwane and the amaNgwane tribe*. Ethnological publi-
    cations 7. Pretoria: Department of Native Affairs.
Vidal, A. O. 1971. Oriki. Praise chants of the Yoruba. M.A. thesis, University
    of California at Los Angeles.
Vilakazi, B. W. 1938. The conception and development of poetry in Zulu.
    Bantu Studies, 12:105–34.
    1942. Some aspects of Zulu literature. *African Studies*, 1:270–4.
    1945. The oral and written literature in Nguni. D.Litt. diss., University of
    the Witwatersrand.
Wainwright, Alexander Theodore. 1979. The praises of Xhosa mineworkers.
    M.A. thesis, University of South Africa.
    1980. The Xhosa *imbongi* at home and on the mines. In Wentzel, pp.
    372–89.
Wainwright, A., McAllister, P., and Wallace, P. 1978. *The Xhosa imbongi
    (praise poet) as a conveyor of social criticism and praise in the min-
    ing industry*. Research report 39/78. Johannesburg: Human Re-
    sources Laboratory, Chamber of Mines of South Africa Research
    Organisation.
Wanger, W. 1923–4, 1925, 1926. The Zulu notion of God according to the
    traditional Zulu God-names. *Anthropos*, 18–19:656–87, 20:558–78,
    21:351–85.
Watts, Ann Chalmers. 1969. *The lyre and the harp: A comparative reconsidera-
    tion of oral tradition in Homer and Old English epic poetry*. New
    Haven: Yale University Press.
Webb, C. de B., and Wright, J. B. (eds. and trans.). 1976. *The James Stuart
    archive of recorded oral evidence relating to the history of the Zulu and
    neighbouring peoples*, vol. 1. Pietermaritzburg and Durban: Univer-
    sity of Natal Press and Killie Campbell Africana Archive.
Wentzel, P. J. (ed.). 1980. *Third Africa Languages Congress of Unisa*. Preto-
    ria: University of South Africa.

West, Martin. 1975. The shades come to town: Ancestors and urban independent churches. In Whisson and West, pp. 185–206.

Westermann, Diedrich (ed. and trans.). 1938. Samuel Edward Kgune Mqhayi, ein südafrikanischer Dichter. In Westermann, *Afrikaner erzählen ihr Leben*, pp. 292–315. Essen: Essener Verlagsanstalt.

Whisson, Michael G., and West, Martin (eds.). 1975. *Religion and social change in southern Africa: Anthropological essays in honour of Monica Wilson*. Cape Town and London: David Philip and Rex Collings.

Williams, Donovan. 1959. Missionaries on the eastern frontier of the Cape Colony. Ph.D. diss., University of the Witwatersrand.

1978. *Umfundisi: A biography of Tiyo Soga, 1829–1871*. Lovedale: Lovedale Press.

Williams, J. E. Caerwyn. 1971. The court poet in medieval Ireland. *Proceedings of the British Academy*, 57:85–135.

Wilson, Monica. 1959. The early history of the Transkei and Ciskei. *African Studies*, 18:167–79.

1969a. Co-operation and conflict: The eastern Cape frontier. In M. Wilson and Thompson, pp. 233–71.

1969b. The Nguni people. In M. Wilson and Thompson, pp. 75–130.

1978. Ritual: Resilience and obliteration. In Argyle and Preston-Whyte, pp. 150–64.

1981. Nguni markers. In Peires 1981c, pp. 145–57.

Wilson, Monica, and Mafeje, Archie. 1963. *Langa: A study of social groups in an African township*. Cape Town: Oxford University Press.

Wilson, Monica, and Thompson, Leonard (eds.). 1969. *The Oxford history of South Africa I: South Africa to 1870*. Oxford: Oxford University Press (Clarendon Press).

Wilson, W. Daniel. 1981. Readers in texts. *PMLA*, 96:848–63.

Woolf, Rosemary. 1976. The ideal of men dying with their lord in the *Germania* and in *The Battle of Maldon*. *Anglo-Saxon England*, 5:63–81.

Wright, H. Curtis. 1977. *The oral antecedents of Greek librarianship*. Provo, Utah: Brigham Young University Press.

Yako, St. J. Page. 1957. *Umtha welanga*. Johannesburg: Afrikaanse Pers Booksellers.

1967. *Ikhwezi*. Lovedale: Lovedale Press.

Yali-Manisi, D. L. P. 1952. *Izibongo zeenkosi zama-Xhosa*. Lovedale: Lovedale Press.

1953. Umnu. J. D. Rheinallt Jones. Trans. F. S. M. Mncube. *African Studies*, 12:72–4.

1954. *Inguqu*. Bolotwa: Khundulu Methodist School.

1977. *Inkululeko: Uzimele-geqe eTranskayi*. ISER Xhosa texts 1. Grahamstown: Institute of Social and Economic Research, Rhodes University.

1980. *Yaphum' ingqina*. ISER Xhosa texts 6. Grahamstown: Institute of Social and Economic Research, Rhodes University.

Zarwan, John. 1976. The Xhosa cattle killings, 1856–57. *Cahiers d'Etudes Africaines*, 16:519–39.

GENERAL INDEX

The following two indexes complement each other: Items in the second are not necessarily incorporated into the first. As far as possible and where appropriate I have supplied dates and names of fathers for historical personages in the general index and izikhahlelo for chiefs and dignitaries, and I have translated all Xhosa entries: the general index is thus intended to serve as a glossary as well. Xhosa orthography has changed over the years, but names sometimes retain older modes of spelling: Thus Mtikrakra, for example, may be spelled Mthikrakra, Mtirara, or Mthirara. I have not aimed for consistency, but rather have chosen the most commonly accepted current spelling of Xhosa names.

INDEX OF XHOSA AND ZULU POEMS CITED

This index is divided into two sections: The first is a list by title/subject and the second, referring to the first, is a list by composer or performer. I have supplied titles to untitled poems and translated Xhosa titles. The titles of written poems are placed in quotes to distinguish them from oral poems. Each title is followed by the name of the poet, the name of the person who recorded or published the poem, and the date of performance if that information is known. The title list is arranged alphabetically by subject and by the surname of the subject where relevant.

Subjects

ancestors, by Masilingane; recorded by McAllister, 121–2
ancestors, by Ndlebezendja; recorded by McAllister, 121, 122

bull, by Geza; recorded by Wilson, 35, 41
bull; recorded by Stuart, 41
Bushman, by Ndzima; recorded by Opland (August 1969), 38, 40, 43

Cape long claw, by Geza; recorded by Wilson, 36, 41
Cape long claw, by schoolboy; recorded by Godfrey, 42
Chakijana's boast, by Vilakazi, 36–7
cock, by Geza; recorded by Wilson, 36, 41
cow, by Geza; recorded by Wilson, 35, 41
crucifixion, by Mabunu; recorded by Opland (December 1970), 255

Dlomo clan; recorded by Kuse, 45
dog; recorded by Stuart, 41
dream, by Mbutuma; recorded by Opland (July 1977), 103–5, 146

"Editor *Isigidimi*," by Mqanda, 208, 240

fiscal shrike, by a Thembu; recorded by Godfrey (1910), 42

Geza's grandfather, by Geza; recorded by Wilson, 35, 37, 40, 43
Goloza, by Jordan, 26

"Paramount Chief Hintsa," by Mqhayi, 216–18, 231
hymn, by Ntsikana; recorded by Philip, 212, 213–15, 220, 230, 231, 240, 243, 244, 246, 255

Isaac's boast, by Geza; recorded by Wilson, 35, 36
Isaiah, by Geza; recorded by Wilson, 35, 36

Joyi, by Mbutuma; recorded by Mafeje (1961), 59, 138, 248

Ian Mackenzie, by Ncamashe; recorded by Opland (March 1977), 98–9, 178–80, 241, 242, 247, 256
"Dr Ian Mackenzie," by Ncamashe, 176–8, 179–80, 241, 244, 245–6, 247, 253, 256
Senator F.S. Malan, by Mpumlwana (1939), 254–5, 256, 261
"Manisi," by Yako, 93
Masingila clan; recorded by Jordan, 46
Masumpa, by Msebenzi; recorded by Van Warmelo, 190
Kaiser Matanzima, by Mabunu; recorded in *Daily dispatch* (September 1979), 268